The Life and Times of Rodrigo Borgia, Pope Alexander VI

THE LIFE AND TIMES

OF

RODRIGO BORGIA

LUCREZIA DANCING BEFORE THE PAPAL COURT.

From a painting by Kaulbach.

Frontispiece]

THE LIFE AND TIMES

OF

RODRIGO BORGIA

POPE ALEXANDER VI.

BY THE MOST REV.

ARNOLD H. MATHEW, D.D.

ARCHBISHOP OF THE OLD ROMAN CATHOLIC CHURCH IN GREAT BRITAIN
AND IRELAND, *DE JURE* EARL OF LLANDAFF OF THOMASTOWN

" Let writers of history remember never to dare to tell a lie nor to
fear to tell the truth."—POPE LEO XIII.

WITH 52 ILLUSTRATIONS IN HALF-TONE.

NEW YORK

BRENTANO'S

Printed in Great Britain

MADE AND PRINTED IN GREAT BRITAIN
BY
SOUTHAMPTON TIMES LIMITED
SOUTHAMPTON

PREFACE

THE object I have in view in writing this book is merely to present as accurate a sketch of the life and times of the principal member of the Borgia family as it seems possible to produce, with the comparatively few contemporary materials that are now available.

The second and third volumes of Monsieur Thuasne's Latin edition of the *Diary of John Burchard* Bishop of Orta, afford much trustworthy information at first hand.

The value of this information has been minimised, firstly, by those who, like Leibnitz, have published merely extracts from it, conveying a false impression of the work itself; and, secondly, by Borgian apologists, who have striven to cast doubts upon the veracity of the Bishop of Orta, or to attribute those entries in his Diary which tell against the Spanish Pope to "interpolators" who were the alleged enemies of his Holiness, and anxious to defame him.

The Diary begins in 1483 and ends, with the death of its author, in 1506. In the short space of twenty-three years, during which Burchard held the office of Pontifical Master of the Ceremonies, no fewer than five Popes had been personally known and served by him. He resided in the Vatican, and, as was customary, kept, for his own private use and information, a daily record of the events which interested him. This Diary was obviously not intended for publication, nor for any other eye than that of Burchard himself. The original Diary is now kept securely locked up in the Vatican, and would probably never have seen the light of day had it not been for Rodrigo Borgia's namesake, Pope Alexander VII. (1655–67), who caused a copy of it to be made for his kinsman, Prince Chigi, who placed it in the library of the Chigi Palace. It thus became accessible to historical and liturgical students, and extracts from it have, from time to time, appeared, whilst all historians of the period it covers have sought information in its pages.

The fact that Burchard did not write the book for publication, or for the public eye, suffices to refute the charges of malevolence and falsehood brought against him by his detractors in their anxiety to vindicate the reputation of the House of Borgia. A man occupying the more or less lucrative appointment of Pontifical Sacristan, deriving his income from the Popes, with whom he was in daily contact and on evidently friendly terms, could have no possible object in jotting down, in his private note-book, details of events which, it is contended, either never took place or were exaggerated.

The style and tone of the entries bear witness to their accuracy. They consist merely of rough notes, usually without comment, and in some cases purposely curtailed, or limited to a few words, sufficient only to recall the incidents, barely recorded, to the writer's memory. The work is by no means a mere *chronique scandaleuse*. It consists chiefly of a protocol of ceremonies and functions at the Vatican, the names of persons taking part in them, the vestments worn, the ornaments used, and so forth. Quite incidentally, and clearly without malice aforethought, other matters are introduced, some of them of historical interest, others sufficiently startling and, at times, even shocking. The Diary is intended primarily and obviously as a mere chronicle of official duties and experiences, and was meant to serve as a book of reference, or a record of precedents for Burchard himself.

Nothing could well have been less like an attack upon the Pope, for the author's impartiality is absolutely conspicuous, in spite of the fact that it has been impugned by Borgian apologists. In the first instance these seem to have derived their animosity against Burchard from his bitter, jealous, and abusive enemy, Paris de Grassis, who succeeded him, and also kept a Diary which one day may see the light.

The contemporaries of Burchard, who corroborate the details given in some of the entries in his Diary, such as Infessura, Sanuto, Guicciardini, Giovio, Machiavelli, and others, are, all of them, condemned as atrabilious, untrustworthy enemies of the Pope, whose statements are not worthy of belief !

An impartial student will be unable to adopt this view, nor is it that of such admirably fair and truth-loving Roman Catholic scholars as Professor Ludwig Pastor and the late Lord Acton.

Borgian apologists, some of them, admit that Pope Alexander was a thoroughly bad man, but they defend him on the ground that he was no worse than his predecessors or than several of his immediate successors in the Papal Chair. This may be true, but it does not excuse the Pope. In accepting the position he held, he, like every other Pope, was bound to be a living representative, a "Vicar" of Christ, and no Pope could ever have been so completely ignorant of the life and teaching of his Divine Master as to suppose he was leading the life and setting the example which the whole Christian world had a right to expect from him when he was living as Alexander lived.

In fact Alexander VI., in his better moments, deplored his crimes and shortcomings, confessed them to be worthy of condign punishment, and promised amendment and "the reform of the Church in its head and in its members."

It was the manifest duty of the Pope to lead and not to follow. The age was, much like every other age, "corrupt and lascivious." Undoubtedly corruption in the fifteenth and sixteenth centuries was more conspicuous, for it was rather gloried in than concealed. The Pope's duty, then, was to rise above it, to denounce the evil and to set a good example to the whole world.

That the gross profligacy of the Papal Court gave rise to scandal, is evident, not merely from the published works of contemporary historians and from the private letters addressed by statesmen, diplomats, and others, to their respective governments, or to personages of consequence, but also from the denunciations of the great Florentine, Friar Jerome Savonarola, of the Order of Preachers, who paid for his temerity in reproving the Pontiff, by suffering the dread penalty inflicted upon the excommunicate and the heretic of the time.

All these accumulated items of independent and separate information form together a body of evidence which cannot be gainsaid. If further corroboration is needed it exists in the few frescoes that are preserved in the Borgia apartments at the Vatican and in the Schiffanoia Palace, the residence of Lucrezia Borgia when Duchess of Ferrara. Unfortunately, the life-history of Alexander VI., which formerly adorned the walls of the Castle of Sant' Angelo in fresco, has been entirely obliterated. It was, probably, there that the painting existed in which the Pope's last-known mistress, the lovely Giulia Bella Farnese, was represented as the Blessed Virgin with the Pontiff kneeling at her feet. The same lady appears, in the Borgia apartments, in the fresco of the Trial of St. Catherine painted by Pinturicchio. There Cæsar Borgia is depicted as the King, Djem Sultan standing on his left; Giulia is St. Catherine, and behind her stand the Pope's young son Giuffredo, Prince of Squillace, with his girl-wife, Sancia of Aragon, whilst Juan Borgia, second Duke of Gandia, the elder brother of Cæsar, who had met with a violent death, is mounted on a white charger at the side. Doubtless other contemporary celebrities appear in the same work.

Giulia Farnese, in a condition of complete nudity is still to be seen as " Justice " in the recumbent effigy which adorns the tomb of her brother, Alessandro Farnese, who became Pope Paul III. (1534–50), and who had been promoted to the Cardinalate by Alexander VI.

Pope Pius IX. (1846–78) was so shocked at the presence of this work of art in the Basilica of St. Peter that he ordered it to be covered with a metal chemise, painted to represent the white marble out of which the statue is carved.

I have to express my acknowledgments to numerous authors for the information collected in the present volume, which does not claim to contain anything that can be called original. I have not noticed that any English author has observed that Alexander's tenth known child, the young Rodrigo Borgia, who became a Benedictine at Salerno, was born in 1503, the year of the Pope's decease. Père Suau, S.J., however, mentions the circumstance in a note, in his *Vie de Saint François de Borja.*

I have to express my indebtedness to Father Ehrle, S.J., of the Biblioteca Apostolica at the Vatican, and to Monseigneur Louis Duchesne, of the École de Rome, for their kindness in furnishing items of information for which I applied to them ; also to the authorities at the British and the South Kensington Museums, for their ready and valuable help in preparing casts of various medals preserved in those unrivalled institutions. To the Curator of the Museum at Nîmes I owe my cordial thanks for a photograph of the portrait of Lucrezia Borgia attributed to Dosso Dossi, and my thanks are also due to the Rector of the Jesuit College at the old Borgian Palace at Gandia, to the Curators of the Museums at Naples, Florence, and Rome, and to Messrs. Spithöver of the Piazza di Spagna in Rome, for the assistance they have given me in the search for Borgian photographs.

CONTENTS

CHAPTER I

CHAPTER II

CHAPTER III

CHAPTER IV

CHAPTER V

CHAPTER VI

CHAPTER VII

CHAPTER VIII

CHAPTER IX

CHAPTER X

The French enter Rome with great ceremony—Vannozza's house plundered—Affairs of Djem; his death—Was Alexander responsible for it?—Abdication of Alfonso of Naples in favour of his son Ferrantino; his last days—Ferrantino's bad fortune—Cæsar Borgia escapes to Rome—Fortune favours the French—They enter Naples, February 22, 1495—Ferrantino takes refuge at Ischia—His uncle Federigo—Siege of Castelnuovo—French attitude towards the Neapolitans—Ferdinand the Catholic appealed to by Ferrantino—Comines at Venice—Charles VIII leaves Naples . . . . . p 208

CHAPTER XI

Homeward march of the French—Charles at Siena and Pisa—Battle of Fornuova—Sufferings of the French troops—Arrival at Asti—Surrender of Novara by the Duke of Orleans—The remnant of the French army arrives in France—Importance of the French invasion of Italy—1495 a disastrous year for Rome—Ferrantino welcomed at Naples—Montpensier attacked by the united forces of Ferrantino and Gonsalvo—Marriage of Ferrantino; his death—Succession of his uncle Federigo to the throne of Naples—The affairs of Pisa—Piero de' Medici attempts to return to Florence—Death of Ludovico's wife, Beatrice d'Este, 1497—Ludovico's grief—Alexander's oppression of the Roman nobility—His predilection for Juan, Duke of Gandia—Cæsar's jealousy—Siege of Bracciano—Defeat of papal troops at Soriano—Gonsalvo da Cordova and the Pope—Murder of the Duke of Gandia—The Pope's sorrow—Fiendish character of Cæsar Borgia . . . . p. 229

CHAPTER XII

Florence after the banishment of the Medici—Piero de' Medici repulsed—The Florentines besiege Pisa—Fate of Paolo Vitelli—Savonarola; his execution—Death of Charles VIII—Accession of Louis of Orleans to the French throne—His matrimonial affairs—Cæsar Borgia returns to a secular life—His magnificent

CONTENTS

CHAPTER XIII

CHAPTER XIV

CHAPTER XV

CHAPTER XVI

Bʙ

CHAPTER XVII

CHAPTER XVIII

LIST OF ILLUSTRATIONS

The Life and Times of Rodrigo Borgia

Pope Alexander VI.

CHAPTER I

Origin of the Borgias—Alonso de Borja : his education—Prophecy
of St. Vincent Ferrer—Alonso elected Pope under the title of
Calixtus III , 1455—His nepotism—Crusade against the Turks—
Victory of Belgrade—Feud with Alfonso of Naples and his heir
—Don Pedro Borgia—Death of Calixtus—Rodrigo Borgia :
parentage and education ; relations with Vannozza Catanei ;
made Archbishop of Valencia and raised to the purple ; Vice-
Chancellor of the Holy See—Election of Pope Pius II —
Rodrigo's conduct at Siena—Reproachful letter from the Pope
—Rodrigo's character and appearance—His munificence at
public festivities—Pius II. continues the crusade against the
Turks—Death of Pius II., 1464—Election of Paul II : his
character ; his death, 1471.

THE remarkable and gifted family of the Borgias,
whose name has been so appallingly conspicuous in
the criminal annals of Europe, had its origin in the
little Spanish town of Borja, on the pleasant, fertile
borders of Aragon, Castile, and Navarre. We have
but scant knowledge of the history of this place ; it
was founded apparently, by the Celtiberians in 960 B.C.,
and in A.D. 1120 we hear of its being bestowed by
King Alfonso I. upon Don Pedro Atarés as a reward

for his help in delivering the neighbouring town of Saragossa from the Moorish yoke.

The said Atarés was a grandson of Don Sancho, a natural son of King Ramiro I., and when Alfonso I. died, in 1134, he might, without undue exertion, have obtained the thrones of Aragon and Navarre. But, in gratitude for miraculous preservation in a storm, Atarés had dedicated his life to piety and good works. Among the latter he is credited with founding the monastery of Venuela, where he spent the evening of his days. He died in 1151, and there is no record of his having left any children. A century later, however, when Jaym I , King of Aragon, undertook the conquest of Valencia no less than eight country squires bearing the name of Borgia figured in his army and assisted in the taking of Xativa. Lands were distributed among them, and they soon established themselves in the new kingdom. We hear of a Rodrigo Borgia who shortly afterwards distinguished himself at the capture of Orihuela, but neither he nor his family owned the lordship of Borja, nor did he take rank as an infante of Aragon. In mentioning the Borgias, Viciana, the chronicler of Valencia, confines himself to remarking that they all came from the town of the same name and that Don Jaym held them in great esteem.

In the thirteenth century the heirs of the conquerors seem to have lived in comparative obscurity, but a century later several of them were prominent in the affairs of Xativa. Some inhabited the town, others the " torre de Canals," and the different branches of the family intermarried. In fortune they were equal, and they boasted the same coat-of-arms, " un bœuf passant de gueule," or, " a bull passant gules." In the fifteenth century an alliance took place between the Borgias and a noble house of Aragon, when one Rodrigo Gil de Borja took to wife Sibila Doms. In the escutcheon of Alexander VI. (grandson of Sibila) we see the union of the arms of the Doms family with the Borgia bull.

The real founder of the Borgia[1] greatness was Alonso de Borja, afterwards Pope Calixtus III. He was the child of Domingo de Borja, Doncel y Señor de la Torre de Canals and Francina de Borja of Valencia, and first saw the light at Xativa, on the last day of the year 1378. He was the only son, but there were four daughters, one of whom, Doña Isabella, married her cousin, Jofré de Borja y Doms, and became the mother of the world-famous Alexander VI.

At the age of thirteen or fourteen Alonso was sent to Lerida to continue his education and to specialise in the study of jurisprudence. He took the degree of Doctor of Civil and Canon Law, eventually winning the reputation of one of the most brilliant jurists of the day. After lecturing in this subject with great success he was appointed Canon of the Cathedral of Lerida.[2] When a young priest he was present at a sermon preached by the great Dominican, St. Vincent Ferrer, at Valencia. At the end of his discourse the friar is said to have singled out Alonso from the rest of the throng and to have addressed to him these prophetic words: "My son, I congratulate thee; remember that thou art destined to be one day the glory of thy country and of thy family. Thou wilt be invested with the highest dignity that can fall to the lot of mortal man. I myself, after my death, shall be the object of thy special honour. Endeavour to persevere in the path of virtue." These words greatly impressed Alonso, who confidently awaited their fulfilment.

Later on he obtained the post of Confidential Secretary to Alfonso V., King of Aragon, who recognised his remarkable diplomatic talent, and was the means of bringing him to Naples. Having carried out various diplomatic missions to the King's satisfaction, and

[1] "Borgia" is the Italianised form of "Borja."
[2] Baron Corvo, *Chronicles of the House of Borgia*, p. 12.

rendered important services to the Papacy, he was appointed Bishop of Valencia by Pope Martin V. in 1429. He declined the offer of the purple because disputes had arisen between Pope Eugenius IV. and Alfonso concerning the kingdom of Naples, but he accepted it upon their reconciliation in 1444.

Although pious and well-intentioned, Alonso had already begun to show signs of the nepotism which was to be so remarkable a characteristic of the Borgia family. His sister Isabella was the mother of two sons—Pedro Luis and Rodrigo (the future Alexander VI.). No sooner was Alonso made Cardinal than he obtained for his favourite nephew Rodrigo, the dignity of Precentor of the Chapter of Valencia. This, however, was but the beginning.[1] In 1455 Pope Nicholas V. died, and Alónso, already an old man of seventy-seven, was elected as his successor, under the title of Calixtus III. Though physically frail and worn, his mental powers were as keen as ever, and, having obtained this exalted position, he proceeded to satisfy the cravings of his ambitious relations. At his first Consistory he appointed Juan Luiz del Mila, the son of his sister Catherine, Cardinal Priest, while Rodrigo, his darling nephew, was made Cardinal Deacon and, later, Vice-Chancellor of the Roman Church. Pedro Luis was overwhelmed with dignities—he was created Duke and Count of Spoleto, Lord of Civita Vecchia, Governor of the Patrimony of the Church, Generalissimo of Holy Church, and finally Prefect of Rome. This last office was given him in the hope that he would hold in check the Roman barons, who resented the advent of the foreigners, or Catalans (as the Romans of the fifteenth century called all Spaniards) from Valencia.

Upon his accession to the Papal Chair, Calixtus III. registered a solemn vow of hostility to the Turks—"the irreconcilable enemies of Christendom." He immediately despatched ambassadors to all the Courts

[1] Baron Corvo, *Chronicles of the House of Borgia*, p 18

POPE ALEXANDER VI. (RODRIGO BORGIA).
Pinturicchio (Borgia Apartments, the Vatican).

POPE SIXTUS IV. (FRANCESCO DELLA ROVERE), GIVING AUDIENCE
TO PLATINA, THE HISTORIAN, WHO IS PRESENTED BY THE POPE'S
SON, CARDINAL GIULIANO DELLA ROVERE, AFTERWARDS POPE
JULIUS II. ANOTHER OF THE POPE'S SONS, CARDINAL RIARIO,
STANDS ON HIS RIGHT.
Melozzo (fresco in the Vatican).

[32]

of Europe, exhorting them to join a crusade against
their common enemy. According to his successor,
Æneas Silvius Piccolomini, he was successful in raising
a large army and a fleet of sixty galleys by dint of
collecting free-will contributions and levying tithes.
A regular system of collecting was organised and
many precautions taken that the funds should be
exclusively devoted to the expenses of the crusade.
In spite of the greatest care, however, a certain
amount of dishonesty crept in and brought discredit
upon the enterprise, though the Pope did his best
to find out and punish the offenders.

Not content with collecting money for the crusade,
the zealous Calixtus did not scruple to annex jewels
from the papal treasury and to dispose of church
property to provide for the expenses of the war. There
is still in existence a lengthy list of valuables sold by
the Pope to the art-loving Alfonso of Naples, in 1456.[1]
He even stripped the volumes in the Vatican Library
of their gold and silver to augment the war fund, an
act which provoked much criticism. Calixtus himself
lived in a simple and frugal style and was not slow to
express his disapproval of the extravagance of his
predecessor, Nicholas V., who had lavished on jewels
and manuscripts wealth which might have been consecrated to the crusade. The buildings begun by the
late Pope were discontinued and the papal revenues
no longer devoted to the encouragement of literature.
Men of letters, indeed, found themselves in little
request under the new regime, when the severest
simplicity prevailed. The aged Pope, indeed, rarely
left his room, and, as Gregorovius remarks, " the
Vatican resembled an infirmary where the gouty
Pontiff spent the greater part of his time by candle-
light in bed, surrounded by nephews and mendicant
friars."

In spite of the Pope's unfailing energy in trying

[1] Baron Corvo, *Chronicles of the House of Borgia*, p. 29

to arouse interest in the crusade, the Catholic princes did not respond to his appeals, but remained steeped in lethargy, even when the Turks planted their standard on the Hungarian frontiers and besieged Belgrade. Calixtus, though grieved to the heart, did not lose courage. Day by day he wrestled with God in prayer, and it was at this time that he instituted the custom of ringing the Angelus bell " I acknowledge and firmly believe, O Almighty God," he prayed " that it is Thy will that I alone should wear myself out and die for the general good. So be it ! I am ready, even if I must myself go into bondage and alienate all the possessions of the Church." His efforts were rewarded, and help arrived in the persons of the Hungarian hero Hunyadi and the saintly monk John Capistran, who, in July 1456, effected the deliverance of Belgrade. The aged Calixtus was overcome with joy at this victory. " The Pope," writes the Milanese ambassador, " praised Hunyadi to the skies, calling him the greatest man that the world had seen for three hundred years." The Turkish fleet also was defeated at Mitylene by the Cardinal Scarampa in August 1457. The Pope, however, was not content with this measure of success, and made plans to advance into Ethiopia and even to carry the war into Granada. He was continually enlisting fresh help, though by this time his treasury was completely exhausted and even his own vestments were pawned.

Meanwhile he had to fight against his former friend, Alfonso of Aragon, who, on the strength of having advanced the Borgia fortunes by his patronage, was not slow to demand unreasonable favours of the Pope. When the latter refused to cede to him the March of Ancona and other lands of the Church, with the words, " Let the King of Aragon govern his kingdom, and leave to Us the administration of the Church," he took the direst umbrage and never forgave the rebuff, in spite of the efforts of Cardinal Rodrigo Borgia to bring about a reconciliation. When Alfonso died, in June 1458, Calixtus refused to acknowledge his son Ferrante as the heir, on the score of his illegitimate birth, and claimed the kingdoms of Naples and Sicily as the property of the Holy See. In a conversation with the Milanese ambassador, he spoke of Ferrante as a little bastard whose father was unknown. " This boy, who is nothing," he said, " calls himself King without our permission. Naples belongs to the Church ; it is the possession of St. Peter. . . . If Don Ferrante will give up his usurped title and humbly place himself in our hands, we will treat him as one of our own nephews."

This, however, Ferrante was in nowise inclined to do. He called on his barons for help, and sent ambassadors to Rome to appeal against the Pope's decree. Duke Francesco Sforza of Milan, the most potent of Italian princes, as well as Cosmo de' Medici, took his part, and it is difficult to say what complications might have arisen, if the death of Calixtus had not intervened, August 8, 1458. Even on his death-bed he did not forget the promotion of his family. The Vicariate of Terracina he bestowed upon his nephew, Don Pedro, who, by his arrogance and love of display, had aroused the envy and hatred of the Roman nobles, especially the Colonna and Orsini. While Calixtus lay dying the storm burst. The nobility and the populace attacked the Castle of Sant' Angelo, in which Don Pedro had shut himself, and threatened to set fire to Rome if he would not surrender the fortress. This he declared himself ready to do on payment of 20,000 gold ducats. His enemies, however, were not satisfied, and demanded his life. At great risk, he succeeded in escaping by night from Rome, with the assistance of the Venetian Cardinal Barbo. He was also accompanied by a troop of soldiers and his devoted brother Rodrigo in disguise. In order to

mislead the enemy, they turned first in the direction
of the Ponte Molle, and then hurried on to the Porta
di San Paolo.   At this gate the two Cardinals left him,
after commanding the soldiers to escort him to Ostia ;
but, so much was he hated, that they nearly all refused
to accompany him, and when, at last, after many
obstacles, the wretched man arrived at Ostia, the
vessel which he was expecting failed him, and he was
obliged to escape in a small boat to Civita Vecchia,
where he shortly afterwards died.

Cardinal Rodrigo returned to Rome after his
brother's flight—an action which required no little
courage on his part.   The same evening (August 6)
the Pope's sufferings ended, and he passed to his rest.
The Romans shed no tears for him, for his death
freed them from the hated yoke of the Catalans.
His burial was conducted with scant ceremony, only
four priests following him to the grave.[1]

The two dominant interests of Calixtus III. were
the crusade against the Turks and the promotion of
his own family.   Apart from his nepotism, his conduct
as Pope does not offer much scope for blame.   On
the whole, he seems to have led a virtuous and honourable life, gentle and indulgent to the failings of others,
but strict and harsh towards his own.   His attitude
toward the Renaissance strikes one as apathetic, but
it must be remembered that the duty of defending
Europe from the infidels absorbed him to such an
extent that he had little time for the encouragement
of art and letters.   He was not, as his accusers have
maintained, actively opposed to their progress, but
simply indifferent.

That the earlier career of Calixtus III. had not
been beyond reproach is proved by the existence of a
bastard son, Don Francisco de Borja, born in 1441,
and of whom we shall hear from time to time in the
course of this history.

[1] Baron Corvo, *Chronicles of the House of Borgia*, p. 57.

The hatred which pursued Don Pedro did not
extend to his younger brother, Cardinal Rodrigo,
who was later to play such a remarkable part in the
history of Italy. As we have already seen, he was
the second son of Jofré de Borja y Doms, a Valencian
nobleman who married Isabella Borgia, sister of
Calixtus III. Rodrigo was thus doubly a Borgia, and
not, as many have maintained, connected with the
family only through his mother.

He was born at Xativa in 1431. Like the rest of
his race, he was distinguished for physical beauty and
strength, and already, at eight years old, was conspicuous in the streets of Xativa for the grace and
gallantry of his bearing. His father died when the
boy was only ten, and his widowed mother took up
her abode at Valencia, a town well provided with
educational advantages. His uncle, Alonso, was at
that time Bishop, and we may suppose that his influence
contributed to enhance the reputation which Valencia
already bore as a literary centre. The little Rodrigo,
we hear, displayed remarkable aptitude for learning,
and soon arrived at the head of his school ; but even
thus early his character showed certain undesirable
tendencies which boded ill for his future career. He
pursued his studies with great zeal, under excellent
teachers, until his eighteenth year, when he went to
the University of Bologna and studied law under the
celebrated Gaspar Veronese. On his return to Spain
he practised as an advocate, earning large sums which
might have been even larger but for his unstable and
volatile disposition. Suddenly he became dissatisfied
with his profession and yearned to distinguish himself
in a military career. Meanwhile he had made the
acquaintance of a widow and her two daughters, and
so great was his depravity that he not only maintained
illicit relations with the mother, but strove also to
enter into a like guilty connection with both the
daughters. After the mother's death he undertook

the guardianship of her children.   One of them he
despatched to a convent, and the other—Catarina (or
Rose) Vannozza Catanei—he retained as his mistress.
Of Vannozza's origin little is known.   She was a
Roman, perhaps of the *petite bourgeoisie* (or, according
to Adinolfi, of a family " non ignobile "), and was born
in July 1442.   Her real name was Giovanna, of which
Vannozza is an adaptation.   We have no authenticated
portrait of her and no very definite description, but
from our limited sources of information we gather
that she was a subtle combination of voluptuous
beauty, amiability, and shrewdness.   She must
certainly have been possessed of some remarkable
magnetism in order to have exercised a permanent
attraction upon so fastidious a man as Rodrigo Borgia.

According to the well-known Roman Catholic
historian, Dr. Ludwig Pastor, his relations with
Vannozza began about the year 1460, when she
became his acknowledged mistress.

Rodrigo's intercourse with Vannozza resulted in
the birth of five children, of whom we shall hear in
another chapter.   They were Don Pedro Luis, First
Duke of Gandia, born probably in 1467; Don Giovanni, born 1474, and assassinated 1498; Don Cæsar
Borgia, who figures so largely in his father's pontificate,
born 1476; Donna Lucrezia, born 1480; and Don
Jofré, born 1481.

Rodrigo was an affectionate father, and did not
stint money to give his children a good education and
a comfortable home.   He did not, however, recognise
them openly before he became Pope.

But to return to Pope Calixtus III.   As we have
already mentioned, his first care was to advance the
fortunes of his family, and in particular, those of his
nephews Pedro Luis and Rodrigo.   The latter, however, was so bound by the fascinations of a life of
pleasure that his uncle's promotion did not give him
as much satisfaction as might have been expected.

Nevertheless, he wrote him a respectful letter of congratulation.

No sooner did the Pope receive the letter than he sent Rodrigo the most cordial reply, expressing his joy in possessing a nephew so skilled in jurisprudence, and inviting him to come immediately to Rome and devote himself to the affairs of the State. But to Rodrigo the idea of leaving his home and amusements and giving up his present lucrative employment was most distasteful. The Pope, all impatient, sent prelates to fetch him, with the offer of a rich benefice to tempt him. Rodrigo, however, still wavered, and turned irresolute, to Vannozza herself. Together they decided that Rodrigo should accept his uncle's invitation to Rome, and that his mistress should establish herself at Venice. Soon afterwards Vannozza set out on her journey, unaccompanied save for two servants and a Spanish noble, Don Manuel Melchior (perhaps the only person who was really aware of her amorous relations), while Rodrigo betook himself to Rome, where he stayed with his friend, Cardinal San Severino.

Soon after his arrival he was summoned by the Pope. Rodrigo cast himself at his uncle's feet, with congratulations upon his promotion. Calixtus, for his part, spoke in glowing terms of his nephew's capabilities, and created him Archbishop of Valencia. A little later—in September 1456—both Rodrigo and his brother, Don Pedro, were raised to the purple in a secret Consistory, though neither of them had the remotest claim to piety. Rodrigo's reputation, indeed, was such as to make his elevation repugnant to the more conscientious of the Cardinals, and it was not until some months later, when they had all left Rome for cooler regions, that Calixtus made the nomination public. It is noteworthy that the Pope did nothing for his own son Francisco, at that time a worthy and pleasing youth of fifteen. Don Jaym of

Portugal was, however, raised to the purple with Don Pedro and Rodrigo. It is pleasant to record that this Portuguese Cardinal continued to live a pure and virtuous life even amid the frightful corruptions of Rome. He died at the age of twenty-five, and his tomb, the work of Antonio Rossellino, is one of the most beautiful monuments of the Renaissance.

Rodrigo's pleasure at being made Cardinal was not unmixed, for he realised that his new dignity would be an additional tie to Rome and an obstacle in the way of his intercourse with Vannozza. But the hope of one day occupying the Papal Chair bore him up. Suddenly, and without any warning, he began to display a most unwonted piety and humility. He paced the streets with sunken head and downcast eyes, paid frequent visits to churches and hospitals, and exhorted the people to faith. He thus acquired a reputation for sanctity quite foreign to his real character.

In 1457 Rodrigo was made Vice-Chancellor of the Holy See as a reward for his services in connection with the disturbances in central Italy. During the hostilities between Filippo Visconti and Alfonso of Aragon, Francesco Sforza had taken possession of nearly the whole boundary-line dividing their States. Hard pressed by Piccinino and other generals, he cast himself upon the domain of Ascoli and appointed Giovanni Sforza as his governor. But a young man named Giosia instigated a conspiracy, banished Sforza from Ascoli, and himself took the reins of authority. Exasperated by his tyranny, the citizens drove him away and appealed to the Church for protection. Giosia, with the help of a few banditti, seized a castle in the neighbourhood of Ascoli and laid waste the surrounding country. The Pope despatched Rodrigo to quell the disturbance, and he performed the errand with so much success that he took the castle and brought Giosia in chains to Rome. On July 4, 1455,

VITTORIA COLONNA.

Muziano (Colonna Gallery, Rome).

VANNOZZA, MISTRESS OF POPE ALEXANDER VI.

Girolamo da Carpi (Borghese Gallery, Rome).

This is one of several existing portraits said to represent Vannozza.

32]

the Cardinal of Siena informed the Cardinal of Sant Angelo of the capture, and the Cardinal of Pavia, in his commentaries, speaks of the skill and decision with which Rodrigo managed the affair.

As long as Calixtus lived Rodrigo seems to have kept his vicious tendencies more or less within bounds. Æneas Silvius Piccolomini, afterwards Pope Pius II., indeed refers to him in the following approving words : " Our Chancellor, Rodrigo Borgia, the Pope's nephew, is young, it is true, but his conduct and good sense make him seem older than his years; in wisdom he is equal to his uncle." But, as will shortly appear, with the advent of the next Pope he began to change his manner of life.

When Calixtus III. died in 1458 Cardinal Rodrigo was the most important personage of the House of Borgia. " Quite unmoved by the hatred of the other Purpled Ones, he entered the Conclave of 1458 for the election of the new Pope, with no such stupid thing as a plan of action, but with a determination to comport himself, according as opportunities arose, so as to improve his position and prospects. . . . To a young man of such temper the gods send opportunities."[1] When the votes were taken it was found that Cardinal d'Estouteville had six, while Cardinal Æneas Silvius Piccolomini of Siena had nine, but neither of them had the minimum majority. A hush of expectation ensued, broken by Rodrigo Borgia, who rose up and proclaimed : " I vote for the Cardinal of Siena." After another silence Cardinals Tebaldo and Prospero Colonna followed his example, and the minimum majority was attained. Thus Æneas Silvius Piccolomini, poet-laureate, ambassador, novelist, historian, Bishop and Cardinal, a man of varied and romantic experience, received the homage of the Cardinals as Pope Pius II. Campano, his biographer, tells us that he burst into tears, so greatly was he moved

[1] Baron Corvo, *Chronicles of the House of Borgia*, p. 60.

CB

by the idea of his new responsibilities. In response to the cheering words of his friends, he answered that none could rejoice at being raised to such a dignity save those who forgot its attendant dangers and toils.

Piccolomini's election was received as tidings of great joy, and all the Italian Powers, except Florence and Venice, breathed more freely now that they had escaped the infliction of a foreign Pope. Although only in his fifty-fourth year, Pius II. was already breaking down in health. Not only did he suffer tortures from an internal malady, but he was often unable to move owing to severe gout. He had contracted this latter affliction by going on a pilgrimage barefoot in fulfilment of a vow made during a storm off the coast of Scotland. But in spite of his physical disabilities his mental powers were keen and bright, and, for the first time for many a long year, the Papal Chair was filled by a broad-minded, travelled, and cultured man who was really fitted to restore the former glory of the Papacy. Those who looked to find in him a literary patron like Nicholas V. were, however, disappointed, for the one aim and object of his reign was the recovery of Constantinople from the Turks. With the assumption of the tiara the pleasure-loving, literary man of the world changed his rôle entirely, and devoted his whole energies to the one purpose for which he considered that God had now called him.[1]

Little is known of the concerns of Rodrigo Borgia during this pontificate. We hear of his going in 1459 on a holiday jaunt with the new Pope, who, not unnaturally, took a special interest in the brilliant

[1] The Roman Catholic historian, Ludwig Pastor, says of him : " In 1444 he confessed to one of his friends that he shrank from entering the ecclesiastical state, *timeo enim castitatem* " He was the father of several illegitimate children. (*History of the Popes*, vol. 1. p. 343.)

young Cardinal who had practically set the tiara on
his head. They visited Florence and chatted with
the little Leonardo da Vinci, then a child of seven.
They also went to Siena and Corsignano, the Pope's
birthplace, where he made arrangements for the
building of a Cathedral, an episcopal palace, and the
Piccolomini Palace for his own family. The super-
intendence of these buildings he confided to Cardinal
Rodrigo, who took advantage of the opportunity to
have their façades adorned with the arms of the
House of Borgia.[1]

In 1460 the Pope, who was recruiting his health
at the Baths of Petrioli, received disquieting rumours
of Rodrigo's proceedings. The young Cardinal, it
seems, was disporting himself at Siena, where he took
part in a bacchanalian orgy and conducted himself
in a manner calculated to bring deep discredit upon
the Church. The following reproachful letter from
Pius II. reveals the situation :

" DEAR SON,

    " Four days ago several ladies of Siena who are
entirely given up to worldly frivolities were assembled
in the gardens of Giovanni di Bichis. We have heard
that you, unmindful of the high office with which
you are invested, were with them from the seventeenth
to the twenty-second hour. In company with you
was one of your colleagues, whose years, if not the
respect due to the Holy See, ought to have recalled
to him his duty. From what we have heard, the
most licentious dances were indulged in ; no amorous
seductions were lacking, and you conducted yourself
in a manner wholly worldly. Modesty forbids the
mention of all that took place, for not only the acts
themselves, but their very names, are unworthy of

[1] Baron Corvo, *Chronicles of the House of Borgia*, pp. 61, 62.

your position. In order that your lusts might have freer course, the husbands, fathers, brothers, and kinsmen of the young women were not admitted. You and a few servants were the organisers of this orgy. To-day every one in Siena is talking about your frivolity, which is the subject of common derision. Certain it is that here at the Baths, where there is a large number of ecclesiastics and laymen, your name is upon every tongue. Our displeasure is beyond words, for your conduct has brought discredit upon your holy office and state; people will say that they invest us with riches and greatness, not that we may live a blameless life, but that we may have means to gratify our passions. This is why the princes and the Powers despise us and the laity mock us daily; this is why our own conduct is thrown in our face when we reprove others. The Vicar of Christ is exposed to contempt because he appears to tolerate these proceedings. You, dear son, have charge of the bishopric of Valencia, the most important in Spain; moreover, you are Chancellor of the Church, and, what makes your conduct all the more reprehensible, is your having a seat among the Cardinals, with the Pope, as adviser of the Holy See. We submit the case to your own judgment: is it becoming for a man of your position to pay court to young women, to send fruit and wines to those whom you love, and to have no thought during the whole day save for all kinds of voluptuous pleasures? We are blamed on your account, and the memory of your blessed uncle, Calixtus, likewise suffers, and he is condemned by many for having heaped honour upon your head. It is useless to seek to excuse yourself on account of your age; you are no longer so young as not to be able to understand what duties your dignities impose upon you A cardinal ought to be above reproach and an example of good living to all. Have we the right to be vexed when temporal

princes bestow disrespectful titles upon us, when
they dispute the possession of our property and
force us to submit to their injunctions? It must be
confessed that we inflict these wounds upon ourselves,
and that with our own hands we prepare these troubles,
by every day diminishing the authority of the Church
through our conduct. Our punishment for it in
this world is dishonour, and in the world to come
well-merited torment. May, therefore, your good
sense put restraint upon irregularities, and may
you never lose sight of the dignity with which you
are clothed, that you may never again be called a
gallant among women and young men. If this
occurs again we shall be obliged to point out that it
is in spite of our admonitions, and that it causes us
great pain. In such a case our censure would cover
you with confusion. We have always loved you and
thought you worthy of our protection as a man of
modest and serious character. Therefore, conduct
yourself in such a way that we may retain this opinion
of you; nothing could contribute further to this
than the adoption of a regular mode of life. Your
age, which is not such as to preclude amendment,
authorises us to admonish you thus paternally.

" PETRIOLI,
   "*June* 11, 1460."

Rodrigo was at this time twenty-nine years of age
—a man of remarkable beauty, tall and dark, with
piercing black eyes. He had gracious and persuasive
manners and a strong and attractive personality.
But he made no effort to subordinate his insatiable
sensuality to his higher faculties, and even when, in
1464, he accompanied the ailing Pope on his celebrated expedition to Ancona, this "essentially low-
minded man" could not refrain from his dissolute
habits. Gaspar Veronensis describes him later as " a
comely man of cheerful countenance and honeyed

discourse, who gains the affections of all the women he admires, and attracts them as the lodestone attracts iron."[1]

To all his physical and mental gifts was added the attraction of wealth. Not only did he inherit the large fortune left by his brother, Don Pedro Luis, but he was the occupant of many lucrative posts. His income from the Church and cloisters in Italy and Spain and the three Cathedrals of Valencia, Carthegena, and Porto was immense. As Vice-Chancellor alone he received 8,000 scudi. His wealth enabled him to live in a princely manner and to sustain a numerous retinue. In his magnificent palace were heaped up treasures of all kinds—silver caskets, precious stones, silk stuffs and gold brocades. His library contained rare and valuable works in every branch of learning and his stables were filled with the most beautiful horses. The whole palace was furnished in a costly and luxurious style, and everywhere was displayed an amazing amount of gold and silver.

But, notwithstanding this abundance, it seems that Rodrigo's housekeeping was of a strangely thrifty kind. The Ferrarese ambassador, writing of him after he had become Pope, says that it was a penance to dine with him, so frugal was his table, and that for this reason Cardinal Monreale and others, whenever possible, evaded his invitations.

In justice to Cardinal Rodrigo, however, it must be said that he was in many respects generous and free-handed, as will be seen by his behaviour under the following circumstances.

In 1462 Pope Pius II., seeking relief from his gout, went to Viterbo, where Rodrigo owned a splendid palace. As the Feast of *Corpus Domini* drew near, the Cardinals and the populace vied with one another in their schemes for decorating the road along which

[1] Baron Corvo, *Chronicles of the House of Borgia*, p. 63.

the sacred procession would pass. But Rodrigo surpassed them all. Gobellino, the Secretary of Pius II., writes: " The space which Rodrigo undertook to arrange contained seventy-four paces. A purple curtain screened statues, reliefs of historical representations, and a richly decorated *stanza* containing a costly throne and a fountain, from which flowed not merely water, but choice wine. At the Pope's approach two young maidens advanced towards him. They sang as sweetly as angels, and when they had, with deference, saluted the Blessed Sacrament and the Pope, they retired towards the curtain and sang in their clear and beautiful voices, ' Open your gates, O Princes, and there shall enter King Pius, the Lord of the world.' Then stepped forward five kings and a band of armed men, magnificently attired, in order to protect the entrance. At the angels' words they exclaimed, ' And who is this King Pius ? ' The angels, pointing to the Holy Sacrament which Pius bore in his hands, cried, ' The mighty Lord of the Universe.' Thereupon the curtain was drawn aside, the entry made free, and the sound of trombones, organs, and many other instruments arose. The kings, amid much applause, intoned a harmonious chant of heroic verses in praise of the Pope. In the procession was a savage, leading a fettered lion with whom he often wrestled. Over the whole space was spread a canopy of rich material, from which hung banners covered with mottoes and symbols of Pope Calixtus and Pedro Luis Borgia, Prefect of Rome. On both sides hung carpets [*arazzi*], valuable both from their material and their artistic execution. The populace and the cultured alike admired them and feasted their eyes upon their beauty. At the exit were armed men arranged in a triumphal arch in the form of a castello. By means of metal machines they contrived to imitate thunder, so that the passers-by were greatly alarmed."

Rodrigo also distinguished himself on the occasion of the splendid festivities of Holy Week, 1462, when the head of St. Andrew was carried into Rome with great pomp and ceremony. According to Gobellino, Cardinal Borgia far outshone the other Cardinals in the brilliance and taste he displayed. He covered the whole of his own house with rich and rare materials, and also superintended the decoration of the neighbouring dwellings, so that the· surrounding space appeared a veritable paradise, full of beauty, music, and song. His palace shone like gold, and the walls were adorned with verses and inscriptions proclaiming in large letters the praise of the Apostle and of Pope Pius II.

Cardinal Borgia's generosity also displayed itself on later occasions, such as the celebrations in honour of the taking of Granada, and the restoration of the Church of Santa Maria in the Via Lata. He contributed liberally to Paul II.'s equipment for the siege of Rimini, as indeed he did to every public undertaking. Pope Paul II. entrusted to him the management of the poor relief fund, and, on the authority of an eye-witness, it is said that the Cardinal saved many needy persons from perishing of hunger.

As we have already mentioned, the necessity for crushing the Turkish power was keenly felt by Pius II. In September 1459 he delivered a great oration showing that, if the Turks conquered Hungary, there would be no check to their descent upon Italy. After futile efforts to rouse the princes of Europe from their apathy, he thought to put them to the blush by leading a crusade in person, fragile and infirm as he was. This heroic decision aroused great enthusiasm among the Cardinals. Rodrigo Borgia, in particular, was ardent in his expressions of approval: " I will be at your side, Pontiff," he exclaimed, " on sea and on land, and even, if necessary, will follow you through fire ! "

The financial needs of the crusade were unexpectedly supplied by the discovery of some alum-mines near Civita Vecchia by a' friend of the Piccolomini family, who gladly contributed to the great cause.

On June 18, 1464, Pius II., weak in body but strong in soul, left the Eternal City for Ancona, the meeting-place of the crusaders. " Farewell, Rome ! " he cried with prophetic insight, " never wilt thou see me again alive ! " In support of Cardinal Borgia's generosity it is mentioned that, not only did he accompany the Pope, but that at his own expense he equipped a fleet. At Ancona Pius II. took up his abode in the episcopal palace while making preparations to continue his journey. But the hand of Death was already upon him. He became seriously ill, and the gravity of his condition was aggravated by the intense heat and the mental distress of disillusionment regarding the success of the projected crusade. He was keenly disappointed at the non-arrival of the Venetian fleet, which he awaited with pathetic persistence. At last, on August 12, their approach was announced. The dying Pontiff rallied for a time and asked to be carried to the window which looked out upon the sea. " A flood of despondency overwhelmed his spirit " as he watched the ships coming in, and with plaintive sadness he whispered : " Until this day the fleet was wanting for my expedition, and now I must be wanting to my fleet."

Two days later the Cardinals gathered round the Pope's death-bed and listened with tears to his last counsels. So much affected were they by his impressive words that for some time not one of them could speak, but finally Bessarion, in the name of all, made a short reply. Only a few hours longer and the brave, worn spirit of Pius II. passed from the fever and the fret of life to its eternal reward.

His death was a severe loss, not only to Western Christendom but also to the Christians of the East, who were already feeling the weight of Turkish oppression. The crusade of which he had been the life and soul now came to an end, and the Venetian fleet returned to Venice.

Those Cardinals who had been in attendance on Pius II. hastened to Rome for the election of his successor. Cardinal Borgia's departure seems to have been delayed, however, by an attack of fever.

On August 28 the Cardinals went into Conclave, and on the 30th the result of the election was made known after only one scrutiny. For a long time it had seemed probable the tiara would fall to Cardinal Bessarion, who was invested with the dignity of Dean of the Sacred College. After him the most note-worthy among the Cardinals were d'Estouteville, the head of the French party ; the zealous Carvajal ; Torquemada, the famous theologian, and his two antitheses, Scarampo and Barbo. [1]   In the first scrutiny Scarampo had seven votes, d'Estouteville nine, and Barbo eleven ; the latter immediately received three more votes by way of *accessit*, and his election was thus secured. The news was welcomed with joy, and the handsome and popular Cardinal received homage under the title of Paul II. He was at this time in the forty-eighth year of his age, " grand seigneur d'esprit léger, tout occupé de statues grecques et de fêtes carnavalesques," says Gebhart, who also remarks that " with Paul II. began that period in the history of the Church when the Popes had nothing apostolic about them." He had originally been intended for a commercial career, and his adoption of the ecclesiastical profession was due to his uncle, Pope Eugenius IV., who undertook the supervision of his education. In 1440 Barbo, together with his rival Scarampo, had been raised to the purple, and in the following years had become, through his gentle-ness, generosity, and charming manners, one of the

[1] See Pastor, *History of the Popes*, vol. iv. p. 5.

most popular personages in Rome. Unfortunately he
took no interest in humanistic studies, and, though his
hostile attitude towards learning has probably been
exaggerated, he certainly contributed but little to
the advancement of literature during his pontificate.
What he lacked in intellectual culture, however, he
sought to make up by the pomp and splendour of
his person and surroundings, which far outshone those
of any previous Pope. His love for precious stones
amounted to a passion, and his tiara was adorned
with the most costly jewels. In appearance he was
tall, handsome, and of dignified bearing. It is said
that for half a century no handsomer man had been
seen in the Senate of the Church. His chief faults
were vanity and jealousy, but these were to a certain
extent counterbalanced by his great kindness of
heart. His goodness to the poor was proverbial, and
he is reputed to have been constant in visiting the
sick, to whom he dispensed medicines gratis. To
the Cardinals he used jokingly to say that, when
he became Pope, each of them should have a beautiful
villa into which he might retire for refreshment during
the hot days of summer.

During the reign of Paul II. (1464–1471) Rodrigo
Borgia remained in favour, and, by reason of his
courtly manners and noble presence, was deputed
to receive the Cæsar, Frederic IV., at Viterbo, upon
the occasion of his state-visit to the Pope in 1469.

Paul did not have so long a reign as his comparative
youth had led people to expect. On the morning of
July 26, 1471, he appeared to be in his usual good
health and held a Consistory lasting for six hours.
He then dined in the garden, indulging in two enormous water-melons, among other delicacies. Later
that night he was seized with an apoplectic fit which
quickly terminated his career. Compared with those
that followed, his reign seems almost praiseworthy,
though his private life and morals would not have

borne a close examination. He had done nothing to forward the plans of his predecessor, and his chief merit lies in his having, to some extent, increased the material prosperity of the Holy See. From a religious point of view his pontificate was unedifying, and tended to pave the way for the grossly immoral and worldly Popes who were to follow.

CHAPTER II

UNDER the dissolute and incompetent rule of Henry IV.
of Castile the country fell into a sorry state. Through
the debasement of the coinage and the depredations
of the nobles, the most shocking confusion prevailed.
Travellers were plundered and Christian prisoners sold
as slaves to the Moors, while the castles of the nobility
became neither more nor less than dens of robbers.
Not only were the King's slackness and incapacity a
source of grievance, but he rendered himself actively
objectionable by making favourites of men of low
degree and promoting them over the heads of the
ancient nobility of the land. But the climax of his
transgressions, which provoked an insurrection of the
nobles under Juan Pacheco, Marquis of Villena, was
Henry's proclamation of his little daughter Juana as
heir to the throne. Thereby hangs a tale. In 1455
Henry had married the sister of Alfonso, King of
Portugal—the gay and sprightly young Princess
Juana. For many years their union proved fruitless,
but in the spring of 1462, the Queen gave birth to a
baby girl. Public rejoicings were set on foot, but
over them all lay the shadow of hypocrisy, for popular

opinion strongly suspected that not Henry, but Beltran de la Cueva, the young Count of Ledesma, was the father of the baby princess. Even as the nobles, prelates, and deputies advanced to swear allegiance to her, words of anger and disdain were uttered beneath their breath, and when she was invested with the nickname of " la Beltraneja," no official remonstrance was made.

Only a fortnight after the Cortes had taken the oath of allegiance to the little princess, Pacheco drew up a secret protest, maintaining her illegitimacy, and before long the rebellion against the King and his favourite, Beltran de la Cueva, came to a head. Ever since the birth of la Beltraneja, Beltran had been treated with almost regal honours by the King, and Villena and his uncle, the Archbishop of Toledo, became more and more filled with resentment. Now that open opposition was declared, the King's position was far from pleasant, and on one occasion he was forced to hide in his own palace from the assaults of Villena's soldiers. After many humiliations and indignities he submitted, and tried to assuage the wrath of his mutinous subjects.

Living at the Spanish Court at this time (1466) was the King's youngest sister, Isabella, a sage and dignified damsel of fifteen. She had been brought up by her mother in deep seclusion in the little town of Arevalo, but in 1462, at Henry's wish, she and her brother Alfonso had been removed to the Court. Here, in the midst of much that was corrupt, Isabella retained her maiden purity and grace, and soon became distinguished for her strength and determination of character. Many wooers sought her hand, among them Don Pedro Giron, Master of Calatrava and brother of Villena. He was a coarse-mannered upstart of shady reputation, and Isabella would have none of him. In spite, however, of her sturdy opposition, King Henry was insistent in his endeavours to promote

this match, and petitioned the Pope to dispense
Don Pedro from his vow of celibacy. But, just as the
dispensation arrived and the exultant bridegroom
set out to claim his bride, his career was suddenly cut
short by poison. It has never been known whether
Isabella was concerned in the plot to kill him, for
although, in these days, the idea of a high-principled
woman's taking part in such a crime is barely credible,
we must remember that the ethical standards of
that time differed in many ways from those of
to-day.

Meanwhile war had broken out. On August 20,
1467, the two armies met on the field of Olmedo.
The Archbishop of Toledo led into battle the King's
half-brother, the boy Alfonso, whom he wished to
set upon the throne, while on the other side Beltran
de la Cueva was conspicuous for his valour. The
result of the battle was indecisive, though indirectly
it went against the King, who appears to have displayed considerable cowardice on this occasion. A
fearful state of anarchy ensued, and the whole country
was divided against itself. Although, after the battle,
an arrangement had been made by which Henry and
Alfonso respectively were to govern the territories
held by their partisans, this was rendered impossible
by the fatuity of one monarch and the extreme youth
of the other.

The crisis was just at its height when the young
Alfonso came to a sudden and mysterious end, July
1468. The fact that his death was publicly announced
some days before it occurred confirms the suspicions
of foul play, and it is commonly supposed that he
died from eating some poisoned trout. The hopes
of his party were now centred·upon Isabella, who in
1467 had left the corrupt Court and thrown in her lot
with her brother Alfonso. Overwhelmed with sadness
at his death, she retired to the convent of Santa Clara
at Avila, refusing the Archbishop of Toledo's request

that she would allow herself to be proclaimed Queen of Castile.   She wished to be reconciled to her brother Henry, she said, and could not entertain the thought of such disloyalty to him.   She was not, however, averse from accepting the position of heir to the throne if the King could be prevailed upon to acknowledge her.

Henry was easily persuaded, and had an affectionate meeting with his sister at a place called Toros de Guisando.   They entered upon a formal agreement by which Isabella was recognised as the heir to the crowns of Castile and Leon (September 9, 1468).

Isabella was now about seventeen, strong in body and mind, and clear-sighted beyond her fellows.   In appearance she was attractive—tall and blue-eyed, with ruddy chestnut hair and clear complexion—" the handsomest lady," says one of her household, " whom I ever beheld, and the most gracious in her manners." Her mother, to whom she was tenderly devoted, had already fallen a victim to the hereditary insanity of the House of Portugal, so that Isabella was obliged to face the world alone.   Her brother Henry was really ill-disposed towards her, and she had no other near relation.

All sorts of plans were now made to procure a suitable husband for Isabella.   Many sought her hand, but the only two to whom she gave any encouragement were the Duke of Guienne, brother of Louis XI., and Ferdinand of Aragon, son and heir of John II. of Aragon.   Ferdinand, who was an engaging youth of her own age, won the day, greatly to Henry's displeasure, for, by the treaty of Toros, his consent was necessary to his sister's marriage. He gave orders for her arrest, but she was taken by the Archibshop of Toledo and Admiral Henriquez to Valladolid, where she was put under the protection of the friendly citizens.   After a time she was joined by Ferdinand, disguised as a servant.   The nuptials

PERHAPS JUAN BORGIA, SECOND DUKE OF GANDIA, SECOND SON OF POPE
ALEXANDER VI.
Pinturicchio (*Borgia Apartments, the Vatican*).

were not long delayed, for, though Pope Paul II.,
who was on the side of the Castilian Court, refused
to sanction the marriage of these second cousins
by a dispensation, Ferdinand and his wily supporters,
John II. and the Archbishop of Toledo, forged a papal
bull in order to quiet Isabella's scruples of propriety.
On October 19, 1469, their marriage was publicly
celebrated at the palace of Juan de Vivero, with
whom the Princess had been staying.   The celebrations
were but simple, for both bride and bridegroom
were poor in this world's goods, and indeed found
difficulty in obtaining the wherewithal to set up their
modest household.   Ferdinand at this time was about
eighteen, a year younger than his bride.   He was
fair-complexioned, with a muscular and well-propor-
tioned figure, an excellent rider and sportsman,
and an eloquent talker.   He maintained his health by
great moderation in eating and drinking combined
with exercise and hard work.   Unlike Isabella, he
had little taste for study, for his literary education
had been neglected.   He had spent more of his boyhood
in the military camp than at school, thereby gaining an
experience of men and things which, later on, stood
him in good stead   Though possessing less refinement
and nobility of character than his wife, he shared many
of her admirable qualities.   He was a master of states-
manship and used to say that chancellors are King's
spectacles, but woe unto those who cannot see with
unprotected eyes.   He was diplomatic, not to say
cunning, and showed great wariness in most of his
proceedings.   The frugality of his *ménage* was remarkable.   " Stay to dinner, Almirante," he would say to
his uncle, " to-day we have an olla."   Isabella is
reputed to have made his clothes with her own hands—
a not overwhelming task, considering the apparent
scantiness of his wardrobe.   It is said that on one
occasion he turned to a courtier who was noted for
his extravagant dress, and, touching his own doublet,
D B

exclaimed, "What durable stuff this is ! it has already lasted me three pairs of sleeves."

The marriage of Ferdinand and Isabella did not harmonise the discord which prevailed in the land. Alfonso of Portugal would not renounce his claims, and doubt was cast over the legality of the marriage. In order to pour oil on the troubled waters, Pope Sixtus IV. (who had become Pope in 1471) despatched Cardinal Rodrigo Borgia on a mission to Spain and Portugal with the object of settling the dispute. The Cardinal took with him the bull of dispensation for Ferdinand's marriage, demanding in return an annual sum of money to be devoted to the war against the Turks.   The Cardinal of Pavia represents Rodrigo's behaviour on this occasion in a most unfavourable light, alleging that his chief purpose was to dazzle the eyes of his countrymen with the magnificence of his display.   It has also been said that he carried on the most scandalous intrigues with the ladies of the Portuguese Court, thereby giving great cause of offence to the King, who treated him with obvious coldness.

However this may be, Rodrigo seems to have had a pleasurable time in his native land, for he stayed there more than a year and many letters from the Cardinal of Pavia were needed to entice him back to Rome.

On his way home, in September 1473, he narrowly escaped shipwreck.   He had embarked on a Venetian galley and designed another for his suite and his baggage, which contained several objects of great value.   Near Pisa a terrible storm arose and it seemed as if the boat would be dashed to pieces, but the Cardinal's good luck did not desert him, and they got safely to land.   The other boat, containing his suite and his treasures, was lost.   No fewer than 180 persons were swallowed up by the waves, among them three bishops and several jurists.

The Spanish confusion was by no means rectified. Henry proclaimed that the Treaty of Toros had been violated by the marriage of Ferdinand and Isabella, since he had not sanctioned it, and declared Juana, whose legitimacy was sworn, to be the heir to the throne. Isabella, on the other hand, was recognised as heir by the Cortes. Alfonso of Portugal united with Henry and the Marquis of Villena, while Isabella's former friend, the Archbishop of Toledo, joined her opponents. The civil war now raged more violently than ever. Alfonso invaded Castile and gained considerable successes, which, however, he did not know how to follow up. The Portuguese troops pushed forward to Zamora, but found the town so ably protected that they retired towards Toro. Ferdinand followed them and a bloody battle was fought on the ledge of rocks separating the two towns. The royal standard was defended with marvellous bravery by Duarte de Almeida, who fought until both hands were hacked off and he fell down exhausted, still clinging to the banner with his teeth. But another knight, Gonzalo Pirez, who subsequently received the nickname of Bandiera, tore the banner back from the enemy. Ferdinand, it seems, had but little share in the victory, and his wife, with some reason, blamed him for the unknightly conduct which had made him flee when threatened with personal risk. Alfonso, on the other hand, fought like a lion in the thickest of the fray, and did not retreat until all hope was lost and the Castilians were sure of their victory. By this battle of Toro, 1476, the fate of Castile was decided. By degrees the adherents of King Alfonso fell away from him and he and his son Juan were obliged to retire to defend the Portuguese boundaries. The civil war was definitely ended in 1479 by the Peace of Alcantara which recognised Isabella's claims to the throne of Castile, and gave the last blow to the hopes of the

Beltraneja. Few victories have been more complete than that of Toro, and when Ferdinand's old father —John of Aragon—died in 1479, Ferdinand and Isabella—" the Catholic Kings "—reigned over the whole of Spain from the Pyrenees to the Pillars of Hercules with the one exception of the Moorish realm of Granada.

The kingdoms of Castile and Aragon were now united though they still remained independent of one another. There was some difference of opinion between the King and Queen as to which should have the first place ; Castile and Leon had hitherto taken the precedence of Aragon in all political transactions ; but Ferdinand now maintained that, as Isabella's husband, his titles should rank higher than those of his wife, Isabella, however, was firm, declaring that, while acknowledging the supremacy of Ferdinand as her husband, she could never, as Queen of Castile, yield precedence to the King of Aragon. She finally gained her point, and it was arranged that, in all public enactments bearing their joint names, the titles of Castile and Leon should precede those of Aragon and Sicily.

Isabella's Confessor, Torquemada, had imbued her with the idea that the suppression of all heresy within her realms was a sacred duty. She had, therefore, in November 1478, obtained a bull from the Pope, Sixtus IV., for the establishment of the Inquisition in Castile. Many modern writers have sought to reduce her share in the introduction of this terrible institution, but it must be remembered that Isabella herself probably considered it a meritorious action to punish with inhuman barbarity those whom she looked upon as the enemies of the Almighty. In 1480 two Dominicans were appointed by her, as Inquisitors, to set up their tribunal at Seville. Before the end of the year 1481 2,000 victims were burned alive in Andalusia alone   The Pope himself became alarmed and threatened to withdraw the bull, but Ferdinand intimated that he would make the Inquisition altogether an independent tribunal. This it became later for all practical purposes, and its iniquitous proceedings continued unchecked.

In 1483 Torquemada was made Inquisitor-General, and he thus became the most potent personage in the country, "master of Isabella's conscience and feeder of Ferdinand's purse."

The great event of the reign of Ferdinand and Isabella was the war with Granada. For many centuries the existence of this Moorish kingdom had been a bitter pill for the Spaniards to swallow. Isabella in her sincere, though misguided, religious zeal deemed that the subjection of the Moors would be well-pleasing in the sight of Heaven. Ferdinand, though animated by baser motives, supported his wife's desire. The Moorish king, old Muley Abdul Hassan, was a brave and fiery warrior, and the Moors under his lead made a valiant stand for their independence. Space forbids our going into the details of the wearisome and sanguinary war which dragged on until 1491, when the siege of the beautiful city of Granada, the last spot held by the infidel in Spain, was begun. The Moors defended it with wonderful tenacity, but famine and the loss of their most courageous men forced them to capitulate. Their King Boabdil, who had succeeded his father, was feeble and incapable, and, greatly to the indignation of his subjects, was only too glad to accept the not ungenerous terms offered by the enemy. Early in January 1492 Isabella and Ferdinand made their triumphal entry into Granada. The Queen, mounted upon a splendid charger, rode by her husband's side accompanied by the nobility and chivalry of Castile and Aragon and many of their bravest soldiers. At a given signal the city gates were thrown open and a melancholy procession emerged. Boabdil, scornfully called "The

Little," with downcast eyes and dejected mien, advanced towards the royal group ; he was about to dismount and kiss the feet of the Queen and her husband in token of submission, but, with diplomatic generosity, they forbade it. Having delivered up the keys of the fallen city, Boabdil, with his family, and suite, made their way towards the little principality in the Alpajarra mountains which had been assigned to him. From a hill above Granada the sorrowful little cavalcade could view the glories of the noble city which had once been theirs. Tears ran down the cheeks of the unhappy king as he gazed upon it. " Yes, weep ! " said his courageous and high-spirited mother, " weep like a woman for the city you knew not how to defend like a man ! "

Four days after the delivery of the keys, Granada was blessed, and purified with the sprinkling of holy water and made ready for the reception of the Christian monarchs. " The steep, narrow lane leading to the Alhambra from the Gate of Triumph was lined by Christian troops, and only a few dark-skinned Moors scowled from dusky jalousies high in the walls, as the gallant chivalry of Castile, Leon, and Aragon flashed and jingled after the King and Queen. As they approached the Alhambra, upon the tower of Comares there broke the banner of the Spanish Kings fluttering in the breeze, and at the same moment, upon the summit of the tower above the flag, there rose a great gilded cross, the symbol of the faith triumphant.

Then, at the gates, the heralds cried aloud, " Granada ! Granada ! for the Kings Isabel and Ferdinand," and Isabel, dismounting from her charger, " as the cross above glittered in the sun, knelt upon the ground in all her splendour and thanked God for the victory."[1]

The fame of Isabel's victory rang through the whole of Christendom, for the conquest of Granada

[1] Martin Hume, *Queens of Old Spain.*

" marked an epoch, and sealed with permanence and finality the christianisation of Europe." For the first time Spain appeared as a Power of the foremost rank, a fact which quite changed European relations. In Rome great rejoicings were held, and the Spanish ambassadors who had brought the news gave a representation of the Conquest of Granada with an imitation fortress of wood.[1] All eyes were turned towards the warrior-queen, so brave and spirited, yet withal so modest and gentle. That she could be cruel and merciless upon occasion it would be idle to deny, but her whole life was dominated by a fiery, not to say fanatical, zeal for the destruction of all hostility to her faith, and what seems to us like bigoted barbarity was, in her case, undertaken in direct obedience to what she considered was the divine will.

A familiar figure in the Christian camp outside Granada was a tall, fair man with dreamy eyes, who for eight weary years had followed the Court, awaiting the royal convenience to listen to his plans for reaching Asia by a western route. His scheme had already been rejected by the Senate of his native city, Genoa, and Ferdinand and Isabella had been too much engrossed with the exigencies of the war to pay serious attention to this man, who was no warrior, but, as many suspected, a mere visionary and dreamer of dreams. Little did they imagine that, while they were concentrating all their efforts upon the conquest of a petty kingdom, they were unwittingly rejecting the acquisition of a new world.

For this blue-eyed dreamer was none other than the great Christopher Columbus himself. He knew full well that the patronage of a powerful sovereign was necessary to the fulfilment of his splendid schemes, and the gibes and jeers of the Spanish courtiers fell unheeded as he persistently awaited the pleasure of Ferdinand and Isabella.

[1] See Gregorovius's *Lucrezia Borgia.*

When the excitement of the conquest of Granada had to some extent subsided, Columbus, or " Colon," as he called himself, was able to gain the Queen's ear.   But his demands were considered so exorbitant and impracticable that Isabella, after some hesitation, agreed with her husband that they must be dismissed. Columbus, after seven years of fruitless waiting, turned away in bitter disappointment, his once ruddy locks now white with care.

But Luis de Sant' Angel, the Jewish Secretary of supplies, rose to the occasion, and, with all due humility, prevailed upon the Queen to reconsider the matter.   Columbus was recalled, and finally Ferdinand was won over, by his wife's representation, to accede to the explorer's demands.   The money for the expedition was advanced by Luis de Sant' Angel from the Aragonese treasury.   The popular legend of Isabella's pawning her jewels for the purpose has now been completely disproved , indeed, they had already been pawned for the expenses of the war.

The agreement was signed at Santa Fé on April 17, 1492, and on August 3 Columbus set forth on his immortal expedition.   Nine months later, after a triumphal progress through Spain, the great explorer, uplifted with success, entered Barcelona, where he was received by Ferdinand and Isabella with princely honours.   With him he brought dusky natives, gold-dust and nuggets, rare birds and plants, and many curious beasts—all testifying to the value of the country he had discovered.   The Queen was greatly touched by the story of his adventures, and when Columbus ceased his eloquent recital the whole assembly knelt and thanked God for having granted so mighty a favour to the crown of Castile.   The discoverer was overwhelmed with privileges ; the title of Don was conferred upon him and his brothers, and he was treated as a Spanish grandee.   A new scutcheon was blazoned for him, combining the royal castle and

CÆSAR BORGIA.

Giorgione (Carrara Gallery, Bergamo).

PORTRAIT ALLEGED TO REPRESENT CÆSAR BORGIA, BUT
CERTAINLY NOT HIS.

Palmesano (Correr Museum, Venice).

lion of Castile and Leon, with the four anchors of his own coat-of-arms.

When Columbus began in May to prepare for a second expedition to the newly discovered country, he was equipped with vast power in order to enable him to christianize Queen Isabella's new subjects. On May 3 or 4 Alexander VI. granted bulls confirming Castile and Leon in the possession of all lands discovered or to be discovered, beyond a certain boundary line. Ferdinand, however, realised the undesirability of vesting so much authority in the person of an Italian sailor, Admiral of the Indies and perpetual Spanish Viceroy though he might be. A Council of the Indies was formed to control the affairs of the new domain, and the priests who governed it did their utmost to baulk the plans which Columbus had made. The news of this second expedition was at first bright and cheering, but soon came complaints of the high-handedness and tyranny of the Admiral, while he, for his part, had much to say of the lack of discipline and justice among his subordinates. Finally, Columbus was summoned to Spain to give some explanation of his proceedings. In 1496 he had an interview with the Queen at Burgos, and found her sympathetic and full of confidence in his ultimate success. But the tide of public opinion had turned against him, the treasury was empty, and it was only with much difficulty and discouragement that the third expedition was laboriously fitted out. In May 1498 he set out on his third voyage. On his arrival at Hispaniola he found nothing but disorder and oppression caused by the insolence of the Spaniards whom he had left in charge. Complaints reached the King and Queen by every ship, and it was finally decided to send out an ambassador to investigate affairs. The man selected was the tyrannical Francisco de Bobadilla, who, with inexorable harshness, immediately upon his arrival in Hispaniola had Columbus thrown into prison, and then, after collecting all the accusations against him, shipped him back to Spain in disgrace.

He reached home in December 1580. Isabella and Ferdinand sent him a letter of regret for the way in which he had been treated, commanded his immediate release, and summoned him to appear before them at the Alhambra Palace. As, with bowed white head and grief-stricken bearing, the degraded Admiral stood before them, Isabella, overcome with remorse at his pitiful situation, burst into uncontrollable weeping. Columbus, deeply affected, also broke down, and, casting himself at her feet, was unable for some time to restrain the violence of his tears. The King and Queen finally arranged that the title of Admiral should be restored to him, and that a new Viceroy—Nicolas de Ovando—should be despatched with thirty-two ships to take Bobadilla's place. Disaster, however, overtook the expedition, and, though the viceroy arrived in safety, it was with the loss of most of his ships and men.

Although the fame of Columbus's enterprise had brought Castile and its Queen before the eyes of the whole world, the financial gain had been extremely small. For several reasons Ferdinand had never been very favourably disposed towards it, and though, when Columbus asked Isabella's help towards equipping a fourth expedition early in 1502, she was anxious that his plans should not be hindered, she herself was disinclined to assist him. In March 1502, the Admiral sailed westward for the last time. When, nearly three years later, feeble in health and broken down in spirit, he returned to Spain, Queen Isabella was no more. The cares of the last few years had pressed heavily upon her, for she was a woman as well as a Queen. In 1499, after much bargaining between Ferdinand and Henry VII. of England, the young Princess Katharine of Aragon had been married by proxy to Arthur, Prince of Wales. The prospect of a separation from her youngest daughter preyed upon Isabella's mind, and she tried hard to delay her departure. But Henry was in a hurry, and in May 1501, setting aside personal inclinations at the call of political duty, Katharine and her mother endured the sadness of farewell, never to meet again on earth.

In 1497 the Prince of Asturias, Isabella's darling son, was carried to the grave, and the following year saw the death of her eldest daughter, the wife of King Emmanuel of Portugal. Her other daughter, Joan, was also a source of grief, for her obstinacy and eccentricity were already earning for her the title of " Joan the Mad." All the domestic sorrow, added to the peculiar cares of her position, gradually undermined the Queen's health, and, after a lingering illness, she gently breathed her last, November 26, 1504. In her will she expressed a wish to be buried unostentatiously at Granada, the city of her triumph, " but, if the King, my lord " desired to be buried elsewhere, then her body was to be laid by his, " in order that the union we have enjoyed while living, and which (through the mercy of God) we hope our souls will experience in heaven, may be represented by our bodies on earth." All her jewels were left to Ferdinand, " that they may serve as witness of the love I have ever borne him, and remind him that I await him in a better world, and so that with this memory he may the more holily and justly live."

An entry in the Diary of John Burchard, Bishop of Orta, relating to the conquest of Granada, runs as follows : " Monday, 4 February, 1488 There entered the consistory and passed to the second hall about one hundred moors, each one with a large iron ring round his neck and all bound together with a long chain and ropes, all being dressed alike. These were followed by an ambassador from the kings of Spain, who knelt before our most holy Lord (Pope Innocent VIII.), kissing his holiness' foot only, and

presented the letters of the aforesaid King and Queen,
written in the Spanish tongue. The Rev. Father
Antoniotto, Lord Bishop of Auray, read these letters
aloud, to the effect that the King and Queen of Spain
were sending to his holiness about one hundred moors,
a part of their spoils taken in the victory at Granada,
the preceding summer, which moors they presented
as a gift to his holiness and offered to send others."
The Pope divided these slaves among the Cardinals
attached to the Curia.

CHAPTER III

BEFORE Cardinal Rodrigo Borgia reappeared at Rome
after his Spanish mission, Pope Sixtus IV. died (1484),
His reign, as we shall see later, had been one of much
agitation and trouble.   Borgia, who had been instrumental in his election, had consequently enjoyed
the papal favour, receiving in reward for his services
the Abbey of Subiaco, *in commendam.* From the
following letter from the Cardinal of Pavia, dated
November 15, 1476,[1] it would appear, however, that
his manner of life had not become more saintly.   The
Cardinal exhorts Rodrigo to abandon his dissolute
habits :

" May God grant," he writes, " that we may
forget the past and become new men, and that we
may carry out what we have expressed in writing.
For my part, I am honestly determined to do so, and
my letter may serve you as a pledge of my intention.
. . . Do not give this letter, which comes from a
full heart, to your secretary, but shut it in your
writing-table, in a place where you can take it out

---

[1] The year of Cæsar's birth.

every year, when you have time and inclination, and read it over again. . . ."

The new Pope, Innocent VIII. (1484–92), was a mild and colourless person, not altogether devoid of attractions. He seems to have had the virtues of gentleness and benevolence, but he was tame-spirited and immoral and easily led by those around him. Giuliano della Rovere, afterwards Pope Julius II., gained a remarkable influence over him, and came to live in the Vatican. He could obtain whatever he liked from the new Pontiff and is mentioned in a letter from the Florentine envoy to Lorenzo de' Medici as being " Pope, and more than Pope."

Innocent VIII. was the first Pope who publicly acknowledged his children   Nepotism was one of his failings, and he made lavish provision for two of his sons. To the elder, Franceschetto, he gave dominion over Anguillari and Cervetri, as well as a large estate ; but after the Pope's death Franceschetto sold them both and betook himself to Florence, where he lived in retirement with his wife Maddalena, daughter of Lorenzo the Magnificent.

During the pontificate of Innocent VIII., Djem, brother of the Sultan Bajazet, of whose tragic end we shall shortly hear, was brought captive to Rome

From Infessura we get a disapproving account of Pope Innocent VIII. Among other things he relates the following : " The Vicar of the Pope in Rome and neighbourhood, watchful of his flock as befits an honourable man, published an edict forbidding clergy as well as laics, whatever their position might be, to keep mistresses, either openly or in secret. The penalty for so doing would be excommunication and confiscation of their benefices, for it was a practice which redounded to the discredit of priestly dignity and divine law.

" When the Pope heard this, he summoned the Vicar

and commanded him to annul the edict, saying that the practice was not forbidden. And indeed, such was the life led by the clergy that there was hardly one who did not keep a mistress. The number of harlots at that time living in Rome amounted to 6,800, not counting those who practised their nefarious trade under the cloak of concubinage and those who exercised their arts in secret."

From this state of things it is evident how they lived in Rome at that time and how the State of the Church was governed. To Innocent VIII. is due the establishment of a kind of bank at Rome for the disposal of pardons[1] in exchange for pecuniary offerings. After a certain proportion of the money paid had gone into the papal treasury, the rest fell to Franceschetto, his son.

When Borgia had returned from Spain he received several letters from Vannozza, which aroused his desire to see his family. He therefore begged the Pope's permission to go to Venice on important business. Innocent, suspicious, forbade him to leave Rome. Rodrigo, incensed, boldly disobeyed. He journeyed to Marino, where, under pretext of indisposition, he stayed several days. From there he sent a letter to Vannozza asking her to come immediately to Rome and take up her abode in an outlying part of the city. In spite of Innocent's repeated commands to return, the Cardinal, now a man of over fifty years of age, determined to await Vannozza's answer in Marino, and wrote to the Pope to excuse himself on the ground of illness. But through Paoletti, who visited Borgia at Marino, Innocent learned that he was by no means incapable of travelling. Finally, Rodrigo was obliged to make up his mind to return to Rome. Arrived there, he was taken in a chair to St. Peter's, where he performed his devotions before the Confession, and then proceeded to the

[1] Indulgences, i.e. remissions of canonical penances.

Lateran. There he paid his respects to the Pope and besought his pardon. But soon came the news that his family had arrived in Rome and were established in the neighbourhood of the Capitol, in a house belonging to the Monks of del Popolo. Vannozza had hardly reached the Eternal City when the curiosity of one of these monks led him to pry into the circumstances which led her to settle in such a remote part. It is related that the Prior of the Order was attracted by the unusual beauty of her daughter and sought to become acquainted with the family. But Vannozza, prompt to act, left her dwelling secretly, and moved into a house in the vicinity of St. Peter's, where precautions were taken that she might live undisturbed. Her major-domo, Don Manuele, who had accompanied her to Venice, was now announced as her husband; he adopted the title of Count Ferdinand of Castile.

Although her house was luxuriously furnished and Don Manuele had access to the most distinguished social circles of Rome, Vannozza continued to live in the deepest seclusion; she never left the house unless it was for the purpose of meeting Rodrigo, who, under pretext of a close friendship with the so-called Count Ferdinand, often passed his evenings at her home.

Borgia's days were spent in outward piety, visiting churches and hospitals. He realised that the Pope's strength was steadily failing, and, with an eye to the approaching election, did all he could to ingratiate himself with the other Cardinals. He was now a rich and powerful man, senior member of the Sacred College, Dean of the Cardinal-Bishops, and Vice-Chancellor of the Church, and his ambition did not stop short of the tiara itself. Many of the other Cardinals were the creatures of Sixtus IV. or Innocent VIII., and having bought their positions, were now quite willing to sell their votes to the highest bidder. Rodrigo ascertained their demands and laid his plans accordingly, with what success will shortly be seen.

LUCREZIA BORGIA, DUCHESS OF FERRARA.

From a portrait painted on wood, dated MDXX., preserved in the Museum at Nîmes.

Lucrezia died in 1519. This portrait is believed to be a copy of a picture by Dosso Dossi.

According to Infessura, Rodrigo had married Vannozza to Domenico of Arignano in 1476, in order to give an appearance of legitimacy to their son Cæsar. This information, however, is of doubtful accuracy. It seems certain that she was married in 1480 to Giorgio della Croce, a Milanese, for whom Rodrigo had obtained the post of Apostolic Secretary. It is remarkable that in the official record of this marriage Vannozza is described as *widow* of Messer Antonio de Brixa. To Giorgio della Croce she bore a son Ottaviano, who died in 1486, the same year as his father. During her connection with Giorgio, Vannozza increased in worldly prosperity. She appears to have been the lessee of several taverns in Rome, to say nothing of a picturesque country house and a vineyard. After his death she soon married a third husband, Carlo Canale of Mantua, a man of some literary repute, who, through Rodrigo's influence, obtained the office of *sollicitator bullarum*. This marriage resulted in the birth of a child for whom Vannozza requested Lodovico Gonzaga to stand sponsor—a significant fact which sheds a ray of light upon the naive and unblushing effrontery of the age.

Vannozza was fifty years old when Rodrigo became Pope, and was openly recognised as the mother of his four surviving children. Though the days of his passion for her were over, he still regarded her with affection. She herself lived a retired life, so that her name has never become entangled in the criminal annals of the House of Borgia. The historian, Paulus Jovius, who knew her personally, speaks of her as " an honourable woman," and the inscription on her tomb describes her as " upright, pious, and charitable, and deserving much on account of what she did for the Lateran hospital." In a letter to her daughter Lucrezia she signs herself " La felice e infelice Madre, Vannozza Borgia," which implies, perhaps, that she

Eb

felt the embarrassment of her position.   There can
be no doubt that, during her last years, she sought
to atone for past sins by devoting herself to a life of
extreme piety.

On the evening of July 25, 1492, the good-natured
and incompetent Pope Innocent VIII. passed away.
It is related that, during his last illness, the operation
for transfusion of blood was unsuccessfully performed.
This, however, is an error arising from the forgetfulness
of two important facts : (1) that the idea of this
operation could not occur to any one to whom the
circulation of the blood was unknown ; (2) that the
phenomenon of the circulation of the blood was not
discovered until the seventeenth century.   Raynaldus
and Infessura say that a certain Jewish physician
undertook to restore the Pope's health , for this
purpose he drew all the blood out of three young
boys, who immediately died.   With their blood he
prepared a draught, which, in spite of the doctor's
protestations, failed to improve the sick Pontiff's
condition.   The saving virtue of drinking human
blood was no new idea, as may be seen from Tertullian,
Apol. ix. : *Item, illi qui munere in arena noxiorum
ingulatorum sanguinem recentem (de ingulo decurrentem
exceptum) avida siti comitiali morbo medentes hauserunt,
ubi sunt ?*[1]

On August 5 the Pope's body was laid in St. Peter's,
where his memory has been perpetuated by a wonderfully executed monument in bronze—the work of
Antonio Pollaiulo   The lawless state which prevailed
in the capital at this time may be seen from the fact
that, during the seventeen days before the new
election was completed, no less than two hundred
assassinations took place   The disturbances at last
became so serious that some of the barons, at the
instigation of Cardinal Giuliano della Rovere, agreed

[1] Baron Corvo, *Chronicles of the House of Borgia*, p. 79.

to sink their party differences and unite with the Conservators of the city in maintaining order. This had a beneficial effect and succeeded in reducing the confusion.

There are several ways by which a Pope may be elected :

(1) By Inspiration—i.e. when several Cardinals together, as though impelled by an unseen power, shout aloud the name of the one they desire to see elected. By this method other voices are attracted and the minimum majority attained. It is, however, rarely employed.

(2) By Compromise—i.e. when the Cardinals cannot agree, and then appoint a committee of themselves with power to decide the election. In this way John XXII. managed to secure his own appointment, so that the Cardinals determined never again to have recourse to this method without securing it against abuse by stringent precautions.

(3) By Majority—i.e. each Cardinal writes the name of his candidate on a slip of paper and, with much ceremony and genuflection, places it in a large, beautifully decorated chalice on the High Altar of the Chapel in which the Conclave is assembled. These slips are then taken out by a Cardinal specially appointed for the purpose, and carefully compared with the number of persons present. If then one of the Candidates has two-thirds of the votes, he is immediately proclaimed Pope. If, however, after repeated attempts, the necessary majority is not obtained, they have recourse to the Method of—

(4) Accession—i.e. every Cardinal is free to accede to another and to strike out the name of his first Candidate. After the election is finished all the slips of paper are carefully burned, so

that no future reference can ever be made to them.

On August 6, 1492, the Conclave met in the Sistine Chapel. The competitors were numerous, each one having some claim to consideration. Ascanio Sforza was the brother of the first tyrant of Italy. Giuliano della Rovere and Riario were connected with Sixtus IV. Lorenzo Cibò seemed to be the direct heir of Innocent VIII., Borgia was a kinsman of Calixtus III., Orsini and Colonna shared the secular greatness of their families. France and Genoa openly took the part of della Rovere.[1] Borgia opposed to him Cardinal Sforza, but Ascanio, whose house was threatening the whole of Italy, realising that his chances were slight, began to lend a favourable ear to Borgia's attractive offers. The other Cardinals were undecided, but Rodrigo knew how to win them by bribery and flattery. For three days the Conclave resembled a banker's counter. To Sforza, Borgia promised his own palace and furniture, all his benefices, the castle of Nepi, the Bishopric of Erlau, and a large sum of money as well as the Vice-Chancellorship of the Roman Chair. Cardinal Orsini was to receive the two fortified towns of Monticelli and Soriano, the legation of the Marches, and the Bishopric of Carthagena ; Cardinal Colonna and his family the Abbey of Subiaco and all the surrounding villages. Savelli, Michieli, and Pallavicini were to be paid for their votes with bishoprics, and Cardinals Sclafetani, Sanseverino, Riario, and Domenico della Rovere were to receive valuable abbacies and benefices.

In this reprehensible way Borgia managed to secure twenty-four votes, and only one was wanting to complete the minimum majority. Cardinals Caraffa, Piccolomini, Zeno, and Costa, as well as Lorenzo Cibò, Giovanni de' Medici, Cardinal Basso, and Giuliano della Rovere, all held aloof from these

[1] Gebhart.

unrighteous proceedings, but finally the required vote
was wormed out of Gherardo, Patriarch of Venice, an
old man already in his dotage.

Rome was in wild excitement about this election.
From the Diary of John Burchard, Bishop of Orta,
we learn that, a little while before the assembly of
the Conclave, Borgia had sent four mule-loads of
silver to Cardinal Sforza's house, under pretext that
the treasure might be more safely guarded there,
but that really it was the price of the Cardinal's vote.

On the night of August 10–11, 1492, the name of
Borgia was drawn out of the electoral chalice. At
dawn a window of the Conclave was opened and the
election of Pope Alexander VI. made known to the
drowsy city.[1] The newly made Pontiff, deeply excited
and perhaps fearful as to the way in which his simoniacal election might be received, hastened to don
the pontifical insignia.   For the same reason he
desired that the news of his appointment should be
spread speedily, and had pieces of paper, inscribed
with his name as Pope, thrown from the Vatican
windows into the midst of the people.

Alexander had hardly dressed himself in his official
garb when he repaired to St. Peter's for the inaugural
ceremonies. The Cardinal Sanseverino lifted him up
in his powerful arms and placed him on the throne,
and the Sacred College paid him the fisrt Adoration.
Huge crowds assembled to catch a glimpse of the new
Pope, whose election, notwithstanding the known
immorality of his life, was by no means unwelcome.
Rodrigo Borgia appeared to possess all the attributes
of a successful temporal ruler, and the prospect of
his being able to steer the Papacy through a difficult
political crisis outbalanced any disadvantages from
a spiritual point of view. Sigismondo de' Conti
describes him as a thoroughly capable man with
remarkable intellectual gifts. He says : " Few people

[1] Baron Corvo, *Chronicles of the House of Borgia*, p. 86.

understood etiquette so well as he did ; he knew how to make the most of himself, and took pains to shine in conversation and to be dignified in his manners. In the latter point his majestic stature gave him an advantage. Also he was just at the age (about sixty) at which Aristotle says men are wisest ; robust in body and vigorous in mind, he was admirably equipped for his new position. . . . He was tall and powerfully built, and, though he had blinking eyes, they were penetrating and lively ; in conversation he was extremely affable ; he understood money matters thoroughly " (quoted by Pastor).

Borgia's physical beauty, though not altogether in accordance with twentieth-century standards, seems to have been universally conceded.[1] This, combined with a fine presence and a superabundant vitality, was quite enough to recommend him to the sensual, beauty-loving Italians.   Portius thus describes him in 1493 : " He is tall, in complexion neither fair nor dark ; his eyes are black, his mouth somewhat full. His health is splendid, and he has a marvellous power of enduring all sorts of fatigue.   He is singularly eloquent in speech, and is gifted with an innate good breeding which never forsakes him " (Pastor).

Although no reference is made in this description to Borgia's dissolute habits, it must not be supposed that they were unknown.   In a College of gay and riotous Cardinals, Rodrigo had been the gayest and most riotous of them all.   But the level of morality among the higher classes in Italy at this time was so distressingly low that public opinion found no difficulty in condoning the profligacy of the new Pope's previous life.   At the same time, considerable resentment was aroused at the unblushing simony by means of which his election had been obtained.[2]

[1] His portrait in the Uffizi Gallery at Florence is considered to bear a strong resemblance to the late Cardinal Vaughan of Westminster.

[2] Many objections have been raised to the assertion that Alexander's

To return to the morning after the Conclave. From
St. Peter's the Pope went back to the Vatican, where
he addressed the Cardinals for a second time, admonishing them, with pious zeal, to change their manner
of life, and declaring that he would make an impartial
investigation of all accused of simony. It was obvious
that, as Pope Alexander VI., he was not inclined
to maintain his former compacts with the Cardinals.
Indeed, it is remarkable that he had already decreed
the downfall of the very men who had most contributed to his election.   Towards Sforza, Riario,
San Michieli, and others, he subsequently displayed
the greatest cruelty, banishing some, and condemning
others to imprisonment or an unmerciful death.
It was with reason that Giovanni de' Medici, a sage
youth of seventeen, observed to Cardinal Cibò, on
the announcement of the election, "Now we are
in the power of a wolf, the most rapacious, perhaps,
that this world has ever seen ; and, if we do not flee,
he will infallibly devour us."

Never had there been such gorgeous celebrations
at a papal election. The Coronation on August 26

accession to the Papacy was brought about by simoniacal
means. Pastor, in replying to these, calls attention to some documents discovered in recent years   The first of these is Brognolo's
Despatch of August 31, 1492, in which, it is true, A. Sforza is not
named.   But in Frakn6i, in the Erlauer *Diöcesanblatt*, 1833, No 20,
the appointment of Ascanio Sforza to the Bishopric of that place
appears, and the other gifts can equally be substantiated. Thus the
appointment to the Vice-Chancellorship appears from *Decret.
Eximiæ tuæ Circ. industria*, dat Rom, 1492, vii. Cal. Sept. *Regest.*
869, f. 1. See also Cod. xxxv. 94, in the Barberini Library   As to the
handing over of the palace, see Appendix, N. 13. The grant of Nepi
is certain, see Leonetti, 1 61 , Ratti, 1 86, whose apology for Ascanio
is quite futile. Besides this, Ascanio received (*Regest.* 773, f. 15^b)
two Canonries (dat Laterani, 1492, vii Cal. Sept A° 1°) ; f. 45 : the
Priorate of a Convent in the Diocese of Calahorra, which belonged
to Alexander VI (*D. ut S.*) ; f. 167 : an Abbey (*D ut S.*) and various
other favours, f. 187, 260, and 295, all dated vii. Cal., Sept. 1492.
Pastor, *Secret Archives of the Vatican*, v., p. 382.

was the occasion for the most brilliant and resplendent
festivities. The streets were decorated with triumphal
arches inscribed with predictions of a Golden Age.
Alexander was fêted like a divinity, and the following
inscriptions are typical of the inanity and profanity
of the compliments with which he was surfeited :

*Cæsare magna fuit, nunc Roma est maxima, Sextus
regnat Alexander, ille vir, iste Deus ;*

and,

*Libertas pia, justitia, et pax aurea, opes quæ sunt
tibi, Roma, novus fert deus iste tibi.*

The Borgia arms, a bull passant on a field or,
lent themselves to ingenious symbolical representations. By the Palazzo of San Marco was erected the
colossal figure of a bull from whose horns, eyes,
ears, and nostrils flowed water, and from its forehead
wine.

When all the customary ceremonies had been
observed, Alexander bestowed his pontifical benediction upon the people. He proceeded to this first
official duty, says Corio, " patiently as an ox and
fulfilled it proudly as a lion."

That the new Pope was no divinity, but made of
mortal clay, was demonstrated before the coronation
celebrations were ended. In taking formal possession
of the Lateran Basilica, he was so overcome with
emotion and fatigue that he suddenly fainted, and
restoratives had to be administered before he recovered
consciousness. " This," writes the devout Delfini to
a friend, " forcibly reminded me of the instability of
all human things."

The news of Borgia's election excited much displeasure in certain quarters, though we can hardly
credit Guicciardini's assertion that all men were
filled with dismay, and that Ferrante of Naples, one
of the most keen-sighted rulers of the day, told
his wife with tears—tears which he had not shed even
at the death of his two sons—" This election will not

only undermine the peace of Italy, but that of the whole of Christendom."

On the other hand, Alexander's accession was hailed with joy by some of the Italian Powers, especially by Milan and Florence. His true self had not yet been revealed, and many entertained a mistakenly high opinion of his character.

It may be interesting to hear what Guicciardini thought of the new Pope. He writes: "Alexander was very active, and possessed of remarkable penetration; his judgment was excellent, and he had a wonderful power of persuasion; in all serious business he displayed an incredible attention and ability. But these virtues were bound up with still greater faults: his manner of living was dissolute, and he knew neither shame nor sincerity, neither faith nor religion. He, moreover, was possessed by an insatiable greed, an overwhelming ambition, a more than barbarous cruelty, and a burning passion for the advancement of his many children, who, in order to carry out his iniquitous decrees, did not scruple to employ the most heinous means."

The new Pope at once took vigorous steps for the restoration of order in Rome, which had been, during the interregnum, the scene of frightful anarchy and bloodshed. The first assassin to be captured was hanged as an example, and his house destroyed. Alexander also established commissioners for the trial of disputes, and set aside certain times when he himself gave audience to all who had any cause of complaint. "He has promised," wrote the Ferrarese envoy on August 17, "to make many reforms in the Curia, to dismiss the secretaries and many tyrannical officials, to keep his sons far from Rome, and make worthy appointments. It is said that he will be a glorious Pontiff, and will have no need of guardians."

Thus the new reign opened with fair prospects and promises. Even the unfriendly Infessura admitted that Alexander "adminstered justice after a marvellous sort," and the powers of Italy were well pleased. But their pleasure was of short duration for the Pope soon began to show symptoms of the nepotism which was to play deadly havoc with the prosperity of his pontificate. All his relations flocked to Rome, anxious to receive the favours which he was eager to bestow. Gian Andrea Boccaccio declares, in a letter to the Duke of Ferrara, "ten Papacies would not suffice to satisfy the greed of all his kindred," and subsequent events proved that these fears were only too well grounded.

CHAPTER IV.

LET us now follow the fortunes of Rodrigo's children.

His two eldest daughters—Girolama and Isabella—are almost unknown to history. They must have been born before 1470, but the name of their mother is wrapped in mystery. We know that Girolama was married to Gian Andrea Cesarini in 1482, when she was probably about thirteen, and that her brief career ended in the following year. We know, too, that her sister Isabella became the wife of a Roman noble—Pier Giovanni Matuzzi—in 1483—only this and nothing more. In the two marriage contracts Rodrigo Borgia is mentioned as their father, but their mother's name does not appear.

Don Pedro Luis, the eldest son of Rodrigo and Vannozza, was probably born in Spain, though the date of his birth is uncertain. Yriarte[1] gives it as about 1467. Sabatini prefers 1460 as the date.[2]

[1] *César Borgia*, vol. i. pp 33, 34. Pastor, vol. v. p. 364.

[2] *The Life of Cesare Borgia*, p. 39. (Stanley Paul & Co., Ltd.)

Little is known of his career beyond the fact that he served in the army of Ferdinand the Catholic and fought bravely in the war against the King of Granada, distinguishing himself at the capture of Ronda, 1485. The same year he was invested by Ferdinand with the hereditary duchy of Gandia, near Valencia. He was betrothed to Maria Enriquez, the King's cousin, but died before the marriage was completed. The date of his death was probably 1488, when he would have been about twenty-one years old. He bequeathed all his possessions to his brother Juan, who adopted the title of Duke of Gandia and eventually married Maria Enriquez.

This Juan (Don Giovanni) was Rodrigo's second son, born in 1474. At the time of his father's promotion to the Papal See he was already in a wealthy and influential position. When the news of the election reached him, he journeyed to Rome to join the other members of his family. He originally intended to stay only a short time there, and therefore sent his wife back to Spain; but his visit prolonged itself, and on June 12, 1493, he was present at the wedding of his sister Lucrezia with Giovanni Sforza, and presented her with a goblet worth seventy ducats. On June 16 he went with his brother Cæsar to receive the Spanish ambassador, and on this occasion they displayed so much pomp and magnificence that they might have been taken for monarchs. From a letter from the King of Naples appointing him Duke of Sessa and Prince of Teano, it is evident that he tarried in Rome till the beginning of August, when he returned to Spain on board a Spanish galley laden with valuables on which the Roman goldsmiths had been working for two months. Nothing more is heard of him until August 10, 1496, when he came back to Rome. He made his entry into the capital with great ceremony, accompanied by his brother, Cardinal Cæsar Borgia, and the whole papal Court.

A few months later, on May 20, another brother, Jofré, appeared with his wife, Donna Sancia of Aragon, in Rome, where the whole family was now assembled. This family union seemed to portend some great undertaking.

Soon afterwards the Duke of Gandia was appointed Captain of the Church by the Pope, and, in spite of a conspicuous lack of military ability, on June 7, 1497, he was made Duke of Beneventum by the unanimous vote of the College of Cardinals.

Tomaso Tomasi represents Juan as a good and honest man, of no mean ability ; there is little doubt, however, that he led an immoral life, giving himself up to gambling and other less pardonable excesses. His father loved him with a passionate love, and his tragic death, in June 1497, of which we shall hear anon, was a source of deepest sorrow to him. He left two children, Juan, third Duke of Gandia, and a daughter, Isabella, who were piously educated by a saintly mother. Juan married an illegitimate daughter of the Archbishop of Saragossa, himself a bastard, and, strangely enough, the first child of this alliance which united so much family iniquity was Francisco Borgia, fourth Duke of Gandia, who afterwards became a saint.

The third son of Rodrigo and Vannozza was Cæsar, born in 1476. The first authentic document dealing with his life is to be found at Rome in the *Liber Sillabicorum*, published in 1488 by a certain Pompilius. From it we learn that Cæsar, when in his twelfth year, was appointed Protonotary of the Papal Chair, a sinecure with important emoluments. From 1490 to 1492 he studied at the University of Pisa, at that time of world-renown, and rendered doubly attractive by the theological lectures of the celebrated Filippo Decio. Among Cæsar's fellow-students were Giovanni de' Medici, afterwards Pope Leo X., and Alexander Farnese, later Pope Paul III.

Besides the university professors, two Spanish savants, Romolino da Herda and Giovanni Vera d'Arcilla, contributed towards his education, which he apparently pursued with industry.   On September 12, 1491, Innocent VIII. appointed him Protonotary and Bishop of Pampeluna, though only on condition that he should not be consecrated for ten years. When his father was made Pope, Cæsar, at his command, left Pisa for Spoleto, where he arrived on August 26, 1492.   He was still there on October 5, as is proved by a letter written by him to Piero de' Medici, Giovanni's brother, with whom he was on intimate terms.

There is no trace of Cæsar's presence at Rome before March 19, 1493, when the ambassador Boccaccio writes to Duke Ercole of Ferrara : " The day before yesterday I visited Cæsar in his house in Trastevere, just as he was about to go hunting. He was clad in secular garments of silk and only a small tonsure was visible.   We rode part of the way together, as we are on terms of intimacy.   He is a man of great and surpassing cleverness and excellent disposition ; and his manners are worthy of the son of a great Prince.   He is cheerful, even merry, and always seems to be in high spirits.   Owing to his great modesty,[1] he presents a more distinguished and amiable appearance than his brother, the Duke of Gandia   He also enjoys a good income. The Archbishop (Cæsar) has no bent towards the priesthood, though his benefices yield him more than 16,000 ducats.   If he does not marry, his revenues will go to another of his brothers, who is hardly thirteen years of age."

This description confirms the idea that his amiable manners and charm of speech made him irresistibly fascinating, and also proves that he adopted an

[1] It is evident that the word " modesty " has changed its meaning

ecclesiastical career against his inclination. This latter fact makes it all the more credible that he was the instigator of his brother's murder, which afforded him a means of escape from the uncongenial priesthood.

Paolo Giovio represents Cæsar as distinctly unattractive in appearance, having a red face covered with blotches, and deep-set, sinister eyes. On the other hand, the portraits of him by Raphael, Bronzino, and other noted artists depict him as a tall, slender man with interesting features.

Machiavelli sees Cæsar through rose-coloured glasses, and represents him as the embodiment of political wisdom and superhuman sagacity. " Cæsar Borgia," he says, " obtained his high position through his father's lucky star, and lost it after the Pope's death, in spite of the fact that he spared no pains and neglected nothing that a wise and courageous man could do to take firm root in the State which he had acquired through the arms and good fortune of another. . . . In the future he had to face the fear that another Pope would be less favourably inclined towards him, and deprive him of what Alexander had given him. He therefore sought to secure his position by four means :

" (1) By the extirpation of all noble families, whom he had deprived of their States, so that the future Pope might not re-establish them.

" (2) By trying to win over all the Roman nobles and thus hold the Pope in check

" (3) By making as many friends as possible in the College of Cardinals.

" (4) By seeking to acquire so much authority before the Pope's death that he would be able by himself to resist a first attack. At the time of Alexander's decease he had fulfilled three of these aims and the last nearly so.

" If we examine the whole conduct of Borgia we

shall see how firm a foundation he had laid for future greatness. . . . I know no better lesson for the instruction of a prince than is afforded by the action and example of this Duke."

Machiavelli further observes : " When I consider all the actions of the Duke, I find it impossible to blame him with having omitted any precaution. Rather must I hold him up as an example to all who, by fortune or by foreign arms, succeed in acquiring sovereignty."

This view of Cæsar's character must be taken with many grains of salt, for the other writers of the day all agree in describing him as a man who shrank from no perfidy or deed of infamy, if thereby his own interests could be advanced.   .

Soon after Cæsar's arrival in Rome the Pope, who, it is said, " loved and hugely feared his son," appointed him to the Archbishopric of Valencia, and on September 20, 1493, he was made Cardinal of Santa Maria Nuova. To evade the blot on his birth, Alexander by means of false witness, represented that he had been born in wedlock.

At the Court of Alexander VI. Cæsar had an excellent opportunity of gaining an insight into the politics of all the States, for he came into contact with ambassadors from all the monarchs of Europe. When he cast aside the ecclesiastical profession he, as well as his brothers, were recognised by the Pope as his natural children, though before this they had passed as his " nephews." The bulls of legitimation, issued by Sixtus IV., however, establish Cæsar's relationship to Alexander VI.

Lucrezia Borgia, the daughter of Alexander and Vannozza, has been depicted as the Messalina of her century by Burchard, Master of the Papal Ceremonies, and other writers. In later times, however, she has found many valiant defenders, and indeed an unbiassed observer would find it hard to pronounce her guilty of

POPE ALEXANDER VI. PRESENTING GIOVANNI SFORZA (LUCREZIA'S FIRST HUSBAND) TO ST. PETER. *Titian (Museum at Antwerp).*

Giovanni holds the Banner of the Church, as Gonfaloniere. The Banner shows the Borgia arms.

all the terrible and shocking charges brought against her. Guicciardini, whose wake was followed by other writers, asserts that she maintained illicit intercourse not only with her father, but also with her two brothers, and there is good reason to believe that accusations of this nature were brought against her quite early in her career. The first traces of them appear in the writings of the Neapolitan poets, who were embittered against Alexander VI. on account of the part he had taken in dispossessing the House of Aragon, and are therefore not to be relied upon when they criticise his relations with Lucrezia.

Pontano, for example, composed the following epitaph for her, although she outlived him more than twenty years :

> Hic jacet in tumulo, Lucretia nomine, sed re
> Thais, Alexandri filia, sponsa nurus

And Sanazzaro thus apostrophises her :

> Ergo te semper cupiet, Lucretia, Sextus ?
> O fatum diri numinis ! hic pater est.

By later writers this evidence is considered of sufficient weight to drag poor Lucrezia down into the deepest depths of infamy. Even the astute Gibbon writes : " in the next generation the House of Este was sullied by a sanguinary and incestuous race, by the nuptials of Alfonso I. with Lucrezia, a bastard of Alexander VI., the Tiberius of Christian Rome. This modern Lucrezia might have assumed with more propriety the name of Messalina, since the woman who can be guilty, who can even be accused, of a criminal intercourse with a father and two brothers must be abandoned to all the licentiousness of venal love."

In face of these scandalous assertions it will be well to consider the circumstances under which Lucrezia's life was spent, as well as the statements of contemporary

FB

writers who knew and greatly esteemed her when she was Duchess of Ferrara.

She was born on April 18, 1480, when Rodrigo was forty-nine and Vannozza thirty-eight years of age. It was a troublous period in the history of Italy; the Papacy had become divested of all holiness, religion was almost entirely materialised, and immoralities of every description were so common as almost to escape remark. At an early age Lucrezia was taken from her mother's house and placed under the care of Adriana Orsini, a relation of Giulia Farnese and cousin to Rodrigo. Giulia—"La Bella," as she was called on account of her surpassing beauty—had already captivated Borgia as Cardinal and was his mistress at the time of his election to the Papacy. Her brother, afterwards Paul III., owed his appointment to the Cardinalate to her influence, and indeed the conspicuous rôle which the House of Farnese has played in history is probably due to the Pope's infatuation for this beautiful woman.

In 1489 a marriage took place between Giulia, then a golden-haired child of fifteen, and Orsin Orsini the young son of Adriana. Giulia had, like Lucrezia, lived in the family of Madonna Adriana, and while there she probably made the acquaintance of Cardinal Rodrigo; either shortly before, or soon after her marriage, she succumbed to his allurements. It is difficult to understand how a man of fifty-eight could thus have attracted so young and lovely a girl, but there is no doubt that two years after her marriage she was his avowed mistress. Adriana connived at her daughter-in-law's dishonour, thereby gaining an enormous influence over Cardinal Borgia who made her the confidante of all his schemes and intrigues.

Rodrigo, as we have seen, was extremely wealthy, and he spared no money on the education of his children. Lucrezia, like other girls of her time, was brought up to have great respect for the outward forms of religion, though no attempt was made to show her the hideousness of the sin which surrounded her.   In Italy pious exercises always formed the basis of female education, and Lucrezia seems to have become particularly accomplished in this respect. In addition to the study of·"piety," she probably devoted much attention to Italian and Spanish, as well as to Latin and Greek.   She appears also to have learned music and drawing, and to have composed poems in various languages, while her skill in em· broidery was famous.   Considering the times, her education was thorough, and she probably continued it later on in life under the influence of Bembo and Strozzi.   Several hundred of her letters are still preserved ; they reveal sensibility and appreciation, but no depth of mind.

Cardinal Borgia was full of brilliant plans for his children's future, and Lucrezia was hardly eleven years old when she became betrothed to a Spanish nobleman—Don Cherubino Juan de Centelles, lord of the Val d'Ayora in the kingdom of Valencia.   By the legal contract drawn up on February 26, 1491, it was stipulated that Lucrezia should bring her husband a dowry of 300,000 timbres, or Valencian sous, and that 11,000 timbres of this amount should be derived from the legacy of her brother, the Duke of Gandia, while 8,000 were to be provided by her other brothers, Cæsar and Jofré.   It was also specified that Lucrezia should be taken to Spain at the Cardinal's expense within one year from the signing of the contract, and that the marriage should be completed within six months of her arrival in Spain.

But in spite of all these provisions, the marriage was destined to fall through.   Rodrigo, for reasons best known to himself, annulled the betrothal and selected another husband for his daughter.   His choice fell again on a young Spaniard, Don Gasparo,

the son of Don Juan Francesco of Procida, a boy
barely fifteen years of age. The betrothal took place
on the last day of April 1491.[1] But when Rodrigo
became Pope his plans for his daughter's future
increased in brilliancy. Not content with a mere
Spanish noble, he desired to see her married to a
prince. At the instigation of his kinsmen, Ludovico
the Moor and the powerful Cardinal Ascanio Sforza,
Giovanni Sforza, Count of Cotignola and Lord of
Pesaro, sought Lucrezia's hand, to the no small
pleasure of her father. Giovanni had already been
married, but his wife, the beautiful Maddalena
Gonzago, had died in child-birth, August 8, 1490.
He was a man of twenty-six, of attractive appearance
and good education. Lucrezia, it must be remem--
bered, had at this time reached the mature age of
twelve and a half years.

The young Count Gasparo had arrived in Rome
to assert his claims to his betrothed, and was anything
but pleased at discovering a rival in the field. He
became infuriated when the Pope demanded a formal
resignation of his rights, and declared that he would
appeal to all the princes and potentates of Christendom. But he had to submit after a time, and retired
to console himself with the 3,000 ducats which were
paid him as compensation. Thereupon, on February 2, 1493, Lucrezia was formally betrothed to
Giovanni Sforza [2] It was arranged that she should
receive a dowry of 31,000 ducats and should follow
her consort to Pesaro within a year.

The marriage was celebrated at the Vatican on
June 12 amid the most magnificent demonstrations
of joy. The bridegroom had arrived in Rome three

[1] Infessura says that Lucrezia was actually married, and not
merely " betrothed," to Don Gasparo.

[2] This alliance did not take place, however, until another project of marrying Lucrezia to the Spanish Count de Prada had fallen
through.

days earlier. Of his entry Gregorovius writes : " On June 9 he entered by way of the Porta del Popolo, where he was received by the whole senate, his brothers-in-law, and the ambassadors of the Powers. Lucrezia, attended by several maids of honour, was seated in a loggia of her palace in order to watch her bridegroom and his suite pass by to the Vatican. As he rode by Sforza greeted her with gallantry, and his bride returned his salutation. He was graciously welcomed by his father-in-law."

The marriage feast on June 12 was a scene of gorgeous splendour. Alexander had invited the nobility and magistrates of Rome as well as the foreign ambassadors.[1] The fairest of the Roman ladies were presented with silver cups full of sweetmeats, and after the banquet there was a magnificent ball, at which the Pope and his companions passed the whole night. This entertainment was varied by questionable songs and a licentious comedy which has been described by Infessura.

Alexander had taken the keenest pleasure in making the arrangements for this brilliant match, for, as Boccaccio, the Ferrarese ambassador, writes : " He loved her passionately, superlatively." At the ambassador's suggestion, the Duke of Ferrara sent, as a wedding gift, a pair of large beautifuly wrought silver hand-basins with the accompanying vessels. The palace of Santa Maria in Portico, where Lucrezia had already taken up her abode, was chosen as the bridal residence.

During the year 1492 Giulia Farnese had given birth to a daughter, Laura. There is no doubt that Alexander was the father, though she passed officially as the child of Giulia's husband, Orsini. In after-years Donna Laura became the wife of Nicolo della Rovere, nephew of Pope Julius II. So little did

---

[1] Baron Corvo, *Chronicles of the House of Borgia*, p. 100.

' Giulia care for popular opinion that she lived in the Palace of Santa Maria in Portico, as if she were a kinswoman of Lucrezia, while her husband dwelt apart in his castle of Bassanello, one of the estates which he had received from the Pope on his marriage.

A letter written by Lorenzo Pucci, the Florentine ambassador at Rome, gives some insight into the domestic affairs of the Borgias. It is dated December 24, 1493, and describes the following scene in Lucrezia's palace :

" . . . I called at the house of Santa Maria in Portico to see Madonna Giulia. She had just finished washing her hair when I entered, and was sitting by the fire with Madonna Lucrezia, the daughter of our Master, and Madonna Adriana, who all received me with every appearance of pleasure. Madonna Giulia asked me to sit by her side ; she thanked me for having taken Girolama home and told me that I must bring her there again to please her. . . . Giulia also wanted me to see the child ; she is now quite big, and, it seems to me, resembles the Pope *adeo ut vere ex ejus semine orta dici possit*. Madonna Giulia has grown stout, and is become a most beautiful woman. In my presence she unbound her hair and had it dressed ; it fell down to her feet—I never saw such beautiful hair before. She wore a headdress of fine linen and over it a filmy net interwoven with threads of gold. In truth it shone like the sun! I would have given much for you to see her that you might have been convinced of what you have often wanted to know. She wore a lined robe after the Neapolitan fashion, as did also Madonna Lucrezia, who after a time went away to change it. She returned in a gown made almost entirely of violet velvet. When vespers were over and the Cardinals took their departure, I left them."

Lucrezia, who was Giulia's constant companion,

must have been aware of the unlawful relations between her friend and the Pope, and it is little wonder that, in the mind of so young a girl, there should have sprung up confused notions of right and wrong, and that her moral being should gradually have become contaminated by the corrupt atmosphere in which she lived.

Jofré, the youngest son of Rodrigo and Vannozza, was born in 1480 or 1481, but the date of his death is unknown. He married Donna Sancia, a natural daughter of Alfonso II. of Naples, who bestowed on him the title of Count of Coriata, Prince of Squillace, with an income of 40,000 ducats. Jofré Borgia also received important fiefs in the kingdom of Naples, and adopted the title of Duke of Suessa and Prince of Teano.

Lucrezia's husband stayed for some time longer in Rome, where, however, his paid position at the papal Court soon began to be equivocal. His uncles had promoted his marriage with Alexander's daughter in the hope of gaining the Pope's help in their schemes for the overthrow of the House of Naples; but the Borgias now went over to the Neapolitan party and declared themselves as the opponents of Charles VIII.'s expedition. The following extract from a letter written by Giovanni Sforza to his uncle Ludovico the Moor throws light on his embarrassing situation :

" Yesterday his Holiness said to me, in the presence of Monsignor [Cardinal Ascanio] : ' Well, Signor Giovanni Sforza, what have you to say to me ? ' I replied : ' Holy Father, every one in Rome believes you to be in agreement with the King [of Naples], who is an enemy of the Milanese. If this is the case, I am in an awkward position, as I am both in the pay of your Holiness and in that of the State of Milan. If things continue in this way I know not how I can serve one party without abandoning the other, and yet I wish to detach myself from neither of them. I beg your Holiness to be pleased to place me in such a position that I may not become an enemy of my own blood, and that I may not act contrary to the obligations to which I am urged in virtue of my agreement with your Holiness and the illustrious State of Milan.' He answered that I took too much interest in his affairs, and that I should choose in whose pay I would remain according to my contract. And then he commanded the afore-mentioned Monsignor to write to your Excellency what you will learn from his lordship's letter. If I had known, my lord, in what a position I was to be placed, I would rather have eaten the straw on which I lie that have bound myself thus. I cast myself into your arms. I beg your Excellency not to desert me, but to consider my position, and help me with your favour and advice, that I may remain a faithful servant of your Excellency. Preserve for me the situation and the little nest which, thanks to the mercy of Milan, my ancestors have bequeathed me. I and my troops will ever be at the service of your Excellency.

" GIOVANNI SFORZA.

" ROME, *April* 1494."

Soon after this, on April 23, Cardinal della Rovere repaired to France to try to persuade Charles VIII. to invade Italy, not for the purpose of conquering Naples, but to accuse Alexander VI. before a council and bring about his deposition.

At the beginning of July Ascanio Sforza, who now made no attempt to conceal his hostility to the Pope, left Rome and joined the Colonna, who were in the pay of France. Meanwhile Giovanni Sforza, in his capacity as Captain of the Church, had joined the Neapolitan army at Romagna. His wife, Lucrezia, with Vannozza, Giulia Farnese, and Madonna Adriana, at the beginning of June accompanied him to Pesaro, where they were to remain until August. But

THE " DISPUTA " OF ST. CATHERINE.

Pinturicchio (Borgia Apartments, the Vatican).

The two children probably represent Jofré Borgia, Prince of Squillace, fourth
son of Pope Alexander VI., and his wife, Doña Sancia of Aragon. The female
figure behind her may be Lucrezia Borgia.

Giuliana and Madonna Adriana offended the Pope
by leaving for Capodimonte, where Giulia's brother
Angiolo was lying seriously ill. Gregorovius quotes
Alexander's letter to Lucrezia, written on July 24,
1494 :

" ALEXANDER VI., POPE ; by his own hand

" DONNA LUCREZIA, DEAREST DAUGHTER,
    " It is several days since we had a letter from
you, and we are much surprised that you neglect
to write to us more often to give us news of your
health, and that of Don Giovanni, our beloved son.
In future be more attentive and industrious. Madonna
Adriana and Giulia have reached Capodimonte, where
they found the latter's brother dead. This event
has so deeply grieved both the Cardinal and Giulia
that they have both been attacked by fever We
have sent Pietro Caranza to look after them and
have provided physicians and everything necessary.
We trust in God and the glorious Madonna that they
will soon be restored. Of a truth you and Don
Giovanni have displayed little consideration for us
in this departure of Madonna Adriana and Giulia,
since you allowed them to go without our express
permission ; for it was your duty to reflect that so
sudden a departure without our knowledge would
cause us the greatest displeasure. And if you say
that they did so because Cardinal Farnese commanded
it, you ought to have considered whether this would
please the Pope. However, it has now been done ;
but another time we will be more cautious and look
about to see to whose hand to entrust our affairs.
We are in good health, thanks be to God and the
glorious Virgin. We have had an interview with the
illustrious King Alfonso, who has shown us as much
love and obedience as if he had been our own son.
We cannot express to you with what mutual satisfaction and content we parted. You may be sure

that his Majesty is ready to yield his own person and all that he possesses to our service.

"We hope that all suspicion and disagreements in connection with the Colonna will be completely laid aside in three or four days. Nothing now remains but to warn you to take care of your health and to pray diligently to the Madonna. Given in Rome in St. Peter's, July 24, 1494."

The year which Lucrezia spent in her husband's beautiful little domain of Pesaro was probably one of the happiest of her life. After the fettered existence which she had led in Rome, she must have tasted, for the first time, something of the joy of freedom, and the relief of being separated from her father and brother must have more than compensated for the absence of the grandeur and magnificence of Rome. She was still but a child in years, and she had inherited, to some extent, her father's buoyancy of disposition, which we may hope enabled her to shake off the taint of the iniquitous atmosphere in which she had been bred, and enjoy the fairness of the fleeting hour. Everywhere in Pesaro the beautiful young wife was welcomed with pleasure, for as yet her life was darkened by no shadow of the suspicions which fell upon her in later years. Pesaro itself had many attractions, and Lucrezia was able to visit the neighbouring castle of Urbino, which, under the Duke Guidobaldi, was at that time a centre of light and learning.

The Sforza palace at Pesaro is still in existence, though the Sforza arms have disappeared and been replaced by those of the della Rovere family. Here Lucrezia spent the greater part of her time, though in the summer she occupied one of the beautiful villas on a neighbouring hill. The most inviting of these country resorts was the Villa Imperiale, on Monte Accio, which afterwards became celebrated in song and story.

About this time many hideous rumours were floating about the Vatican. In 1496 it was reported in Venice that the Duke of Gandia had brought to Italy a Spanish woman to gratify his father's unholy passions. Don Jofré's wife, the beautiful and frivolous Donna Sancia, was also giving Roman tongues much cause to wag ; it was said that her brothers-in-law, Cæsar and the Duke of Gandia, contested her favours and that several young nobles and Cardinals, such as Ippolito d'Este, enjoyed an unlawful intimacy with her. Rome was indeed at this period a sink of iniquity, even eclipsing in vice the Court of Naples, from which Donna Sancia had been removed. No wonder that the warning voice of the great prophet Savonarola made itself heard in the land.

The origin of the child Giovanni, or Juan, born in 1497 or 1498,[1] is clouded with mystery. In two different documents of 1501 he is described as an illegitimate son of Cæsar Borgia and legitimised by the Pope. In March 1498 the Ferrarese ambassador informs Duke Ercole that Lucrezia was believed by the Romans to have given birth to an illegitimate child. This date agrees with the age of Giovanni as given in September 1501. The documents of legitimation are in the Archives of Este, Lucrezia having probably taken them with her to Ferrara, where the mysterious child was allowed to pass as her brother. Another papal brief of September 1, in the same year, does but increase the obscurity surrounding the *Infans Romanus*, as the boy was called. It unblushingly explains that he was really the offspring of the Pope, but that, " for good reasons," this fact had been suppressed in the preceding document. To quote Alexander's own candid remarks " Since it is owing, not to the Duke named [Cæsar], but to us and to the unmarried woman mentioned,

---

[1] See Pastor (vol vi p. 105), who gives June 18, 1497, as the probable date,

that you bear this stain [of illegitimate birth], which
for good reasons we did not wish to state in the preceding instrument ; and in order that there may be
no chance of your being annoyed in the future, we
will arrange that the document shall never be declared null, and of our own free will, and by virtue
of our authority, we confirm you, by these presents,
in the validity of all that is specified in the said instrument." Ronchini has rightly pointed out that
the second bull was meant to be kept secret until a
necessity arose for divulging it ; thus Gregorovius is
incorrect when he speaks of open and shameless
legitimation. The dukedom of Nepi, including Pales-
trina, Olevano, Paliano, Frascati, Anticoli, and other
places, was conferred upon this infant of tender years
by the Pope, his father.

The suggestion that Giovanni was Lucrezia's son
is now generally repudiated, and it is considered
morally certain that Giulia Farnese was his mother.
He seems to have been brought up with Lucrezia's
little boy, Rodrigo, and we shall hear of him later
at the Court of Ferrara, recognised and welcomed by
the Duchess as her brother.

From the *Regesta* of Pope Leo X. (fasc. vii. p. 166),
it appears that Alexander's tenth child, Rodrigo,
son of Giulia Farnese, was born in 1503, the year of
the Pope's death. Very little is known of him beyond
the fact that on the 18th of the Kalends of September
1515 (August 15), he received a dispensation from
Leo X. enabling him, notwithstanding his illegitimacy,
to enter the monastery of the Benedictine Order,
that of the Blessed Virgin Mary of Vietro, in the
diocese of Salerno.

Giovanni Sforza had by this time fallen quite into
disfavour with the Borgias, who realised that no great
advantage was likely to accrue to them from his
marriage with Lucrezia.

The House of Sforza had lost much of its former

prestige, and it seemed that Lucrezia might profitably adorn a more brilliant sphere. Giovanni's position at the Vatican had become unbearable, and at last he was requested voluntarily to renounce his wife. This he naturally refused to do, whereupon he was threatened with extreme measures.

Gregorovius writes : " Flight alone could save him from the dagger or the poison of his brothers-in-law. According to the chroniclers of Pesaro it was Lucrezia herself who helped her husband to flee, thus giving proof of her sympathy with his sad position. One evening, it is said, when Jacomino, Lord Giovanni's chamberlain, was in Madonna's room, her brother Cæsar entered, and, at her command, Jacomino had concealed himself behind a screen. Cæsar talked freely with his sister and said, among other things, that the command had been given to take Sforza's life. When he had gone Lucrezia said to the chamberlain : ' Did you hear what was said? Go and tell him.' This Jacomino immediately did, and Giovanni Sforza threw himself upon a Turkish horse and rode with hanging stirrups to Pesaro, where the beast dropped down dead."

According to letters of the Venetian ambassador in Rome, this flight took place in March, during Holy Week. Sforza, under some pretext, went to the Church of St. Onofrio, where he found a horse in readiness for him.

The Borgias now demanded a divorce, a request which hardly emanated from Lucrezia, for a coolness seems to have arisen between her and her father and brothers, with the result that, early in June, she sought an asylum at the Convent of San Sisto, on the Appian Way, thereby creating a great sensation in Rome.

Her conduct towards her husband is difficult to understand. At first she seems to have stood by him, but later there was a complete rupture between

them. At the divorce proceedings instituted by
Alexander she declared her willingness to swear that
their marriage had never been consummated, and
that she was still a "virgin," an announcement
which excited universal derision and mirth in Italy.
In vain did Giovanni protest against the assertion of
his impotence, but finally, persuaded and intimidated
by his kinsmen, Ludovico the Moor and Ascanio, he
yielded and made a written declaration to the effect
that there had been no consummation of their union.
The formal dissolution of the marriage was pronounced on December 20, 1497, and Sforza was
requested to return his wife's dowry to the amount
of 31,000 ducats.

While admitting that Alexander VI. forced Lucrezia
to consent to this shameful divorce, it cannot be
denied that she gave proof of much weakness of
character in the whole affair. But her punishment
was not delayed. Sforza, in revenge for his humiliation, attributed to the Pope the most horrible motives
for desiring the divorce, crediting him and his family
with crimes "which the moral sense shrinks from
putting into words." Lucrezia thus became the
subject of public scandal, and her fair fame was
sullied by hints of the most shameful and revolting
kind. Scandalous tales went the round of all the
Italian Courts, were repeated by Malipiero and
Paolo Capella, formed the subject of satires by
Sannazaro and Pontano, crept into the chronicles
of Matarazzo, and survived in the histories of Guicciardini and Machiavelli.[1]

[1] See Symonds, *Age of the Despots*, p. 330.

CHAPTER V

WORN out in body and wearied in mind, Piero
de' Medici passed to his rest, December 3, 1469.
His elder son Lorenzo, a brilliant and capable youth
of twenty-one, immediately took up the reins of
authority. His was a remarkable personality, for
his many natural gifts had been fostered by a wise
education and the influence of a pious and cultured
mother. Though singularly unprepossessing in appearance himself, he adored beauty in others, and
in his early youth became enamoured of a lovely
and amiable maiden. But just as her charms were
at their height, Death claimed her, and she was borne
to an early grave, leaving behind her many sorrowing
lovers. Lorenzo, though greatly saddened by this
event, did not refuse to be comforted. He poured
out his soul in sonnets to his lost love, but before
long we get the following relation from his own pen:

" A public festival was held in Florence, to which
all that was noble and beautiful in the city resorted.
To this I was brought by some of my companions
against my will, for I had for some time past avoided
such exhibitions. . . . Among the ladies there assembled, I saw one of such sweet and attractive manners
that, whilst I regarded her, I could not help saying, ' If this person were possessed of the delicacy,
the understanding, the accomplishments of her who

is lately dead—most certainly she excels her in the charms of her person. . . . '

" Resigning myself to my passion, I endeavoured to discover, if possible, how far her manners and her conversation agreed with her appearance, and here I found such an assemblage of extraordinary endowments that it was difficult to say whether she excelled more in her person or in her mind. Her beauty was, as I have before mentioned, astonishing. She was of a just and proper height ; her complexion extremely fair, but not pale ; blooming, but not ruddy. Her countenance was serious without being severe ; mild and pleasant, without levity or vulgarity. Her eyes were lively, without any indication of pride or conceit. Her whole shape was so finely proportioned that amongst other women she appeared with superior dignity, yet free from the least degree of formality or affectation. In walking, in dancing, or in other exercises which display the person, every motion was elegant and appropriate. Her sentiments were always just and striking, and have furnished materials for some of my sonnets ; she always spoke at the proper time and always to the purpose, so that nothing could be added, nothing taken away. Though her remarks were often keen and pointed, yet they were so tempered as not to give offence. Her understanding was superior to her sex, but without the appearance of arrogance or presumption ; and she avoided an error too common among women, who, when they think themselves sensible, become for the most part insupportable. To recount all her excellences would far exceed my present limits, and I shall therefore conclude with affirming that there was nothing which could be desired in a beautiful and accomplished woman which was not in her most abundantly found. By these qualities I was so captivated that not a power or faculty of my body or mind remained any longer at liberty, and I could

LORENZO DE'MEDICI.
Uffizi Gallery Florence.

CARDINAL ALESSANDRO FARNESE, AFTERWARDS POPE
PAUL III.
Raphael (National Museum, Naples).
He was brother of Giulia Farnese, "La Bella," to whose
influence he owed his promotion to the Cardinalate;
hence he was known as "The Cardinal of the petticoat."

96]

not help considering the lady who had died as the planet Venus, which, at the approach of the sun, is totally overpowered and extinguished "[1]

The lady with whom Lorenzo became thus infatuated bore the name of Lucrezia. She was a member of the Donati family, and numbered among her ancestors the famous Curtio Donati, whose military talents had been the admiration of the whole of Italy. But Lorenzo's dreams of bliss were destined never to be fulfilled. For political reasons, he entered into a prosaic and highly respectable alliance with Clarice, a daughter of the celebrated Orsini family. The match was promoted by Piero de' Medici, and the wedding took place on June 1, 1469. But although the romantic element was entirely lacking in this *mariage de convenance*, the young couple soon developed a mutual respect and affection; this may be seen from a letter written by Lorenzo to his wife in the following July from Milan, where he had gone to witness the baptism of the eldest son of Galeazzo, the reigning Duke. It runs as follows :

" LORENZO DE' MEDICI TO HIS WIFE CLARICE

" I arrived here safe and sound, and I think that this news will be more welcome to thee than any, saving only that of my return ; so, at least, I conclude from my own longing to see thee. Seek to be often in the society of my father and sisters. As much as possible I will hasten the time of my home-coming, for the time of our separation seems like a thousand years. Pray for me, and if thou shouldst desire anything of me, here, let me know betimes.

" Thy

" LORENZO DE' MEDICI.

" MILAN,

"*July* 22, 1469 "

[1] Roscoe, *Life of Lorenzo de' Medici.*

GB

GB

Lorenzo, who was acting as his father's deputy during the illness of the latter, seems to have been received with great respect at Milan, which was at that time under the authority of Galeazzo Maria, son of Francesco Sforza. Upon his departure Lorenzo presented the Duchess with a gold necklace and a diamond worth three thousand ducats, and the Duke, not to be outdone in amiability, expressed a wish that he would act as godfather to all his children.

As we said before, Piero de' Medici did not long survive his son's marriage The latter had already given ample proof of his administrative capacity, and, though it seemed at first as if the Medici power might be endangered, the Florentines, influenced by the representations of Tommaso Soderini, approached him with respect, inviting him to take upon himself the government of the city, as his father and grandfather had done before him.

Lorenzo's younger brother, Giuliano, was only sixteen at the time of his father's death—too young to take any active part in the government. Both brothers were highly cultured and showed a disposition to encourage men of talent and to promote the revival of learning. Unlike Lorenzo, Giuliano was attractive in appearance, and his amiability and generosity, as well as his propensity for public merry-making, caused him to be extremely popular with the people of Florence.

The management of state affairs which Lorenzo now assumed did not render him neglectful of his private concerns. The commercial transactions of his house were continued, though Lorenzo proved himself but an indifferent financier, and disbursed the family riches with more zeal than discretion. The enormous wealth of the House of Medici was such that, during the last thirty-seven years, they had spent on public charities alone no less than 665,755 florins.

The particular branch of traffic from which the Medici derived their colossal wealth is not known, but it is probable that the trade in eastern commodities was the original source of their prosperity. They also obtained considerable revenues in other ways ; as, for example, from the great country estates of Poggio Cajano, Caffagiolo, etc. But the main bulk of their riches probably proceeded from the great banking establishments which they had erected in almost all the important trading centres of Europe. In those days the rate of interest was regulated according to the need of the borrower, and tremendous profits must have been made by such institutions to which even princes and sovereigns did not hesitate to resort when pressed for money

In March 1471 the Milanese alliance with Florence was consolidated by a visit from Duke Galeazzo Sforza to Lorenzo He and his wife Bona arrived in Florence accompanied by a large and gorgeous retinue, which was entertained at the public expense. There were no less than a hundred armed cavalry, five hundred infantry, fifty richly clad in silk and silver, and the same number of courtiers. Including the retinues of the latter, there were altogether about two thousand horsemen, to say nothing of five hundred couples of dogs and an unlimited number of falcons

In spite of the amazing splendour of his own equipment, Galeazzo was overcome with admiration at the princely treasures of Lorenzo Especially was he impressed by the priceless works of art— rare paintings, gems, and statuary—which abounded in the palace and garden. Lorenzo's celebrated collection of manuscripts and other curiosities also attracted him, and, though he could not perhaps value them at their true worth, the Duke had the tact to acknowledge that gold and silver were as nothing in comparison with these marvellous works of art.

Galeazzo's eight days' visit was the occasion for the display of unbridled luxury and extravagance in Florence Even the Florentines, who were far from being strait-laced, were scandalised by the licentiousness and laxity of the Milanese courtiers, who, in the enjoyment of their mad and merry holiday, openly disregarded the rules for Lenten fasting. The portrait of Duke Galeazzo, painted during his stay in Florence by one of the Pollaiuoli, is still to be seen in the Uffizi Gallery.

The Medici were the representatives of Florentine hospitality, and Lorenzo, who was of a studious disposition, probably yielded to these dissipations from necessity rather than choice He found his highest enjoyment in the companionship of literary men, among whom one of his most intimate friends was Poliziano, the celebrated scholar and poet.

As an example of Lorenzo's desire to promote the claims of learning may be mentioned his labours on behalf of the University of Pisa. This institution, once of great repute, had fallen upon evil times. In 1348, when the Black Death was raging in Italy, a similar seat of learning had been established at Florence , but, owing to the expenses of living and the number of distractions which the city offered, the scheme did not prosper The Florentines decided, therefore, to re-establish the University at Pisa, which, since 1406, had been under the jurisdiction of Florence. The task was entrusted to Lorenzo and four other citizens. Lorenzo was the moving spirit and supplemented the state grant by large sums from his private purse.

In 1471 Pope Paul II. was succeeded by the gifted and impetuous Francesco della Rovere, under the name of Sixtus IV. The early relations between Lorenzo de' Medici and the new Pope were nothing if not amiable. Lorenzo, at the head of the Florentine embassy, repaired to Rome to congratulate him

upon his promotion. He met with a most favourable reception, and Sixtus confided to him the care
of the papal finances, an office which contributed
much to the enrichment of both Lorenzo and his
maternal uncle, Giovanni Tornabuoni Lorenzo was
further allowed to buy part of Paul II 's collection
of jewels at a very reasonable price, and was also
granted the valuable lease of the papal alum-mines.
Encouraged by these marks of favour, Lorenzo, who
was of a practical turn of mind, ventured to remark
that his most cherished desire was to see a member
of his family admitted to the Sacred College. Sixtus,
who seemed unwilling to refuse him anything, lent
a ready ear to this request, and Lorenzo left Rome
well content with his reception, and laden with every
token of the Pope's favour.

At the time of his accession Sixtus IV. was the
father of several sons, who passed as his " nephews."
He lost no time in raising them to important ecclesiastical dignities and bestowing upon them riches
which they, with equal speed, proceeded to squander.
One of them, Pietro Riario, who was at one and the
same time Cardinal of San Sisto, Patriarch of Jerusalem, and Archbishop of Florence, expended no less
than 20,000 ducats on one single festivity in honour
of Leonora of Aragon, who passed through Rome in
June, 1473, on her way to marry Ercole, Duke of
Ferrara. The Square of Santi Apostoli was converted
into a banqueting-hall, and the banquet, at which
the Seneschal changed his dress four times, was served
by silk-clad waiters. There were wild boars roasted
whole, peacocks, fishes covered with silver, storks,
cranes, and stags Sugar castles full of meat were
stormed and their contents thrown to the people
outside In short, the display of luxury was unex-
ampled and unbridled. Pietro's brother, Girolamo,
who enjoyed a like reputation for extravagance and
profligacy, was made a Count by the Pope, and, that

he might have the wherewithal to support this dignity, 40,000 ducats were spent on purchasing the province of Imola from the Manfredi. The Medici wished to buy Imola themselves, and their bank did its utmost to prevent the money negotiations of Sixtus IV. The latter, who was anxious to gain possession of the town of Castello, sent Giuliano della Rovere to capture it. Giuliano had more of the soldier than the priest in his composition and Vitelli, the governor of the town, was finally obliged to capitulate, notwithstanding the help of Florence and Milan The Pope's party, not without reason, attributed his lengthy resistance to the financial help of Lorenzo, who was not inclined to stand idly by and watch Castello, on the very borders of Tuscany, fall a prey to the enemy. One consequence of this event was an alliance between Milan, Florence, and Venice for their mutual security (1474).

In spite of Lorenzo's popularity with the Florentines, he was soon to fall a victim to a plot which has perhaps no parallel in history His overbearing ambition had made him many enemies, and, as before mentioned, his support of Vitelli had excited the animosity of Pope Sixtus, who saw in the removal of the Medici the main hope of future security for the Papacy. His views were warmly supported by Girolamo Riario, whose ambitious projects had been stimulated by his marriage with Galeazzo's daughter, Caterina Sforza, a woman of strong and determined character.[1] The Pope's displeasure had been further excited by the league between Florence, Venice, and Milan, in which Lorenzo had played a leading part. As a first token of resentment, Sixtus deprived Lorenzo of his office of Papal Treasurer and bestowed it upon Francesco Pazzi, whose family owned a bank in Rome and who had advanced three-fourths of the purchase

[1] *Catherine Sforza*, by Pasolini, French translation by Marc Hélys (Perrin & Cie, Paris, 1912).

money for Imola, when the Medici refused their co-operation. The Pazzi were a noble and influential Florentine family whose fortunes, owing to the Medici ascendancy, had lately been declining. It was one of Lorenzo's leading principles to prevent the other nobles from becoming too powerful, and this attitude could not fail to embitter the Pazzi, who, though they continued to live on terms of apparent friendliness with the Medici, were quite ready to make common cause with Girolamo Riario and the Pope. According to Poliziano, Giacopo Pazzi, the head of the family, was an unprincipled profligate, who, having squandered the paternal inheritance in riotous living, sought occasion to hide his own downfall in that of his native city. He had no children, but an abundance of nephews and nieces, one of whom, Guglielmo, had married Lorenzo's favourite sister Bianca. Another, Francesco, had for some years resided in Rome, as his bold and domineering nature could not resign itself to the growth of the Medici power in his native city.

The real cause of the enmity between the two families is not clear. Machiavelli mentions a wrong inflicted by the Medici on one of the Pazzi in connection with some inheritance. But as this took place many years before the death of Piero, when his sons were still children, it seems improbable that the grievance could have produced such far-reaching effects.

The conspiracy had its origin in Rome, where Francesco de' Pazzi and the Count Girolamo Riario, incited by Sixtus IV., entered into a compact to bring about the downfall of the Medici. In the event of their being successful, the Pope hoped to take possession of Tuscany and to place the Pazzi and Riario in authority at Florence. The most active agent in the plot was Francesco Salviati, who had lately been promoted to the Archbishopric of Pisa, much to the displeasure of the Medici. Poliziano describes him as a man of vicious habits, addicted to gambling, and of inordinate vanity. Great cunning and surpassing impudence were among the other characteristics which rendered him remarkably unfit for his high ecclesiastical position. The other conspirators were Giacopo Salviati, brother to the Archbishop; Giacopo Poggio, a celebrated scholar of the day; Bernardo Bandini, a man of dissolute life; Giovanni Battista Montesecco, of military fame; Antonio Maffei, a priest of Volterra, who had been led to take part in the plot through grief for the misfortunes of his native city, whose ruin he attributed to Lorenzo; Stefano de Bagnone, one of the apostolic scribes; with several others of less importance.

As the Medici were extremely popular with the majority of the Florentines, the conspirators saw the necessity of providing an adequate military force for the support of their undertaking. King Ferrante of Naples, who was at that time on friendly terms with Pope Sixtus, was persuaded to lend his countenance, and Girolamo directed his nephew, Cardinal Riario, to comply with the commands of the Archbishop of Pisa, who now issued orders that two thousand men should advance by different routes towards Florence, so as to be in readiness to support them in case of need.

Just at this time, in the spring of 1478, the Archbishop despatched Cardinal Riario to Florence, where he took up his abode at a country villa belonging to the Pazzi, about a mile from the city The assassination of the Medici brothers was planned to take place at Fiesole, where Lorenzo had a residence to which it was expected that he would invite the young Cardinal and his suite. The conspirators were right in this supposition, for Lorenzo made ready a magnificent banquet to which Riario and his attendants were bidden. Giuliano, however, was absent from the festivity, on plea of indisposition, so the attempt was postponed to a more favourable occasion.

After consideration, it was decided that the assassination should take place on the following Sunday, during the High Mass in the Church of the Reparata, now known as Santa Maria dei Fiori.

To Francesco de' Pazzi and Bernardo Bandini was entrusted the murder of Giuliano, while Lorenzo was to be slain by the hand of Montesecco But the latter, at the last moment, refused to commit murder in a church, before the High Altar, not daring " to make Christ witness of a crime " Thereupon, two ecclesiastics, Stefano de Bagnone, the Apostolic Scribe, and Antonio Maffei were chosen in his place Neither of them appears to have suffered any qualms of conscience at the idea of desecrating the sacred place with so hideous a deed.

Cardinal Riario had expressed a desire to be present on the following Sunday at High Mass in the Church of the Reparata. Lorenzo, therefore, invited him to Florence, where he and his suite were received with magnificent hospitality. To the dismay of the conspirators, however, Giuliano did not appear, and when all were assembled in the church, and he still remained absent, they began to fear that their plan would again fall through Francesco de' Pazzi and Bandini, in concern, hastened to his palace to fetch him. Giuliano, all unsuspecting, accompanied them back to the church. On the way they engaged him in merry conversation, and even threw their arms round him in token of apparent friendliness Their real object, however, was to discover whether he was wearing armour under his clothes. Reassured on this point, they entered the church with him and seated themselves close by his side.

The critical moment had arrived. The appointed signal for action seems to have been the beginning of the canon of the Mass The bell rang ; the priest elevated the Host ; the congregation bowed their heads. At the same instant Bandini thrust his dagger into Giuliano's breast. The victim staggered a few steps forward and sank helpless upon the ground. With incredible brutality, Francesco de' Pazzi sprang upon him and continued to stab him even after he was apparently dead. Such was the vehemence of his rage that, in his excitement, he gave himself a severe wound on the lip.

Meanwhile Bagnone and Maffei had attacked Lorenzo. Maffei, however, miscalculated his aim, and, instead of plunging his dagger into the throat of his victim, succeeded only in slightly wounding his neck. Lorenzo defended himself with vigour. Twisting his cloak round his left arm to serve as a shield, he drew his sword and managed to repel his assassins. The latter, recognising their defeat, sought refuge in flight, having first wounded a friend of Lorenzo's who had hastened to his assistance.

Bandini now attempted to fall upon Lorenzo, but was driven back by a faithful servant of the House of Medici—Francesco Nori. Though his interference cost him his life, the interruption gave Lorenzo's friends time to flock to his help. They hurried him into the sacristy, where Poliziano immediately had the brass doors of Luca della Robbia closed upon him.

It was feared that Lorenzo's injury had been caused by a poisoned dagger, and Antonio Ridolfo, a youth of distinguished family, gave practical proof of his devotion by undertaking to suck the wound. Great consternation ensued, and so great was the tumult that many thought that the building was falling in. The panic-stricken people crowded to the exit, but no sooner did they realise that Lorenzo's life was in danger than the whole scene changed. The wounded man was surrounded by a number of Florentine youths, who formed themselves into a bodyguard and led him to his palace, going out of their way that he might not meet the dead body of his brother.

As had been previously arranged, the Archbishop and his followers were seeking to take possession of the Seigniorial Palace Stationing the other conspirators in different apartments, Salviati himself went into the room where Petrucci, the Gonfaloniere, and several other magistrates were assembled. Upon his entrance Petrucci, out of respect to his position, rose to greet him. This action seems to have disconcerted the Archbishop, for the Gonfaloniere was well known for his courage and decision of character. However this may be, Salviati's nerve deserted him at the crucial moment, and, instead of intimidating the magistrates, he merely proceeded to inform Petrucci that the Pope had conferred an ecclesiastical appointment upon his son. The hesitation and confusion of his manner and the apprehensive way in which he glanced towards the door were so striking that Petrucci's suspicions were aroused, and he rushed from the room to summon the guards. The Archbishop attempted flight, thereby tacitly acknowledging his guilt. Petrucci, in pursuing him, came into contact with Giacopo Poggio, whom he seized by the hair and delivered into custody. The other magistrates seized upon any weapons at hand—not disdaining even kitchen pots and pans—in order to defend themselves and the Seigniorial Palace. The doors were barricaded and the conspirators were so violently handled that they were obliged to relinquish all attempt at resistance.

Nor had Giacopo de' Pazzi been any more successful in his endeavours to incite the citizens to revolt. Standing outside the Palace at the head of about a hundred soldiers, he tried to stir up the people with cries of " Liberty ! " The palace gates were stormed and several of the insurgents pressed their way in. They were, however, driven back by the magistrates and the gates again barricaded as far as possible until a reinforcement of friends came to their help. Now, for the first time, Petrucci and the magistrates heard of the murder of Giuliano. The news filled them with the deepest indignation, and, with the common consent, Giacopo Poggio was hanged from one of the palace windows in sight of the whole populace. Petrucci, at the same time, gave orders for the arrest of the Archbishop, his brother, and the other leaders of the conspiracy. Only one escaped; he was found a few days later hiding behind some wainscoting, half dead from hunger, and was pardoned out of consideration for his sufferings All the others were slaughtered or thrown, half alive, through the palace windows. After having been kept in confinement from April 26, the day of the murder, until June 12, the young Cardinal Riario, who had taken refuge at the altar, was eventually set free through the intervention of Lorenzo. Whether the latter believed in his innocence is doubtful. Perhaps he was moved to compassion by the Cardinal's pitiable condition. So abject was his terror that it is said that he never recovered his normal health and complexion. His servants were all slain, and the streets strewn with their mangled corpses. Francesco de' Pazzi was discovered at his uncle's house, confined to his bed by the state of his wound He was dragged naked to the Palace, where he met with the same fate as his colleague. According to Poliziano, Archbishop Sal-viati, who was hanged at the same time, seized Francesco's body with his teeth, not loosing his hold even in the agonies of death.

Giacopo de' Pazzi had meanwhile fled from the town. The following day, however, he was brought back to Florence and delivered up to justice by the neighbouring peasants, heedless of his entreaties that they would put him to death. His guilt was sufficiently obvious to the authorities, and he was speedily executed   The fate of his nephew Renato, who suffered death at the same time, excited universal compassion ; he was an inoffensive person of studious tastes, and his only crime had been that of silence regarding the conspiracy. Although Giacopo was dead and buried, his body was was not allowed to rest in peace. A violent and incessant rain which set in soon after these disturbances was attributed by the superstitious people to the displeasure of Heaven that so great a criminal had been interred in holy ground instead of outside the walls of Florence. The magistrates, either from desire to gratify the people, or because they too shared this belief, commanded that the corpse should be removed. The next day it was dragged from its tomb by a band of gutter children, who, regardless of remonstrance, hauled it through the streets, and, after the most disgraceful outrages, flung it into the Arno. It was never seen again, and it was popularly supposed that the devil had taken it.

The other members of the family were punished with imprisonment or exile. The only exception was Guglielmo de' Pazzi, the brother-in-law of Lorenzo, in whose house he found a refuge from the fury of the populace. He was afterwards commanded to remain at his own country house, about twenty-five miles from Florence

The priests who had taken part in the plot were discovered in a Benedictine cloister on the third day after the attempt. On their being brought forth the populace, beside itself with rage, fell upon them and hewed them in pieces. Indeed, it was with difficulty that the monks who had sheltered them were preserved from sharing the same fate. Montesecco was seized a few days later and beheaded on May 1. Before his execution he made a full confession of the circumstances in connection with the

conspiracy. His disclosures are of great importance
in their bearing upon the question of the Pope's
participation in the affair. There seems to be no
doubt that Sixtus was intensely anxious to bring
about the downfall of the Medici, but whether he
countenanced the actual shedding of blood is still
a matter for dispute. The most that can be said
for him is that he managed to keep within the letter
of the law.

The last to meet his fate was Bernardo Bandini.
He had succeeded in escaping to Constantinople,
but the Sultan Mohammed II , on being apprised
of his crime, had him seized and taken in chains to
Florence. Esteem for Lorenzo, it is alleged, was
the mainspring of this action. Bandini arrived in
December 1479 at Florence, where he met with well-
merited retribution An embassy was afterwards
despatched in the name of the Republic with a message
of thanks to the Sultan.

The utter failure of the Pazzi conspiracy was a
striking witness to the affection in which Lorenzo
was held by the Florentines. The remarkable out-
burst of popular emotion rendered it unnecessary
for him to take any steps in his own defence Indeed,
he did his best to restrain the fury of the people
and to prevent further bloodshed. In spite of his
wound, he addressed a crowded audience in the most
touching terms, begging that the punishment of the
wrong-doers might be left to the magistrates, lest
haply the innocent might suffer with the guilty.

Giuliano was universally lamented, for his humanity
and generosity had made him the darling of Florence
He is described by Poliziano as tall and powerful,
with dark complexion and glowing eyes. Although
gentler and less ambitious than Lorenzo, he was
distinguished for great courage, and displayed strength
and dexterity in all physical exercises He loved
music and the fine arts, and was in the main dominated

by religious principle. His burial in the Church of San Lorenzo was celebrated with great magnificence. Many young Florentines, who had looked up to him with admiration, donned mourning garb out of respect to his memory. Guiliano died unmarried, but soon after his death Lorenzo heard of the existence of a child by a woman of lower rank, either posthumous or born immediately before the father's murder. He was taken into the Medici household, whence he passed, forty-five years later, to the papal throne as Clement VII.

Montesecco's confession had revealed the Pope's animosity to Lorenzo, who, at the same time, realised that the King of Naples would probably ally himself with Sixtus. Ferrante was already desirous of engaging in war for the sake of his son, who had acquired a considerable degree of military repute. Lorenzo, in his anxiety to protect himself against this impending danger, wrote to all the Italian States, as well as to the Kings of France and Spain, protesting against the treachery of a Pope who spared neither virtue nor rank to attain an end which would endanger the whole of Italy. Several of the Italian States, including Ferrara and Venice, declared themselves on the side of the Florentines, and the Kings of France and Spain assured Lorenzo that they would use all their influence in his favour.

Lorenzo's preparations for the defence of Florence angered the Pope still more. In the first heat of his displeasure he decreed the confiscation of the Medici property and that of all the Florentines then in Rome, as well as the imprisonment of the Florentines themselves. He would have been even more severe in his treatment had he not entertained apprehensions as to the fate of his son Cardinal Riario, who was still in prison. With the view of appeasing his anger, the Republic of Florence despatched to Rome Donato Acciajuoli, a scholar renowned for his skill

in managing public affairs.   But the Pope, instead
of giving heed to his representations, threatened to
have him imprisoned in the Castle of Sant' Angelo.
He would indeed have carried this threat into execution if the legates from Milan and Venice had not
interfered, declaring that they would look upon any
such infringement of the rights of the people as a
personal affront   Sixtus thereupon armed himself
with spiritual weapons, and solemnly anathematised
not only Lorenzo but the Gonfaloniere and the other
Florentine magistrates.

In the bull which the Pope issued for this purpose
on June 1 Lorenzo is called a " son of iniquity and
a   child   of perdition," while equally opprobrious
epithets are bestowed on the magistrates.   Lorenzo
is accused of numerous offences against the Papal
Chair, and the Pope's own forbearance and long-
suffering are extolled.   Following in the footsteps of
our saviour, he had long suffered with patience the
injuries of his enemies.   He would have borne with
them still longer if Lorenzo and the Florentine
Council, possessed by diabolical fury, had not laid
violent hands on the Lord's anointed and, *proh dolor
et in auditum scelus*, hanged the Archbishop, imprisoned the Cardinal, and destroyed their followers
in various ways.   He thereupon proceeds to pass
sentence of excommunication upon Lorenzo and the
Council, proclaiming them to be incapable of owning
any property or receiving any inheritance, and
prohibiting the acceptance of any ecclesiastical office
by any of their descendants.   At the same time all
the bishops and clergy of the Florentine territories
were deprived of their benefices.

If the Pope had been content to denounce merely
those who had been implicated in the punishment
of the Archbishop and the ecclesiastics, he might
have attained his end ; but, by including in the ban
the Florentine bishops and clergy who were not

personally concerned in the conspiracy, he outran the bounds of his authority. It naturally resulted that the papal edict was disregarded by all, including the enraged clerics. The Bishop of Arezzo, Gentile d'Urbino, summoned a convocation in the Church of the Reparata, and a document was drawn up accusing the Pope of having instigated the recent crimes, and exonerating Lorenzo and the Florentines from the offences laid to their charge. It is to be regretted that this defence (*Synodus Florentina*) was couched in terms as passionate and unmeasured as those of the papal bull itself. In it Pope Sixtus is alluded to in such choice terms as " the Vicar of the Devil," and " the adulterers' minion." There can be little doubt that, by thus overstepping the limits of decorum, its promoters did no little harm to their cause. The Pope's conduct aroused the indignation of Christendom. Venice, Milan, Ferrara, and Rimini, all took Lorenzo's part. Louis XI. of France gave his special sanction to the league, and sent Comines, the historian, to represent him at Florence, while the Emperor and Matthias Corvinus of Hungary despatched envoys to remonstrate with Sixtus.

CHAPTER VI

POPE SIXTUS IV., who had hitherto concealed his
hatred of Lorenzo under a cloak of craftiness, now
threw aside his disguise and made open and un-
abashed attempts to get rid of him. The King of
Naples was persuaded to send an embassy to Florence
admonishing the citizens to deliver Lorenzo over
to his enemies or at least to banish him from Tuscany.
The Florentines, however, rose to the occasion and
absolutely refused to accede to this proposal, declaring
themselves ready to endure any hardships rather
than betray their leader. They, moreover, ordered
their Chancellor, Bartolomeo Scala, to draw up a statement concerning the conspiracy, declaring Sixtus IV.
to have been its instigator and promoter.

When Lorenzo realised that the Pope's animosity was directed against him personally rather than against the State, he convened a meeting of three hundred citizens and begged them earnestly not to allow their anxiety for the safety of his person to blind them to the welfare of the State, maintaining his willingness to sacrifice his life and property in the cause of peace. But the Florentines remained loyal, and Giacopo de' Alessandri, in the name of the whole assembly, declared that they were prepared to defend him even at the risk of their lives.

Preparations for fighting now began. The papal forces were led by the Duke of Urbino and the Neapolitan troops by Alfonso, Duke of Calabria. The Florentines appointed Ercole d'Este, the Duke of Ferrara, as their Commander-in-Chief.

The allies advanced towards Florence, carrying devastation in their train. Having plundered several unimportant places, they turned their attention to Arezzo. The Florentines were prepared to oppose them with vigour, but the enemy, who were somewhat discomfited by the spirited defence of the citizens of Arezzo, decided that discretion was the better part of valour, and refrained from any engagement. The Duke of Urbino's proposal of an armistice was welcomed by the Duke of Ferrara, greatly to the displeasure of the Florentines, who felt aggrieved at having incurred the expenses of the campaign without having gained any corresponding advantage. Both armies thereupon retired into winter quarters.

Lorenzo took advantage of the truce to make further overtures ; but, in spite of the interest which Milan and Venice professed in his cause, neither of them seemed disposed to send him any practical help. The Emperor and the Kings of France and Hungary were unsuccessful in their attempts to reconcile the Pope and Lorenzo, for Sixtus, quite unmoved, repelled all friendly advances.

During the winter the Florentines had gained the services of three experienced generals—Ruberto Malatesta, Rudolfo Gonzaga, and Costanzo Sforza of Pesaro. Venice finally decided to send auxiliary troops under the leadership of Carlo Montone and Deifobus Anguillari Thus reinforced, the Florentines adopted the offensive. They divided their troops into two parts, one of which was to invade the papal domains while the other advanced against Alfonso, Duke of Calabria At Montone's approach, the papal forces beat a hasty retreat, but their courage was renewed by his unexpected death, and they encountered the Florentines on the shores of Lake Trasimene. The remembrance of Hannibal's victory on the same spot, however, so unnerved them that they made but a feeble attack and were easily repulsed. The Florentines thereupon proceeded to ravage the country as far as Perugia.

The troops who were fighting against Duke Alfonso did not fare so well. Dissension sprang up among the various generals, in consequence of which the Duke of Ferrara withdrew his forces. Alfonso seized the opportunity to attack the Florentines, who, having lost confidence in their leaders, fled ignominiously at the first onslaught. In Florence the consternation was indescribable, for the route to the city now lay open to Alfonso. Fortunately for the Florentines, the Duke showed no disposition to follow up the victory, but frittered away his time in plundering and besieging unimportant towns, until the troops came back from Perugia to inspire the citizens with fresh courage. Contrary to all expectations, the Duke of Calabria proposed a three months' truce. This was hailed with joy by the Florentines, who hoped thus to obtain relief from the increasing anxieties and expenses of war

But this lull in the storm produced very little improvement in Lorenzo's critical situation. He had seen the terror with which the Florentines had viewed the Duke of Calabria's victory, and knew that, as the war was being waged against him personally, the mere fact of his surrender to the enemy would put an end to the strife. He realised too, that, in spite of the protestations of the citizens, a feeling of discontent was growing up in Florence and that he might be betrayed at any moment. The truce had given the Florentines time to estimate their position, and complaints were arising that the commerce of the city was ruined and the public treasury exhausted. Enough blood had already been shed, it was said, and Lorenzo would do better to sue for peace than continue his preparations for war.

Feeling the ground thus tremble beneath him, Lorenzo made up his mind to a bold step. He determined to throw himself upon the mercy of Ferrante, King of Naples, at the same time endeavouring to convince him of the injustice of the war and persuade him to agree to a separate peace. He was not unmindful of the enormous risk involved in this undertaking, but he felt that it was impossible for things to continue under their present conditions. At the beginning of December, 1479, then, he left Florence covertly, without communicating his intention to his fellow-citizens, and proceeded to San Miniato, whence he despatched to the Florentine magistrates the following letter :

" It was from no lack of respect that I took my departure without assigning any reason. Rather was it from the conviction that, in the present critical condition of our town, action is more prudent than deliberation It seems to me that peace is essential, and, since all other means of procuring it have failed, I have decided rather to incur danger to my person than to leave the town any longer in her present precarious position. With your permission, therefore,

I shall proceed directly to Naples, for, as our enemies
are especially aiming at my person, I believe that
to surrender myself into their hands will be the
speediest way of bringing peace to my fellow-citizens.
It must be conceded that either the King of Naples
is, as some believe, and as he himself has declared,
friendly to our State, seeking rather to do us service
even by this hostile action than to rob us of our
freedom, or, that he is desirous of bringing about
the ruin of the State Should he be favourably
disposed, I can best put his disposition to the proof
by surrendering myself unreservedly to him. This
seems to me to be the only way of making an honourable peace. If, on the contrary, the King's hand
is against us, we shall, in this way at least, be in a
position to estimate his attitude, and this knowledge
had better be obtained at the sacrifice of one than
of many.

" Since I am the person principally involved in
this affair, I am willing to take the risk upon myself.
It may be that nothing further than my own destruction is desired. And, as I have enjoyed among
you honour and distinction beyond my deserts,
perhaps in a greater degree than any other citizen
of our times, so I feel a special obligation to advance
the welfare of my native place, even though it may
be at the cost of my own life. It is in this spirit that
I set out on my journey.

" It may be the will of Providence that, since this
war opened with the shedding of my blood and that
of my brother, I should be instrumental in bringing
it to an end. My one desire is that, in life or in
death, in fortune or in misfortune, I may contribute
to the prosperity of my native place. Should the
result of my project be favourable, I shall rejoice
in having obtained peace for my country and safety
for myself. Should it be otherwise my distress
will be alleviated by the idea that my misfortune

was necessary for the welfare of my country. If our enemies are merely aiming at my destruction, I shall be in their power, and if their intentions go further, they will then be obvious to every one. In the latter case, I do not doubt that all my fellow-citizens will unite in defending their freedom to the last extremity, and I have confidence in the divine Providence which has hitherto favoured our fore-fathers. With this conviction I take farewell of my native town, beseeching Heaven that I may be enabled on this occasion to act as befits a loyal citizen.

" SAN MINIATO,
    "*December* 7, 1479."

This letter was exactly calculated to work upon the feelings of the emotional Florentines. Upon reading it, says Valori, the magistrates could not restrain their tears. Some of the citizens, however, suspected that Lorenzo had already received from Ferrante the assurance of a hospitable reception, while others gave expression to their fears of an impending change in the Government.

Lorenzo was received at Naples with all respect. His friend, Prince Federigo, and the King's grandson, Ferrantino, met him at the landing-stage and conducted him to the King. His arrival excited the liveliest interest; everybody was anxious to obtain a glimpse of a man whose character and talents commanded universal admiration.

For twelve anxious weeks Lorenzo remained at Naples, divided between hopes and fears. By the charm of his personality he soon won the friendship of the King's chief minister, Diomede Carafa, and he had powerful allies in Federigo and the Duchess of Calabria. The King, too, seemed favourably inclined towards him and lent an attentive ear to his representations. He said that while the interests of Naples and Florence were so closely connected, it would

redound to the injury of the former if he took part
against the Florentines. Lorenzo also warned him
against the ambitious projects of the Papal See, which
had already often interfered in Neapolitan affairs,
and thus had a most detrimental effect upon the
State. Nor did he omit to refer to the Pope's part
in the conspiracy which had cost his brother's life.
So effective were these remarks that, although the
King did not immediately accede to Lorenzo's desire,
he gave him reason to hope that the affair would have
a favourable issue, and treated him with the utmost
deference.

But Lorenzo's mind was not yet at rest. Alfonso
had broken the truce and obtained fresh victories
over the Florentines, including the conquest of
Sarzana, the one great Medicean acquisition. The
Pope had received intelligence of Lorenzo's sojourn
at Naples, and did not cease to urge Ferrante to
remain constant to the alliance He begged him
either to keep his visitor at Naples or to send him to
Rome to make his submission to the Holy See.
Although Lorenzo was well aware of the dangers
which threatened him, he betrayed no apprehension,
and continued zealously to pursue his object. With
the wonderful adaptability which distinguished him,
he threw aside his cares and succeeded in gaining
great popularity with the Neapolitans. He bought
galley-slaves and restored them to liberty, gave
gorgeous banquets to the nobles, and presented many
poor girls with dowries. Little wonder, then, that
one whose wealth and generosity alike seemed
boundless, should speedily win the hearts of the
pleasure-loving citizens.

Ferrante was at length persuaded to accede to
Lorenzo's proposals, and, having once made up his
mind what course to pursue, he had no difficulty
in arranging a peace which was acceptable to both
parties. Thus, Lorenzo, who had arrived at Naples

ST. CATHERINE, FROM THE " DISPUTA."
Pinturicchio (Borgia Apartments, the Vatican).
The portrait appears to be that of Giulia Farnese, Mistress of Pope Alexander VI.

defenceless and embittered, left it after three months
the acknowledged friend and ally of King Ferrante.
He hastened his homeward journey as much as possible,
but no sooner had he departed than a papal envoy
came to the King with a proposal which would not
only have put an end to the truce, but have involved
serious danger to Lorenzo. The latter, however,
deemed it discreet to ignore the urgent message
of recall sent after him by Ferrante. He was
welcomed at Florence with every manifestation of
joy. People of all ranks thronged to congratulate
him on his safe return, and, though the terms of peace
were not all that they might have desired, there
were few open signs of discontent.

Pope Sixtus, however, was by no means disposed
to relinquish his plans for Lorenzo's destruction,
and, urged on by Girolamo Riario, he began to make
fresh preparations for war. Alfonso of Calabria,
too, notwithstanding the peace stipulations, remained
with his troops at Siena, whence they continued to
be a source of disquietude to all the surrounding
country. But the situation was saved by an invasion
of the Turks. " As it pleased God," writes Zarducci,
" it came about by His consummate miracle that,
on the sixth day of August, 1480, the fleet of the
Turk came to Otranto and besieged it ; whence
Alfonso, by order of the King, was forced to return
to the Kingdom in defence of that town." All Italy
was seized with alarm, for Mohammed II. the conqueror of Constantinople, ravaged the neighbouring
coast, putting the inhabitants to death by torture
or carrying them into slavery. But all this turned
to the advantage of the Florentines, so much so indeed
that there were not wanting people who accused
Lorenzo of having encouraged the Sultan's attack.
Not only were they rid of Alfonso's objectionable
presence, but they received overtures of peace from
Sixtus IV. Towards the end of 1480 deputies,

under the conduct of Soderini, Bishop of Voltera, were despatched to Rome in order to make terms with the Pope. On the first Sunday in Advent Sixtus gave them audience beneath the portico of St. Peter's, where, on their knees, they craved absolution. The Pope, in his reply, gave free vent to his displeasure and reprimanded them severely for their transgressions against the Church. Finally, however, he received their submission and released Florence from the interdict.

Girolamo Riario, in his insatiable thirst for revenge, now sought other means of getting rid of Lorenzo. In conjunction with some Florentine citizens of shady reputation, he set on foot a fresh scheme against his life. The place chosen was the Church of the Carmelites, and Battista Frescobaldi, lately consul at Pera, undertook to do the deed on Ascension Day, May 31, 1481. But Lorenzo's friends, who, since the Pazzi conspiracy, had jealously guarded his safety, had their suspicions aroused and arrested Frescobaldi. While in prison he made a full confession which resulted in the speedy execution of his accomplice and himself.

Universal consternation was excited in Florence by this new plot, and henceforward Lorenzo generally appeared in public surrounded by a number of tried and trusty friends, prepared to protect him against any malicious attack.

The whole of Italy (with the exception of Venice, which was suspected of having given them encouragement) united in the endeavour to drive the Turks out of Otranto. But the latter made a valiant resistance, and it was doubtful how the war would end, when a sudden illness put an end to Mohammed's career (May 3, 1481). His death was the occasion of public rejoicings in Rome, and processions of thanksgiving, in which the Pope himself took part, were ordered during three days. A dispute between his two sons, Bajazet and Djem, led to the recall of the Turkish troops which were destined for the relief of Otranto. On September 10 the town capitulated, and by the terms of the treaty the Turks were allowed to depart in freedom. But the Duke of Calabria, in defiance of this, retained about 1,500 of them as prisoners, afterwards employing them in his various campaigns.

Meanwhile, the Venetians sought to take possession of Ferrara, and, through the influence of Girolamo Riario, endeavoured to win the Pope for their side. Ercole d'Este, Duke of Ferrara, seeing his country threatened, also turned to Sixtus for help. But the latter treated his request with indifference, and showed no inclination to take his part. Ferrara belonged to the States over which the Papal See claimed authority, and, though the Pope was in no position to prevent its conquest, he was well aware that the other Italian States would not tolerate such an aggrandisement of Venice. He hoped, too, to be able eventually to place the government of Ferrara in the hands of his beloved Girolamo Riario, who was making energetic preparations for war.

The Duke of Ferrara had married the daughter of Ferrante, King of Naples, greatly to the displeasure of the Venetians, who looked upon the alliance as a threat. Ferrante proved a faithful friend to his son-in-law, who was further supported by Lorenzo de' Medici, the Duke of Milan, the Marquis of Mantua, and Giovanni Bentivoglio of Bologna. The command of the united troops was undertaken by Duke Federigo of Urbino.

With the view of discovering the Pope's real attitude towards them, Ferrante approached him with the request that he would allow the Duke of Calabria, with some Neapolitan troops, a free passage through his territories A decided refusal enlightened him. Without delay Alfonso adopted hostile tactics, and, seizing Terracina, Trevi, and other towns, advanced to within forty miles of Rome. At the same time the Florentines took possession of Castello, and, greatly to the joy of its inhabitants, restored it to the guardianship of Niccolo Vitelli

The Duke of Calabria had meanwhile arrived so close to Rome that daily skirmishes took place between the outposts Ruberto Malatesta, who, at the Pope's request, had taken command of the papal troops, drove Alfonso to such straits that the latter, unable to wait for reinforcements from Naples, was forced into an engagement at Campo Morto in the Pontine Marshes. If we are to believe Machiavelli, this was the most gory battle which Italy had seen for fifty years. The Duke of Calabria was utterly defeated, but, thanks to the courage of those Turks whom he had unlawfully detained after the capitulation of Otranto, he was able to escape with his life.

Malatesta, to whom was due the credit of thus delivering the Pope from danger, was warmly received in Rome, where he retired to enjoy his triumph. Shortly after his arrival, however, he died mysteriously. His death has been attributed to various causes, among others, to poison administered through the malice of Girolamo Riario. But it is probable that his colossal exertions amid the unhealthy swamps of Campo Morto were quite enough to account for his sudden illness Sixtus IV showed every respect to the saviour of his capital, and with his own hands administered Extreme Unction. By command of the Pope, a marble monument was erected to him in St. Peter's.

Riario on the other hand, at the head of the lately victorious army, hastened to dispossess Pandolfo, Malatesta's illegitimate son, of his inheritance of Rimini, a circumstance which tended to confirm the suspicions of foul play. His attempt would probably have been successful if Pandolfo had not turned for help to Lorenzo, who sent some Florentine troops to his relief. Riario (who, though less talented than Cæsar Borgia, seems to have been but little his inferior in depravity) then turned his attention to Castello, which was bravely defended by Vitelli, and Pesaro, which was under the authority of Costanzo Sforza.

The Venetians, meanwhile, had captured several towns in the dukedom of Ferrara, in spite of the resistance of the Duke of Urbino. The death of the latter and the ill-health of the Duke of Ferrara contributed to the further success of the republic. The Pope, who had lent them no assistance and could therefore claim no part in their conquests, began to view with alarm the growing power of the Venetians. Under the influence of Giuliano della Rovere, he decided to detach himself from them and to enter into negotiations for a separate peace. With the support of the Emperor's ambassador a truce was made between Rome on the one hand, and the King of Naples, the Duke of Milan, and the Florentines on the other (April 1483). The Venetians refused to give up hostilities, with the result that Pope Sixtus laid them under excommunication.

A congress was now held at Cremona, with the object of arranging some efficacious plan for humbling the Venetians. It was decided that the Duke of Milan should attack the Venetian territory, and that Alfonso of Calabria should make an effort to relieve the Duke of Ferrara. In this way the progress of the Venetians was checked, and, on being foiled in their attempt to conquer Ferrara, they showed themselves inclined for peace. The Duke of Milan was approached and persuaded to relinquish the cause of the allies. His defection moved the others to unite with Venice in the Peace of Bagnolo, August 7, 1484, by which the Ferrarese were delivered from the fear of conquest.

Upon receiving the news of this peace, which was practically a victory for Venice, the Pope was so overcome with excitement and anger that for fifteen hours he lay as one dead, and finally passed away in the night of August 12. It was said that he lived on war, and that peace must needs be his death. Though not without many good points, Sixtus had been completely under the corrupt influence of Girolamo and Pietro Riario, to whom he could deny nothing. His nepotism has become a byword, and he openly and shamelessly offered ecclesiastical offices for sale, not even hesitating to create new ones for the increase of his treasury.

Burchard, in his Diary, gives a vivid account of the disgraceful obsequies accorded to the dead Pope His rooms were pillaged in the twinkling of an eye by his valets and prelates. The chaplain himself seems to have undertaken to prepare the body for burial. "We washed the corpse," he says, "but, as there was no towel, I tore up the shirt which he was wearing at his death and used that instead. We dressed him, without a shirt, in a short cassock, and a pair of slippers given by the Bishop of Cervia."[1]

Terrible days followed the burial of Sixtus IV. The populace rose in fury against his nephews and burned their palaces, while the Orsini and Colonna factions massacred one another in the streets and the Cardinals and nobles barricaded the entrances to their houses.

The new Pope, Giovanni Cibò (Innocent VIII), like his predecessor, owed his election to simony. Cardinal Borgia had hoped to be elected, but, on finding that he had small chance of success, sold his votes to Cibò. As we have already seen, the latter was a person of no character, with a strong tendency to let others do his thinking for him. He cherished a

[1] See The Diary of John Burchard, Bishop of {Orta, vol: i. English translation).

great admiration for Lorenzo, and sought his advice on all important occasions. Lorenzo, who knew how to estimate the far-reaching influence of the Papacy over Christendom, made every effort to confirm himself in Innocent's good graces. By so doing he paved the way to the brilliant position to which his family, in spite of many obstacles, afterwards attained.

During the confusion which followed the Pazzi conspiracy the town of Sarzana, occupying an important position near the Genoese and Florentine boundaries, had been seized by bandits. This was a serious loss to Florence, and as soon as Lorenzo was free from the dangers which threatened him he made preparations for its reconquest. The first thing to do was to take Pietra Santa—no easy task Lorenzo's presence, however, animated the Florentines with fresh courage, and, after a few days' siege, the town capitulated, under condition that the inhabitants should be no further molested. The victory was a costly one, and through the ravages of war and fever Lorenzo lost many of his best friends. The troops were exhausted after the campaign, so that instead of proceeding to the attack of Sarzana, they were obliged to cease hostilities for a time. Lorenzo, moreover, was suffering severely with gout, for which he was compelled to seek relief at the baths of San Filippo.

But before his health was restored Lorenzo was agitated by the revival of the ill-feeling between Ferrante and the Papacy, the seeds of which had been sown in the latter years of Sixtus IV. The Neapolitan nobles, whose liberty Ferrante sought to restrict, became discontented and struggled to regain their old rights. The populace, who had suffered much from the caprice and tryanny of the upper classes, would undoubtedly have come to the King's help if he had not succeeded in suppressing the insurrection himself. When Innocent VIII. became Pope the nobles represented to him in bitter terms their miserable condition under Ferrante, " a demon for dissimulation, treachery, and avarice " (Symonds), and his even more tyrannical son, Alfonso. The Pope's feelings were thus worked upon to such a degree that he. consented to engage in a war which, said his advisers, could only redound to the honour and glory of the Papacy. Considerable forces were raised and the command undertaken by Ruberto San Severino. The papal standard was erected at Salerno, which was the first town to display open rebellion.

Although Ferrante was aware of the amicable relations between the Pope and Lorenzo, this did not prevent him from turning to the latter for help. Lorenzo immediately left the baths of San Filippo and hastened to assure the King of his support, though at the same time deprecating his arbitrary attitude towards his nobles. The Medici policy was one of peace, but Lorenzo took Ferrante's side, on the ground that an increase in the papal power would disturb the equilibrium of Italy. The Florentines, however, were of a different opinion. They were in no wise disposed to make war upon the amiable Pope, especially as they were apprehensive of the interference of Venice. Lorenzo, however, knew his own mind, and was not to be deterred from his plan.

Meanwhile the unrest at Naples was growing apace. Ferrante's confidential ministers were in secret correspondence with his enemies, and Alfonso, who had advanced towards Rome in order to hinder the papal troops from uniting with the rebels, was completely routed by San Severino and obliged to flee to Florentine dominions. Lorenzo, although ill and unable to visit Alfonso, did his best to deliver him from his unenviable position, and gave him money to continue the campaign   He also influenced Ludovico Sforza, the Duke of Milan, and the Orsini family to take part against the Pope. At the same

time he endeavoured to convince the latter of the futility and danger of his policy, assuring him that the struggle could, at best, end only in the accession to the Neapolitan throne of some adventurer who would be a more dangerous enemy to the Papal See than the House of Aragon had been. Innocent's martial zeal now began to wane. San Severino was left without further reinforcement, and the war, though not abandoned, was continued but languidly. On May 8, 1486, a battle was fought. It lasted for several hours, during which, Ammirato informs us, no one was even wounded, much less killed. San Severino was obliged, nevertheless, to retreat from the field. The results of this bloodless battle were important. Ferrante sought to make terms with the Pope, proposing to pay him a certain sum of money and to grant a complete amnesty to the rebellious nobles, at the same time acknowledging the Pope's supreme jurisdiction over Naples Thereupon the war came to an end.

Lorenzo was now free to turn his attention to the conquest of Sarzana, which he had very much at heart. The Florentine troops were commanded by Giacopo Guicciardini and Pietro Vittorio. The defence was so obstinate and the siege so protracted that Lorenzo, impatient, himself visited the troops, hoping to revive their courage. His appearance was as successful as it had been at Pietra-Santa, and the garrison surrendered unconditionally. Lorenzo's presence prevented the pillage of the town, which, now incorporated with the Florentine State, formed a bulwark against the attacks of the Genoese.

In July 1487 Lorenzo lost his wife, Clarice. He seems to have mourned her sincerely, but his grief was mitigated by his pleasure in the promotion to the Cardinalate of his young son, Giovanni. In spite of the Neapolitan war, Lorenzo remained on good terms with Pope Innocent VIII. and did not cease to

IB

importune him to bestow the Red Hat upon the little
Giovanni, who from his babyhood had been destined
for the Church.   He also appealed earnestly to Ascanio
Sforza and Rodrigo Borgia to exert their influence on
his behalf   Lorenzo's request was finally granted in
March 1489, but only on the condition that during
the next three years Giovanni should neither wear
the insignia of the Cardinalate nor have a seat or
vote in the College of Cardinals.   Lorenzo in vain
sought to set aside these unwelcome restrictions.   The
Pope for once, remained firm, insisting that the
boy should give the full time of probation to the
study of theology and canon law.   Lorenzo's letter
to his son on the joyful occasion of his promotion to
the full privileges of his rank (1492), has become a
classic.   It is indeed a remarkable combination of
shrewd worldly wisdom and religious principle.   The
young Cardinal is recommended to show his gratitude
to God for the honour done him by living a pious
and exemplary life.   He is warned against the difficulty of remaining virtuous in Rome, " that sink of
all iniquity," "where there would be no lack of evil-
minded persons anxious to drag him down into the
abyss into which they themselves have fallen."
" Counting upon your youth," continues the letter,
" they will expect to find this an easy task.   Thus it
behoves you to set yourself to prove that this hope
is unfounded, particularly because at present the
College of Cardinals is so poor in men of worth. . . .
The less your conduct resembles that of those who
now compose it, the more beloved and respected you
will be. . . . You can easily understand how much
depends upon the personality and example of a Cardinal.   If the Cardinals were such as they ought to
be the whole world would be the better for it ; for
they would always elect a good Pope, and thus secure
the peace of Christendom.   Endeavour, therefore, to
be such that it would be well for all if the rest

resembled you. . . . You are not only the youngest
member of the College, but the youngest person that
has ever been raised to the rank of Cardinal.   You
should, therefore, in all that has to do with your
colleagues, be observant and respectful and keep
yourself in the background in the Papal Chapels and
Consistories, or in deputations.   You will soon learn
which among them are deserving of esteem.   You
must avoid both being and seeming to be intimate
with those whose conduct is irregular.   In conversation keep as far as possible to generalities.   On public
occasions let your equipage and dress be rather below
than above what is permissible.

" Spend your money rather on keeping a well-
appointed stable and servants of a superior class than
on pomp and show.   Endeavour to lead a regular
life, and gradually get your household into strict
order—a thing which cannot be done immediately
where both master and servant are new.   Silks and
jewels are not suitable for persons in your position,
and your taste will be better shown in the acquisition
of a few valuable antiques and handsome books and
by your circle being well-bred and learned rather
than numerous.   Also, it is better for you to entertain your friends at home than to dine out often ; but
in this matter you should follow a middle course.
Let your food be simple, and take plenty of exercise ;
for those in your situation are liable, without great
caution, to contract infirmities. . . . Let it be your
rule to rise early.   Setting aside the advantage to
your health of the practice, it gives you time to get
through the business of the day and to fulfil your
various obligations. . . .

" Another very necessary precaution, particularly
on your entrance into public life, is to call to mind
in the evening what will be the work of the day
following, so that you may never be unprepared for
your business.   If you speak in the Consistory, it

seems to me that, considering your youth and inexperience, it will be most becoming for you to adhere
to the wise judgment of the Holy Father. You will
be pressed to intercede for the favours of the Pope.
Be cautious, however, that you trouble him not too
often, for his temper leads him to give most to those
who are least clamorous. You should be on the
watch to say nothing that would annoy him, but
rather tell him things likely to give him pleasure ;
and, if you should be obliged to request some kindness
from him, let it be done with that modesty which
corresponds best with his own disposition. Take
care of your health."

It is difficult to reconcile the tone of this letter
with the morality of its writer. Lorenzo is said to
have ruined the happiness of countless homes, and to
have even seized the dowries of Florentine girls to fill
his own coffers.

Lorenzo's low opinion of the College of Cardinals
at this time was, alas ! but too well founded It is
true that it possessed a few worthy members, but their
influence was quite outweighed by that of the majority,
who lived the lives of secular princes steeped in luxury
of the most debased and licentious kind. Prominent
among the most corrupt and vicious of them were
Ascanio Sforza, Orsini, Riario, Giuliano della Rovere,
and, most of all, Rodrigo Borgia Of these two
subsequently wore the tiara—Borgia as Alexander VI.,
and della Rovere as Julius II.

Lorenzo never saw his favourite son again after the
celebrations in honour of his promotion. His malady
was becoming so serious that, towards the end of
March 1492 he left Florence for his villa at Capreggi,
hoping to benefit by the country air. But it was in
vain. He rapidly became worse, and his illness is
said to have been aggravated by the medical treatment, in particular by a draught of crushed pearls
and powdered precious stones. His friend, Poliziano

and his favourite sister, Bianca, were with him to cheer
his last days, and it was the former who broke to
him the news of his rapidly approaching end   Lorenzo
sent for Savonarola, the friar whose name was then
on every tongue, in order to receive absolution.
What passed between them is not certain.   One
account says that before the Prior would hear his
confession he asked the dying man whether he felt
himself to be in the true faith of God.   Lorenzo
answered that he fervently believed it.   Thereupon
Savonarola asked him if he would restore all that
he had unlawfully acquired.   After some hesitation,
Lorenzo agreed, but when he was desired to restore
liberty to Florence he indignantly dismissed the
Prior without having made his confession.   The Last
Sacraments were, however, administered by another,
and Lorenzo had a long interview with his son Piero.
Shortly afterwards he breathed his last, April 8, 1492.

Thus died Lorenzo the Magnificent, the man
whose " pregnant parts and quick inventive brain "
have been the wonder of his own and subsequent
generations.   His character, a fine one in many
respects, was full of the strangest inconsistencies, and
the ease with which he could turn from the most
serious occupations to the most frivolous amusements
gained him the reputation of possessing two souls in
one body.   He appears to have had genuine claims
to piety, yet he was rarely free from some amorous
intrigue.   " One day would find him disputing in the
Academy on virtue and immortality and inditing
pious poems , on the next he might be seen in the
midst of his dissolute friends, singing loose carnival-
songs, or listening to Luigi Pulci declaiming the
wanton lyrics of his *Morgante*."   The words and
example of such a man, and the evil splendour of such
a Court, could not fail to have a corrupting influence
on Florentine life.[1]   On the other hand, it must be

[1] Pastor

remembered that, on the whole, he sought to promote the peace and happiness of his country and never prostituted his undoubted military talent to a purely selfish ambition. He may, perhaps, have been intent on personal ends in the first instance, but throughout the whole policy of this " miniature Augustus " there was woven " a genuine fibre of patriotism."

The news of Lorenzo's death gave rise to universal sorrow in the city of the lilies, for as Guicciardini once wrote : " Florence could not have had a better or more delightful tyrant." He left behind him three sons—Piero, " the mad," Giovanni, " the wise," and Giuliano, " the good." The eldest, Piero, was hardly twenty-one, and it was only by special arrangement that the magistrates, out of respect to his father's memory, allowed him to take public office. He was a wild young fellow, absolutely unfit to assume the direction of the State, as events soon proved. His portrait by Botticelli, to be seen in the Uffizi, shows a handsome and interesting face with a great bush of dark hair. He was tall and commanding in figure, and possessed of extraordinary strength and agility. Indeed if his moral nature had been as well developed as his physical, he might have made an excellent ruler His manners were, on the whole, agreeable, though at times haughty and overbearing. From the Florentines he demanded a blind obedience, and he constantly ignored the advice so often given him by his father, " to remember that he was only a citizen of Florence." Persons with any claim to positions of importance were looked upon by Piero with the greatest suspicion. There still existed other members of the Medici family who might, with almost equal right, have taken upon themselves the conduct of affairs. The sons of Piero Francesco Medici, Lorenzo and Giovanni, although descended from the younger branch, had hardly less claim than Piero to posts of authority in the State. But this branch of the Médici, although possessed of great wealth, had never taken any part in the government, probably because the connection with the older branch of the house was considered honour enough. Nevertheless, there arose between the two a spirit of rivalry which was not without important effects.

Another source of disturbance was the preaching of Girolamo Savonarola, who was stirring all hearts with his denunciations of the prevailing immorality and self-indulgence. Under his influence men and women laid aside their former luxuries and adopted the simplest and barest form of living. So completely, indeed, did this remarkable man dominate the popular mind that it was not difficult to foresee that he would shortly influence the domain of politics to a like extent.

It is possible that Piero might have attained his end by banishing Savonarola from Florence; but the Prior was so much beloved by the people that such a step would have been ill-advised. Piero himself was no favourite with the Florentines, for he was quite devoid of his father's tact and moderation.

Lorenzo's uncle, Piero Francesco Medici, had left behind him two sons, the aforesaid Lorenzo and Giovanni, who cherished a not unwarrantable grudge against Piero. Giovanni was much admired for his handsome appearance, and found no difficulty in capturing the hearts of the beautiful ladies of Florence. It happened that, one evening, he and Piero were at a masked ball where both sought the favour of the same lady. But to tolerate such a position was impossible to the haughty Piero, who, infuriated at the success of his rival, bespattered with ink his garment of silver cloth.

Giovanni bore the insult as well as he could. Perhaps he did not recognise Piero, or did not feel inclined to begin hostilities. But another masked ball was held at which both rivals were again present. Piero, unable to brook the idea that another should dare to aspire to the favour of the lady in question, rushed angrily up to Giovanni and tore the mask from his face. The latter, who was surrounded by friends, drew his dagger and plunged it into Piero's breast. Happily for the latter, he was wearing armour underneath his clothes, so that no harm was done.

The next morning Piero brought the case before the magistrates, desiring that the Medici brothers might be severely punished. Fearing, however, that he would be reproached with undue severity towards his own kinsmen, he contented himself with their temporary banishment from Florence.

Nevertheless, both brothers preserved an undying animosity for Piero, and lost no opportunity of trying to injure him. Through the mediation of Ludovico Sforza, they entered into an alliance with Charles VIII. of France, who was planning an invasion of Italy. They gave him clearly to understand that the Florentines were already out of conceit with Piero and that the situation was now ripe for overthrowing the Medici rule and restoring Florence to her original condition.

On the other hand, the vain and ambitious Piero had attached himself to the King of Naples   Alfonso, who had now succeeded his father, Ferrante, appears to have promised to try to procure for him the title of Prince and the power of a despot, and, in return for this, was to be allowed to shelter his fleet in the harbour of Livorno and to count on Piero's assistance in repulsing the attacks of the French.

In this way were the members of the same family divided into two hostile camps, one of which encouraged Charles VIII. in his invasion of Italy, while the other favoured the claims of the House of Aragon. Their private enmity was thus the cause not only of the discord in Florence, but, also, to a certain extent, of the undoing of Italy.

CHAPTER VII

Illness of Louis XI. of France—The Hermit of Calabria summoned
to heal him—His fear of death—His character and administration—His successor, Charles VIII.—Anne of Beaujeu her wise
rule—Civil war in Brittany—Landois his terrible fate—Battle
of St Aubin du Cormier—La Trémouilles' treatment of his
prisoners—Death of Francis of Brittany—His daughter Anne—
War continued—Betrothal of Anne of Brittany—Anne of
Beaujeu gradually withdraws from her position of authority—
Release of Louis of Orleans—Marriage of Charles VIII and
Anne of Brittany—Character and appearance of Charles VIII.

It was evident that Louis XI of France would never
be well again. In March, 1480, he had been suddenly
deprived of sense and speech by a paralytic seizure.
For three days he remained in this condition, and
though he afterwards recovered his faculties, he had
never really regained his strength. The thought of
death filled him with terror, and in his extremity
he sent for the Hermit, Robert of Calabria, whose
prayers were reputed to restore the sick to health.
This holy man had lived for thirty years under the
shadow of a rock, during which time he had tasted
neither fish, flesh, eggs, nor milk. He was an un-
learned man, "ni clerc ni lettré," but in saintliness
none could compare with him. Pope Sixtus himself
bowed before the Hermit's wisdom and piety, and
on his journey through Italy the people everywhere
honoured him as an apostolic messenger and saint.
When he arrived at Tours, King Louis, on his knees,
implored him to prolong his life. The Hermit tried
in vain to turn his thoughts to the life beyond the
grave, assuring him that with God alone lay the

power to lengthen his days. Comines tells us that he often overheard his ministrations to the King, and declares that his words were most certainly divinely inspired, being void of any earthly taint.

Nevertheless, Louis's condition grew nothing better, and, as he became weaker, his state of mind grew even more pitiable. He was painfully conscious that he had unduly oppressed his subjects, and now lived in a constant state of suspicion and dread that they would avenge themselves. In terror he shut himself in his Château of Plessis, near Tours, keeping his Scottish guards at hand both day and night. At the same time he was most anxious to conceal his true state from the people, and, from fear of losing his authority, he dealt out severe punishments, and conferred and arbitrarily withdrew offices and dignities with the object of proving that he was still capable of governing. By dint of thus unpleasantly asserting himself there was little danger that his existence would be ignored. Another of the whims by which he hoped to deceive his subjects as to his failing strength was to lay aside his usual sordid garb and appear before them in the most gorgeous apparel, in spite of his pitiably wasted appearance.

When Louis realised that his end was near he sent for his son Charles, whom he had neglected for several years, and gave him some parting words of good advice, recommending him to retain his old servants, to avoid quarrelling with Francis, Duke of Brittany, and to keep the peace right and left until he came of age. So great was his fear of death that his attendants were forbidden to mention the word in his hearing. Nevertheless, he passed away (August 30, 1483) more peacefully than do many braver and better men. " A cry of thankfulness," it is said, " went up from every heart in France when his death was known. . . ."

Louis XI. has been called an universal spider. He

was sly and suspicious, but displayed great shrewdness and wariness in the conduct of affairs.   Cruel and unsympathetic in disposition, it is said that he had more than 4,000 people put to death during his reign.   One of his political enemies, Cardinal de Balue, was kept shut up for many years in an iron cage as a punishment for his offences.   Both his first and second wives suffered much from his harshness and neglect, and he made but little effort to bring up his son Charles in a way befitting the future King of France. Although proud and haughty in manner, Louis displayed a distinct propensity for pleasures of the lowest kind, and engaged in amorous intrigues with an abandonment which seems hardly compatible with the superstition and caution of his character.

But, notwithstanding his many and glaring faults, Louis XI. was a great king.   Under his administration the disturbed country acquired some semblance of order ; he stamped out feudalism and substituted autocracy for anarchy, and, by breaking the power of the nobles, he laid the foundation of France's future greatness   He also gave an impetus to commerce, and to him is due the credit of establishing the silk industry.   Though himself no scholar, he encouraged learning, and set up a printing press at the Sorbonne, while the Greek savants who sought refuge in France after the conquest of Constantinople found in him a powerful protector.

Charles was only thirteen at the time of his father's death, and his guardianship was entrusted to his elder sister, Anne of Beaujeu, wife of Pierre de Bourbon.   She was a strong-souled and capable woman, and for nine years continued to be the virtual ruler of France.   History has never given Anne her due, but she undoubtedly deserves the highest honour for the wonderful vigour and skill with which she guided the affairs of France during this time.   "Her very. success has doomed her to the neglect of posterity; she was neither tragical nor wicked, and the historians of the time have passed her by almost without a word. She dealt sharply with Philip of Comines after the death of Louis XI., as indeed he justly deserved; and the historian has meanly avenged himself on her by omitting from his *Memoirs* the years of her admirable government, and " even the very mention of her name." Her accession to authority gave great umbrage to the nobles, in particular to Louis of Orleans, who himself wanted to be in her place. Anne, or " Madame la Grande," as she was well styled, was alarmed at his attitude, and did all she could to impress the people in her favour. She liberated prisoners, recalled the banished, reduced the taxes, and brought Jean Doyrac and Olivier Daim to justice. Olivier, a barber beloved of the late King, was hanged for his many crimes, while Doyrac, who had insulted Anne's husband, the Duke of Bourbon, was banished, after having been publicly whipped in Paris and having his tongue and his ears removed.

Anne came out victorious in the struggle which had been set on foot to overthrow her. The States-General had met at Tours to consider the matter, but Anne showed so much ability in the conduct of her case that her fame spread throughout the whole country. Her success, however, did not interfere with her temperate and tactful policy. In order to conciliate Louis of Orleans, the Duke of Angoulême, and Dunois, Louis's illegitimate son, each of them was given a yearly pension and a company of a hundred lancers.

Peace seemed to be restored, when there arose fresh disturbances which were eventually to bring about the union of Brittany and France.

By the last will and testament of Francis de Montfort, Duke of Brittany, it was decreed that, in the event

of his family's dying out, the dukedom should fall
to the Lord of Penthièvre and his niece, the Lady
of Brosse. As he possessed two brothers, an uncle
and a cousin, the extinction of his house seemed so
improbable that no one took much heed of this
provision. Strange to relate, they all died, except
the cousin, Francis II. of Brittany, who had only
two daughters.

Louis XI. persuaded the Lady of Brosse to sell
her claims to him. Francis II., who lived in mortal
terror of Louis, sought help from Edward of England,
Maximilian of Austria, and his son Philip the Handsome, offering one of his daughters to each of the latter
But neither of these could aid him ; Edward was prevented by the confusion arising from the ambitious
plans of his uncle Richard, and Maximilian was
occupied by internal strife and the revolt of Ghent.

There were two other claimants—Davaugours, the
legitimised bastard of Francis II., and the Vicomte
Rohan, who had married a daughter of Francis I.
Rohan had two sons, for whom he coveted the Duke's
daughters Francis refused to entertain the idea of
such an alliance in spite of the exhortations of his
nobles.

Francis II. was completely under the influence
of his minister Landois, who, originally a tailor, had
been raised to the highest position of honour. His
bold and domineering ways made him greatly disliked,
and his conduct with regard to the Chancellor
Chauvin made him the object of universal hatred.
This unfortunate Chancellor was allowed to perish
of hunger in an infected dungeon, and the jailer,
fearing to be accused of his death, displayed the terribly emaciated corpse in public. Landois bestowed
the dead man's property upon the Davaugours, thus
making Francis his accomplice.

Shunned by all, Landois sought help from Louis
of Orleans, who hastened to Nantes to meet him.

Rendered still more impudent by this alliance, Landois promoted his nephew, Guibé, to the bishoprics of Rennes, Nantes, and d'Alby, and finally made him ambassador, legate, and Cardinal. Another nephew he appointed Coadjutor of Rennes, an office which was to prepare his way to becoming President of the States-General. Despinay, who then occupied this position, was a hindrance to Landois's plan, so he got rid of him as he had already despatched Chauvin, in 1484.

The nobles now determined to bear his tyranny no longer. Thronging to the Duke's palace, they implored him, on their knees, to grant them justice. Francis, although terrified out of his wits, refused to deliver up his favourite Another party of nobles tracked Landois to his country house, but he escaped just in time and returned the next day in triumph to the palace.

Brittany was now divided into two parties : Landois united with the Duke of Orleans, while the conspiring nobles joined Anne of Brittany, daughter of Francis II. Since his coronation festivities, the young King Charles had been a fervent admirer of Louis of Orleans, who on this occasion had distinguished himself in the tourney. He was also beginning to look upon his good sister Anne as an obstacle to the exercise of his authority, interfering with his plans and separating him from his friends. Among these were the three chamberlains, Maillet, Pot, and Gouffier. They had made up their minds to kidnap the King, and were actually in his room, persuading him to flee, when Anne rushed in upon them, and, animated by the spirit of her dead father, so intimidated the conspirators by her threats that they fled ignominiously from the Court. Charles, who was a weak and good-natured youth, gave in without resistance. The Duke of Orleans, as the prime mover of the plot, dared no longer to show his face at Court. Anne, who dreaded opposition from the Parisians (whose governor was an Orlean), had her brother carefully watched and guarded by troops, and took him to Montargis in order to await developments.

The Duke of Orleans meanwhile sought to curry favour with the people, by taking the part of the oppressed against the oppressor. So secure of his position did he feel that in January 1485 he, as first prince of France, laid claim in Parliament to the Presidency of the States-General He was, however, repulsed by the leader, Jacques de la Vacquerie, who remarked that the greatest blessings for the country would be unanimity and peace, and that the princes of the blood should set the people a good example. Louis then turned to the University, which at that time numbered about 25,000 students, but was here even more frigidly received

Anne of Beaujeu now thought it time to act. She sent to Paris armed soldiers who would doubtless have taken Louis prisoner had not his allies, Gui, Pot, and Louhans, discovered his danger, set him on a mule and helped him to escape. At the same time Anne entered the city.

However, Louis was not yet quelled. In conjunction with Duke Francis of Brittany and the able Dunois he collected a force of 10,000 men and attacked the Regent. Her cause seemed hopeless when affairs suddenly took a favourable turn Orleans was about to take the bridge spanning the Loire and join his allies on the other side when Anne, noticing this manœuvre, sent Duboucheage to oppose it. The citizens of Orleans came to her assistance, and Louis, pursued by la Trémouille, was obliged to yield at Beaugency.

The French nobles set their hopes on Landois, who had meanwhile collected a considerable army. But he, too confident of success, plundered and burned the possessions of many important Bretons who were absent in Ancenis. By this barbarity he drove them to unite with Charles VIII. Not content with this, he ordered his troops to seize the nobles in Ancenis. Anne of Beaujeu sent the militia from Guienne to their help. The two armies met, but, instead of fighting, they effected a reconciliation, indignant that the interests of so infamous a scoundrel should lead to a civil war.

Landois, nothing daunted, continued his resistance, supported by Duke Francis. Several nobles withdrew from the troop, and, in conjunction with the inhabitants of Nantes, demanded his surrender. Quaking with fear, the favourite fled to the Duke, who despatched the Cardinal de Foix and the Vicomte Narbonne to allay the uproar. They returned, however, without having effected their object. The insurgents came nearer and nearer, demanding that Landois should be delivered over to them. The latter, green with terror, hid in a cupboard. On hearing the Chancellor and his enemies approaching, Duke Francis, with incredible infatuation, continued to support him. "Why did the people want him? What evil had he done?" he asked. And not till they appeased him by pretending that they wanted to shelter Landois from the rage of the populace, and that he would be given a chance of vindicating himself, did the Duke produce him from his hiding-place. Taking Landois by the hand, he admonished the Chancellor to consider the interests of justice, which the latter, without any breach of the truth, had no difficulty in promising.

Landois came to a sad, though well-merited end A confession of part of his crime was wrested from him by torture, and then he was put to death by hanging. Afterwards two parties were again formed, the one adhering to Charles VIII. and Anne of Beaujeu, the other to the Emperor Maximilian, who was to marry Anne of Brittany, daughter of

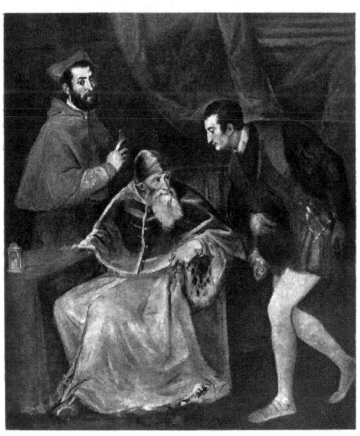

ALESSANDRO FARNESE, POPE PAUL III., WITH HIS GRANDSON CARDINAL ALESSANDRO
FARNESE, AND HIS NEPHEW JUAN BORGIA II., DUKE OF NEPI, FIFTH SON OF POPE
ALEXANDER VI., BY HIS MISTRESS GIULIA FARNESE, SISTER OF POPE PAUL III.

Titian (National Museum, Naples).

Francis II. To Maximilian's adherents belonged Louis of Orleans and his inseparable companion Dunois, as well as Francis II. and his new favourite, Lescun. After the death of the Seigneur of Brosse, his widow, Nicoli, had made over his property of Penthièvre to France, to the huge indignation of Duke Francis and Lescun. Spurred on by them, Maximilian seized Mortagne and Terouenne, and sent his herald to Paris demanding that Anne of Beaujeu should be removed from the Court of his son-in-law, Charles VIII., and the States-General summoned. All this was with the idea of restoring peace, but his tactics aroused universal displeasure. "The time when Germany was subject to France may be remembered," exclaimed Graville, lord of Beaujeu, Vendôme, and Montpensier, "but not the time when France was subject to Germany." Notwithstanding the indignation produced, the Regent had a foreboding that a plot was being prepared, and she turned to her brother-in-law, the Constable de Bourbon, entreating his support. With some difficulty she succeeded in bringing him over to her side. At the same time a messenger was intercepted bearing letters which proved beyond a doubt the existence of a plot. Maximilian, the Duke of Orleans, the Duke of Lorraine, and others, as well as the greater part of Brittany, Navarre, Gascony, and Guienne, had conspired against her, though the soul of the plot was Dunois.

Anne stood alone against them all. She appealed, however, to the towns for assistance, and her confidence was not misplaced. Thus intimidated, many of the conspirators went over to her side and the danger which had threatened her faded into insignificance.

Intrigues and agitations continued, but through the remarkable skill with which the energetic Regent conducted affairs, most of the fortified places of

KB

Brittany fell at last under her sway, while Duke Francis remained possessed of little besides Nantes and Rennes. She owed much to the loyalty of la Trémouille, who worked under command of the Constable de Bourbon. Her young brother, whom she had hardly allowed out of her sight since the last attempt at kidnapping, was then able to return to Paris.

The Regent, who had hitherto been distinguished for her moderation, now took a step which gave rise to a new war. Before Parliament she accused her brother-in-law, Louis of Orleans, of felony, and the Duke of Brittany and the Grand-duke Philip, Count of Flanders, of withholding their feudal homage from the King. The Duke of Bourbon, the Counts of Nevers and Angoulême, either from disinclination or from motives of propriety, absented themselves from the session. This circumstance brought Anne to her senses, especially as the magistrates hesitated to confirm her accusation. She therefore withdrew it provisionally.

The Duke of Orleans and Francis II. now appealed to Henry VII. of England, who sent a few thousand men to the support of Marshal Rieux. The latter was thereby enabled to reconquer Vannes and Ploermel Meanwhile la Trémouille also entered the field and reduced Ancenis, Châteaubriant, and Fougères to ruins, to the no small discomfiture of the Bretons.

On July 27, 1488, a battle took place at St. Aubin du Cormier. After two hours' fighting, la Trémouille defeated the Breton troops. The number of dead and captured amounted to 8,000. Among the latter were the Duke of Orleans, the Prince of Orange, and several well-known French nobles. Although conscious of their precarious situation, the prisoners did not lose courage, especially as la Trémouille treated them with consideration. With alacrity they accepted his invitation to a banquet, little suspecting the fate that awaited them   During dessert la Trémouille rose and deliberately announced that the two Princes would await the King's decision as to their punishment, but the leaders, who had been taken while fighting against their King and country, would be allowed only a moment in which to prepare for death. All in vain were their supplications for delay. La Trémouille was obdurate, and they were all straightway executed

The two Princes were dragged from one prison to another. The Prince of Orange was taken to Angers, where the raging crowd threatened to tear him in pieces. Orleans was confined at Bourges, where, so strict was his supervision, that every night he was locked up in an iron cage

Duke Francis of Brittany bound himself over to pay 200,000 golden guldens as war indemnity, to banish all foreigners from his dukedom, and not to give his daughter in marriage without the King's consent. As a pledge of good faith, he delivered up to France his strongest fortresses, and swore an oath of fealty. He died, however, almost immediately afterwards. His death is ascribed by some to grief at the loss of his independence, by others to a fall from his horse (1488). By his will he left the dukedom of Penthièvre to the Duke d'Albret, who had loyally supported him in all his wars. The regency was to be undertaken by Marshal Rieux with the aid of d'Albret, Lescun, and Dunois. D'Albret's sister, Françoise de Dinan, Comtesse de Laval, was to supervise the education of Francis's two daughters. One of these, Isabeau, died soon after her father, and the other, Anne, was only about twelve years old. She was, however, a capable young person, of resolute will and with decided opinions of her own. D'Albret, notwithstanding his grey hairs and the possession of eight children, now took it into his head to try to win the hand of this young heiress. Apart from his age, his whole conduct and appearance were such as to make the thought of marrying him repugnant to any right-minded girl.   Moreover, Anne regarded herself as betrothed to the good-natured Archduke Maximilian, who however never appeared to take much notice of his affianced bride.   The Regent, too, came to her aid and persuaded the Pope Innocent VIII. to refuse the marriage dispensation.   Dunois also supported her, and succeeded in winning over to his side the German leaders, several Breton gentlemen, and even the Seigneur of Montauban, the Chancellor of Brittany.   There now arose two parties ; on one side were Lescun, d'Albret, and de Rieux, and on the other, the Chancellor, Dunois, and the Princess Anne.

Meanwhile the French army advanced.   Without any open declaration of war, it had been despatched by the Regent in order to fan the flame of discord. Dunois and the Duchess no longer felt safe in Rennes, and were obliged to seek refuge in Nantes.   But de Rieux had the gates closed and refused to admit his sovereign.   Dunois approached the town, hoping that the citizens would take their part.   De Rieux advanced against him with a strong force, meaning to take the Princess prisoner.   Dunois, always prompt in action, drew up his little escort in battle-array, keeping Anne close behind him.   This acted admirably, for de Rieux, restrained by a kind of shame from drawing his sword against the lady to whom he had sworn fealty, returned to Nantes without carrying out his plan ; but the next day, repenting of his weakness and spurred on by d'Albret, he came back with a still larger troop.   Dunois, unable to resist him, entered into negotiations.   He undertook to surrender the Duchess Anne, and gave up his best friend, de Louhans, as hostage.   He and the Duchess found hospitality in the outskirts of Nantes, but, on his arrival in the town, de Louhans realised that there was no hope of escape. He sent a message to Dunois telling him how matters stood, and offering to release him from his promise.

Dunois was in desperate straits, for he wished to sacrifice neither the Duchess nor his friend. But he did not give up hope, and began negotiating with his enemies in order to gain time. The latter, sure of victory, agreed to the proposals, which were of slight importance in themselves. After a fortnight, however, they were startled out of their complacency by the news that Dunois had escaped with the Duchess to Rennes The inhabitants of this town, angry at d'Albret's unprincipled conduct, had invited Anne and Dunois to take refuge with them.

Torn by disruption and strife, Brittany seemed near her downfall. Henry VII. of England sent 6,000 English to the help of d'Albret. German and Spanish troops were also despatched to Brittany ; but, instead of uniting to drive out the French, they only fanned the flame of civil war which was smouldering all over the country. ,

Anne of Beaujeu was meanwhile observing these proceedings from her Château at Plessis les Tours, and, without apparent interference, managed, with her wonted ability, to turn things to her own advantage. She endeavoured to reconcile her enemies and restored to freedom the Prince of Orange, Comines, and Bussy who had been taken prisoners in the battle of St. Aubin. Her most dangerous opponent, the Duke of Orleans, was kept in captivity. Through this leniency she won the adherence of Dunois. The fate of Brittany seemed sealed. Rohan, at the head of the French troops, had taken possession of almost the whole of the dukedom, and hardly anything but Rennes remained to the young Duchess Maximilian, who would have come to her help, was detained by disturbances in the Netherlands. He was her only hope and had won her heart by his endeavours to aid her. No one knew that they had secretly devised a plan which had, at first, some success, but eventually proved useless. Maximilian sent the Duke of Nassau to Paris to insist upon the fulfilment of the compact which Francis of Brittany had made with France. He was received by the Regent with the greatest affability She had no suspicion as to the real object of his visit, and even provided him with an escort to Rennes. No sooner had he arrived there than the betrothal of the young Duchess and Maximilian took place by the curious ceremony of procuration. But instead of going to Rennes in person to complete the marriage, the phlegmatic bridegroom betook himself to the Danube, anxious to recover the hereditary duchies of Austria after the death of the Hungarian King, Matthias Corvinus, in the interest of the moment forgetting his affianced wife in Rennes, his daughter in Paris, and his son in Flanders.

This marriage, if marriage it may be called, brought the young Duchess into an extremely dangerous position. Rohan advanced more boldly, d'Albret seized Nantes as security for a reconciliation with France, de Rieux permitted the slaughter of all the German troops who had come to her help, and the English soldiers, far from defending the country, ravaged it like enemies.

Anne of Brittany, neglected by her betrothed, turned for advice to Henry VII. of England, who urged Maximilian to return. He also sent envoys to Spain to stir up Ferdinand But Anne of Beaujeu recognised the danger that would accrue to France if England were to menace Normandy and Guienne, Spain, Roussillon and Cerdagne ; and Maximilian Artois, Burgundy, and Franche-Comté, while at the same time all three were labouring to secure the independence of Brittany. When she heard of the betrothal of Anne of Brittany she was seized with consternation, and would have sent a French army to occupy Brittany, had she not been afraid that Anne would flee to Maximilian. She then changed her tactics and treated the marriage as a joke, at the same time seeking to win the young Princess for her brother Charles, and showing her every respect and consideration.

Dunois, the Prince of Orange, and almost the whole of the Breton nobility were now on Anne of Beaujeu's side. But nothing could persuade the fourteen-year-old Princess to consent to a marriage with Charles VIII. Even Dunois was obliged to appear to side with her, if he did not wish to lose her confidence.

In 1491 Charles attained his twentieth year, and it was noticed that the Regent now somewhat relaxed her strict supervision and often absented herself from Court in order to inspect her property. It seemed that her influence was on the wane, and that the Orleans party would gain the upper hand. People reproached her with having allowed her private grudge against the Duke of Orleans to affect her treatment of him. The Duke of Angoulême, Dunois, and the Prince of Orange all joined the chorus against her. Above all, her own sister Jeanne, wife of Louis of Orleans, opposed her. Wearing deep mourning, Jeanne cast herself at the King's feet and implored mercy for her husband. In vain did Anne of Beaujeu try to make a stand against all this hostility ; the time of her power was over and gone.

Encouraged by this abatement of the Regent's authority, Miollars, the King's Senator, and Cossé, Overseer of the Court Bakery, ventured to reproach the young King with his lack of independence and to challenge him to manifest his power by restoring the Duke of Orleans to liberty. But Charles would not openly defy his sister's authority. Under pretext of a hunting party, he went to Montrichard, and from there despatched d'Aubigny with orders to liberate the Duke. Upon meeting they fell into one

another's arms and wept for joy. The long imprisonment had altered Louis. Instead of laying claim to
the hand of Anne of Brittany, he was now a zealous
supporter of her marriage with Charles.

The Regent, on hearing of Louis's release, recognised that her authority had had its day and ceased
to be. Charles was now entirely under the influence
of her enemies, and she was filled with apprehensions
as to what might befall her. The young King was,
however, too good-natured to allow any injury to be
done to his sister. In answer to her humble letter of
self-justification, he sent her a reassuring communication, protesting that he would close his ear to all
hostile insinuations, and ending affectionately with
the words—" Vous disant à Dieu, ma bonne sœur,
ma mie, qui vous ait en sa garde. . . ."

As Anne of Brittany remained unmoved by all
representations on behalf of her marriage with Charles,
force had to be employed. Three troops under
Rohan, la Trémouille, and the King, advanced and
conquered the whole country as far as the capital
in which the Duchess remained. For Charles to
reduce Rennes to ruins and take forcible possession
of the lady would hardly have been seemly, so Louis
of Orleans undertook to act as mediator. By his
eloquence and amiability he contrived to move her,
and on November 15, 1491, a secret marriage contract
was signed.

Nevertheless Anne, who was far from being meek-
spirited, demanded a capitulation in which her
personal freedom and that of her troops and depen-
dents should be expressly granted. Perhaps she
wished to spare the German troops who surrounded
her, or felt ashamed that they should regard her as
Queen of the Romans while she was secretly betrothed
to Charles.

Her bridegroom awaited her at Langeais, in Touraine,
whither she escaped secretly with two nobles and

HIERONYMI FERRARIENSIS A DEO MISSI PROPHETÆ EFFIGIES

CAROLVS VIII GALLIÆ REX

her Chancellor, Montauban. Everything was prepared for the marriage. Dunois alone was absent. Just as the wedding contract was signed, he died, December 6, 1491.

Through her marriage Anne's rights as sole heiress to Brittany were transmitted to Charles. His former betrothed, Marguerite, was calmly sent back to her father Maximilian. Anne seems to have got over her dislike to him, and on the whole made him a good and suitable wife.

From the historian Comines we get no very attractive account of Charles VIII. He describes Charles as lacking in intelligence, capricious, and easily influenced by unwise counsellors. Guicciardini, while confirming this mention of his feeble mental powers, comments on his great passion for governing and acquiring renown. He had little confidence in his nobles, but was much under the influence of men of low degree who were susceptible to bribery.

His external appearance did not belie his character. Short of stature, and short-necked, with parrot-like nose, of enormous dimensions, it was little wonder that Anne of Brittany had not found him alluring. Baron Corvo describes him thus. " A self-conceited little abortion—of the loosest morals even for a King, of gross Semitic type, with a fiery birth-flare round his left eye, and twelve toes on his feet hidden in splayed shoes, which set the fashion in foot-gear for the end of the fifteenth century in Italy."

In 1495 Charles and Anne lost their only son. From Comines we gather that the bereaved father was not overwhelmed with grief. Though he wore mourning in seemly fashion, it was supposed that there lay deep in his heart of hearts a grim kind of satisfaction that his son was no more, " parce qu'il était bel enfant, audacieux en parole et ne craignant point les choses que les autres enfants sont accoutumés à craindre, et vous dis que pour ces raisons, le père en passa aisément son dueil, ayant desja douté que tost cet enfant ne fust grand et que continuant ses conditions, il ne luy diminuast l'authorité et puissance : car le Roy ne fut jamais que petit homme de corps et peu étendu : mais estoit si bon, qu'il n'est point possible de voir meilleure créature."

Queen Anne, however, was inconsolable. Not only did she experience the natural grief of a mother on losing her child, but she foresaw the injury which would accrue to the State through his death. The King, hoping to cheer her, commanded several nobles to come and dance before her—among them Louis of Orleans, who was already thirty-four years old, and passed as the next heir to the throne. The Duke had so much difficulty in concealing his joy at the Dauphin's death that the royal pair were deeply offended, and for a long time refused to speak to him.

Both Charles VIII. and Louis of Orleans were destined to be intimately connected with the fate of Italy.

CHAPTER VIII

UPON the death of the illustrious Francesco Sforza,
in 1466, his eldest son, Galeazzo Maria, succeeded to
the throne of Milan. Galeazzo was a fiend in human
form, and the corruptness of his life and morals gave
cause for scandal even in those shameless times.
His mother, Bianca, tried to induce him to reform
his evil ways, and her death was attributed to poison
administered by him in resentment at her interference. Afterwards he continued his iniquities un-
restrained, abandoning himself to the most appalling
and monstrous immoralities. Like most profligates,
he was mercilessly cruel, and revelled in the torments
of his victims. As Bishop Creighton remarks : " There

was a superfluity of naughtiness in the insolence with
which he disregarded all restraints in gratifying his
appetites, and punishing those whom he suspected "
One offender was shut up in a chest and buried alive ;
a peasant who had caught a hare was made to eat
his capture, skin and all, until the unhappy wretch
died. A priest who had offended the Duke by pre-
dicting that his reign would not last more than
eleven years, was immured in a dungeon and slowly
starved to death. A small loaf, a glass of wine, and
the wing of a roast capon were put before him with
the message that he would never get anything else
to eat. Galeazzo delighted in the sight of corpses
in a tomb, and enjoyed nothing more than being
present at executions. Many other revolting in-
stances of his barbarity might be mentioned, but
enough has been said to illustrate the fact that he
was a tyrant of the most vicious kind. He oppressed
the people with heavy taxation and extorted money
from the rich. Nevertheless, he was not absolutely
devoid of good qualities. He loved and encouraged
the arts, and his Court was one of the most brilliant
in Europe. To his courtiers he showed himself
generous and amiable, and he granted a willing audience
to his subjects. His Council consisted of the most
capable and distinguished men, for he recognised
virtue and disliked double-dealing and self-conceit.
During his reign he caused many buildings to be
erected, and fortified Novara and Galiate. He was
well read, an astute politician, and an eloquent
speaker, excelling in this respect all the other princes
of the day.

The time arrived when the people of Milan could
no longer endure their Duke's tyranny. A conspiracy
was formed, headed by three young people of distinguished families whose dignity had been outraged.
They were Giovanni Andrea Lampugnano, Girolamo
Olgiati, and Carlo Visconti. Inspired by the scholar

Montano, they planned to murder the Duke on St. Stephen's Day, December 26, 1476, in the Church of St. Stephen. On that particular day the weather was so cold that Galeazzo wished to hear mass in his own residence, the Castle of Porta Giovia ; his chaplains, however, had already gone on to the church, so he finally decided to follow them. He and his suite started forth on horseback, accompanied by the ambassadors of Ferrara and Milan. The Duke was richly dressed in crimson, brown, and sable ; but, unhappily for himself, he wore no breastplate. As he entered the church where the conspirators, well armed, were assembled, Lampugnano moved as if to clear the way before him, then suddenly drew his knife and thrust it into the Duke's neck and abdomen. Olgiati pierced him in the throat and breast, while Visconti dashed forward and dealt him three deadly thrusts, and a certain Franzoni wounded him in the back with a sword. With the cry, " O nostra Donna ! " the Duke expired. Thereupon Franzoni fell upon one of his servants, Francesco da Riva, and slew him as well. The congregation, recovering from the stupefaction in which the sudden attack on the Duke had plunged them, drew their swords and rushed upon the conspirators. Lampugnano, who tried to slip away amongst the women, was slain by Gallo Mauro, one of the Duke's guard. His corpse was dragged through the city by street-urchins, hewn in pieces, and thrown into the river. The other two conspirators escaped, but were soon captured and executed, together with Franzoni. Olgiati, who was only about twenty-two years of age, was cruelly tortured ; as the executioner was cutting open his breast with a blunt knife, the victim, though fast losing consciousness, made a last effort and exclaimed : " Courage, Girolamo, the memory of this deed will endure for ever ; death is bitter, but glory is eternal ! "

On hearing the news of Galeazzo's murder, Pope Sixtus IV. exclaimed : " To-day the peace of Italy is dead," and it certainly appeared as though the political system of the country were radically over-thrown The new Duke, Giovanni Galeazzo Sforza, was only a child, and his mother Bona, to whom was entrusted the regency, was a woman of little account, not likely to be able to withstand the schemes of the ambitious King of Naples. Sixtus immediately issued a brief to all the Italian potentates, urging them to use their influence on behalf of peace and to recognise and support the Regent. The taxes devised by the late Duke were suspended and his creditors paid. A large quantity of grain from Sicily was sold to the people at less than cost price. These prompt measures were mainly due to the State Secretary, Cicco Simonetta, who had already conducted the affairs of State under Francesco Sforza and his son Galeazzo, and was now Bona's most trusted minister But he found violent opponents in the five brothers of the murdered Duke. Of these, Filippo Maria and Ottaviano were already in Milan, and the other three now returned from banishment, Ascanio from Rome, and Ludovico the Moor[1] and Sforza Maria, Duke of Bari, from France. They all united with Ruberto San Severino, Donato del Conte, and Ibletto Flisco to devise schemes for ousting their sister-in-law and her adviser. The hatred between the two parties grew so intense that a catastrophe seemed inevitable when Luigi Gonzaga, Marquis of Mantua, came to Milan on a visit to the young Duke, to Bona and to the brothers Sforza, to whom he was much attached. With the help of the papal legate he succeeded in bringing the adversaries to terms. The Duchess

---

[1] So called from his swarthy complexion, says Guicciardini, but Paul Jovius asserts that Ludovico was fair It is probable that the nickname " il Moro " arose from his having adopted the mulberry-tree for his device.

Bona was to pay each of the brothers a yearly sum of
12,500 ducats, and to give up to them the revenue
of Cremona, which belonged to the dowry of their
mother Bianca. In addition, each of them received
an imposing palace in Milan. Having thus amicably
arranged matters, Luigi Gonzaga returned to Mantua.

But the reconciliation was not lasting. The ambitious Ludovico still strove for the mastery, and
his schemes were favoured by the unrest prevailing
in northern Italy, where the old dissension between
Guelphs and Ghibellines was revived. The Genoese
nobles rebelled, but they could not stand against
the Sforza brothers, who compelled them to return
to their former dependence. The Swiss also prepared
for war, secretly incited by Sixtus IV., who, like the
King of Naples, was annoyed with the Duchess for
remaining faithful to her alliance with the Florentines.

After the suppression of the Genoese rising, the
Sforza brothers, in conjunction with San Severino
and Donato, busied their brains with plans for overthrowing Cicco; but the latter was equally clever
in baffling them. At Whitsuntide Donato was
invited by the Duchess and the Council to the Castle.
Hardly had he arrived when he was seized, tortured,
and thrown into the Monza prison, known as il Forno.
Thereupon the Sforza and San Severino despatched
Stefano Stampa to demand his release. On meeting
with a refusal they laid siege to the Porta Tosa,
where an army of 6,000 men soon rallied round them.
The Ghibellines were incited to revolt, and Milan
was divided into two factions. The Sforza brothers
offered to lay down their arms as soon as Donato,
who had often risked his life for the State, should be
set free. The other party replied that Donato
should be liberated as soon as they had laid down
their arms. Finally, after the intervention of the
Florentine and Neapolitan envoys and several important citizens, matters were satisfactorily settled.

Ruberto San Severino, somewhat suspicious at the trend of events, with a few of his veterans, crossed the Ticino and visited a castle owned by the brothers Giovanni and Francesco Cocconati. Here he learned that Gorella di Caravaggio was pursuing him with an armed troop. In order to escape him, he told the Cocconati that Borella was fleeing on account of having insulted the Duke, and that when he reached the castle they would do well to take him prisoner. Thereupon San Severino rode on in great haste. Borella soon afterwards turned up at the castle, and begged assistance in capturing Ruberto; but the brothers seized and imprisoned him instead By this cunning did San Severino escape the danger which threatened him. Ibletto Flisco fled to Villanova, but was captured and incarcerated in one of the towers of Milan Castle.

Worst of all fared it with the young Ottaviano Sforza, who escaped in the direction of the Adda. At the Duchess's command he was pursued by peasants, and, in trying to cross a ford, he was borne away by the current, though his horse arrived uninjured on the other side. His body was found after three days, brought to Milan, and entombed in the Tempio Maggiore.

Sforza, Duke of Bari, Ludovico, and Ascanio Sforza were banished on account of their part in the disturbance—Sforza to Bari, Ludovico to Pisa, and Ascanio to Perugia. Donato tried to escape from prison by twisting his bedclothes into a rope and letting himself down from the window. But the rope broke and he fell from a considerable height. He was taken back severely injured, but, in spite of assiduous nursing, died in a few days.

The young Giovanni Galeazzo was crowned in the Cathedral at Milan, 1479, amid popular rejoicing. About the same time the Swiss invaded the north and occupied a rocky valley. When the Milanese

THE SARCOPHAGUS OF ALEXANDER VI, IN THE CRYPT OF ST. PETER'S.

THE EXECUTION OF SAVONAROLA AND HIS DOMINICAN BRETHREN IN THE MARKET-
PLACE AT FLORENCE, MAY 23, 1497.
St. Mark's Museum, Florence.

army advanced against them they withdrew to the mountains and rolled stones down on the pursuing troops, who fled in alarm, not realising the small numbers of the Swiss. The latter then gave chase. A panic broke out among the Milanese, who took flight in great disorder along unknown mountain paths. Many, to escape death, cast themselves into the river and were borne away by the force of the current. In this way more than 8,000 men perished.

In February 1479 war broke out anew with Genoa. Sforza, Duke of Bari, and his brother Ludovico, incited by Ferrante of Naples, had entered Genoese territory and united with San Severino and Ibletto. The young Duke, Bona, and Cicco sent large sums of money to Ercole d'Este and Federigo Gonzaga in order to gain their assistance against the Sforza. They also obtained the help of Ruberto Malatesta of Rimini and Costanzo Sforza of Pesaro (of another branch of the family), who were both willing to take part against the Pope. Both brothers Sforza and San Severino were declared rebels, and their revenues, together with their maternal inheritance of Cremona, confiscated.

The Sforza then betook themselves to Tuscany, and, after engaging in successful marauding expeditions, returned to Liguria. Ferrante and the Pope, who was bitterly hostile to the Florentines, despatched an army against them. The Duke of Milan, Federigo Gonzaga, the lords of Rimini and Pesaro, and even the Venetians, came to their assistance. All Italy was up in arms, and a universal war seemed imminent.

Meanwhile Sforza, Duke of Bari, had died, and King Ferrante bestowed the dukedom of Bari upon Ludovico il Moro. The latter, always greedy and grasping, straightway invaded Tortona, which, by dint of bribing the governor, he succeeded in annexing. He then advanced towards the Po, taking possession

LB

in the Duke's name of several small fortresses on his way.

Cicco, alarmed at these proceedings, opposed Ludovico, in company with Ercole d'Este, Gian Giacopo Trivulzio, and several other captains. But another party in Milan, headed by Bona's lover, Tassino, tried to bring about a reconciliation between Ludovico and Bona, to which the latter, realising the power of her brother-in-law, was nothing loth to agree.

The court of Milan was now cleft in twain. At the head of one party was Cicco, who for fifty years had conducted the affairs of State ; at the head of the other was Antonio Tassino of Ferrara, who, originally a small tradesman, had been appointed Chamberlain to the Duchess Bona by Galeazzo Maria. Though not handsome, he was young and well dressed, and after the Duke's death steadily grew in favour with Bona, who consulted him on all the affairs of State, to the great annoyance of Cicco. The latter, indeed, could hardly conceal his contempt for the young upstart, thereby incurring his implacable hatred.

At Tassino's suggestion, Bona decided to summon Ludovico to the Court. He was greeted with effusion by the Ghibellines, and received at the Castle with all politeness by Bona and the young Duke.

This reconciliation between the Duchess and her brother-in-law filled Cicco with the greatest consternation. " Illustrious Duchess," he remarked, " I shall lose my head, and you your rule, in the course of time." This prophecy was fulfilled. He sought in vain to win Ludovico's good opinion by showing himself friendly, but the latter was persuaded by his companions, in particular by Pusterla, that he would never be able to live in peace as long as Cicco Simonetta was free. At the same time Pusterla united with the Ghibelline leaders and incited them to arms.

He also sent a message to San Severino, Cicco's bitterest foe, summoning him to prepare for war. Ludovico still seemed undecided, but Pusterla, without consulting him, seized Orfeo Aricco, a friend of Cicco's and paymaster of the forces. His son Alexander was taken to the Borromeo Palace, from which he managed to escape disguised as a miller. When Ludovico heard this he no longer wavered, and determined that Cicco should be arrested. The latter, since Galeazzo's death, had occupied rooms in the Castle, and twice refused to appear before Ludovico. At the third summons, however, he yielded and was immediately taken captive. His brother Giovanni, and many of his adherents, met with the same fate. Cicco's rooms and his house, Torre di Capponi, were plundered.

Cicco and his brother were shortly afterwards sent to Pavia and placed in the charge of Count Giovanni Attendolo. Orfeo Aricco was taken to Trezzo, and the others were set free. Ludovico was now appointed co-regent with Bona. Envoys were despatched to the King of Naples to negotiate between him and the Florentines. Venetian ambassadors appeared at Milan, and Ascanio Sforza was recalled from banishment. Ferrante, for his part, sent envoys to Milan, and peace was concluded on November 20, 1479. But the Venetians refused to come to terms, and rather incited the Swiss to war against the Milanese. The misunderstanding between Ferrante and Lorenzo the Magnificent still prevailed, and gave rise to Lorenzo's already mentioned journey to Naples. Not only did he win the King's favour, but he succeeded in bringing about an alliance between Sixtus IV. and Ferrante and the Duke of Milan and Florence.

Ascanio Sforza, Bishop of Pavia and Apostolic Legate *a latere*, through jealousy of his brother, favoured the Ghibelline party Ludovico, who had formerly been on their side, now began to oppress them. When Ascanio arrived at the Castle of Milan he, with several leading nobles of his party, was arrested and the Ghibellines were forced to deliver up their arms. Ascanio was banished to Ferrara.

In response to the appeals of several of Ludovico's friends, he sent lawyers to Pavia to pronounce judgment upon Cicco. Ludovico, who knew that Cicco had laid by considerable sums in foreign banks, offered to release him on payment of a ransom of 40,000 ducats. But the prisoner sturdily resisted this proposal. He had been unjustly and disgracefully treated, he said, in return for long and faithful service. If he had offended in anything, he was willing to receive an appropriate punishment, but his property, acquired by honourable work, should pass to his rightful heirs.

Cicco's appointed judges were Colla, Capitano di Giustizia, and Ambrogio Oppizone, Doctor of the College of Judges. Oppizone, however, withdrew from the responsibility; so Colla, alone, decided on the death-sentence, which was mainly grounded upon the imprisonment of Donato. After having been cruelly tortured, Cicco, with maimed limbs, was taken to the castle ramparts at Pavia, where he was executed, 1480. He was seventy years old, and displayed remarkable fortitude during his torture and in face of death. The following lines were carved upon his tomb :

> My country's faithful servant and my Lord's,
> I perished by the guile of treacherous words.

Now that Cicco was out of the way Tassino's arrogance grew and flourished, particularly as the Duchess Bona daily showed him fresh signs of favour. He did not scruple to keep Ludovico and the first nobles of the land waiting in his anteroom while he combed his hair carefully, and he displayed an overbearing haughtiness to every one with whom he came in contact. He persuaded the Duchess to make his father, Gabriello, Governor of Milan Castle, in place of Filippo Eustachio; but the plan was frustrated by Ludovico's party. Tassino and his father were driven out of Milan, and, with the treasure of gold and precious stones which they had accumulated through the favour of Bona, betook themselves to Venice. The Duchess, however, could not endure this separation from her lover, and, throwing decency and dignity alike to the winds, decided to follow him. Nothing could turn her from this decision. Regardless of the fate of her son, she delivered the regency to Ludovico, who promptly had a legal document drawn up to that effect. Then she started forth, like one demented, in pursuit of her lover. But her quest was doomed to meet with failure. At Abbiategrasso she was arrested by order of Ludovico, and condemned to live sequestered from the world. Thus it may be seen how an insignificant man like Tassino proved to be the prime cause of the loss of Milan by the House of Sforza.

The young Duke was under the sway of Eustachio and Pallavicini, so Ludovico adopted a friendly policy towards them. From this there resulted what might almost be called a triumvirate; San Severino, displeased at this development of affairs, demanded an increase of salary. On being refused he left Milan in dudgeon and went to Castelnuovo, where he began to prepare for war. Ludovico summoned Costanzo Sforza, an illegitimate son of Sforza, from Florence.

The Florentines and Ferrante sent envoys urgently begging San Severino to return to Milan, but he refused to trust himself to Pallavicini and Eustachio. He now entered into negotiations with Pietro dal Verme, who was the master of Vaghera as well as many small fortresses, Piero Maria Rosso, and many other nobles of Parma, who were discontented with the new government   They were also joined by Ibletto

In 1482 4,000 cavalry and 2,000 infantry were ordered out by Ludovico. Part of this force was sent to help the Duke of Savoy, who was attacked by the Bishop of Milan, while the rest, under the leadership of Costanzo Sforza, marched against San Severino. Ibletto Fliṣco, who, with a large number of adherents from Liguria, was about to unite with San Severino, was overtaken by Costanzo Sforza, forced into an engagement, and utterly routed. This defeat greatly discouraged San Severino's friends, especially dal Verme, who realised how slight was their chance against the Duke   The danger of his situation soon began to dawn upon San Severino also, and he withdrew with a few veterans to Genoa, whence he and thirteen of his men went by sea to Siena. His son Gasparo escaped to France, but their wives and Ruberto's younger son were led captive to Milan.

Ludovico now despatched Costanzo against Piero Maria Rosso, under pretext that he had disobeyed the Duke's summons to Milan. The real reason, however, was that Ludovico wished to seize his possessions, which were many, and included twenty-two castles in Parman territory   Costanzo tried hard to compromise, for Rosso had done important service to Francesco Sforza, and he shrank from witnessing the ruin of so illustrious a family. But, mainly through the influence of Pallavicini, Costanzo's representations were unavailing, and Pietro Bergamino and Trivulzio were placed in command of 6,000 men and despatched against Rosso.

Rosso, recognising that he had no chance against such a force, gave himself into the hands of the Venetians. They appointed San Severino Commander-in-Chief and sent him with an army of 17,000 against Ercole d'Este, who, at the suggestion of his son-in-law, Ludovico,[1] had blocked the way so that they could not go to Rosso's help Ercole, in his extremity, turned to Ludovico. The whole of Italy was now in arms. On the side of Milan were Ferrante of Naples and Florence, while Venice was supported by Sixtus IV. and Genoa. The Duke of Urbino was appointed General-in-Chief of the Milanese by Ludovico.

The Duke of Ferrara was already too old to cope with San Severino The latter crossed the Po, near Ferrara, and established his camp in the Park of Garcos, where he planted the banner of St. Mark. At this the Duke was almost beside himself with rage, so that his wife (Ferrante's daughter) had to take over his responsibilities. Rumours of his death soon spread ; the people were seized with the greatest consternation which was not allayed until he appeared on a balcony in public.

The Duchess, who was most anxious to maintain the courage of the soldiers, summoned a hermit from Bologna. In passionate terms he admonished the people to sacrifice blood and property as in a sacred cause. His words had the desired effect, particularly as he promised to equip a fleet of twelve galleys which should annihilate the Venetians. The whole town was stirred, and the hermit was revered as a magician. On a certain day all the inhabitants, greatly excited, repaired in procession to the enemy's camp in order that San Severino might be converted by the eloquence of the wonderful man.

On seeing this strange sight the Duke of Urbino cried, " Tell the Duchess that it is not processions which are needed to disperse her enemy, but rather money, artillery, and soldiers ! " In Romagna the Venetian and papal troops were victorious, and the Duke of Calabria was utterly defeated at Campo Morto after a desperate and bloody fight.

[1] Ludovico had married the seventeen-year-old Beatrice d'Este.

Sixtus IV., perturbed at the Venetian success, united with Ferrante of Naples and the Florentines ; they were joined by many petty princes who were alarmed at the Venetian threat of taking Ferrara. The Pope pronounced anathema against Venice, but, with the exception of a few monks, his decree was ignored by all the Venetian clergy, who appealed against the Pope to a Council.

The Milanese now appointed Ferrante's son, Alfonso of Calabria, as their leader, but the Venetians boldly opposed this alarming alliance. San Severino, indeed, gained sundry advantages over the allies, but in the battle of Argenta the Venetians suffered a total defeat at the hands of Alfonzo and Costanzo Sforza. Fifteen thousand of their men suffered death or imprisonment, and they began to lose hope. San Severino now succeeded in gaining possession of the bridge over the Adda at Trezzo. When the news reached Milan a panic arose, for the Court feared a revolution, but, as nothing alarming occurred, Ludovico plucked up courage and continued the war with renewed energy.

The Venetians now summoned the Duke of Lorraine to the command of their troops. Ludovico, with the idea of intimidating Ferrara, advanced against Bergamo, but San Severino hastened to its defence, leaving the Duke of Lorraine with part of the Venetian troops before Ferrara. Strategic manœuvres were employed on both sides in order to mislead the enemy and to avoid an actual engagement.

A Venetian fleet was meanwhile threatening the coasts of Naples and plundering the neighbouring places. The Neapolitan galleys, on the other hand, laid waste the coast of Dalmatia, but could not succeed in enticing the Venetians from Naples. Ferrante was therefore obliged to recall his troops and turn his attention to the defence of his own States.

The league against the Venetians had already

become weakened through the many selfish interests of its members, and threatened to become extinct. Alfonso, whose daughter was affianced to the young Duke of Milan, saw through the ambitious schemes of Ludovico, now supreme governor of Milan. The Florentines, too, who had nothing to gain from the war, were beginning to weary of the state of affairs.

Notwithstanding the vigorous opposition of the papal envoy, the Treaty of Bagnolo was concluded, by which the Duke of Ferrara was bound to restore to the Venetians all the privileges which they had formerly enjoyed in Ferrara, and also to cede to them further territory.   On the other hand, all conquests made by the Venetians were to be returned to the Duke.   Milan and Mantua were to restore all conquests made on Venetian ground.   The towns which the Venetians had possessed in Naples were to go back to Ferrante, and in return they were to enjoy commercial privileges in his States. Ruberto San Severino, as Captain-General of the Venetians, was to receive a salary of 140,000 ducats, of which 50,000 were to be contributed by Milan, 50,000 by Venice, and the other 40,000 by the Pope, Ferrante, the Florentines, and the Duke of Ferrara.

This treaty, while to the advantage of the chief Italian Powers, bore hardly on the smaller Princes and States.   To Sixtus IV, who had hoped to enrich his nephews with the lands taken from the Duke of Ferrara and the Venetians, it was as gall and wormwood   Upon the news of its conclusion reaching him, he exclaimed, "This peace is a shame and disgrace, which will in time be more productive of evil than of good.   I can neither bless nor sanction it!" (August 12, 1484).   Seeing that the Pope was becoming speechless from fear and anger, the envoys begged him to bless the peace which could not now be altered.   Drawing his gouty hand from its sling, he made a sign which some regarded as a refusal, others as compliance. After this he spoke no more, and died the following night, August 13, 1484.[1]

Ludovico's behaviour was now exciting considerable displeasure, for it was obvious that he intended to usurp the authority which belonged to his nephew, Giovanni Galeazzo. Not only did he entirely renounce the Ghibelline party, but, whenever possible, raised to the most important positions those who had always been hostile to the Sforza family. His relations with Bona, too, were such as to arouse discontent. This universal dissatisfaction culminated in a plot to murder Ludovico. The conspirators were Francesco, brother of Eustachio of the Ordine Bianco, Fra Ugo Barattino, the Father Confessor of the Duchess Bona, Luigi Vimercato (with the connivance of Pasino, whom Ludovico had insulted), a certain Sant' Angelo, stipendiary, and Guido Eustachio and his brother Filippo. All these were supported by several of the nobles and patricians of Milan. On the appointed day they stationed themselves at the entrance to the church which Ludovico was in the habit of attending, but, on account of the throng, he entered by another door, thus frustrating their plan. Nothing daunted, however, they assembled at the gate of the citadel, for it was his custom to go every day to the Pallavicini and the Castellan. When Ludovico arrived he asked for Eustachio, and, on hearing that he was engaged at his midday meal, he turned and went into his rooms, followed by Vimercato to spy upon his movements. But Ludovico's servants saw the gleam of an unsheathed dagger which he was wearing under his doublet. Their master, on being informed, had him arrested, and, after a short trial, he was beheaded, quartered, and his limbs fixed up on the gates of Milan (February 27, 1484). Pasino, after being repeatedly tortured, was condemned to lifelong imprisonment in the Castello of Sartirano, where,

[1] See Chapter VI.

by Ludovico's orders, he was tortured every year on St. Ambrose's Day.

In 1485 Milan was ravaged by the plague, and Corio, the historian, withdrew into retirement from fear of infection. It was at this time that he began to write the work which was to be of such great importance to the student of history

At the same time Alfonso of Calabria, Ferrante's eldest son, summoned an assembly of the barons at Chieti, under pretext of arranging certain business matters. He profited by this occasion to have Count Montone and his wife arrested and imprisoned in a dungeon at Naples. The new Pope—Innocent VIII.—thereupon united with the Count's relations and declared war against Ferrante.

The unpopularity of the King of Naples did but increase when Alfonso began to take part in the government. Comines writes: " There existed no more vicious, cruel, and wicked scoundrel than Alfonso. His father was more dangerous, because no one could guess what were his thoughts or with whom he was angry, for even while he flattered and entertained, he did not scruple to betray. From Ferdinand no one ever obtained mercy, nor was he ever moved by sympathy, as his nearest relations and friends have told me , never was his heart touched by the sufferings of the poor whom he oppressed by taxation. In his anxiety to engage in the commerce of the State, he farmed herds of pigs for half profits. He had them fed by farmers in order to command a better price, and he also insisted on being paid for those which died. In places where olive oil was produced, such as Apulia, he and his son bought it up at a favourable price ; in the same way they bought corn before the harvest and afterwards sold it for as high a profit as possible. And, if it began to fall in value, they forced the people to buy it. Indeed, when they had corn to be bought no one else dared to offer any for sale."

Thus, by creating fictitious famines, did Ferrante make his profits. His starving subjects were compelled to buy his provisions, however abominable these might be. One of his victims writes : " The bread made from the corn of which I have spoken was black, stinking, and abominable. One was obliged to consume it, and from this cause sickness frequently took hold upon the State."

Although Pope Innocent VIII. had been brought up at the Court of Naples, this did not prevent his cherishing a secret grudge against King Ferrante ; the latter had displeased him by desiring a remission of a considerable part of the money usually paid by Naples as church tribute, giving, as an excuse, the heavy expenses incurred by the Turkish crusade. The discontented barons hoped now to find an ally in the Pope, and formed a conspiracy. A deed of violence perpetrated by Alfonso gave Innocent an opportunity of giving his displeasure vent.

The little mountain town of Aquila enjoyed the freedom of a republic, though it was really in subjection to the King of Naples. For more than a century the Count of Montorio had exercised over it much the same kind of authority as that of the Medici over Florence. This independence rankled in the mind of Alfonso, and he determined to deprive the town of its privileges. His troops were now ·quartered at Chieti, whither he summoned the Count. The latter, all unsuspecting, responded to the call, whereupon he was immediately arrested, and, with his wife, conveyed to Naples. At the same time Alfonso despatched his troops in small detachments to Aquila, by which means the whole army succeeded in entering the town without exciting suspicion. When, at last, the citizens guessed his intention, they repeatedly begged the King to remove his men, as it was contrary to their privileges to be obliged to receive troops in their town. As he turned a deaf ear to their entreaties, the citizens armed themselves and slaughtered part of the garrison, putting the rest to flight. They thereupon declared their independence of King Ferrante and placed themselves under the protection of the Church. Innocent welcomed them cordially and prepared for war. Ferrante, for the sake of appearance, liberated the Count of Montorio. The Pope, however, allowed the vassals of the Colonna to advance against Aquila. The King then summoned a parliament at Naples, but the Count of Fondi, the Duke of Amalfi, and the Prince of Tarento were the only nobles who had the courage to appear. All the other barons escaped to Melfi, convinced that to fall into Ferrante's power would mean the loss of their lives. They determined that they would no longer be trampled upon, but Alfonso, who was well aware of their intentions, seized the Count of Nola, took all his strongholds, and sent his wife and two sons as prisoners to Naples. He also made up his mind to capture the other rebellious barons one by one, before they had time to unite their forces; but his enemies were more numerous than he had expected, and he was therefore obliged to be wary in his movements. However, neither Alfonso nor the malcontents were ready for war, so negotiations were set on foot, with a view of gaining time rather than of making peace. Ferrante sent to Florence and Milan to demand auxiliary troops, which they, as allies, were expected to provide.

Ludovico, following his usual obscure policy, returned an ambiguous reply, but Florence, which was dominated by Lorenzo de' Medici, promised the King powerful support. Ludovico was therefore obliged to declare his readiness to help, and the war costs were to be shared between Milan and Florence. The Count of Pitigliano, the Lord of Piombino, and all the generals of the House of Orsini, were subsidised, and began fighting in November.

The Pope, on the other hand, strove to show himself friendly to the Venetians, and released them from the ecclesiastical censures laid upon them by Sixtus IV. But the Republic of Venice was only just beginning to enjoy the benefits of peace after lengthy warfare, and did not feel inclined to plunge into fresh hostilities. They, however, offered the Pope the services of their General, Ruberto San Severino, and his two sons. Innocent VIII., in this predicament, summoned to his assistance the Duke of Lorraine, whom he regarded as the representative of the House of Anjou, and offered him the investiture of the kingdom of Naples. But the Duke was just then engaged in disputing his grandfather's will, by which he was deprived of his inheritance, and could therefore be of little help.

Ferrante, meanwhile, had given the barons to understand that he was willing to listen to their complaints. They therefore despatched the Count Bisignano as their representative, with many requests Ferrante, with his usual power of dissimulation, appeared to acquiesce in their demands, and sent his second son, Federigo, to their assembly with power to grant them. But the barons, who knew the treachery of their King, were alarmed at his seeming complaisance, and refused to accept peace under the conditions which they themselves had proposed. When Federigo arrived at Salerno, in the belief that matters were pacifically arranged, the Prince of Salerno convened a meeting of the barons, and sought, in strong and energetic terms, to induce him to accept the crown in his father's stead, assuring him that they would defend his throne at the sacrifice of their lives and property

Federigo, who was in truth a noble Prince, moved by no prospects of self-advancement, thanked them for their proposal, but refused it with decision, declaring his unwillingness to defy the law and treat his father and brothers with contumely.

The conspirators were seized with rage and desperation, and, as they could not make Federigo King, they
took him prisoner instead.   They further took up
their stand under the papal banner and openly declared
themselves hostile to the King.   Ferrante determined
to avenge the affront by an attack on the States
of the Church, and sent Alfonso to the frontier of
the Kingdom.   When he realised that the soldiers
as well as the leaders had religious motives for warring
against the Pope, he summoned a meeting of commanders and barons in Naples Cathedral and publicly
explained that he only desired to defend his boundaries
and that he had no wish to fight against the Holy
See, of which he remained a dutiful son (1485).   At
the same time he issued commands to all the bishops
and prelates of his kingdom that they should leave
the Roman Court and repair to their own dioceses.
The revenues of the Archbishop of Salerno and the
Bishops of Melito and Teano, who did not comply
with this order, were confiscated.   A second force
under command of Duke Alfonso's son, Don Ferrantino,
was sent to Apulia, accompanied (on account of the
inexperience of the leader) by the Counts of Madde-
loni and Marigliano.

Nothing decisive occurred at first.   Alfonso and
the Orsini blocked the way of San Severino, who
wished to pass through the Papal States in order to
join the revolting barons.   Thereupon all the towns
on the boundaries of Romagna rose in rebellion,
renouncing their adherence to the Pope and declaring
themselves republican.   The Baglioni provoked insurrection in Perugia, and the Vitelli in Citta di Castello,
while Giovanni dei Gatti asserted his rights to Viterbo.
In Assisi, Foligno, Montefalcone, Todi, Spoleto, and
Orvieto a party was formed which wished to join
with the Florentines.

Meanwhile on May 8, 1486, the troops of Duke
Alfonso and San Severino had an encounter at the

Bridge of Lamentana, where San Severino's son, Fracasso, received a dangerous wound. Alfonso took a number of his men prisoners, and forced him to retreat. Thereupon he united with the Orsini and cast terror into the heart of Rome. At the same time Federigo escaped to Naples, where he was rapturously received by his father and the citizens.

The wily Ferrante did not cease to try to win over to his side the rebellious barons who were annoyed with the Pope because their soldiers received no pay. The Cardinals, too, assailed Innocent with complaints and requests, so that he at last made up his vacillating mind to enter into negotiations with Ferrante. The barons likewise resolved to make up their quarrel with the King, but they proceeded with the greatest caution. The Pope, knowing the treacherous character of Ferrante, desired that the Duke of Milan, Lorenzo de' Medici, and the King and Queen of Castile should act as guarantors for his promises.

Peace was concluded on August 11. Ferrante acknowledged himself as a direct vassal of the Church, and undertook to pay the Pope an annual tribute. In spite of the guarantee of the King of Spain and the Duke of Milan, the barons knew Ferrante's faithlessness and Alfonso's cruelty well enough to be greatly alarmed at this peace.

The Chief Seneschal of the kingdom, Pietro di Guerrara, died of a broken heart, and the other barons banded themselves together to defend their castles, and, if possible, to obtain help from Rome and Venice. But Ferrante and Alfonso, in their crafty way, treated them graciously and promised them every security. The Prince of Salerno alone refused to be entrapped by their wiles; he fled to Rome, but perceiving that the Pope's thoughts were no longer of war, he betook himself to France.

Ruberto San Severino, dismissed by the Pope, now journeyed with 1,600 cavalry in the direction

LOUIS XII., KING OF FRANCE.
Uffizi Gallery, Florence.

ST. JEANNE DE VALOIS, WHOSE MARRIAGE WITH LOUIS XII.
WAS ANNULLED BY POPE ALEXANDER VI., 1480.

She founded the Order of the Annonciades at Bourges, and
died in the odour of sanctity, 1504.

of Ravenna. Alfonso, however, was on his track, and Ruberto could do nothing but disband his force, and, hurling maledictions on the Pope, escape secretly by night to the Venetians, in company with about one hundred cavalry. His soldiers, like sheep without a shepherd, dispersed in all directions. Some of them were captured and robbed by peasants, others by the Florentines and Bolognese, while others entered the service of Alfonso.

Ferrante and Alfonso were meanwhile deliberating as to how they could revenge themselves on the barons. They determined, first of all, to compass the ruin of the Count of Sarno and the Secretary Petrucci, on whom the other barons laid all the guilt. They hastened the wedding between Marco Coppola, the Count's son, and the daughter of the Duke of Amalfi, a grandson of the King. In the midst of the festivities in the great hall of Castelnuovo, constables rushed in and seized the Count of Sarno and his sons Marco Coppola and Filippo, the Secretary Petrucci, the Counts Carinola and Policastro, together with several others. Not content with this, the King gave orders for the plundering of their castles, which treachery excited violent protests. He therefore appointed four judges to pronounce sentence on the prisoners, who were all condemned to death and their property confiscated.

The King apparently wished to prolong the pleasure of seeing them die, for he refused to have them all executed on the same day. The Secretary's sons were the first to suffer; they were executed on a scaffold erected in the middle of the market-place A few months later Petrucci himself and the Count of Sarno were beheaded at the gate of Castelnuovo, in sight of the whole town, May 15, 1487. Ten days later he commanded the arrest of the Duke of Altamura, Prince Bisignano, the Duke of Melfi, the Duke of Nardi, the Count of Morcone, the Count

MB

of Lauria, the Count of Melito, the Count of Nola, and many other cavaliers. At Alfonso's instigation the King, at various times and in various ways, brought about their deaths.

To complete the tragedy, Marino Marzano, who for twenty-five years had languished in prison, was handed over to the executioner. The fate of the last batch of victims remained a secret until it was noticed that the hangman was adorned with a gold chain belonging to the Prince of Bisignano. Rumours spread that they had been killed and thrown in sacks into the sea, while their sons and wives, accused of further insubordination, were arrested and deprived of their goods

Ferrante, emboldened by the annihilation of so many barons, now abandoned all pretence of deference to the Pope, and refused payment of tribute, at the same time coolly disposing of benefices without any reference to the Holy See. Innocent despatched the Bishop of Cesena to Naples to remonstrate with the King on his conduct. The latter insolently replied that as far as the tribute was concerned, he had already spent so much on behalf of the Church that he could justly claim dispensation ; also that he knew his subjects better than did the Pope, and would therefore continue to distribute benefices as he thought good   Truly, this was the most shameful peace ever entered upon by the Holy See.

In 1487 Northern Italy was invaded by the Swiss, who were successful until the Duke of Milan despatched a powerful army against them. They thereupon made peace and restored what they had conquered. But war soon broke out again. The Swiss asserted that they were accused by the Italians of plundering the churches, and laid siege to Domodossola, the strongest castle of the whole country. Ludovico Sforza advanced as far as possible, and Renaldo Trivulzio undertook to raise the siege. A terrible encounter took place, in which many were killed and wounded. The Swiss, who displayed the greatest bravery throughout, were finally obliged to yield. One part of them fled to the mountains, while another continued to defend the bridge of Crea, at the entrance to the Antegoria Valley. They held out with phenomenal courage until the number of slain fallen into the river was so great as to make a kind of bridge across which the enemy passed and attacked the Swiss on the flank. The latter all perished, and a like fate overtook those who had sought refuge in the mountains. Some were killed by the soldiers, others by the peasants, while those who escaped died of starvation, and were found with grass and leaves in their mouths. The fiendish cruelty displayed by the Italians during this war was a disgrace to humanity. It is even said that there were women who roasted parts of the corpses and served them at meals.

Genoa also was not free from disturbances. Ibletto Flisco and Battistino Campofregoso took up arms against the Cardinal Archbishop Paolo, who, in the name of the Duke of Milan, held the regency of Liguria. Archbishop Paolo withdrew to the casteletto and bombarded the town, which fell into strife and disorder. The Duke thereupon sent Francesco San Severino with large troops to Genoa. Ibletto finally united with Adorno and Spinola and became reconciled to the Duke, so that only the castle and Savona remained in Paolo's hands But Ludovico Sforza, who intended to seize Genoa for himself, made an arrangement with Tregoso that Savona should be ceded to him on payment of 4,000 ducats yearly, and that Chiaro Sforza, daughter of Galeazzo and widow of Dal Verme, should be betrothed to his son Tregesino. Paolo now yielded the fortress to San Severino, who entrusted it to the care of Zanone da Lavello a man both brave and

loyal, and himself set sail for Rome.   But Ludovico,
when he had the castle in his power, forgot Tregoso,
and appointed as Governor of Genoa the able Agostino
Adorno.

In 1487 began preparations for the marriage of
the young Duke of Milan and Isabella, daughter of
Alfonso of Calabria, who had been betrothed since
1480. The Duke's natural brother, Hermes, was
sent to the Neapolitan Court that he might act as
escort to the bride. He was accompanied by the
most distinguished nobles of Milan, who vied with
one another in the display of magnificence. All
were clothed in gold and silver stuffs, and decorated
with costly pearls and precious stones ; but the most
gorgeously apparelled was the Marchese Rolando
Pallavicino, whose jewels were valued at 25,000
ducats. The very servants wore silken garments
with the arms of their masters embroidered in silver
and pearls upon the left sleeves.

At Genoa six galleys awaited the Marchese Hermes
in order to take him to Naples. On December 24,
1488, he reached his destination with a company of
450 persons, not including the Genoese ambassadors,
who were there as a sign of respect for the Duke.
Having concluded the arrangements for the wedding,
he set out on his homeward way with the bride, who
had many Neapolitan lords and ladies in her train.
At Civita Vecchia they were received and entertained
by Monsignore Ascanio, uncle of the bridegroom,
while at Leghorn the bride was waited upon by a
deputation of Florentines, who invited her to go
into the country to recover from the fatigues of
her journey. She remained in Leghorn four days,
during which the Florentines inaugurated brilliant
festivities in her honour.

On January 17, 1489, Isabella arrived at Genoa,
where she met with an enthusiastic reception. The
approach of the little fleet was signalled by the firing

of salutes. The highest nobles of the town came forth to greet her, and, amid the pealing of bells, she was escorted under a canopy to the ducal palace. Here she stayed for five days, and then went on to Tortona, where Ludovico and her bridegroom advanced on horseback to meet her. The young Duke greeted her with effusion, and would have embraced her, instead of kissing her hand in Neapolitan fashion, if the restlessness of the horses had not prevented him. The town was gaily decorated, and everywhere hung festoons of laurel with gilded apples nestling in the foliage. The people hailed the bride with shouts of joy, and she was escorted by the crowd to the Episcopal Palace, which was arranged for her reception. Who could, at such a moment, foresee that Isabella was destined to become one of the most unhappy Princesses of Italy? The next day they continued their way to Abbiatagrosso, where the Duchess Bona met her and accompanied her to Milan.

Three litters were specially built to convey the bride and her suite to the bridegroom's home. The one destined for her own use was decorated with red velvet bearing the impress of the ducal arms, and furnished inside with the greatest luxury. A few miles from Milan she was met by a deputation of welcome, consisting of Philip, uncle of the young Duke, several ladies of the highest rank, and sixty of the most beautiful maidens of Milan.

Near San Cristoforo, Ludovico, with a retinue of senators and ambassadors, advanced to greet her and escorted her to Milan. At the harbour of Porta Ticinese the Duke, with more than 500 nobles and a bodyguard, came to meet his bride. At the same moment cannon thundered, trumpets crashed, and bands played in order to announce the happy arrival of the young Duchess. Hand in hand, the bridal pair made their way to the Castle. In the courtyard the walls were draped with azure cloth from which hung festoons of ivy. Everywhere there was evidence of joy and welcome. Upon entering the Castle they were received by the Duke's sister, Bianca Maria, who embraced the bride and led her to the bridal-chamber. The bed was of untold value, both from an artistic and a pecuniary point of view; upon the counterpane were embroidered five lions in pearls. All around were spread wonderful carpets, and the whole room was decorated with crimson satin.

The next day the marriage ceremony took place in the Cathedral. Cloths in the Sforza colours were spread in the streets; all the houses were decorated with carpets, satin cloths, and festoons of laurel and ivy. The goldsmiths displayed in the middle of their street an immense gilded globe adorned with four golden griffins; a silvered column bearing a lion was on the top, while at the foot of the globe stood a child dressed as Cupid, who sang festal verses as the bridal pair passed by. In the Cathedral place triumphal arches were erected, upon them depicted the most distinguished deeds of the Sforza family.

The wedding procession was led by the pages and serving nobles; then followed the ducal trumpeters and minstrels, together with those of the other gentlemen, and then the ambassadors and the chief nobles in pairs. The ducal sword was borne by Viscount Francesco Bernardino, and immediately after him rode the bridal couple under a canopy of gold cloth lined with ermine. The bride's horse was led by the Marchese Giovanni Pallavicino and the Count Giovanni Borromeo, while by her side walked Alexander Sforza, in readiness to help her dismount. Fifty of the most beautiful ladies in Milan rode at the end of the procession, which was joined by the clergy. Priests and monks in their full vestments formed a line which reached from the Castle to the Cathedral.

Amid cries of joy the bride and bridegroom reached the church, where a solemn mass was celebrated. Then a priest handed the wedding-rings, which lay upon the altar, to the Bishop, who blessed them, and, after a long address, gave them to the Duke. The latter placed one of them on the bride's finger, while he himself received the other from Ludovico. After a solemn *Te Deum* several of the nobles were knighted by the newly married Duke. Finally the procession wended its way back to the Castle in the same order in which it had come.

But in spite of all these manifestations of good-will to the young Duke, Ludovico retained the management of state affairs in his own hands, and only allowed the merest pittance for the maintenance of the ducal household. He gave important offices to his adherents and made himself loathed by his system of oppression. Not only did he take upon himself the command of the army, but he seized upon the ducal treasure and disposed of the annual revenues. His sovereignty, indeed, was supreme, and Giovanni Galeazzo and his young wife were repressed in every way. Isabella, who was a girl of spirit, could not brook this humiliating treatment, and sent the following appeal to her father, Alfonso :

" It is now several years, my father, since you arranged for me an alliance with Giovanni Galeazzo, with the idea that he should, on reaching a proper age, govern his States as his father Galeazza, his grand-father Francesco, and his ancestors, the Visconti, have done before him. He has now attained the requisite age, and is already a father ; yet his authority has been completely stolen from him. Only with difficulty can he obtain the necessaries of life from Ludovico and his ministers. Ludovico manages everything as he pleases, decides upon war or peace, makes laws, confers diplomas, exempts from taxes, imposes rates,

distributes favours, appropriates treasures—all according to his pleasure. We, on the other hand, deprived
of all assistance, and without money, lead the life
of private persons; Giovanni Galeazzo does not
appear as the Lord of the State, but Ludovico stations
the prefects in the fortresses, surrounds himself with
soldiers, augments the Council, and usurps all the
exclusive privileges of the ruler. Not long ago he
became the father of a son, who, according to the
popular belief, is destined to be Count of Pavia, and
later to succeed as Duke. Meanwhile, the mother
is honoured as though she were the Duchess. We
and our children are despised, and are indeed not
without risk to our lives under his rule, so that one
day, in order to bring to an end the hatred which is
openly and on all sides manifested to us, we may be
swept out of the way, and I can already imagine
myself an inconsolable and deserted widow. And
yet I still feel in me courage and strength. The
people love and sympathise with us, while they hate
and abhor our tyrant, who has sucked their blood in
order to satisfy his avarice. But I bow beneath the
unequal weight, and submit to the ignominy which is
laid upon us.

" It thou has any bowels of compassion, if thou
dost cherish a vestige of affection for me, if my tears
can move thee, if there is in thy heart a spark of
generosity, so let me entreat thee to free thy daughter
and thy son-in-law from cruel bondage, insults, and
death, and raise them to the throne. But, carest
thou nothing about our fate, better would it be for
me to take my own life than that I should continue to
bear the yoke of tyranny and suffer every reverse
under the eyes of my rival."

On receiving this epistle Alfonso was filled with a
mighty anger against Ludovico. He went to his
father, Ferrante, and told him what disgrace had

ALFONSO D'ESTE, DUKE OF FERRARA, LAST HUSBAND OF
LUCREZIA BORGIA.
Dosso Dossi (Uffizi Gallery, Florence).

PIETRO LUIGI FARNESE, DUKE OF PARMA, SON OF CARDINAL ALES-
SANDRO FARNESE, AFTERWARDS POPE PAUL III. BORN 1490,
ASSASSINATED 1547. FATHER OF CARDINAL ALESSANDRO FARNESE,
JUN., BORN 1520, DIED 1589.
Titian (National Museum, Naples).

come upon the House of Aragon, urging him, with vehemence, to interfere on behalf of the young Duke.

Ferrante realised the extent of Ludovico's authority, and he thought that the matter would be more prudently settled by negotiation than by war. Cool and self-possessed, he awaited an opportunity for revenge. He never allowed himself to exhibit anger or displeasure, and appeared to disregard insults as though he had not understood them. Finally, he despatched two ambassadors to Ludovico, who received them with every appearance of amiability. They, with great moderation, explained to him that, his nephew having now attained a suitable age to undertake the government of Milan, King Ferrante begged that the sceptre of authority might be yielded to him. Ludovico, however, sent the messengers back to Naples without any decisive answer. Ferrante was informed by Isabella of the unsatisfactory result of the embassy, and he finally agreed with Alfonso that force would have to be employed before the young Duke could be restored to his rights.

CHAPTER IX

MEANWHILE, as we have already seen, Pope Innocent
VIII. had been gathered to his fathers, and Rodrigo
Borgia, as Alexander VI., was now occupying the
Papal Chair.

In 1493 King Ferrante prepared to take active
measures against Ludovico the Moor. He gave
command of the army to his son, Alfonso, who,
possessed of no small military skill, was only too
ready to undertake an expedition in defence of his
daughter's interests. Ferrante imagined that the
war would be but a trivial one, since its only object
was to place the rightful prince upon the throne, and
he knew that the people strongly disapproved Ludovico's behaviour to his nephew, the young Duke
Galeazzo. Alexander Sforza, the Duke's half-brother,
had visited Naples and assured the King that the
citizens were already ripe for revolt against Ludovico's
hated rule.

But Ludovico, through his spies, managed to keep
well abreast of Ferrante's plans, and made up his
mind to resist them at any cost. So astute a man

could not fail to realise that he had given his subjects
genuine cause for complaint. Taxation and all
manner of extortions, deprivation of property, banishment, insults, death, outrages, the promotion of
favourites of low degree, ingratitude for service
rendered, utter ruin for all whose riches excited his
avarice or against whom he bore a secret grudge—all
these were of constant occurrence, and caused him
to be hated by all. Now, when he was about to fight
in an unjust cause, Ludovico deemed it advisable
to obtain help from outside. France seemed to him
the most suitable source to which to appeal, for the
House of Anjou had never yet renounced her claim
to Naples. He therefore despatched the Count of
Belgiojoso to the Court of Charles VIII. to persuade
the King to act as his ally. The Count fulfilled his
mission with all the skill of an accomplished courtier ;
he interviewed all who were likely to have any influence
over their monarch, bribing some with gold and
others with promises of great possessions in Naples.
By this means he won over many of the nobles to
his side, among them Stephen de Vere, a former
Chamberlain of the King's, afterwards Seneschal
of Beaucaire, and Briçonnet, the financier. The
frivolous young King, secure in his shallow-pated
ignorance, airily consented to undertake the invasion
of Naples, " but there was none save himself and two
lesser folk who found it good." These two lesser
folk were Briçonnet and de Vere, who hoped by
means of the expedition to increase their possessions.
But those who had more at heart the welfare of their
King and country tried to discourage the undertaking.

Ludovico wrote a letter to Charles VIII., referring
to the friendly relations which had always existed
between France and the House of Sforza and inviting
him to attempt the reconquest of Naples, which had
been illegally annexed by the House of Aragon. He
also represented that Naples was most admirably

situated for the headquarters of a campaign against the Turks, since a fleet could easily be equipped and an army collected Promising to support the French with arms, money, horses, and soldiers, he conjured the King not to refrain from an undertaking which would have the countenance of all the Princes in Italy, to say nothing of Heaven itself. From Naples, he continued, it would be a light matter to attack the Ottoman Empire, conquer Jerusalem, and win everlasting fame. " All the thousands banished from their country by the despot Ferrante cry to thee for help, through thee they expect to be restored to their homes ; they call to thee for support with the same anguish with which the Patriarchs in limbo once looked to Christ for deliverance. Everything foretells victory ; thou hast nought to fear, either from without or within, and, if anything deters thee, remember that I will see that thou art obeyed, followed, and received by all with honour."

Charles, dull of wit, lazy, and yet boastful, began serious preparations for his invasion of Italy, after an arrangement had been made with Ludovico that the French army should be granted a free passage through Italy. Ludovico further undertook to furnish him with 500 lances and to allow them to equip as many ships at Genoa as they should find necessary ; he also agreed to provide Charles with a loan of 200,000 ducats upon his departure. On the other hand, the French King undertook to defend the dukedom of Milan and Ludovico's authority, to invest the town of Asti (the property of the Duke of Orleans), with a garrison of 200 lances, which should always be in readiness to fight for the House of Sforza, and also to bestow the princedom of Tarento upon Ludovico after the conquest of Naples.

This compact was secretly arranged, and when the rumour of the impending invasion spread and Ludovico was suspected of being in alliance with the

French, he feigned to be no less alarmed than the others at the prospect of the intruders' arrival.

The claims of the House of Anjou to Naples were as ill-founded as those of the House of Aragon. Both parties deduced their rights from a gift. In order to prove the validity of this gift, it had first to be settled whether the kings of Naples held their crown as vassals of the Holy See and whether the Pope could, under certain circumstances, again lay claim to it. It was presumed that the power with which one Prince had been endowed by another might, at will, be transferred to a third, and that only the consent of the Church would be necessary to render the transference valid.

If prescription of that which had been acquired by force or cunning could legalise its possession, then the House of Anjou had certainly the first claim to Naples, since it had governed that kingdom for almost two hundred years. When, in 1442, Renatus was driven from Naples by Alfonso of Aragon, the kingdom was lost to the House of Anjou, and through several successive legacies its rights were inherited by Louis XI , who bequeathed it to his son Charles VIII.

On the other hand, exception might be taken to the claims of Ferrante. He derived them from Manfred, the natural son of Federigo II., and they were only transmitted to him through the female line. Ferrante, moreover, was himself illegitimate, though acknowledged by his father. But the same power which invested the House of Anjou with Naples had, on a later occasion, bestowed the same kingdom upon Alfonso, Ferrante's father. The feudal power of the Papacy, to which both sides appealed, had therefore to be regarded as the final arbiter.

Ferrante inherited the throne from his father Alfonso, and could consequently be regarded *de jure* and *de facto*, as the rightful king.

Charles VIII., who was anxious to be on good

terms with the Florentines, sought by promises and threats to turn them from their alliance with Ferrante. But they were reluctant to proclaim themselves definitely on his side, and their envoys, the Bishop of Arezzo and Piero Soderini, who were despatched to the French Court at Toulouse, expressed themselves so dubiously as only to excite suspicion.

Through de Briçonnet and the Seneschal Beaucaire, Charles sounded the ambassadors as to their intentions. The latter begged that he would not compel them to take part against Ferrante. The ruin of their State would profit him little, they said, while Ferrante was great and powerful, and enjoyed the Pope's support, and they would be subjugated before France could help them. Charles, who regarded this statement as a mere subterfuge, became furiously angry, and commanded the removal of all Florentines from his States, as well as the confiscation of their property. Fortunately, however, he allowed himself to be dissuaded from such an extreme measure.

In order to further his ends, he overwhelmed the brothers Lorenzo and Giovanni de' Medici with favours, hoping that they would overthrow Piero, who was unpopular. They themselves were much loved in Florence for their generosity and amiability, while Piero, by his pride and ambition had aroused universal dislike.

Both brothers, rendered arrogant by the King's marks of favour, openly boasted of their power and influence, and persuaded many of the citizens to join their party. But the gravest suspicions were aroused when d'Aubigny stayed in Florence on his return to France and was received by them with every demonstration of respect. Piero, under pretext that they were a danger to the State, had them arrested ; their goods were seized, and their speedy execution followed. But the Senate began to see through Piero's ambitious plans, and the people took up arms on Lorenzo's behalf. Piero now pretended that he meant to overlook the offence, being unwilling to shed the blood of a kinsman. They were, however, banished and forbidden to come within a twenty-mile radius of Florence. Thus was Florence divided into two factions.

Charles sent an embassy to Rome for the purpose of securing the sympathy of the new Pope, Alexander VI.; but the latter replied evasively, calling his attention to the fact that Naples was a fief of the Church, and that, in the event of a quarrel about it, it was the province of Rome to decide the affair. But when Charles sent a second embassy, the Pope's attitude seemed to have changed entirely, and he had gone over to the Neapolitan side. A match had been arranged between Sancia, the illegitimate daughter of Alfonso of Calabria and Jofré, then Alexander's youngest son. The King of Naples heaped favours upon the young couple, and the Pope was thus quite drawn over to the Neapolitan party. He now gave Charles to understand that the House of Aragon had already been enfeoffed three times by the Papal See, and that, if he had no better claim to advance, the right of the Aragons to Naples could not be disputed.

The other Powers, with the exception of Ercole of Ferrara, Cardinal Giuliano della Rovere (Alexander's implacable foe), and Lorenzo, son of Piero Francesco de' Medici, now showed a strong disposition to support the Pope. Ferrante of Naples was in high glee. "Be of good cheer," he wrote to his envoy in France, "for perfect harmony now reigns between me and the Pope."

But before Charles could set out on his campaign, he wanted to make sure of the friendship, or at least of the neutrality, of the other European Powers. His relations with Maximilian of Austria were, to say the least, unpleasant. Not only had Charles repudiated his betrothal to Maximilian's little daughter, Margaret, who was ignominiously sent back to Austria, but he had added insult to injury by marrying Anne of Brittany, the Emperor's affianced bride. Ambassadors were sent to the King of France demanding compensation for his offence, but the affair ended amicably, for every one was tired of war. It was arranged that Philip, Maximilian's son, should receive the part of Artois which Charles had annexed and which had already been made over to France as a portion of Margaret's dowry.

Comines, in his *Memoirs*, relates that he asked many doctors of theology whether Anne's marriage with Charles was valid, and that some gave answer in the affirmative, others in the negative. It seems, however, that neither this match nor that of Margaret, who afterwards married the Prince of Castile, turned out happily. Anne's three sons all died very young, and Margaret lost her husband in the first year of their wedded life. Shortly after his death she gave birth to a still-born son, " qui a mis en grande douleur les Roy et Reyne de Castile, et tout leur Royaume."

Amicable relations had also to be established between France and Ferdinand of Spain, who was a kinsman of the reigning House of Aragon in Naples. Ferdinand had once borrowed 100,000 ducats from Louis XI., giving him, as security, Roussillon and Perpignan. But when a few years later, he was prepared to pay back the money, Louis steadfastly refused to give up these two provinces. As soon, however, as Charles had decided on the Italian expedition, he sent envoys to Ferdinand announcing his readiness to restore them, and asking nothing but his friendship in return. The transfer really took place, and Ferdinand promised not to interfere in the affairs of the House of Aragon.

The Venetian response to Charles's request for help and advice was unsatisfactory. They could

THE TORTURE OF " THE QUESTION," COMMONLY APPLIED IN THE FIFTEENTH
CENTURY IN ROME.

From a fresco in the Church of San Pietro in Gessate.

not undertake to support him, they said, for they always had to be on their guard against Turkey; that it would be presumption on their part to offer advice to so wise a King, but that they were more disposed to help than to hinder him. With these evasive words Charles had to be content.

In August 1494 King Charles set out gaily, almost flippantly, on the great campaign which was to change the face of Europe. His first stopping-place was Lyons, where he tarried for several weeks, wasting his substance in riotous living. Cardinal Giuliano della Rovere and the Duke of Salerno, who had escaped from the snares of King Ferrante, hastened thither to persuade Charles to attack Naples. His sagacity soon perceived that he must turn for help to Stephen de Vere and Briçonnet rather than to the King. Their policy consisted of shameless flattery and indulgence, by which means they maintained a strong influence over the weak-minded Charles. The Duke represented the Italian invasion and the conquest of Naples as an undertaking to which the House of Anjou (whose claims devolved on Charles) was in honour bound. Thus the way was smoothed for Ludovico's ambassador, Galeazzo, brother of Count Cajazzo of San Severino, who shortly afterwards arrived. He was received by the King with the greatest affability and brilliantly entertained. Ludovico had won over the Genoese, who had formerly been attached to the House of Aragon. It was arranged that the Duke of Orleans should go with a fleet of 3,000 Swiss to Genoa, while d'Aubigny was to be sent to Milan with 200 lances and 3,000 Swiss But the King was undecided as to whether he should go backwards or forwards.

Comines observes that the cost of equipping the ships for Genoa was so great as to cripple the King's monetary resources. He continues. " Car, comme j'ai dit, il [Charles VIII.] n'estoit point pourvue,

NB

ne de sens, ne d'argent, n'y d'autre chose nécessaire
à telle entreprise. . . . Je ne veux point dire que le
Roy ne fust sage de son age ; mais il n'avait que
vingt et deux ans, ne faisoit que saillir du nid."

Ludovico, who was by this time extremely unpopular in Italy, did all in his power to urge the King
to set out. Finally Charles prepared to start, but
again wavered, and Comines was told that everything
was broken off. On the same day, however, the
King borrowed 500,000 ducats from a merchant in
Milan, for which Ludovico had to provide security.
Before this he had already borrowed 100,000 francs
from the Bank of Genoa, for which he had, in four
months, to pay interest amounting to 14,000 francs.
Ferrante sought by negotiations to hinder Charles's
advance towards Naples, and even volunteered to pay
him an annual tribute. Thereby, however, he only
served to confirm the King in his plan. These negotiations did not prevent Ferrante from making active
preparations for war. He equipped a fleet of forty
galleys and assembled a land force of 7,000. But
death suddenly freed him from his embarrassments
on January 25, 1494. Burchard relates that he had
become unwell at his country house of Trapergola,
and had therefore returned to Naples. In mounting
his horse he fell down unconscious, and the next
day passed away, *sine luce, sine cruce, sine Deo.* He
was seventy-one years of age.

Alfonso, Duke of Calabria, now succeeded to the
throne of Naples, and every one looked anxiously to
see what attitude the Pope would adopt towards
the new King, who did everything in his power to
propitiate him. Early in February Alexander warned
the French ambassadors against attacking Naples,
and also wrote a letter to Charles VIII. expressing
surprise that he should entertain hostile designs
against a Christian Power when a union between
all European States was necessary in order to thwart

the Turks. On May 7, 1494, Alfonso was crowned by the Cardinal of Monreale, and soon afterwards was celebrated the betrothal of Sancia of Aragon and the thirteen-year-old Jofré Borgia. Alexander exempted the new King from the annual tribute, and in return Alfonso invested the Pope's eldest son, Giovanni the Duke of Gandia, with the princedom of Tricaria and other crown lands, which yielded an annual income of 12,000 ducats. Neither was Cæsar forgotten: a considerable portion of crown land was assigned to him. The bride's dowry amounted to 200,000 ducats, and the alliance was celebrated by the most brilliant festivities, as if they wished to forget the danger that was threatening the country. But Alfonso was quite conscious of the gravity of the position. He determined to undertake the command of his troops himself, and entrusted that of the fleet to his brother Federigo.

On August 23, 1494, Charles left Vienna and advanced towards Asti. At Suza he was met by Galeazzo San Severino, who accompanied him to Turin. The Regent Bianca, widow of the Duke of Savoy, received him with astonishing splendour. De la Vigne, in his *Vergier d'honneur*, describes the magnificence of the display. Dazzled by the number and value of the diamonds worn by the Duchess and her suite, Charles was unable to refrain from borrowing them, upon which he immediately pawned them for 12,000 ducats. As Comines naïvely remarks : " Et pouvez voir quel commencement de guerre c'estoit, si Dieu n'eut guidé l'œuvre."

In Chien Charles stayed for several days, enjoying himself in his own fashion. Dramas of doubtful morality were performed in his honour, but the chief attraction seems to have been the charms of a certain Anna Solari (De la Vigne and Ségur).

Asti was the appointed meeting-place, and Ludovico Sforza, Ercole of Ferrara, and Guiliano della Rovere were there to greet the French King. Ludovico was accompanied by his wife Beatrice and fifty beautiful Italian ladies, who, moreover, were not troubled with many scruples of morality. , The King's weak brain was dazzled by the loveliness of these women, who were adorned in the richest manner and by no means sought to conceal their charms. They made their entry into the town in six carriages covered with gold cloth and red velvet and drawn by six-and-twenty horses. Charles, who had at first been inclined to harbour suspicions of Ludovico, changed his opinion in two days, for he was quite overwhelmed by the splendour of his reception.

King Alfonso had despatched two armies towards Charles. The one, led by his son and Virginio Orsini, was opposed by the tried and trusty d'Aubigny, a Scotchman by birth, and distinguished both for his bravery and his generalship. The other, which had embarked with the idea of conquering Genoa, was commanded by Federigo, Alfonso's brother. With the help of Flisco (Fiesco) and several disaffected Genoese, Federigo hoped to have little difficulty in effecting his object. But unfortunately for his plans, Louis of Orleans appeared at the crucial moment and drove back his troops. The cannon which the French had installed on their vessels, and which, up to that time, had not been used in Italy, contributed greatly to the victory. A great galley belonging to Comines, and furnished with heavy artillery, was seriously damaged. The Swiss, under the leadership of the Bailiff of Dijon, advanced towards the Neapolitans, who fled before them. Many prisoners were taken, but they received no further injury than, after the Italian custom, being stripped to their shirts and then set free. Among them was Fregoso, a natural son of Paul Fregoso, Cardinal-Archbishop and former Doge of Genoa.

The Swiss guards, who took the war seriously

however, plundered Rapallo and killed many of the inhabitants ; but when they brought their booty to be sold at Genoa, the Italians rose in revolt and several Swiss were slain. Order was restored by Adorno, who held the reins of government.

While Charles was at Asti he received news of the success of Louis of Orleans at Genoa. The outlook seemed promising when the King was taken dangerously, ill with a disease which, though called small-pox, was probably the result of his dissolute habits. He got better, however, and continued his way to Casale, the capital of Montferrat. Here he was heartily welcomed by the Margravine, and he did not neglect the opportunity of borrowing her jewels with the intention of pawning them in Genoa.

Chance favoured Charles in a surprising way. Don Ferrantino, at the head of the second division of the forces of his father, Alfonso, had advanced with his men as far as Ferrara, and was burning with anxiety to fight d'Aubigny. But his men lacked cohesion, being made up of soldiers from different Italian States who were, again, under the command of their own leaders ; moreover, the news of the French victory at Rapallo had discouraged the Italians   Although they exceeded the French in number, a council of war decided that it would be indiscreet to venture upon a battle. Orsini, in particular, was opposed to the idea of fighting, although Pescara and Trivulzio were of a different opinion. Subsequent events proved that d'Aubigny was right in supposing that Ferrantino's troops would soon be disbanded if left alone. The Colonna, who had always been rivals of the Orsini, declared themselves on the side of the French, seized upon Ostia, and summoned Charles to take possession of that important harbour.

The Pope thereupon withdrew the troops which he had sent to Ferrantino's help, while d'Aubigny was reinforced with fresh men. The favourable moment was gone; but Ferrantino would not yield, for he still reckoned on the support of the Princes of Romagna. Mordano, near Imola—a strong fortress—resisted, but the French stormed the town with incredible fury. The garrison—men, women and children—were all massacred, and when d'Aubigny entered he found nothing but the corpses of the inhabitants. Don Ferrantino then withdrew to Rome.

While at Casale Charles gave audience to Constantine Arianités, claimant to the crowns of Servia and Macedonia. He assured the King that European Turkey, weary of Bajazet's tyranny, was now ripe for rebellion. Ludovico, too, had approached Charles at Asti, and had, with much eloquence, expounded the same theory. "Quand vous me voudrez croire," he said, "je vous aiderai à vous faire plus grand que ne fut jamais Charlemagne, et chasserons ce Turc, hors de cet empire de Constantinople aisément, quand vous aurez ce Royaume de Naples."

Charles, who from the outset had cherished remarkable dreams of covering himself with glory by crushing the Turkish power, was encouraged and strengthened in his childish schemes by these words. He now proceeded to Pavia, where the luckless Gian Galeazzo, Ludovico's ill-treated nephew, was languishing in captivity. Ludovico was greatly alarmed when he heard that the King desired to speak with his cousin (the mothers of Charles and Galeazzo were sisters, Princesses of the House of Savoy), for he feared that the chivalrous instincts of France might be aroused at the sight of the unhappy Prince. The latter was only about twenty-five years old, but he had been a prisoner for ten years. His chief pleasure lay in the affection of his wife Isabella and his little son, for whom he pathetically entreated the French King's protection. Galeazzo's physician, Theodore of Pavia, was present at the interview, and Charles gathered, from his behaviour, that his patient was suffering from the effects of a slow poison. As Comines says, he would willingly have warned him, " mais il ne vouloit déplaire en rien au dit Ludovic." At a certain moment a secret door opened and the young Duchess, clad in deep mourning, entered. She threw herself at the King's feet, imploring him to protect her husband and pardon her father ; but Charles, though affected, answered that it was now too late to help her.

The poor young wife, with her little children, shut herself up like a prisoner in a room into which the light could not penetrate, and lay for a long time upon the hard ground.   Her rival, the gay Beatrice d'Este, could now for a short time enjoy her triumph.

Ludovico, now more than ever anxious to win the King's favour, provided him with gold and weapons and tried to urge him forward.   Charles soon left Pavia for Piacenza, but no sooner had he arrived there than news reached him of Galeazzo's death.[1]   This event caused him considerable remorse, for he was conscious of having done nothing to improve his fortunes. He was also mistrustful of Ludovico, who hastened to Milan to make arrangements for the coronation of Galeazzo's little son.   Meanwhile Charles had the obsequies of his cousin celebrated in the most lavish and magnificent manner, inviting the whole of Piacenza to take part in them.

From Asti Comines was sent with letters of recommendation from the Duke of Milan to his ambassador in Venice.   He received a monthly salary of 100 ducats, together with a beautiful dwelling and three gondolas. The Venetian envoy in Milan was treated with equal consideration, only, as Comines ingenuously remarks, there no gondolas were placed at his disposal, because in Milan it was customary to use horses.   He journeyed through Brescia, Verona, Vicenza, and Padua, and

[1] There is good reason to suppose that Ludovico hastened his end by poison.

was everywhere received with the greatest respect, and worthily entertained. Everything was arranged for him, but, alas! no one thought of paying the minstrels and tambourine players, so that the poor Comines was not much the gainer.

As Comines approached Venice he was received by twenty-five nobles richly clad in red silk. They escorted him to the Church of St. Andrew, where the other nobles and the ambassadors from Milan and Ferrara were already assembled. Afterwards he was taken on board a luxuriously equipped boat, much larger than an ordinary gondola and capable of holding about forty people. To Comines was given the place of honour between the two envoys, and away they went down the Grand Canal, "the most beautiful street in the world." He was greatly impressed by the splendour and beauty of the houses which they passed, many of them decorated with marble and precious stones. It was the richest town that he had ever seen, and, as he remarks, the best governed.

Escorted by fifty nobles, Comines visited the Cloister of the Black Monks of San Giorgio, where an apartment was assigned to him. The next day he appeared before the Signor and delivered his credentials to the Council, which was assembled under the presidency of the Doge. The latter (Barbarigo) is described as a gentle, wise, and amiable old man, with a wide understanding of Italian affairs. His palace was very beautiful, and contained four large and richly gilded halls of marble, though the court itself was small. From it Comines could hear mass being sung at St. Mark's, the richest Cathedral in the world, full of marvellous treasures and precious stones.

For eight months Comines stayed in Venice, enjoying himself at the public expense. He has nothing but praise for the good management and sagacity of the Seignory. When the latter heard of Galeazzo's death they asked Comines whether Charles VIII. would be inclined to take up the cause of the little five-year-old heir. But Comines thought it unlikely on account of the friendly relations between the French King and Ludovico, who, regardless of the child's claims, was proclaimed Duke at Milan. In order to gain this end, he had invited the French to Italy, knowing that the Italian Powers would never allow this usurpation.

It was not long before the deference which the Italians had, at first, accorded the French, diminished, for their rapacity and unseemly conduct were making them universally unpopular. The French now found themselves in considerable embarrassment. Their treasury was completely exhausted, and Briçonnet advised a return to France. But this would have been no easy matter. At the same time the King was assured by the brothers Medici, and others, that Florence was waiting open-armed to receive him. Ludovico, too, was ready with promises of help. Nevertheless Charles, in order to continue the march, was obliged to raise 150,000 gold ducats upon his crown lands, and the clergy advanced 15,000 on the understanding that the freedom of the Gallican Church should be granted in Rome. While these transactions were going on, Pope Alexander sent a message to Charles forbidding him to set foot in the papal province. But the King replied that he had long since taken a vow to make a pilgrimage to the Apostle Peter at Rome, and that he must fulfil it even at the risk of his life.

This command of the Pope only served to rouse the French spirit, and it was now merely a question as to which route the army should take Venice, to the north-east, was neutral; the Pope had finally decided to oppose the French; in Florence opinion was divided—the citizens were prepared to welcome

Charles and were confirmed in their views by Savonarola's predictions that a scourge should chastise Italy.
Piero de' Medici, on the other hand, was in league
with Naples. It was finally decided to take the
rough and stormy route of the Via de Pontremoli,
rather than the shorter and more convenient one
through Bologna and Rimini. They would thus
avoid Prince Ferrantino of Naples, who had been sent
by Alfonso to hold the Romagna. The Duke of
Montpensier had orders to move towards Pontremoli
with the vanguard, while Charles soon followed with
the remaining troops.

When the French reached the Florentine fortress
of Tivizzano, the garrison opposed them with decision.
But the Marquis of Malaspina, who knew the neighbourhood well, offered himself as guide and disclosed
the weakest point in the fortress. After a vigorous
attack, the Duke of Montpensier and his troop
gained an entrance and slew the whole garrison
with great slaughter. Little was gained, however,
by this cruelty, for the French progress was checked
by the impregnable fortresses of Sarzana and Pietra
Santa. Both these places, on their steep heights,
needed only to keep their gates shut to render further
advance impossible. The French were thus placed in
an awkward plight, for to besiege the fortresses would
have been extremely risky, owing to the difficulty of
obtaining provisions in that sterile district. People
were justified in thinking that Ludovico had enticed
Charles into a trap.

The situation was saved by the discord just then
prevailing in Florence. Piero de' Medici, hated for
his extortions and misrule, thought to escape from
the atmosphere of distrust which surrounded him
by imploring the protection of Charles. He was
evidently influenced by the example of his father
Lorenzo, who, under similar circumstances, had appealed to the Neapolitan Court. But Piero was cast in

a less heroic mould; he lacked both courage and skill to carry through his enterprise, and only succeeded in getting permanently banished from Florence.

From Empoli Piero despatched the following letter to the Government :

" I will not try to justify my hasty departure, for I think it no wrong to adopt a measure which, in my humble opinion, is not only calculated to restore peace to my native town, but is also attended with less difficulty and danger for the State and its inhabitants (myself alone excepted) than any other. I have decided to go in person to his Most Christian Majesty in the hope of mitigating the displeasure which the town has been obliged to cause him by fulfilling her contracts with other States. For, it seems to me that this is the only respect in which the King desires a change. As I have been hitherto regarded as the cause of his ill-will, I will either justify my conduct or at least attract his revenge to my person rather than to the State. My family has already often set the example of such a sacrifice, but I hold myself under a deeper obligation than any of my forefathers, because I, more than any of them, have been honoured beyond my merits. The less I deserve the distinctions which have fallen to my share, the more I consider myself bound to carry out my present plan. Neither difficulty nor expense, nay, not even life itself, do I esteem ; but I would willingly sacrifice myself for each of you in particular, much more for the whole Republic. On this occasion I shall probably give you a proof of my sincerity, for I shall either return with good news for you and the Republic, or I shall surrender my life in the attempt to serve you. By the love and loyalty which you owe to the ashes of my father, the great Lorenzo, and by the kindness you have ever displayed towards me, I conjure you to remember me in your prayers. Also, if it be the will of Providence that I should not return to you, I commend to your care my brothers and children. To-morrow I set out on my journey from here.

" PIERO DE' MEDICI.

"GIVEN AT EMPOLI,
  " *October* 26, 1494."

From Empoli Piero proceeded to Pisa, whence he sent a message to the Neapolitan envoy in Florence to the effect that, though his devotion to the House of Aragon never failed, he lacked friends, money, and credit to continue a war in which he had been involved through friendship for the royal House of Naples.

On October 30 Piero arrived at Pietra Santa, where he heard that Orsini, who had been sent to reinforce Sarzana, had been attacked and defeated by Montpensier—a circumstance of trifling importance considering the strength of the two fortresses. But Piero was afraid to enter the camp of Sarzana without a letter of recommendation from the French King. Briçonnet and de Piennes were despatched to meet him, but when Piero arrived at the camp he completely lost his head, and knelt, cowed and discomfited, before the King, whose reception of him was cool and a trifle contemptuous. The French demands were by no means modest, but Piero agreed meekly to all that was proposed. Sarzana, Pietra-Santa, Librafratta, Pisa, and Livorno were to be surrendered until the conquest of Naples should be completed, and Florence was to be the pledge of reconciliation. Comines tells us that the French were highly amused and astonished that Piero should concede so much more than they had ever expected.

The Florentines were furious when they heard of Piero's irresponsible folly. " It was time," said Piero Capponi, in the Council of November 1, " to shake off this baby government." They sent an embassy of five citizens, headed by Savonarola, to Charles, hoping to obtain some amelioration of the hard conditions. But neither their representatives nor the threats and predictions of Savonarola could move the King. From the demeanour of the envoys Piero could see how greatly the Florentines were offended by his action. He therefore begged his kinsman Paolo Orsini, the commander of the Florentine army, to follow him to Florence with as large a troop as he could muster. On November 9, he presented himself, with a considerable retinue, at the Town Hall, intending to summon a general parliament and take the government into his own hands; but his entry was prevented by Corsini, Nerli, and others, who hurled the most bitter reproaches at his head. Piero, disconcerted, retired to his palace, and, arming himself and his servants, begged Orsini to defend him from his enemies. But the whole of Florence was in rebellion. Everywhere sounded the cry, "Liberty! liberty! down with the Balls!"[1] Even the sight of Piero's brother, the popular Cardinal de' Medici, produced no effect upon the excited crowd. The very street-boys assailed Piero with stones and hisses; the tumult became more and more violent, until he saw that all hope was gone, and that nothing remained but the memories of the family. The magnificent works of art collected by Lorenzo in the garden of San Marco, which had been for the Florentines a kind of Art Academy, were all stolen or destroyed. Even the very trees which he had planted were demolished.

Charles VIII., meanwhile, was moving onwards. From Sarzana he went to Pisa by way of Lucca, where he refused to see Cardinal Piccolomini, who had been sent by the Pope to try to make terms with him. On November 9 Charles entered Pisa, where

[1] The Medici arms.

the citizens hailed him as their deliverer. They had suffered oppression from the Florentines for no less than eighty years, and consequently hated them with a deadly hatred. A mighty throng advanced to meet the French King, entreating him to relieve their city from the yoke of Florence.

A certain Rabot, Councillor of the Dauphiné Parliament, advised Charles to grant the request of this ill-treated people. The King, who certainly had no power to bestow freedom upon the Pisans, nevertheless obligingly promised them his protection. Rabot, amid many demonstrations of joy, communicated his answer to the people. In their excitement they hastened to the Arno Bridge, where stood the statue of a colossal lion erected in token of the Florentine supremacy; this they threw down and raised in its place an image of the King, who, sword in hand, was mounted on a horse which trampled with its hoof the overthrown lion.

On the same day were banished the Florentine authorities, who were only saved from actual ill-treatment out of respect for Charles. The King's untimely complaisance was to result in a bloody strife, which disturbed the peace of Italy for many a weary year.

D'Aubigny was meanwhile gaining important successes in the Romagna. He had taken several fortresses and compelled the bold Catherine Sforza, widow of the late governor of Imola and Forli, to renounce her alliance with the Pope. He then advanced to Faenza with the object of attacking Ferrantino, but the latter was so much terrified at this proceeding that he beat a hasty retreat to Cesena. There he received news of the surrender of Sarzana and the Florentine rebellion. No longer feeling safe, he marched towards Rome, but his obvious alarm had weakened confidence in his power to such an extent that serious resistance seemed improbable.

Charles only stayed in Pisa a few days and then continued his way towards Florence. At Empoli he received disquieting news of the rebellion of the Florentines and the banishment of the Medici. Florence, it is true, was prepared for the defence, but, at the same time, she did not omit to send ambassadors to the French King, with costly presents for his propitiation.

CHAPTER X

ON November 17, 1494, the French army entered
Florence. Charles VIII., welcomed by the shouts
of the people, rode under a rich canopy borne by
elegant youths of noble descent. " The monarch's
appearance was in strange contrast with that of
the numerous and powerful army behind him. He
seemed almost a monster, with his enormous head,
long nose, wide, gaping mouth, big, white, purblind
eyes, very diminutive body, extraordinarily thin
legs and misshapen feet. He was clad in black
velvet, with a mantle of gold brocade ; bestrode a
tall and very beautiful charger, and entered the
city riding with his lance levelled—a martial attitude then considered as a sign of conquest. All
this rendered the meanness of his person the more
grotesque "[1]

[1] Villari

THE TRIAL OF ST. CATHERINE.

With him was the imperious and warlike Cardinal della Rovere (afterwards Pope Julius II.), who was filled with the ambition to depose Alexander VI., as a simoniacal usurper.

Having been escorted by the Seignory, amid deafening cries of " Viva Francia ! " from the excited populace, to the Church of Santa Maria del Fiore, where mass was celebrated, Charles was installed with much ceremony in the luxurious palace of the Medici. The owner of the said palace, Piero de' Medici, had meanwhile arrived in Venice, where he encountered Comines and poured out his woes to him To such a pass had things come, he said, that he had actually been refused credit for a piece of cloth (to make clothes for himself and his brothers), worth about one hundred ducats. This was indeed a humiliation for a member of the rich and prosperous house of Medici.

King Charles remained for several days in Florence, enjoying the festivities which were arranged for him. A representation of the Annunciation was given in the Church of San Felice, with such brilliant success that the King begged for a repetition of it. Each day was filled with pageantry and feasting, and at night the city was so brilliantly illuminated that it seemed like midday

But this pleasant state of affairs was not to last. Philippe de Brienne, who was staying with Lorenzo Tornabuoni, a friend and kinsman of Piero de' Medici's, used all his influence to persuade the King to recall Piero. This Charles was not disinclined to do, and an invitation to return was sent to him, with the assurance that he should be reinstated in his former dignities. Piero, however, who received the letters while in Venice, was misguided enough to ask advice of the Council; the latter, who were by no means anxious for the complete restoration of peace in Florence, warned him against placing too much reliance on the King's promises, and gave orders

OB

that he should be carefully watched in order to prevent his leaving the town.

When the news of Piero's recall spread through Florence, the people fell into a state of tremendous excitement, which was increased by the French King's declaration that he would establish a new constitution and appoint the Seignory himself. The citizens, goaded to rebellion, protested that the town would defend herself to the bitter end rather than consent to lose her freedom. The people thronged round the palace, and fighting would undoubtedly have begun there and then if a few of the French leaders, combining with some members of the Seignory, had not interfered. Nevertheless, the French pride had received a severe blow, and they realised that Florence was not to be conquered by entering it " chalk in hand and lance to hip."[1]

The Seignory took advantage of the opportunity to try to abate the King's unreasonable pretensions, and soon the terms of the agreement were settled. Charles was to receive the title of Restorer and Protector of the Liberty of Florence, with the right to hold the fortresses for two years, on condition that they should be restored directly the war was ended; the Florentines were also to pay him a large sum of money, but a fresh dispute arose as to the amount. Finally, Charles ordered his secretary to read his conditions aloud, declaring that he would yield no further. When the magistrates again refused to accept them the King, in anger, exclaimed: " Then we will sound our trumpets ! " Thereupon the capable, energetic Capponi seized the document, tore it up, and made his famous reply: " Then we will ring our bells." These decisive words were not without their effect upon Charles, who realised the undesirability of a fight with the Florentines.

---

[1] The French made chalk-marks on the houses they intended to occupy.

Capponi, who had left the hall in dudgeon, was recalled, and the King, who had known him personally as an envoy to the French Court, called out facetiously: " Ah, Ciappon, Ciappon, voi siete un mal Ciappon ! " Thus, thanks to Capponi's prompt action, a compromise was made without much difficulty.

The Florentines bound themselves to pay 120,000 ducats, in three instalments ; they were to change their coat-of-arms for that of the French King. The latter, in return, took them under his protection and bound himself not to retain the fortresses for more than two years, and, if the Neapolitan expedition ended before that time, to give them up without delay. The Pisans were to be pardoned as soon as they returned to their old allegiance to Florence ; the decree putting a price on the heads of the Medici was to be revoked, but the estates of Giuliano and Giovanni were to remain confiscated until all Piero's debts were paid, and Piero himself was not to come within two hundred miles of Florence. After this agreement had been drawn up in official form, the contracting parties met in the Church of Santa Maria del Fiore, November 26, 1494, and took a solemn oath of observance.

On November 28, stimulated by the warnings of Savonarola, the King, to the unspeakable joy of the citizens, left Florence for Siena. Among the many causes of grievance against the French was the plunder of the splendid palace in which they had been so lavishly entertained. Even the King himself had not thought it beneath his dignity to make off with objects of the greatest value, among them an intaglio representing a unicorn, estimated by Comines to be worth about 7,000 ducats. The officers, nobles, and common soldiers busied themselves in the same way, and shamelessly took possession of everything that tempted their greed.

At Siena Charles stayed several days, enjoying the

festivities inaugurated in his honour and indulging his propensity for amorous adventures. His further progress was not without danger, for his soldiers were exposed to great privation on the bare and frozen fields. Comines wrote to the King that Alfonso was about to establish himself at Viterbo, while his son Ferrantino was to defend Naples. He was thus protected in the rear by Rome and the Orsini possessions. But Cardinal Riario, who was in Viterbo and in league with the Colonna, surrendered the town to Charles. Fortune favoured the French; all the fortified places in the neighbourhood of Viterbo yielded, and even as they journeyed through the Orsinsi domain they met with no resistance.

From Brazzano, one of the largest of the Orsini towns, where the French army had found a plentiful supply of food, the King despatched Cardinal Riario to Ostia, a place of great importance under the dominion of the Colonna Through the quarrels of the two houses of Orsinsi and Colonna Rome was divided into two factions, and, according to Comines, it was only this constant strife and ill-will that prevented the States of the Church from being the happiest States on earth.

Before Charles's entry into Viterbo he had sent envoys to Rome in order to negotiate with Pope Alexander VI., whose friendship he considered would be worth an army to him. The Pope, who had let Ferrantino and his troops into the capital by night, dismissed the envoys, but retained Cardinal Ascanio Sforza, brother of the Duke of Milan, and Prospero Colonna as hostages.

More and more were the French spreading themselves over the papal domains. As the Pope's mistress, Giulia Farnese, her sister Girolama, and Madonna Adriana were going to visit Cardinal Farnese in Viterbo, they fell into the hands of a body of French scouts under the captaincy of d'Allègre. They and

their suite were taken captive to Montefiascone, and
when the captain discovered their identity, he placed
their ransom at 3,000 ducats, at the same time informing King Charles of the affair.   The latter,
however, refused to see them.

Alexander was filled with anxiety upon hearing
of this adventure and begged Cardinal Ascanio to
intercede on behalf of the captives.   He also wrote
to Galeazzo of San Severino, who was accompanying
the King to Siena, and who, anxious to please the
Pope, urged Charles to release them.   The King
complied, and sent the ladies, with an escort of 400
Frenchmen, to the gates of Rome.   The Pope, it is
said, went to meet them arrayed in the most festive
lay attire, much to the amusement of the people.
Ludovico reproached Cardinal San Severino and
Monsignore Ascanio for surrendering them, for, since
these beautiful women were " the heart and eyes "
of the Pontiff, " they would have been the best whip
for compelling him to do everything that was wanted
of him ; for he could not live without them."

Charles rejected Alexander's request for an armistice
for himself and Alfonso, and sent envoys to negotiate
with him.   But the Pope, instead of listening to their
proposals, had them arrested, though he very soon
released them.   He was indeed in a vacillating temper,
and " grew more helpless from hour to hour."   At one
moment he wanted to defend himself, the next to
come to terms ; then, again, he thought of leaving
the city.   On December 18 Burchard relates that
" everything in the Vatican down to the bedding and
table service, was packed for flight."[1]

On December 17 the French took possession of
Civita Vecchia, and on the same day the Orsinsi went
over to the French King and admitted him to their
Castle of Bracciano.   After much wavering, the Pope
decided to give up opposing Charles and to allow

[1] Pastor.

him to enter the city. During Christmas night three French envoys had arrived in Rome, and their retinue calmly installed themselves in the chapel in the places reserved for the prelates. Burchard, Prefect of the Ceremonies, was anxious to turn them out; but the Pope, in terror, exclaimed: "You will cost me my head, let the French put themselves wherever they please!"

After considerable difficulty, the Pope and the King came to an understanding. Charles promised to respect Alexander's rights, both temporal and spiritual, and the whole of the city on the left bank of the Tiber was given up for the occupation of the French troops.

On the last day of the year 1494 Charles made his formal entry into Rome. At the Porta del Popolo the keys of all the city gates were delivered over to the King's Grand Marshal It is said that the entry of the troops lasted from three o'clock in the afternoon till nine in the evening—a sight witnessed by mighty throngs of spectators. Cardinals Ascanio Sforza and Giuliano della Rovere rode beside the King, and many Italian nobles and generals were conspicuous among the French nobility. The imposing procession struck terror into the hearts of the Romans, who were particularly impressed by the weight and size of the bronze cannon. The Pope himself was so much alarmed and unnerved that, notwithstanding the King's assurance that he should be treated with respect, he had fled to the Castle of Sant' Angelo. The Cardinals, in particular Riario and Ascanio, urged Charles to depose him and consent to a new papal election. Twice were cannon pointed towards the castle, but "tousjours le Roy par sa bonté y resista."

During the first days of the French invasion a number of houses were plundered by the soldiers, and several inhabitants suspected of hostility to Charles were murdered. The home of Vannozza was ruthlessly ravaged ; some of her servants were ill-treated, and she herself exposed to coarse insults. One can imagine her feelings at being subjected to the affronts of insolent soldiers, while her treasures, the result of long saving, were plundered beneath her very eyes. Her first impulse was to hasten to the Pope to beg him to have the French quarters burned down, but she was prevented by the reflection that this might lead to the complete downfall of the Pope and his house.

At last a compromise was made. The Pope agreed to yield Civita Vecchia and other strongholds of the States of the Church to Charles until he had conquered Naples. The helpless Djem, too, was to be delivered over to the French, though Alexander was to retain the 40,000 ducats which Bajazet annually paid as pension for his brother. Cæsar Borgia, "who seemed to have been born only that there might be in the world one man wicked enough to carry out the designs of his father, Alexander,"[1] was to accompany Charles to Naples as hostage.

The sudden appearance of Djem upon the scene may perhaps require some explanation. He was the son of Mohammed, the conqueror of Constantinople, and brother of Bajazet, the reigning Sultan. Although younger than the latter, he far surpassed him in intellect and courage. Supported by a large party, he revolted against his brother. A bloody fight ensued in which Djem was worsted and obliged to flee. At first he sought shelter with the Knights of St. John at Rhodes, but the Grand Master was base enough to have him arrested and, later on, for greater security, delivered up to Pope Innocent VIII., who kept him in the greatest subjection. Bajazet did all he could to win the Pope's favour, and even sent him the Holy Spear which was supposed to have

[1] Guicciardini.

pierced the body of Christ. He also undertook to
pay an annual sum of 40,000 ducats for the maintenance of his brother, who for the rest, lived quite
pleasantly at Rome during the last years of Innocent VIII. and the first of Alexander VI.   He took
part in all the papal festivities, and when he rode
with the Duke of Gandia, the latter always treated
him with the greatest consideration.

When Charles VIII. was preparing for his journey
to Naples, which was to be followed by the more
important oriental enterprise, it was understood that
Djem had instigated a rebellion against Bajazet.
But the farther Charles advanced, the more did
Alexander realise the impossibility of resisting him,
and he decided, together with Alfonso, to enter into
negotiations with the Sultan.   Two envoys—Camillo
Pandone and Giorgino Bucciardo—were therefore
despatched as apostolic ambassadors to Constantinople.
They met with a favourable reception, but, as Bucciardo was returning to Rome in company with an
envoy from the Sultan, they were shipwrecked between
Sinigaglia and Ancona, and completely plundered by
Giovanni della Rovere, Lord of Sinigaglia. In this
way they lost the 50,000 ducats which the Sultan was
sending to the Pope, as well as all their important
papers.   They were then set free, but, in spite of the
Pope's appeal to the Venetians, who owned the control
of the Turks in the Adriatic, the money was never
restored, and the papers were handed over to King
Charles, who was still in Florence, by della Rovere,
the Pope's enemy. There were five letters from
the Sultan to Alexander, one of them containing an
offer of 300,000 ducats and the holy seamless robe of
Christ in return for the death of his brother Djem.

Although the envoy had lost these letters he had
not forgotten their contents, which he was able to
impart to Alexander VI. The offer of so considerable
a sum, as well as the desire to thwart the French King's

THE MARTYRDOM OF ST. SEBASTIAN.

Pinturicchio (Borgia Apartments, the Vatican).

plans, must have been a great temptation to the Pope to take Djem's life. "He knew the secret of a slow poison[1] devoid of taste and smell, and resembling powdered sugar in appearance, with which he could easily effect his object." Djem, who, with a sum of 2,000 ducats, was delivered over to Charles, already bore death in his heart. In bidding farewell to Alexander and Cæsar, he thanked them in touching words for their kindness, and begged them to recommend him to the King's favour. This recommendation was quite unnecessary, for it was to Charles's interest to keep him alive. Nevertheless, on February 25 the unfortunate man died, greatly to the satisfaction of Bajazet, who, it is said, promptly handed over the blood-money. The statement is, however, disputed.

Paul Jovius, Guicciardini, and Marino Sanuto all speak of the popular suspicions that Alexander VI. was responsible for Djem's death. On the other hand, Burchard, whose testimony is worthy of credit, simply writes that Djem died after having eaten "something that did not agree with his stomach"[!] Another contemporary biographer asserts that he died from rheumatism, increased by the neglect of the French King His physician appears to have ascribed his death to catarrhal affection of the chest,[2] and the same cause is mentioned in a letter from the Venetian Government to their ambassador at Constantinople. The writer continues: "He died a natural death, that is very certain."[3] But the

---

[1] Probably a cumulative poison was meant.

[2] No reliance whatever can be placed upon the evidence of a physician at this period, more especially when he may have been an interested witness,

[3] See l'Epinois, article on "le Pape Alexander VI." *Revue des Questions Historiques*, April 1881.

Pastor (vol. v p 465) gives additional evidence in favour of Alexander's innocence. Nevertheless, the damaging fact remains that

circumstances of the death were less well known then than they are now.

When the contract with Charles had been, signed, Alexander ventured to emerge from the Castle of Sant' Angelo, and a meeting took place between him and the French King in the garden of the papal palace.   Extreme amiability prevailed at this interview, and they vied with one another in the display of politeness.   Having embraced affectionately, the problem arose as to which could remain longer with uncovered head.   The Pope solved it by reaching forward for the royal head-gear and obliging Charles to put it on while he put on his own.   Thus were both the august heads covered at one and the same time.   It is noteworthy that Charles kissed neither the hand nor the feet of the Pope.   No doubt the latter had arranged for the meeting to take place in the garden to prevent the need of demanding homage from the King.   At a second interview, however, Charles, as an obedient son of the Church, kissed the papal feet.

'Alexander, in his first fright, had given a kind of promise to bestow upon Charles the investiture of Naples ; but now he steadily refused to commit himself to anything definite, merely promising to bring the King's desire before the College of Cardinals.

During the month which Charles spent in Rome, he comported himself exactly as if he were the legal owner of the city, and kept the Palace of San Marco always filled with Cardinals and the highest officials of State.   His long stay there, however, instead of

---

Alexander applied to Bajazet for the sum he had offered to the Pope as a fee to be paid for the murder of Djem.   If the death had been due to natural causes, it may well be asked why Alexander demanded payment, since Djem was no longer in his custody when his death occurred.   We have always suspected that Cæsar, before his flight from the French camp, administered the poison or made arrangements for its administration.

injuring his cause, rather served to prepare his way
to Naples, for many of the Neapolitan nobles fell
away from Alfonso and declared themselves on the
French side.

The once bold and warlike Alfonso, his son Ferrantino, and the Orsini were now afraid to remain
in Rome. Alfonso indeed, fell into a state of deep
dejection. If the waves roared at night he imagined
that they were calling " France, France ! " and the
very trees and stones seemed to him to shriek the
hated name.

When the young Ferrantino got back to Naples
Alfonso deemed it advisable to abdicate the crown
(January 23), for, on account of his cruelties and
oppressions, he was so much detested that he felt
his throne tremble beneath him. This was not
surprising, for a more depraved and vicious tyrant
would have been hard to find. After signing his
abdication in favour of his son, he betook himself
in obvious terror, to the harbour, where four galleys,
laden with his treasures, awaited him. He was
conveyed safely to Mazara, in Sicily, a country seat
owned by the widowed Queen of Naples. Here he
was permitted to pass the last days of his wicked life
in peace and safety.

Guicciardini relates that the spirit of King Ferrante appeared three times to Alfonso's physician,
enjoining him to tell his son Alfonso that all resistance
against the French would be futile, as it was fore-
ordained that his family should die out after the
loss of his crown. The reason assigned for this
punishment was the cruelty of which the House of
Aragon, especially Ferrante, had been guilty towards
its subjects. The same historian further relates that
the forms of murdered ones often appeared to Alfonso
in his sleep, and that he dreamed that the people
were dragging him away to a bloody revenge.

Alfonso now led the life of a penitent and took a

vow of retirement from the world. He served God at all hours of the day and night, fasted, gave alms, and lived the life of a holy man. At last he was attacked by a painful disease, which he bore with great patience. He was about to retire to a cloister in Valencia when death overtook him. Comines closes with the words, " et selon sa grande repentance, il est à espérer que son âme est glorieuse en Paradis."

Ferrantino, who was a brave and promising youth, did his best to avert the dangers which surrounded him. He liberated the prisoners and restored their property, and granted extensive privileges to the people. But it was too late. If this leniency had been displayed earlier a reconciliation might have taken place, but now every one suspected that it was only the result of fear, and it therefore failed of its intended effect. Most of the nobles and office-holders had already joined the French party, and the prospect of Charles's approach filled Ferrantino with terror. Nevertheless, he assembled a considerable troop, of which the command was taken by Giacopo Trivulzio and the Count of Pitigliano, Niccolo Orsini. With this army he proceeded to San Germano, which, from its favourable position, served as the key to the kingdom, for on the one side it was obscured by steep mountains, and on the other by deep morasses, and in front by the river Garigliano. He might certainly have retarded the advance of the French had not the cowardice or treachery of his generals rendered resistance impossible.

Meanwhile Charles was drawing near to Naples. At Velletri it was discovered that the wily Cæsar Borgia, who had been sent by the Pope as a guarantee of good faith, had slipped away to Rome. This was looked upon as an omen of Alexander's faithlessness. Montefortino was stormed by the French on their march, and all the inhabitants slain. Valmontona, which belonged to the Colonna, was not attacked, but they planted their cannon in front of Monte San Giovanni, which, after a very heavy siege, was taken. Charles now approached San Germano, which was occupied by Ferrantino's troops. It seemed that now, if ever, the advance of the French might be checked; but before they reached San Germano Ferrantino had fled, with his disorganised forces, to Capua. Here his men were refused admission though he and a small retinue were allowed to enter. Ferrantino did not stay in Capua, but hastened on to Naples, where a rebellion had broken out. On his return he found that Virginio Orsini and the Count of Pitigliano were on their way to Nola. Both were taken captive with their men, and, though no injury was done them, they suffered considerable losses.

The instigator of this treachery was Trivulzio, who, immediately after Ferrantino's departure, had delivered the town to Charles and gone over to the French. The latter pursued Ferrantino on foot, and, in order to advance more rapidly, were obliged to leave their heavy artillery behind.

The surrender of Capua was soon followed by that of all the most important places in the kingdom, with the exception of Brindisi, Reggio, and Gallipoli. Everything conspired to favour the French progress; even the weather was mild and pleasant, and the meadows brilliantly green and covered with spring flowers. "In the short space of a few weeks," remarks Ricciardi da Pistoja, "the French conquered, as by a miracle, a whole kingdom, almost without striking a blow." "The French," said Alexander VI., "came in with wooden spears, and found they had nothing to do but the quartermaster's work of marking the doors with chalk."

Ferrantino, deserted by all, summoned the most important Neapolitan nobles, released them from their oath of fealty, and gave them permission to negotiate with Charles. Although this could not fail to make the people more favourably disposed towards him, it was obvious that his cause was hopeless. The Neapolitans lost no time in plundering his palace, and the lives of the royal family were no longer safe. Ferrantino managed to escape to Ischia, where he sought refuge in the castle for himself and family. With some reluctance, the governor consented to admit the King alone, probably with the intention of surrendering him to the French; but as soon as the door was opened Ferrantino drew a pistol from his cloak and shot him on the spot. The garrison, impressed by this practical demonstration of the King's courage and presence of mind, allowed him to take possession of the castle without resistance.

On February 22, 1495, Charles entered Naples in triumph. Never was a King more joyfully received, for the people believed that they were now delivered from the tyranny of the House of Aragon. Calabria and Apulia, as far as Brindisi, declared themselves for the French, and all the nobles of the kingdom came to Naples to pay homage to Charles.

In Ferrantino's flight to Ischia he had been accompanied by his uncle Federigo. The latter was afterwards summoned to Naples by Charles, who offered him a dukedom in France for his nephew if he would renounce his claim to the throne. In vain did Federigo beg that Ferrantino might receive a portion of Naples with the title of King, and also that he himself might retain his title and possessions. Charles would not yield, and, after a second futile interview, Federigo returned to Ischia.

Now began the siege of Castello dell' Nuovo, where Ferrantino had left a German garrison under command of the Marquis of Pescara. Chance at last brought the siege to an end, for the uninterrupted firing of ten days had not been able to force the place to surrender. A powder magazine exploded and caused terrible devastation; nevertheless, the garrison held out bravely. But misfortunes rarely come singly. The wind blew a lighted fuse into a storehouse of pitch, resin, and other inflammable materials. A terrible fire immediately arose, and streams of burning pitch and sulphur poured into the courtyards and ruins of the castle where lay the mutilated and wounded. Things seemed desperate, when Caspar, a captain who had already distinguished himself, came to the front. He forced Pescara to take flight, plundered the treasure, which he divided among his German soldiers, and then capitulated. On March 5, 1495, the trusty captain knelt on the breach, his hands extended, his white head bared, and begged for mercy. Castello dell' Nuovo could no longer hold out against the heavy artillery of the French, and surrendered on March 15

Charles now had himself crowned and took up his residence in the Castello Capuano. To the people he behaved kindly, reducing their taxes and freeing them from oppression, but he treated the nobles, especially the adherents of the House of Anjou, with great arrogance. The Aragons, particularly the Carafas, were dealt with more graciously. All offices and landed property were given to the French.

The self-respect of the Italians was wounded by the King's attitude, and they felt keenly the contempt shown to their nobles. While the French, who were unacquainted with the manners and customs of the country, managed everything as they pleased, it was only with difficulty that the Italians could approach the King. They were obliged to wait for hours in the anterooms of the French minister, and days at the King's door begging for an audience; and if, at last, after being exposed to the contemptuous glances of the courtiers, they reached the royal presence, fresh humiliations awaited them. They yearned, with a kind of home-sickness, for their former habits and customs, which were now so much despised by their conquerors. The very drama which the French introduced must have been a source of deep annoyance to the Italians, who were not spared the infliction of many insults from the stage. Indeed, the French, from the courtiers and generals down to the common soldiers, took no pains to hide their contempt for the cowardice of the Neapolitans.

Charles, however, troubled himself little about the humours of his new subjects. He was mightily enjoying the pleasures of the south, and spent much of his time at knightly tournaments and plays. Every morning he conscientiously performed his devotions at one of the churches of Naples, and he also devoted himself to the "healing" of epileptics and those afflicted with the King's Evil. According to the popular belief, the King of France had the power of healing these diseases by the laying on of hands. When he attended divine service in the Church of St. Januarius, the head of the saint and the reliquary in which his blood was preserved were displayed in the King's honour. The blood seemed at first as hard as stone, but when he touched it with a little silver staff it immediately became liquid. Charles and his suite were astonished, for this miracle was reputed to happen only at the prayer of the faithful and on rare occasions.

Ferrantino had meanwhile hastened to his father, Alfonso, whom he found at Messina surrounded by monks. They consulted as to the best means of banishing the French from Naples, and decided to turn for help to the Spanish King, Ferdinand the Catholic, a step which proved to be a fateful one for the Aragonese House of Naples and Sicily. Ferdinand was indisputably the heir of Alfonso I. of Naples and Sicily, whose crown was illegally transferred to his natural son Ferdinand I. Although the King of Spain had raised no claims at Ferrantino's coronation,

and had even given him his sister in marriage, it was supposed that this was only for lack of power to maintain them at that time. Without considering this danger, the King of Naples despatched his secretary to Madrid, where he was favourably received by Ferdinand the Catholic, and, although he had promised Charles not to interfere with his plans of conquest, it was represented that the treaty had only been concluded on the condition that the French King could exhibit legal claims to Naples.

The King of Spain equipped a large fleet and placed it under the command of "The Great Captain," Gonsalvo Fernandez Aguilar da Cordova, who without delay set sail for Sicily.

The other Powers also began to feel uneasy about the French King's conquests, and all sent ambassadors to Venice. The King of the Romans sent the Bishop of Trent, together with two knights and a doctor. They were well received, and allowed ten ducats a day, in addition to free lodging. Soon afterwards the Spanish ambassador arrived, followed by the Bishop of Como and Francesco Bernardino Visconti, both dispatched by Ludovico. All were treated in the same manner. At night they met in secret council, and the Milanese tried to deceive Comines about their mission. The latter, however, was well aware of their plans. He appealed to the great Council to repress a league which was being formed against Charles, but the Doge told him to give no heed to such rumours, since in Venice every one was free to speak as he liked, except concerning the affairs of the State

When the news of Charles's entry into Naples and the surrender of the fortresses reached Venice, Comines was summoned by the Doge. He found him ill, but able to communicate the tidings with an appearance of cheerfulness. None of those present were able to dissemble with the same ease, and many

PB

of them, by their dejected bearing, revealed the sadness of their hearts.

Comines immediately informed Charles of the situation, and begged him either to equip himself with money and supplies or to make up his mind to return to France as soon as possible after the fortified places had been provided with garrisons. He also advised the Duke of Orleans, who was at Asti, to prepare for the attack which would doubtless follow.

One morning Comines was summoned to appear before the Great Council. The Doge, upon his entry, informed him that Venice had concluded a league with the Pope, the King of the Romans, the King of Spain, and the Duke of Milan. Their object, he said, was threefold: (1) to protect the Christian States against the Turks, (2) to defend Italy against all outside attacks, and (3) to maintain and protect the Italian States. At the same time he commissioned Comines to acquaint Charles VIII. with the formation of the league. All present, we are told, bore their heads high and looked much more cheerful than they had done on hearing of the conquest of Naples.

Although they assured Comines that they bore no ill-will to the French King, their intention of banishing him from Italy and cutting off his return was obvious.

On the afternoon of the same day all the envoys of the League, in company with a band of musicians, went in gondolas past Comines's windows, but " the Milanese ambassador appeared not to recognise him." In the evening there was great jubilation, including fireworks, bonfires, and the roar of cannon. For three days Comines and his companions refrained from entering the town, so that no unseemly word was addressed to them. At the Pope's wish the League was made known publicly on Palm Sunday, and that not merely in Italy but also in Germany and Spain. All the Princes and envoys were to bear olive-branches in token of peace. In Venice a carpeted way led from the Doge's Palace to the end of the Place of San Marco, and a magnificent procession of magistrates, envoys, and their retinues passed along it. They were all magnificently attired in red velvet. Even the servants had received new garments, " mais elles estoient bien courtes," Comines quaintly remarks. At a column of porphyry the decisions of the League were read aloud. All who were present received the general absolution from the papal legate. Comines, though invited, was not present. During the short time which he afterwards remained in Venice he was treated as before, and when and he left for Florence, where he was to await the King, he was provided with a safe escort and the expenses of his journey as far as Ferrara were paid for him.

Charles was now in an unenviable position, for the Neapolitans, who had formerly welcomed him as their deliverer, loathed the French from the bottom of their hearts. The military heeded neither the laws nor the customs of humanity, and even the nunneries were not safe from the indulgence of their bestial sensuality. Charles realised that he must depend upon his own troops since Ludovico of Milan had failed him. But before leaving Italy he made another effort to persuade the Pope to confer upon him the investiture of Naples ; but Alexander, who had refused this before, was still less inclined to gratify him now.

Charles, however, could not bring himself to say good-bye to Naples without making a considerable parade of his departure.

On May 12 he made a brilliant entry into the town as King of France, Sicily, and Jerusalem. He was received by some of the most distinguished citizens, who presented their children to him, begging that he would grant them titles of nobility. Before the ceremonies were ended the King took a solemn oath binding himself to maintain the privileges of his new subjects, who, for their part, undertook to render him loyalty and obedience.

Charles now made preparations for departure. In spite, however, of the admonitions of Comines, he neglected to garrison Reggio in Calabria and other important towns, which had formerly adhered to France, but, since the formation of the League, had gone over to the House of Aragon.

As Governor of Naples Charles installed the Duke of Montpensier, "bon chevalier et hardy; mais peu sage, ne se levant qu'il ne fust midy," as Comines informs us. In Calabria the French were represented by d'Aubigny, a brave and canny Scot of the House of Stuart, who was appointed Chief Constable of the Kingdom, Count of Acri, and Marquis of Squillace. The other fortresses Charles confided to his most experienced generals. All of them proved faithful to their trusts except Gabriel de Montfaucon, a man held by the King in high esteem, but who surrendered the fortress of Manfredonia within four days, although they had no lack of provisions. In Tarento, Georges de Suilly distinguished himself by his valour; he defended the town until hunger forced him to submit. He himself died of the plague.

They all suffered from an alarming scarcity of money as the expected supplies did not arrive. The Princes of Salerno and Bisignano, as well as the Colonna, were provided with more than thirty places to defend; but they soon began to get discontented and to intrigue against the King, instead of winning honour and glory by remaining loyal to their oath of fealty.

CHAPTER XI

ON May 20, 1495, Charles VIII. took leave of Naples
and began his homeward march. His soldiers were
overjoyed at the prospect, and it was easy to recognise
those who were appointed to return to France, by
their cheerful bearing, while those whom duty called
to stay behind showed deep depression. Even the
King could not conceal his pleasure at departing,
and expressed compassion for those who were left.

Rome was reached on June 1. To the great disappointment of the French, they found that the
Pope had already left the city, although Charles had
sent an envoy assuring him of their homage, and
begging him to await their arrival. The League,
having doubts of Alexander's loyalty, had, it appears,
persuaded him to retire to Orvieto, after having
placed a strong garrison in the Castle of Sant' Angelo.

Charles's second entry into Rome was much less impressive than his first had been. He refused the offer of residence in the Vatican, preferring what he considered less risky quarters in the Borgo. Once more he begged an interview of the Pope, who agreed to meet him at Viterbo, but, on arriving there, he found that Alexander had already taken his departure for Perugia. Charles, however, was received with great pomp, and tarried there three days awaiting the arrival of his rearguard and artillery. Meanwhile, he went to view the dead body of the sainted Rosalia, who looked as if merely sleeping, as indeed the monks declared she was.

The French now gave full vent to their hatred of the Italians, and behaved as if they were in the land of an enemy. While the King was at Viterbo the vanguard stormed Toscanella, which had refused their admittance, and slaughtered the inhabitants. Charles, it is said, was extremely vexed at this, for Toscanella belonged to the papal dominions. But the anger of so mild and inconsequent a monarch was not very alarming, and the Bastard of Bourbon, who was responsible for the attack, sought to appease the King by making him an accomplice. Among the prisoners was a young girl of ravishing beauty. The Bastard brought her to Charles and left them alone together. The maiden, realising her danger, fell on her knees before the image of the Madonna, and in terror besought her protection. The King was so touched by her despair that he began to make inquiries about her circumstances. She confessed that she was betrothed, but that her bridegroom and all her possessions had been lost in the Toscanella disaster. Fortunately it was discovered that he had escaped the massacre and was among the prisoners. The King sent for him, gave the young couple his blessing, and presented them with 500 ducats.

At Siena Charles was received by an embassy of

the most distinguished citizens. Comines was there, too, and after two days he tried to persuade the King to resume his march, since the allies were still unprepared for war. But he stayed almost a week longer, for the Sienese entertained him in a manner after his own heart, and "luy monstrenent les Dames." Leaving a garrison of three hundred French in Siena, Charles proceeded to Pisa, his original idea of going to Florence having been changed by the news that the Florentines were equipping themselves for war. As Jacopo Nardi relates, it was marvellous to see how rapidly men and boys took arms, and how private citizens competed with the Commissioners of the Seignory in stocking the city with weapons and supplies (Villari). The French King was filled with indignation to hear that the whole town was preparing as if for the approach of a foe, while the Florentines suspected that he was about to reinstate Piero de' Medici. Savonarola, of whom Charles had a kind of superstitious awe, was sent to Poggibonzi (June 1495) to remonstrate with him; but, though the King seemed impressed at the time by his warning words, they had no permanent effect.

At Pisa Charles was welcomed with delight. All the houses were decorated, and the children of the nobles, dressed in white silk woven with lilies, came forth to meet him. On the great bridge was erected his statue, with his horse treading on the Lion of Florence and the Serpent of Milan. Tables groaning under rare wines and delicacies were set up in the street, and even the least of the French soldiers were invited to partake. One day, as the King was returning from mass, he encountered a procession of all the loveliest women in Pisa, robed in black, with flowing hair, bare feet and ropes about their necks; they besought him, with cries and plaints, not to deliver them up to the tyranny of the Florentines.

But though Charles appeared touched, he would give no promise. A French garrison was established in the citadel, commanded by d'Entragues, a man of shady reputation.

The King now continued his march by way of Lucca, where, according to de la Vigne :

> Il fut festié moult honorablement
> En submettant la ville entièrement
> Les corps, les biens des hommes et des femmes,
> A son plaisir et bon commandement,
> Pour le servir de cœur, de corps et d'ames

From Lucca Charles went on by way of Pietra Santa to Sarzana, where he received news that the Genoese were about to detach themselves from Milan. He therefore sent troops to their help, and a French fleet from Naples was also despatched. But the rumour proved false, and the fleet was defeated at Rapallo.

The Duke of Orleans, whose troops were occupying Asti, and had also conquered Novara, as a descendant of the House of Visconti, laid claim to Milan. He was supported by the Margravine of Montferrat, though against the King's wishes.

From Lucca, Charles went on through Pietra-Santa and Sarzana to Pontremoli, at the foot of the mountains. He sent the vanguard, under Marshal Gié and Trivulzio, to request an entrance, which was granted. But there soon arose a quarrel between the inhabitants and the Germans belonging to the King's troops, with the result that thirty or forty of the latter were killed. Their compatriots, infuriated, flew to arms, plundered the town, and burned all the provisions they could lay hands on. This outbreak, united to the King's bad reputation, did great harm to the French cause. The army suffered much privation from lack of provisions, though the Germans did their best, by the vigour of their service, to compensate for the misfortune they had caused. Owing to their energy the King, with all his baggage and artillery, were safely conveyed over the precipitous mountain paths of the Apennines. The vanguard, under Marshal Gié, was already thirty miles in advance, in camp near the village of Fornuova, only half a mile away from the troops of the allies. The latter, luckily for the French, were led, by the expectation of greater booty, to wait until the rest of the army had arrived.

In the camp at Fornuova the French were able to renew their stock of provisions. The peasants brought very black bread, much-watered wine, and a little fruit, which they sold at exorbitant prices. The soldiers at first feared that the food might be poisoned, and hesitated to taste it, especially as two Swiss died. But before midnight their hunger overcame them, and they followed their horses' example by making a good supper. Comines remarks that it was greatly to the credit of the Italians that no poison had been employed.

The two armies were separated by the river Taro, which could easily be crossed at low water. Comines was deputed to enter into negotiation with the allied forces, for the French army had to cross the river before continuing its march. He set out reluctantly on his mission, and, though an interview took place, it led to no result. The same night there broke over the camp a terrible storm, in which many saw a presage of evil. The French position was indeed critical. In front of them was a large and powerful army commanded by the daring Marquis Francesco Gonzaga, and it seemed as though their scanty troops could have little chance against it. But when, on Monday, July 6, Comines found Charles fully armed on a beautiful black horse, he recognised such a change in the King's usual faltering and undecided demeanour that the words of Savonarola, " This time you will escape from the danger which threatens you," recurred to him and gave him fresh courage.

Everyone saw that a battle was inevitable. The strength of the French was concentrated in the vanguard under Trivulzio and Marshal Gié ; the main corps was commanded by the King, and the rearguard by la Trémouille and the Comte de Foix.

The army of the League was divided into four parts, three of which were destined for the attack while the fourth was to defend the camp. The first corps, under Galeazzo San Severino, was to cross the river on the upper side of the French vanguard and proceed to the attack. The centre, under Gonzaga, consisted of about 14,000 men, including many hardy Stradiotes. Their task was to cross the Taro and attack the French centre, while a strong reserve under Montefeltro were to await the signal of attack on the river bank. The third corps, commanded by Forte Braccio, was to fall upon the French rearguard.

Of the fight which followed Comines gives a wonderfully detailed account, but the reports of contemporary Italian historians differ considerably. There is no doubt, however, that Charles VIII. displayed remarkable bravery and did not shrink from the greatest personal risk. Both sides suffered much, for the fight, though short, was sharp. The French army would probably have been utterly destroyed if it had not been for the untrained Bohemians in the Italian forces, who hastily began to plunder the enemy's baggage. The French were thus enabled to cut their way through, though not without heavy damages. The royal standard, the headquarters, and an immense amount of valuable booty fell into the hands of the Italians, and it is not surprising that they laid claim to the victory, although the object of the battle had not been gained. The well-known

Madonna of the Victory, now in the Louvre, commemorates this claim. The French, for their part, considered themselves victorious, since they were now able to continue their march.

The Italians, who were little accustomed to bloodshed in war, seem to have regarded this battle as remarkably gory, while Comines mentions it as a comparatively insignificant skirmish. The French slaughtered all their prisoners, but the Italians treated theirs with humanity. The Marquis of Mantua, in an interview with Comines, recommended to him those who had been taken captive, and in particular his uncle Ridolfo, under the delusion that they were still alive. " Mais je scavoye bien le contraire," says Comines, " toute fois je classeuroye que tous les prisonniers seroyent bien traités. . . . Les prisonniers par nous détenus estoyent bien aisés à panser, car il n'y en avoit point."

To an unbiassed observer it would seem that great errors were made on both sides. Charles ought to have proposed a battle with the allies instead of allowing his vanguard to cross the river, and thus deprive himself of their support. Just as blameworthy was the conduct of the allies, who, by their great superiority in numbers, might easily have gained a victory over the weary French troops ; but their forces were split up into too small portions, which were not well under the control of their generals.

On their homeward march the French troops suffered sadly from lack of provisions and water. Their thirst, we are told, was so terrible that they were obliged to drink muddy ditch-water. Comines sometimes went for two days with nothing to eat but a little bad bread, yet he was among those who suffered least It was most praiseworthy, he thinks, that there was no murmuring. This was the most fatiguing and painful march in which he had ever engaged, although he had followed the Duke of Burgundy in many a hard campaign.

At last the hungry and weary troops arrived at
Asti, where they were cheered by an abundant supply
of provisions. Here they received news that Louis,
Duke of Orleans, was about to surrender Novara
owing to lack of food. Charles immediately hastened
to Vercelli, hoping to be able to cross the Sesia and
go to the Duke's assistance ; but, owing to the heavy
rains, the river was swollen into a rushing torrent,
and the camp was cut off from help. The King,
however, rose to the occasion and himself superintended the building of a bridge of boats, which,
alas ! was speedily swept away by fresh floods of
rain. While they were considering the erection of
another bridge the Duke of Orleans surrendered, only
thirty Frenchmen being left in the citadel. Two
thousand men had died of hunger, and of the remaining
5,000 less than 600 were capable of fighting. The
others were so emaciated as to appear more dead
than alive.

Although French historians represent the reconquest of Novara in a not unfavourable light, it cannot
be denied that it was one of the most acute humiliations which they had encountered in the whole
campaign. The town was completely invested by
the allies, and the garrison suffered the most terrible
privation. Charles was obliged to ask for an armistice,
which the Duke of Milan only granted with reluctance.
The Duke of Orleans and a few friends were allowed
to visit the King at Vercelli, but only on condition
that they should return to Novara in the event of
no peace being concluded. After lengthy negotiations,
the Duke of Milan finally decided to leave the allies
and enter into a private treaty with Charles. The
latter was thus permitted to equip a fleet in the
harbour of Genoa, and received promise of a free
passage through Milanese territory, and assistance
in troops and money in the event of his undertaking
a fresh campaign against Naples.

The French, who had lost 2,000 men through hunger and pestilence, now set out to join their King at Vercelli. More than three hundred of them, however, died on the way, and as many more collapsed immediately upon their arrival. The King treated his troops with great consideration, and Comines, it is said, saved more than fifty lives by nursing many of the invalids in the little Castle of Camariano.

With his army now reduced to one-third of its original numbers, Charles pushed homeward by way of Turin. Here he tarried for some time, but on October 22, 1495, he took his departure and was soon back in his own dominions. His wonderful conquest of Naples was already a thing of the past, though its effects were far-reaching indeed.

In spite of its evanescent character, the invasion of Charles VIII. was a great factor in the history of the Renaissance. It marks a turning-point from which dates the spread of culture in Europe. Italy, in all her glory, was at last revealed to the nations of the north. " Like a gale sweeping across a forest of trees in blossom, and bearing their fertilising pollen to far-distant trees that hitherto have bloomed in barrenness, the storm of Charles's army carried far and wide through Europe the productive energy of the Renaissance."[1]

The year 1495 had indeed been a disastrous one for Rome. It had twice witnessed the invasion of the French, and before its close one of the most terrible floods ever known in Italy had set its mark upon the city. In some parts people were drowned in their beds, and many others died from the effects of cold and hunger. " There were great floods," writes a Venetian correspondent, " in the reigns of Pope Sixtus IV. and Martin V., but never one like this. Many are filled with terror and think there

[1] J. A. Symonds, *Age of the Despots*, p. 358.

is something beyond nature in it ; but it is not for
me to say anything on this point. . . . These parts
of Rome have suffered so much that it makes the
heart ache to see it. The Pope has ordered processions to implore the mercy of God."

A belief arose that the Divine wrath was about
to burst forth upon the city and utterly destroy it.
Strange and ominous tales were spread, one in particular of a monster said to have been found on the
banks of the Tiber The Venetian ambassadors
describe it as having " the body of a woman, and a
head with two faces. The front face was that of an
ass with long ears, at the back was an old man with
a beard. The left arm was human, the right resembled the trunk of an elephant. In the place of
a tail it had a long neck with a gaping snake's head
at the end ; the legs, from the feet upwards and the
whole body, were covered with scales like a fish."
On all hands signs and tokens were thought to portend
fresh disasters, and the voice of Savonarola thundered
forth the most terrible prophecies of evil to come.

As soon as the young King Ferrantino heard that
Charles had left Naples he landed on the coast of
Calabria with about six hundred men. Gonsalvo
da Cordova joined him, but d'Aubigny, whom
Charles had left behind to defend Naples, defeated
them at Seminara. Ferrantino retreated to Messina,
and Gonsalvo fled over the mountains to Reggio.
In this battle Ferrantino was saved from death by
the loyalty of his page, Giovanni of Capua, who
paid for his heroism with his own life.

At Messina Ferrantino equipped a small fleet and
sailed in the direction of Naples, hoping to be kindly
received by the Neapolitans. In vain he cruised
about the coast for three days, and he was already
about to retire when a boat from Naples brought
him news that the people were longing for his return,
but, from fear of the French garrison, they dared

not welcome him ; if, however, he would attempt a landing they would stand by him. On the day after the battle of Taro, therefore, Ferrantino landed at Maddalena, about a mile from Naples. An insurrection arose ; the gates were closed behind the French, and only opened again to receive Ferrantino, who was greeted by the populace with loud cries of joy.

The Duke of Montpensier made a brave defence, but was finally obliged to flee to Salerno. Here he received reinforcements, and, returning to Naples, almost compelled Ferrantino to beat a retreat. But, fortunately for the latter, the Pope sent a few troops to his aid, and, with the help of Prospero and Fabricius Colonna, he was able to repulse the French attack.

Ferrantino also sought help from the Venetians. The Senate, no longer hiding its hostility to France, sent him a considerable fleet and a land force under the Marquis of Mantua, who had won a great reputation in the battle of Taro. In return for this assistance, they demanded the surrender of Brindisi, Trani, Gallipoli, Otranto, and other towns on the shores of the Adriatic.

Montpensier, who had withdrawn to Atella, was reinforced by a number of Swiss. D'Aubigny, also, though himself in need of support against Gonsalvo, sent him both money and men. These were commanded by Count Moreto and Albert San Severino, who, however, were surprised and captured on their march by Gonsalvo. At Atella, Montpensier was so violently attacked by the united forces of Ferrantino and Gonsalvo that he was obliged to negotiate. An armistice of thirty days was granted on condition that, if in that time no fleet came to his help, he must surrender not only Atella but also all the Neapolitan fortresses still in the possession of the French.

But Charles, having once safely arrived in his own country, troubled little about the brave warriors left behind in Italy. The stipulated time passed, and the hoped-for succour did not arrive. Montpensier, therefore, had to fulfil the conditions of the treaty ; but Ferrantino, instead of keeping his promise of letting the French troops immediately set sail for Provence, sent about 6,000 of them to the island of Procida and other unhealthy parts, where almost two-thirds of them died from hunger and disease. Montpensier died at Pozzuoli, but d'Aubigny, after tarrying in Calabria until he heard of the surrender of Atella, withdrew his troops and led them safely back to France.

Ferrantino, whose claim to the throne of Naples was no longer disputed, now turned his attention to matrimony. He had long loved Joanna, a beautiful girl of fourteen, the half-sister of his father Alfonso, and, now that his kingdom was in a state of comparative peace, he gained the Pope's dispensation for the marriage. Their near relationship was looked upon askance by many. "Ce me semble horreur," says Comines, "de parler d'un tel mariage, dont on eut fait deja plusieurs en cette maison." The King, however, did not long enjoy his married life, for he died shortly after the wedding celebrations. As he left no children, the crown passed to his uncle Federigo, a Prince of considerable virtue and kindliness, who, under more propitious circumstances, might have reorganised and tranquillised the kingdom of Naples.

Before Charles VIII. left Italy he had given the Florentines a definite promise that, in return for the loan of a much-needed sum of money, he would restore Pisa to them. D'Entragues received orders to evacuate the citadel, but he surrendered it to the Pisans for 12,000 ducats, whether at the King's counter-order, or merely from a desire for money, is not certain. The Florentines thereupon had recourse to arms ; but the Pisans raised forces and

THE STORY OF ISIS AND OSIRIS.
Pinturicchio (Borgia Apartments, the Vatican).

turned to the other Italian States for help, promising subjection if they would free them from the hated yoke of Florence. The Venetians and the Duke of Milan prepared for the defence.

Meanwhile the Florentines, under Viletti, attacked the unfortunate town, but were forced to retreat by the fire of artillery from the citadel.

There now appeared a new candidate for the possession of Pisa, no less a person than the Emperor Maximilian. In October 1496 he marched into Milanese territory, where the Duke had made brilliant preparations for his reception. He then proceeded in the direction of Pisa. But the Venetians, who were ever seeking to increase their power, and kept a jealous eye upon their neighbours, placed a strong garrison in the town, and obliged Maximilian to withdraw. They tried to persuade him to renounce his claims, but he, angry at his failure, was eager to ravage the whole province of Tuscany. A terrible storm arose, however, and scattered his fleet, so that he was obliged to beat a hasty retreat to his own domains.

For the last year Piero de' Medici had been living a degraded and vicious life in Rome. He had never given up hope of being reinstated in Florence, and thought that the Emperor's arrival in Pisa would provide a suitable opportunity for him to try to return. The Pope and the Venetians supported him, and he had many friends among the youth of Florence who encouraged him in his undertaking. With the help of Virginio Orsini, who, during the battle of the Taro, had escaped from captivity, Piero marched into Umbria with a considerable force, and reached Rapollano in the middle of winter. But the Florentines had taken all necessary precautions. Arezzo and Cortona were reinforced and all disposable troops gathered to Florence, while the friends of the Medici were carefully watched.

QB

It was thus almost impossible for the advancing forces, who relied as much on their friends as on their own strength, to venture an assault. Virginio, therefore, merely set fire to the outlying villages, having first plundered them for the maintenance of his men. While in this critical situation he received a command to take service with the French King, who was withdrawing his troops from Naples. Notwithstanding the grudge he bore to Charles for having unjustly detained him in prison, Virginio lost no time in marching towards Naples with his troops, leaving Piero and his friends in the lurch. His treachery met with its reward, for he, together with the Duke of Montpensier, was taken prisoner at Atella, and they both died in captivity. Piero's army was now disbanded.

About this time domestic troubles pressed hardly upon Ludovico of Milan. Three of his sons died and soon afterwards, in January 1497, he lost his wife, Beatrice d'Este, after the birth of a still-born child. Ludovico, who was absolutely callous to the miseries of his fellow-men, nevertheless suffered agonies of grief at her death, for she had been the loyal sharer of all his joys and ambitions, to say nothing of his crimes. At his command she was splendidly entombed in the Chapel of Santa Maria delle Grazie, which was decorated in the most lavish manner. Beatrice was only twenty-three at the time of her death ; her strong personality had always exercised a remarkable influence over her wicked husband, and when she was no longer on earth to advise him, his fortunes began steadily to decline. Ludovico ordered that the day of her death should be observed as a fast, and he himself always celebrated the anniversary with deep abasement of spirit, standing with rent garments at the table where his courtiers dined.

Now that Alexander VI. had no more to fear from

France, he adopted measures for the oppression of the Roman nobility, proceeding to enrich his beloved children at their expense. He was especially anxious to promote the fortunes of Juan, Duke of Gandia, upon whom he hoped to found the future greatness of his house. The Duke, though immoral, was of a gentle and amiable disposition, and was as much loved as his brother Cæsar was hated and feared. The Pope, indeed, loved Juan with a far more tender affection than that which he bore to the brilliant Cæsar. The latter, who longed for the proud position of heir of the House of Borgia, was consumed with jealousy of his elder brother. Juan, however, was still young, while Alexander was getting on in years, so that in the natural course of events Cæsar would never have the first place in his father's favour. A horrible plan was already seething in his brain; he had reduced crime to a fine art and found no difficulty in devising a way of removing this hindrance from his path. How he succeeded will shortly be seen.

Alexander VI. had always been at enmity with those Roman nobles whose possessions excited his greed. Upon becoming Pope he had lost no time in attacking the Orsini, until the French invasion had forced him to desist. At the same time, he pursued the Colonna, who had seized upon Ostia. He confiscated their property and had their palaces demolished; but, on account of the Pope's treaty with Charles VIII., to whom the Colonna were attached, he was obliged to give up molesting them for a time. After the French retreat, however, he renewed his hostilities against the Orsini, who had remained faithful to France, while the Colonna were more inclined towards the House of Aragon.

The task of overthrowing the Orsini was entrusted to Juan, Duke of Gandia, whom the Pope summoned from Spain for this purpose. When he arrived in Rome (August 10, 1496), the French garrison at

Atella had already been forced to surrender, with the result that Virginio, the Orsini leader, was imprisoned. This seemed a good opportunity for attempting the further conquest of the Orsini strongholds. The Duke of Gandia, though by no means remarkable for military skill, was, amid much pomp and circumstance, appointed Commander-General of the papal troops. On October 27 the expedition started from Rome. Gabera, Scrofano, Formello, Campagnano, and finally Anguillara, speedily succumbed.

" The next step was to proceed to lay siege to the family castle of Bracciano. This majestic fortress, with its five round towers, still crowns the height above the blue lake in grey and massive grandeur. Here the whole clan, with all their forces, were assembled. The youthful Alviano, with his high-spirited consort, Bartolomea, Virginio's sister, commanded the defenders." [1] Bartolomea threw her whole energies into the cause of her family, and sacrificed her riches, her jewels, and even her wedding-robe in order that the soldiers might be paid. Her husband, Alviano, also distinguished himself by wonderful fearlessness, energy, and presence of mind. The Duke of Gandia, on the other hand, was inexperienced and not very capable, so that no progress was made until the end of November, when the guns which the King of Naples had lent the Pope arrived. Even then Bracciano continued to hold out bravely, though the besiegers displayed the most inhuman cruelty. Cæsar Borgia, who was indulging in the pleasures of the chase at Monte Mario, was nearly taken prisoner, and was only saved by the fleetness of his horse. The Pope was frantic at the non-success of his troops, and on Christmas Day was quite incapacitated by anxiety.

The French King, meanwhile, did not abandon the Orsini cause. He sent them money and a few

[1] Pastor, vol. v. p. 489.

troops under Carlo, a natural son of Virginio Orsini, and Vitellozzo. Many old soldiers again enlisted under their banner, and they were also joined by the Baglioni, the Prefect of Rome, and other important nobles who feared the Borgia rapacity. Only the Colonna and Savelli held back. They were now as friendly to the Borgias as they had formerly been hostile, and gave no heed to the popular saying that "the Borgias would dine on the property of the Orsini, but that they expected to sup on that of the Colonna."

The approach of these reinforcements compelled the papal army to raise the siege. The two armies met at Soriano an January 25, 1497, and the battle resulted in the absolute defeat of the pontifical troops. The Orsini, though at a disadvantage in the beginning, fought lustily, and five hundred men were killed or taken prisoners; the rest saved themselves by flight. The Duke of Gandia was wounded and Urbino captured, and the Apostolic Legate died a few days later from the effects of fright.

The Orsini were now masters of the Campagna. The Pope was terrified at the news of the defeat, and contrived to patch up a kind of peace with his enemies. Virginio Orsini, however, derived no benefit from the success of his house, for he had died, presumably from poison, before the battle took place.

Ostia still remained in the power of Cardinal Giuliano della Rovere, the declared enemy of the Pope. The latter now turned to the only friend whom he could trust—Gonsalvo da Cordova, the Spanish General, and commissioned him to reconquer it for the Papal See. As peace prevailed in Naples, Gonsalvo united his Spaniards with the papal forces and began to fire upon the fortress; but before many shots had been exchanged, Menaldo, the commander of the garrison, surrendered (March 9, 1497). At the same time Alexander VI. decided, on his own responsibility, to deprive Cardinal Giuliano della Rovere of his benefices, and his brother Giovanni, who had supported Vitellozzo, of the Prefecture of Rome.

On March 15 Gonsalvo and the Duke of Gandia, " the one an able general and statesman, the other a mere stage prince bedizened with ornaments and tinsel," arrived in Rome. They were welcomed at the gates by the Pope's sons, all the Cardinals, and a goodly multitude of people. Gonsalvo was at once conducted to the Pope, who kissed him on the cheek, and, in presence of the Cardinals, conferred on him the golden rose. The Spaniard gave proof of his magnanimity by begging that Menaldo might be liberated. His request was granted, and Menaldo was allowed to retire to France.

Modern writers have maintained that Gonsalvo took the opportunity of remonstrating seriously with the Pope on his evil ways, but there seems to be no mention of this in contemporary chronicles. There can be no doubt, however, that such reproof was urgently needed, for Alexander's nepotism and iniquity were unbounded. It was about this time that Cardinal Peraudi remarked to the Florentine envoy : " When I think of the lives of the Popes and some of the Cardinals, I shudder at the idea of residing at the Court."

The Pope, who was anxious to form a party of Cardinals to support his schemes, had made himself very unpopular in 1496 by conferring the red hat upon several Spaniards. In June, 1497, a Secret Consistory was held, at which he proposed to invest the Duke of Gandia with the Duchy of Benevento as well as the cities of Terracina and Pontecorvo, hoping thus to prepare his way to the throne of Naples. Though there were twenty-seven Cardinals present, Piccolomini was the only one who had the courage to protest against this alienation of church property, and his remonstrances were disregarded. In the same month Cæsar Borgia, despite the great disapproval of the College of Cardinals, was appointed Legate to Naples, where he was deputed to anoint and crown the new King Federigo. At the close of the Consistory, Cæsar retired to his rooms and shut himself in ; it is probable that he was already busying himself with the plans for his brother's murder. The time had come when his jealousy could no longer be contained and he determined, by foul means, to oust the Duke of Gandia from his position as heir of the Borgia fortunes. Several contemporary historians impute to him the desire of getting rid of a rival for Lucrezia's favours. This, however, can hardly be credited, for Lucrezia was already on distinctly unfriendly terms with her father and brothers after the dissolution of her union with Sforza. It cannot be denied that Cæsar possessed some demoniacal kind of influence over his sister, but there are no fixed facts to prove the appalling suspicions which have been promulgated by enemies of the House of Borgia. There is, however, little doubt that both Cæsar and the Duke of Gandia maintained immoral relations with Donna Sancia, their sister-in-law. Some have regarded this as an additional motive for the murder.

Burchard, the Master of the Papal Ceremonies, gives in his Diary a blunt and detailed account of the Duke's murder, which, however, bears upon it the impress of truth. " On June 14," he says, " the Cardinal of Valencia [Cæsar] and the Duke of Gandia, both sons of the Pope, were present at a banquet given by their mother, Vannozza, who lived near the Church of San Pietro in Vincoli. As it grew late, the Cardinal reminded his brother that it was time to return to the Papal Palace. They and a small escort therefore mounted their horses, or mules, and rode as far as the Palace of Cardinal Ascanio Sforza, where the Duke informed the Cardinal that he wished to pay a visit to his mistress before going home.   Thereupon he dismissed his entire suite with the exception of his valet and a masked person who had visited him daily for the last month.   He let this domino sit behind him on his mule and rode as far as the Ghetto, where he gave his servant orders to wait for him until a certain hour, but, if he did not get back by that time, to return to the palace. The Duke took this masked person up again behind him and rode on.   But in the night he was murdered, and his body thrown into the Tiber.   The servant who waited for him was also attacked and fatally wounded, and, although everything was done to revive him, he did not recover consciousness enough to give any comprehensible information about his master's fate.

" When the Duke had not returned by the following morning his people became uneasy, and one of them informed the Pope that his sons had passed the whole night in revelling, and that the Duke had not yet reappeared.   At this news the Pontiff was overcome with anxiety, though he suspected that Gandia had spent the night with some hired prostitute, and, not wishing to compromise himself by leaving her house in broad daylight, was waiting the shades of evening.   But when the night came and he did not appear, the Pope became acutely miserable, and, sending for various people, questioned them minutely. Among them was a workman, Schiavoni by name, who had spent the night in a boat on the Tiber, guarding some wood which he had been unlading. To the question whether he had seen any one thrown into the river on the preceding night he replied that he had noticed two foot-passengers come down the street, and look carefully round to see if anybody was passing.   As nothing stirred, they turned back, and soon two other men appeared.   They looked

THE ARMS OF POPE ALEXANDER VI.
Pinturicchio (Borgia Apartments, the Vatican).

about just as the others had done, and, as everything remained quiet, made a signal to their companions. Thereupon a man mounted on a white horse rode up ; in front of him was a corpse, whose head and arms hung down on one side of the horse and his feet on the other ; it was supported by the two men he had just seen, to prevent its falling down. As soon as they reached the place where the town-refuse was cast into the Tiber, the rider and both the men seized the body by its hands and feet and hurled it into the river. The horseman asked them whether it lay right in the current, and they answered, ' Yes, signore.' Thereupon he himself looked into the river, and, perceiving a cloak floating on the water, asked what the black thing was. They told him, and one of the men threw a stone upon it and caused it to sink. On being asked why he had not informed the authorities of the occurrence, Schiavoni answered that he had, during his lifetime, seen over a hundred corpses thrown into the Tiber, and had never heard any inquiry made about them." This remark was truly significant of the shocking state of Rome under Alexander VI.

Orders were given that the Tiber should be dragged, and after a time the body of the Duke of Gandia was hauled out. The Roman wits did not lose the opportunity of making epigrams upon Alexander VI., " the true successor of St. Peter, and indeed a fisher of men." The Duke's throat had been cut, and there were eight ghastly wounds on other parts of the body. His purse, however, and his rich garments had not been touched, so it was obvious that robbery had not been the motive for the murder. The corpse was taken to Sant' Angelo, where it was clothed in ducal robes and then carried on an open bier to lie in Santa Maria del Popolo.

The Pope, who had loved his son with a great love, grieved for him with a great grief. He shut himself in his room, overcome with sorrow, and wept bitterly, so that the noise of his weeping was heard afar off. From Wednesday evening till Sunday morning no food passed his lips, neither did he lose his trouble in sleep from Thursday morning till Sunday. When the first transports of grief were over, remorse seemed to seize him. He summoned a Conclave of the Cardinals, humbled himself with tears before them, and instituted a commission for the amendment of the abuses which he had sanctioned in the Church.

An interview with Vannozza appears to have soothed the Pope's troubled soul. It is probable that she reasoned with him, and pointed out the fact that the brilliant Cæsar was more fitted to uphold the majesty of his house than had been the less gifted Duke of Gandia. " The miserable father rose from the earth, dried his eyes, took food, put from him his remorse, and forgot, together with his grief for Absalom, the reforms which he had promised for the Church."[1]

Roscoe assumes that Gandia was attacked and murdered by a jealous rival, because, in Schiavoni's account of the event, there is no hint of Cæsar's guilt, and also because, after the murder, Cæsar was apparently received with friendliness by both his father and sister. But there is very little evidence to support this theory. Even if it is true that Cæsar did not leave his palace that night, this is no proof of innocence ; he had no need to commit the crime in person since in Don Michelotto, the leader of his band, he had always a ready instrument for any deed of infamy. That jealousy of the Duke's love for Lucrezia was the motive for killing him, as is imagined by Tomaso Tomasi and Gordon, is most improbable, but Cæsar undoubtedly felt that his brother stood in the way of his worldly advancement. He had adopted an ecclesiastical career very much

[1] J. A. Symonds.

against his inclination, and it was only through the Duke's death that he could hope one day to attain the position of an independent Prince, the summit of his ambition. He alone had anything to gain from his brother's removal, and, as we have already seen, his character was such that he shrank from no iniquity which might in any way be of advantage to him. Alexander and Lucrezia probably realised his infamy, but did not dare to oppose him. " The Pope loves and hugely fears his son," says the Venetian ambassador. Platina, too, tells us how much Alexander feared the power of his ferocious offspring, and adds that Cæsar, who had begun to despise the Cardinal's Hat, murdered his brother for no better reason than that he wished to lead the papal troops in his stead.

The Duke of Gandia's wife, Donna Maria Enriquez, was in Spain at the time of the murder. Upon hearing the sad news from the Pope's sister, Donna Beatrice Borja y Arenos, she lost no time in appearing before the tribunal of the kingdom of Valencia to claim the duchy of Gandia and the Neapolitan fiefs of Suessa, Teano, Carinola, and Montefoscolo on behalf of her three-year-old son, Don Juan. He was accordingly recognised as the legal heir.

Cæsar was now released from all ecclesiastical ties, by the Pope, who devoted his energies to building up the fortunes of his fiendish son. As time went on this monster of iniquity became more and more inhuman in his cruelty. It is said he actually stabbed Perotto, the Pope's minion, while the boy was taking refuge in Alexander's arms. On another occasion " he turned some prisoners sentenced to death into a court-yard of the palace, arrayed himself in fantastic clothes, and amused the papal party by shooting the unlucky criminals. They ran round and round the court, crouching and doubling to avoid his arrows. He

showed his skill by hitting each where he thought fit.
. . . Other scenes, not of bloodshed but of grovelling
sensuality, though described by the dry pen of Burchard, can hardly be transferred to these pages"
(Symonds).

One of Cæsar's most striking qualities was the
coolness with which he regulated his passions. He
lost nothing by impatience, but would calmly await
the psychological moment in order that he might
taste the exquisite pleasure of revenge and enjoy its
flavour to the full. The Pope, who, for his part,
could control neither tongue nor impatience, looked
with admiration and astonishment upon the trans-
cendent genius of his son, " le véritable virtuose de
la famille."

CHAPTER XII

SINCE the banishment of the Medici, many changes had passed over Florence, and the reins of government were now in the hands of the mob. The real leader of the citizens, however, was Savonarola, who was determined upon the reformation and purification of the city. Through negligence on the part of the magistrates a famine arose, which proved that the government was by no means an ideal one. With the co-operation of the leading inhabitants, a Gonfaloniere was elected in the person of Bernardo del Nero, an old man well stricken in years, while the other offices of State were filled with men who did not belong to Savonarola's party. Piero de' Medici, encouraged by this turn of affairs, and upheld by

promises of support from Venice and the Pope, resolved to make an effort to reinstate himself. He and
his brothers collected a troop, at the head of which
they placed Bartolomeo d'Alveano, who had already
distinguished himself in connection with the papal
forces. Stealthily they advanced towards Florence,
but, just as they were about to approach the gates,
a violent rain set in causing confusion among the
soldiers and a delay of several hours. The Florentines,
meanwhile, had got wind of the enemy's approach,
and, led by Paolo Vitelli, took energetic measures to
defend their town. The Medici partisans were taken
into custody, so that Piero could no longer expect
any help from his friends. His men had to abandon
their plan of attacking the gates, and withdrew to
the States of the Church, where they occupied themselves with plundering the villages Nardi relates
that, on this occasion, Piero was so near the city walls
(April 28, 1497) that the Florentines could recognise
him, and that they congregated in bands to gaze
upon him and his followers, though no sign of friendliness was shown.

Nardi further mentions that the poet Benivieni,
himself a passionate enthusiast, was sent to inquire
of Savonarola what would be the result of this dreaded
attack of the enemy. The Prior, who was reading,
looked up and answered: " O thou of little faith,
why doubtest thou? Knowest thou not that God
is with thee? Go, tell thy superiors that I will pray
for the town, and that they must not be afraid, for
Piero de' Medici will not come beyond the gates, and
having accomplished nothing, will retreat." And it
happened just as he had predicted.

Four of the most important adherents of the
Medici were convicted of holding communication
with the enemy and condemned to death. The aged
Gonfaloniere, Nero, was included in the same punishment for having known, yet not disclosed, the enemy's

plans. Great discontent was aroused in Florence by this severity.

Meanwhile the Florentines besieged Pisa. The Duke of Urbino, who had purchased his freedom for 30,000 ducats, Bartolomeo d'Alveano; who had formerly been on the opposing side, Paolo Orsini, Ludovico the Moor, and Venice, which was then at the height of its power, took the part of the Pisans. The Florentine troops were led by Paolo Vitelli, while the Marquis of Mantua had command of the allies. Both parties prepared for war. The Pisans were returning from plundering Volterra when they were attacked by the Florentines in the valley of San Regolo. A battle ensued, in which Florence sustained an utter defeat.

In their extremity the Florentines turned to Ludovico Sforza. It was not difficult to convince him of the undesirability of any increase in the Venetian power, and he consented to support Florence; the treaty, however, was to be kept secret until a suitable opportunity occurred to withdraw his troops from the allies.

This secret alliance with the Florentines was much more harmful to Venice than an open breach would have been. Ludovico persuaded several leaders who had formerly adhered to Pisa to come over to the side of Florence, and a large and powerful army entered the field under the command of Paolo Vitelli. They advanced against Pisa, garrisoned all the approaches to the town, and directed their batteries against Vico Pisano, a fortress in the neighbourhood. The latter surrendered, and the enemy proceeded to the conquest of Pisa.

The Florentines proposed to settle their dispute with Pisa by arbitration; but Venice, conscious of her power, preferred to continue the war, in the expectation of uniting Pisa to the Venetian possessions.

But, as Vitelli continued the siege with great vigour

and persistence, the allies became more inclined to listen to the Florentine proposals. After lengthy negotiations, the judgment was entrusted to Duke Ercole of Ferrara, who passed the following sentence (1499) : The Venetians were to withdraw their troops from the dominions of Florence and Pisa ; Florence was to pay them 180,000 ducats as compensation for the expenses of the war, and Pisa was again to be restored to Florentine authority.

Universal discontent was aroused by this decision, and it was decided to return to the fight.

The walls of Pisa were very strong, the town well provisioned, and the garrison numerous and capable ; but the Florentines made vigorous efforts to gain the victory, especially as the Venetians withdrew the greater part of their troops under the pretext of dissatisfaction with the behaviour of the Pisans, though really in order to seize upon part of their domains.

Vitelli first attacked the fortress of Stampace, on which the Pisans set their chief hopes. The inhabitants resisted bravely, men, women, and children taking part in the defence ; but the garrison was utterly defeated. Most of them were shot down and the rest fled to Pisa. Vitelli might have followed up his victory by forcing an entry into the town, but this, for some reason or other, he neglected to do. The Pisans thereby gained time to recover from their consternation. But, although Vitelli may have let slip a favourable opportunity, it must be admitted that he spared no effort to force the town to surrender, employing every means at the command of a skilful general. Luck, however, was against him. The plague broke out among the Florentine troops, who were encamped in a marshy district. The putrefying corpses of the slain contributed to aggravate the evil, and although fresh reinforcements arrived from Florence, the death-rate became so high that the siege had to be abandoned

SERVANTS WITH SPORTING-DOGS AND HORSE OF THE
MARQUIS GONZAGA.
Mantegna (Mantua).

THE MARQUIS GONZAGA, WITH HIS SON, THE
CARDINAL FRANCESCO GONZAGA.
Mantegna (Gallery at Mantua).

256]

Vitelli now journeyed to Cascina, where he was awaited by an embassy of Florentines. He was declared prisoner and conveyed to Florence, where he was accused of meeting with the Medici at Casentino and of set purpose allowing them to escape. He was also severely censured for his conduct at the siege of Pisa. As he refused to admit his guilt, he was put to the torture; but, as the cruellest torments could wrest from him no confession, he was condemned to death and was beheaded on the night after his trial.

The Florentines had by this time begun to grow restive under the domineering influence of Savonarola. Already, in 1496, he had given great offence by the fiery outspokenness of his Lenten sermons, which were quite frankly directed against the Pope, the Roman clergy, Ludovico Sforza, the Medici, and the Florentines themselves. Ludovico the Moor and Piero de' Medici urged the Pope to take active measures against this inconvenient reformer, whose position was hourly getting more precarious There arose a hostile party anxious to have him bound and cast into the Arno as a heretic, but the Friar Preacher still had many supporters, and they dared not lay hands upon him.

Unfortunately for Savonarola, a Seignory hostile to him now came into power. At one of their assemblies a Franciscan accused the Prior of heresy and fraud, challenging him to prove the truth of his doctrine by the Ordeal by Fire. Savonarola refused, but Fra Domenico, his faithful supporter, took up the gauntlet and a day was fixed for the ceremony. The Franciscan, however, now cast about for an excuse to withdraw the challenge, saying that his quarrel was with Savonarola alone, and that he would have nothing to do with Fra Domenico. But, in spite of the Franciscan's faint-heartedness, and the fact that Savonarola severely reproved Fra Domenico for his excess of zeal, the

RB

matter was not allowed to rest "If Savonarola enters the fire," said his enemies, " he will be burned ; if he refuses to enter it, he will lose all credit with his followers ; we shall have an opportunity of arousing a tumult, and during the tumult we shall be able to seize on his person." The members of the Seignory were quite willing to help forward this plot, which could only result in the shedding of innocent blood.

April 7 was the day finally fixed for the ordeal. Savonarola, accompanied by his friars, walked in procession to the Piazza singing the psalm, " Let God arise, and let His enemies be scattered." The Franciscans, who had made no demonstrations, were already there, and stood silently on their side of the Loggia while the Dominicans prayed aloud. A vast multitude of people had gathered together to witness the sight ; the windows, balconies, and even the roofs of the neighbouring houses were crowded with spectators. All was ready when a dispute arose between the two parties as to what each champion should be permitted to take with him into the flames. Fra Domenico was desirous of taking the crucifix, but to this the Franciscans raised resolute objections. Finally, he announced his willingness to take the Sacred Host instead ; but this proposal was emphatically opposed by the throng of spectators as well as by the Franciscans. The discussion lasted so long that the shades of night were already gathering before the matter was settled, and, after waiting a whole day for the ordeal to take place, the disappointed and angry mob dispersed at the command of the Seignory.

The conduct of Savonarola and his followers aroused universal condemnation ; even the Piagnoni declared that he ought to have entered the fire alone if no one would go with him. The whole of Florence tingled with indignation and resentment, and the Friar's fate was already sealed by his own act.

On the morning of Palm Sunday, April 8, Savonarola,

in direct opposition to the command of the Seignory, preached a sermon in St. Mark's. His words were few and melancholy; he offered his body as a sacrifice to God, and took a sad but calm farewell of his people. Before the day was over Francesco Valori, the Prior's chief supporter, was murdered and the Convent of San Marco stormed. Savonarola, amid the jeers of the populace, was led before the Seignory, which received the Pope's authority to institute proceedings against him. Painful days followed, in which strange confessions were alleged to have been forced from the Prior by torture, though statements thus extorted can hardly be accepted as proofs of guilt. The trial, as all had foreseen, resulted in sentence of death by hanging being pronounced upon Savonarola, Fra Domenico, and Fra Silvestro. On the following day, May 23, they went forth calmly and courageously to meet their fate, after a night spent in prayer. Before being delivered over to the executioner they were degraded from the priesthood as " heretics, schismatics, and contemners of the Holy See." As Savonarola mounted the ladder to the place of execution he looked round upon the crowd assembled to see him die, and cried aloud, " My people, what have I done to you that you should treat me thus? "

When life was extinct the bodies were burned and the remains cast into the Arno. It is said that a little child afterwards saw the Friar's heart unhurt among the ashes, and for many years flowers were placed upon the spot where his body fell, on every anniversary of his death.[1]

On April 7, the very day fixed for the Ordeal by Fire, Charles VIII. came to his end. The cause of his death is uncertain, but it is generally attributed

[1] St. Philip Neri regarded Savonarola as a saint, and always wore his medal It is not unlikely that the excommunicated Dominican may, like Joan of Arc, be raised to the altars of the church.

to apoplexy following a blow on the head. It is related that he and his Queen were entering a gallery in the Castle at Amboise, in order that they might watch the courtiers playing at tennis, when the King struck his head against the top of the low doorway. Not taking much notice of the blow, he entered into conversation with the people around him, saying to one of them that he hoped never to commit another wilful sin as long as he lived. While thus speaking he fell down unconscious, and, in spite of the ministrations of several doctors, passed away in a few hours.

Charles, though remarkably faulty in character, appears to have won the affection of his subjects, who mourned long and loud for him. Comines arrived at Amboise three days after his death and prayed by the coffin of the dead King. Never was such grief seen, he says, for Charles had always shown himself gentle, kind, and generous, never giving cause of offence to any one.

As he left no legitimate children he was succeeded by his distant cousin, the already mentioned Louis, Duke of Orleans, who as Louis XII. ascended the throne without any opposition. Europe was not long left in suspense as to the new King's projects; he had set his heart not only upon overthrowing the House of Sforza, but also upon conquering the kingdom of Naples. Under his rule began an Italian war which continued after his death, bringing nameless miseries in its train.

When quite a youth, Louis had married the Princess Jeanne, third daughter of Louis XI. She was a woman of blameless life, but sickly and unattractive in appearance and her husband now sought a divorce upon the grounds of her having given him no heirs and also of her near relationship to him. At first the slighted wife resisted the attempt to dethrone her, but finally, rather than submit to further indignities, she gave in.

The true cause of Louis's repudiation of Jeanne lay in the passion which he had long ago conceived for Anne of Brittany before she became the wife of Charles VIII. He was also much attracted by the idea of uniting the crowns of Brittany and France. The papal consent ought to have been obtained before the new marriage was concluded, but Louis, in his hurry, took upon himself to dispense with it. Alexander VI., anxious to keep on good terms with him, overlooked this offence, and sent his son Cæsar to France to deliver the dispensation.

But, before this, the Pope had summoned a Consistory for the purpose of releasing Cæsar from his ecclesiastical ties. Cæsar himself explained that he had only adopted this estate in order to please his father, that it was distasteful to him, and that he had a desire to marry. The Cardinals replied that they were not opposed to his wishes, but that they would leave the whole affair in the hands of the Pope. The latter, though he had at first been averse from the idea, thereupon gave his consent to the change.

Cæsar immediately resigned his red hat and donned secular garments of French fashion, August 17, 1498. On the same day Louis de Villeneuve, the French ambassador, arrived in Rome for the purpose of accompanying Cæsar to France. The preparations for the journey were, however, so extensive that they did not start until the beginning of October. Before this the Pope sent an autograph letter to Louis XII. commending Cæsar to his kindness as one who was more precious to him than anything else on earth. He is mentioned as Duke of Valentinois, so that the principality must have already been conferred on him, though the formal investiture had not yet taken place. With the dukedom was included an income of 20,000 francs, to which the French King added the appointment of Captain of one hundred lances, an appointment also worth 20,000 francs a year.

The Pope, who was always overshadowed by the fear of being called to account for his abuses of church property, thought to safeguard himself by a friendship with the King of France. Ferdinand and Isabella were much perturbed at this alliance, which, could only be prejudicial to them. They sent envoys to the Pope deploring the fact of Cæsar's mission to France, an alliance with which would run counter to the interests of the other States. Alexander sought to assuage their agitation, but they soon saw through his intentions and turned from complaints to accusations. Bitter words were said, and the Pope ended by declaring all who contradicted him to be " bastards of the Church." One of the envoys pertly replied that there were in Rome plenty of bastards whom one would be reluctant to harbour in the Church. This remark so angered the Pope that he averred that all that he had done had been rightly done, and that he would do the same again, in defiance of those who had had the hardihood to contradict him. Thereupon he turned an angry back upon them and shut himself in his room.

But the envoys were likewise filled with wrath and indignation, and declared that they would not budge before drawing up a legal protest. They so far forgot themselves, indeed, as to stamp their feet in resentment, until the Pope, more enraged than ever, emerged from his room and showed them the door.

Meanwhile Cæsar had arrived in France, where, by Louis's command, he was given a magnificent reception. They surrounded him with a guard of honour, and the people thronged to see him in such multitudes that one of his suite wrote home from Chinon saying that he had seen neither trees, walls, nor villages in France, but only men, women, and the rays of the sun. Even Cæsar, who had no modest opinion of himself was astonished at the sensation he was causing.

On December 19, 1498, Cæsar entered the royal camp at Chinon with a splendour never before witnessed in France. Accompanied by a gorgeous procession of men and mules, the Duke himself appeared riding on a richly saddled and bridled battle-horse. He wore a garment of red silk and gold stuff elaborately decorated with embroidery and precious stones. His cap was adorned with five or six rubies " as big as beans," which shone like fire. Upon his gloves were a quantity of precious stones, and his boots were covered with pearl embroidery and gold laces. Round his neck alone he wore jewels to the value of 30,000 ducats, and his horse was decorated in the most extravagant manner with pearls and precious stones.

The French King watched the procession from a window, making mock of this extravagant display. As he remarked to his courtiers, it was " too much for the petty Duke of Valentinois."

Apart from the delivery of the papal dispensation, the main object of Cæsar's journey was to win the hand of Carlotta, daughter of the King of Naples, who had been brought up at the French Court. To his no small chagrin, however, not only did Federigo refuse to sanction the match, but the lady herself stoutly refused to have anything to do with him.

The Pope, however, was determined to marry one of his children into the royal House of Naples, and prevailed upon King Federigo to consent to a marriage between Lucrezia and Don Alfonso, younger brother of Donna Sancia and illegitimate son of Alfonso I., a young Prince only seventeen years old. According to the contract, Alfonso was to remain in Rome for a year, and Lucrezia was not bound, during the Pope's lifetime, to follow him to Naples. It was only out of fear that the King had acquiesced in this alliance, and he remained firm in denying Cæsar the hand of his daughter. Lucrezia, apparently, had conceived a genuine affection for her new consort,

" the handsomest young man ever seen in the Imperial city," and she suffered keenly when, shortly after their marriage, he was torn from her by a violent death.

When Cæsar saw how frail was his prospect of obtaining Carlotta's hand, he decided not to give up the Pope's dispensation until King Louis had lent him his support. Although every one knew that he had received it, he, in the most barefaced way, denied his possession of it. But Louis summoned an assembly of theologians, and put before them the question whether his first marriage had not been legally dissolved and his marriage with Anne legally concluded, especially as there was no doubt that the Pope had already conferred the dispensation. With one voice the theologians declared him to be in the right, and Cæsar could do no less than hand over the dispensation. He, however, vented his rage upon the papal legate, who had betrayed the fact of its despatch, and " gave him a dose of the poison which he always kept in readiness for those who offended him." That luckless legate died a few days later in great wretchedness.

At the French Court Cæsar met two men who were destined later to have considerable influence on his career. They were Georges d'Amboise, for whom he had brought a Cardinal's Hat, and Giuliano della Rovere, who had hitherto been the Pope's bitterest foe, but who was now won over to the Borgia cause through the mediation of Louis XII.

A new alliance was projected between Cæsar and the charming Charlotte d'Albret, sister of the King of Navarre. She, less scrupulous than Carlotta of Naples, accepted the hand of Cæsar, who thus gained an entry into the royal house of France.[1]

Cæsar started with renewed energy on his downward career. The Pope and Lucrezia quailed before his

[1] See *Duchess Derelict*, by E L. Miron.

domineering spirit, for no one was safe from his poisonous powders or from the depredations and murderous assaults of his bandits, who remorselessly removed any one who stood in the way of his insatiable ambition.

Now that King Louis was assured of the Borgia support, he concluded an alliance with the Venetians by which he was to deliver over to them Cremona and Ghiaradadda as soon as his conquest of Milan should be completed.

Louis had now quite made up his mind to undertake an Italian campaign, in spite of the dissuasions of some of his courtiers on the ground of inadequate means. The King, however, stood firm, and despatched a large force of cavalry towards Piedmont. The troops destined for the conquest of Milan were commanded by Trivulzio, de Ligny, and the Count d'Aubigny. Louis himself went only as far as Lyons, leaving the administration of the campaign to his generals and to luck. With him were Cæsar Borgia and Cardinal della Rovere.

The army, which consisted of about 14,600 men, met with remarkable success. Louis's progress was as speedy and bloodless as that of his predecessor; all the Lombard towns opened their gates, and Milan rose in rebellion against Ludovico. The latter had hoped for help from the German Emperor and Federigo of Naples, but Maximilian was engaged in warring against the Swiss, and, upon hearing that Alessandria had succumbed to the French, Federigo abandoned his original idea of opposing the Pope. Ludovico therefore sought refuge in the Tyrol, deeply depressed that so many of his former friends had become his foes. The Milanese sent envoys to the French camp announcing their readiness to yield Milan as soon as King Louis arrived. This example was followed by the other towns of the duchy, who all surrendered. Even Bernardino da Corte, to

whom Ludovico had entrusted the citadel of Milan,
yielded to bribery, and delivered it over to the enemy.
But his treachery was so much despised by Italians
and French alike, that he was utterly boycotted,
and, shunned by his fellows and tormented by conscience, he shortly afterwards died from pain and
shame.

Louis XII., who was now at Lyons, received news
of the brilliant success of his troops, and hastened to
Milan, where, on October 6, 1499, he was welcomed
by the populace with indescribable joy. He was accompanied by Cæsar Borgia, the Cardinals d'Amboise
and Giuliano della Rovere, the Duchess of Ferrara
and Savoy, and many other people of note.

The Milanese satisfaction was not, however, of.
long duration. It is true that Louis reduced their
taxes, but they wished to be entirely freed from
them, and much secret murmuring and discontent
arose. Trivulzio, himself an Italian, was made governor of the city, and Louis received homage from
the States of Milan and Genoa. The young heir,
son of the unfortunate Galeazzo, was despatched to
a cloister in France, while his mother Isabella retired to Naples, where she had the unhappiness of
beholding the downfall of the House of Aragon.

Alexander VI. was unable to conceal his delight
at the French success, for he saw in it a promising
prospect for the aggrandisement of his children.
On August 24, 1499, two Portuguese envoys were
sent to remonstrate with him on his nepotism,
on Cæsar's resignation of the Cardinalate, and on the
French alliance, which was injurious to the peace
of Europe. Alexander, though disquieted at their
attitude, did not change his conduct, and shortly
made arrangements for Cæsar to conquer the Romagna.

The Pope, after holding a Consistory, sent his
major-domo, Giacopo, to Cæsar, at Lyons, with
despatches containing the whole scheme that the

Borgias should found an independent dominion through the downfall of the noblest princely house in Italy, and though Alexander carried on these proceedings with the greatest secrecy, Ludovico became aware of Giacopo's journey. As soon, therefore, as the latter reached Milanese territory, he was arrested and his despatches seized. When the Pope heard this he was furiously angry; he had all the gates of Rome shut, and gave orders to arrest the Milanese envoy. But the latter had already taken flight, fearing the Pope's vengeance. The Sforza party were greatly alarmed at this, and placed themselves under the protection of the Colonna. This precaution proved not to be unneeded, for Alexander wished to wreak his revenge on Sforza's adherents. He sent a message to Cardinal Colonna demanding the surrender of the fugitives. This the Cardinal was disinclined to grant, but, as the Pope threatened to employ force, he saw that he must either deliver up his friends or draw down the papal anger upon himself and his family. Nevertheless, he resolved to try flight, and sought refuge with his friends at Nettuna, one of the Colonna possessions.

The Pope gave orders that the palace of the Milanese envoy should be searched, but nothing was found save empty walls. It having transpired that the envoy had hidden all his furniture and treasure in a cloister, Alexander sent messengers to seize upon them, with strict commands to bring him the twelve valuable silver statues representing the Apostles.

It was about this time that the Pope appointed Lucrezia regent of the dukedom of Spoleto, with the life-long enjoyment of its privileges and revenues. At their father's command, Lucrezia and her brother Jofré made a brilliant and pompous entry into the town (August 1499). The magnificence of their display almost rivalled that of Cæsar's visit to Chinon. They were welcomed with great honour and respect.

On August 15 Lucrezia received the priors of the city, who swore allegiance to her, and later on the Commune gave a state banquet in her honour. Her stay in Spoleto was short, for her regency was only a token that she had actually taken possession of the territory.

Lucrezia was at this time in an extremely trying position. Her husband, Don Alfonso, after having lived with her at Rome for a year, had disappeared on August 2. The reason of his flight is not quite clear, but it was probably encouraged by the advice of Ascanio Sforza, who knew the plans of Alexander and Cæsar, and realised that Louis XII. was aiming not only at the conquest of Milan, but also at the fall of the House of Naples. Whether Lucrezia knew of her husband's intended flight is uncertain. A letter written from Rome by a Venetian on August 4 simply says : " The Duke of Bisceglia, Madonna Lucrezia's husband, has secretly fled and gone to the Colonna in Genazzano ; he deserted his wife, who has been with child for six months, and she is constantly in tears." (Diary of Marino Sanuto, quoted by Gregorovius.)

Lucrezia was now utterly in the power of the Pope, who, enraged at her husband's flight, banished his sister, Donna Sancia, to Naples. Alfonso, for whom his wife seems to have had a sincere affection, sent a pressing message urging her to follow him to Genazzano ; but the letter fell into Alexander's hands, and he compelled her to write to her husband demanding his return. It was perhaps to avoid the sight of Lucrezia's sadness that the Pope sent her from Rome and entrusted her with the government of Spoleto.

Alfonso decided to obey the papal command and return to his wife. Alexander desired him to go to Spoleto and then come with Lucrezia to meet him at Nepi. Nepi, although always under ecclesiastical government, had several times changed masters. Alexander himself had been appointed governor by his uncle Calixtus, but when he became Pope he conferred the position on Cardinal Ascanio Sforza. At the beginning of 1499, however, Alexander again took upon himself the control of the city, and he now delivered it, together with the castle and domain of Nepi, into the hands of Lucrezia. On September 4, 1499, Francesco Borgia, the Pope's treasurer, took possession of it in her name.

On October 10 the Pope despatched a brief to the city of Nepi commanding the municipality thenceforth to render obedience to Lucrezia, Duchess of Biscegha, as their true sovereign. Two days later he invested his daughter with the power to remit some of the taxes to which the inhabitants had been subject. On October 14 Lucrezia returned to Rome, and on November 1 she gave birth to a son, who was named Rodrigo, out of compliment to the Pope. He was baptized with great ceremony on November 11, in the presence of ambassadors from England, Venice, Naples, Savoy, Siena, and Florence, as well as many other dignitaries.

Cæsar Borgia, who was now in high favour with Louis XII., had, with the papal troops and some French reinforcements, set out on his campaign against the Tyrants of the Romagna. His intention was to attack the Sforzas of Pesaro, the Malatesta of Rimini, the Manfredi of Faenza, the Riarii of Imola and Forli, the Varana of Camerino, and the Montefeltri of Urbino. When Alexander returned from Nepi to Rome, rendered confident by Cæsar's alliance with France, he had Giacopo Caetani, Protonotary of the Roman Chair, arrested on an unjust pretext, in order that he might seize his possessions. Caetani soon died in the Castle of Sant' Angelo, whereupon his son, Niccolo, heir to the property of Sermoneta, was seized and strangled, by the Pope's command. Hardly was the victim dead when Alexander announced that the town of Sermoneta and the other possessions of the Caetani had fallen to the Papal See.

There can be no doubt that the Pope was at this time completely under the malignant influence of Cæsar, who was the moving spirit in many deeds of infamy which his father would hardly have conceived unaided.

The troops which Louis of France had promised to the Borgias consisted of 300 lances under the command of d'Allègre, and 4,000 Swiss, who, nevertheless, were to be paid by the Pope. After forcing Imola to surrender, Cæsar proceeded to besiege Forli, whose citadel was bravely defended by the spirited and beautiful Caterina Sforza. She was a woman of extraordinary courage and skill, yet with the few resources at her command she was in no position to hold out for any length of time. If, however, the plot of one of her faithful servants had succeeded not only Caterina, but also the whole of Italy, would have been freed from the tyrannical yoke of the Borgias. Tomasino, one of the Pope's musicians, a native of Forli, went to Rome with forged letters from the citizens, begging the Pope to make peace. These letters, it is said, "were charged with so virulent a poison that the death of the person who opened them was assured." They were rolled up inside a hollow reed, and Tomasino confided the secret to one of Alexander's servants, who promised his support. But the plot, in spite of every precaution, reached the Pope's ears and both the conspirators were arrested. From Burchard we learn that, in answer to the Judge's question how he could expect to escape when he had been contemplating so dreadful a crime, Tomasino said that his only thought had been for Caterina, that Imola and Forli would have thereby been freed from Cæsar's tyranny, and, moreover, that death for such a cause was to him of little moment.

The fate of the two culprits is unknown, but judging from the temper of the Borgias, their punishment could have been no light one.

On January 12, 1500, the citadel of Forli capitulated, overcome by the violent attacks of the enemy and the cowardice of some of the officers of the garrison. Caterina herself fell into the hands of Cæsar. According to the reports of the time, he led her in golden chains to Rome, where the Pope assigned her rooms in the Belvedere, and where she remained in terror of Cæsar's poison. After a futile attempt at flight she was taken to the Castle of Sant' Angelo ; but some French gentlemen, in particular Ivo d'Allègre, persuaded the Pope to set her free and to allow her to retire to Florence, after having spent a year and a half in captivity. She spent her last days in a convent and died there in 1509, leaving behind a son of the same bold spirit as herself—Giovanni Medici. He was the last of the great *condottieri*, and became famous as the leader of the Black Bands.[1]

During the siege of Forli Cæsar committed a crime of which only a mind in the last stages of depravity could have been guilty. Juan Borgia had been chosen by the Pope as legate *a latere*, and journeyed to Forli to parley with Cæsar, who, though he hated him on account of his predilection for the Duke of Gandia, received him graciously. Cæsar invited him to a banquet and had poison mixed with his food. The unhappy Cardinal had hardly tasted it when he began to feel unwell ; nevertheless, he continued his journey to Rome. At Urbino, however, he was seized with such violent sickness that he nearly died. While he was fighting against death he heard of the capture of Forli, and, notwithstanding his condition, he decided to go and congratulate Cæsar on his success. He had hardly reached Fossombrone when he succumbed to the effects of the poison. Some maintain that he did not suspect Cæsar's treachery until a few minutes before his death, and

[1] *Catherine Sforza*, by Count Pasolini. French version by Marc Hélys (Paris, 1912).

that with his dying breath he gasped: "I see now only too clearly that Cæsar wishes us all to go the same way as the Duke of Gandia."[1]

· At the same time Cerviglione, Captain of the papal troop, was murdered by command of Cæsar, whom he justly suspected of carrying on an amorous intrigue with his wife. The Pope seemed little concerned at his son's iniquities. Indeed, Rome and the whole States of the Church were just then overrun with assassins, so that one crime more or less was a mere trifle. The Borgias, secure in their alliance with France, openly robbed some by force of arms, while they had others secretly murdered in order to prey upon their riches. Thus Agnelli, Archbishop of Cosenza, was poisoned at his own table by one of the Borgias' hired assassins. The Archbishop, who with his relations and friends had enjoyed a merry meal, was the next morning found dead in bed with every symptom of poisoning. "His face was so much disfigured that it was terrible to look upon."

Alexander immediately seized upon the dead man's riches and sent them to Cæsar. The Archbishopric he bestowed upon Francesco Borgia, son of Calixtus III., while his post as Secretary of the Apostolic Chamber he bartered for 5,600 ducats to a Genoese merchant named Ventura Benessai.

It was the Pope's pleasant custom to claim for his own all the possessions left by deceased clerics, regardless of any last will and testament left by them. The benefices were sold in so shameless a manner that Cardinal Bembo remarked that the only way of remedying so great an evil would be for the secular princes to forbid their subjects to purchase them under pain of life-long banishment and confiscation of their goods.

[1] Pastor considers the story of Cæsar's having poisoned his nephew to be groundless. See *History of the Popes*, vol vi p. 73

Hardly five months had passed since the entry of Louis XII. into Milan when the Milanese, exasperated by the cruelty and infamy of the French, turned again to Ludovico Sforza, whose harsh rule seemed mild in comparison with that of France. Sforza, who had appealed in vain to Maximilian for help, now took 8,000 Swiss into his pay and united his forces and those of Ascanio, who came over the mountains into Italy and seized Como. On February 5, 1500, the gates of Milan opened to receive Ludovico, who was now apparently re-established as Lord of Milan.

But the King of France was not inclined to submit tamely to this snatching away of his conquest, and sent an army under la Trémouille to expel Ludovico. A battle was fought at Novara, whose citadel was still occupied by the French, although they had been driven from the town. The Swiss refused to fight against their kinsmen in the French army, and remained obdurate when Sforza, with promises and tears, begged them at least to convey him to a place of safety. On April 10, 1500, he was taken prisoner, probably through the treachery of some of his Swiss soldiers, who were tempted by the high price which la Trémouille set upon his capture.

Ludovico was taken to Lyons, where, upon his arrival, a huge crowd collected eager to witness the downfall of so mighty a Prince. After staying two days there without being allowed to address the King, he was taken to the terrible state prison in the Castle of Loches, where he languished for ten years, at first in a subterranean dungeon and afterwards in an upper chamber. Such was the pitiful end of the false and passionate Ludovico Sforza, whose vaulting ambition had thus o'erleapt itself.

Cardinal Ascanio Sforza, who had fallen into the hands of the Venetians and been delivered over to the French, was treated with greater humanity. He

SB

was taken to Bourges and kept in honourable captivity where King Louis himself had been imprisoned a few, years before.

The news of Ludovico's fall reached Rome on the evening of April 14, 1500. The Pope is said to have rewarded the messenger with 100 ducats, and the Orsini gave expression to their joy by means of bonfires.

The rising in Milan forced Trivulzio to beg troops from the Venetians. At the same time he withdrew the French soldiers who were with d'Allègre in the Romagna, thus leaving him with his forces so much weakened that he was unable to continue the war. He retired with his troops to Rome (February 26, 1500), where a brilliant reception awaited him The Pope could hardly control his impatience for his son's arrival ; he was feverish and agitated, " weeping and laughing at the same time." His heart was filled with pride at Cæsar's wonderful abilities, for he had displayed extraordinary powers of organisation during the campaign. All the Cardinals were commanded to send their retinues to meet the conqueror, and all the magistrates, ambassadors, and other dignitaries were requested to join in the procession Cardinals Orsini, Farnese, and Giovanni Borgia went as far as Civita Castellana to welcome him. Having been greeted by the Cardinals, he continued his way through the Corso to the Castle of Sant' Angelo. First came a number of carriages, followed by fifty noblemen richly clothed ; then a troop of trumpeters and minstrels, who, however, were forbidden to play, three heralds—Alfonso, Duke of Bisceglia, Lucrezia's ill-fated husband, and Jofré, Duke of Squillace, Cæsar's younger brother. Finally came Cæsar himself, riding between two Cardinals. He was clad in black velvet, with a finely wrought chain of gold round his neck. After him marched a hundred servants on foot, each one clothed in black velvet and bearing a stick in his hand. Lastly came the foreign ambassadors, each of whom had an Archbishop or Bishop on his right.

The proceedings were unpleasantly disturbed by a dispute between the English and Neapolitan envoys and the two representatives of the King of Navarre as to their order of precedence. The question could not be satisfactorily settled, and the Navarrese left the procession in a state of high dudgeon.

As Cæsar rode past the Castle of Sant' Angelo he was honoured as no one had been before him. The whole garrison stood on the walls and ramparts, under arms, with unfurled banners bearing allusions to the Duke's exploits, while a triple salute was fired by the artillery.

The Pope, meanwhile, viewed the proceedings from a balcony, in company with the Cardinals Monreale and Cesarini. As soon as his son reached the portico of the Vatican, Alexander rushed into the Papagallo room to welcome him. The throne, steps, and floor were decked with gold brocade. Cæsar advanced gravely to the threshold, inclining himself ceremoniously. Burchard, who was present in his official capacity, heard him thank his father, in Spanish, for all the favours which he had showered upon him. As he bent down to kiss the Pope's foot, Alexander could no longer restrain himself, and, with a passionate gesture, caught hold of his son and pressed him to his heart. Cæsar's triumph seemed indeed to be complete. The Duke of Gandia's murder was apparently forgotten, and Valentinois, " biondo e bello," was the admired of all beholders on that festive day.

Although the Jubilee year (1500) had hardly begun, the Pope inaugurated a masked fête in order to give his son a chance of displaying his unbridled luxury. It was at this time that Cæsar, taking the Roman Emperor for his model, adopted the device, *Aut Cæsar, aut nihil.* On the Piazza Navona was produced a representation of the Triumph of Julius

Cæsar. The procession opened with twelve triumphal chariots, in the last of which sat Cæsar himself, magnificently attired, and accompanied by a numerous suite. It moved slowly towards the Vatican, that the Pope might behold the wondrous spectacle.

Alexander was clearly overwhelmed with a sense of his son's marvellous abilities. Not long after this he summoned a Consistory, and with the Cardinals' consent made him Gonfaloniere and General-issimo of the Church, at the same time presenting him with the Golden Rose.

CHAPTER XIII

The Jubilee Year, 1500—Florence renews her efforts for the over-
throw of Pisa—Narrow escape of Alexander VI —Murder of
Alfonso of Bisceglia—Lucrezia sent to Nepi to indulge her grief—
Raising of money for Cæsar's campaign—His entry into Pesaro
described by Pandolfo Collenuccio—Surrender of Rimini and
Faenza—Astorre Manfredi—The wife of Caracciolo, the Venetian
General, falls into Cæsar's power—Louis XII pursues his plan
of attacking Naples—Cæsar turns his attention to Florence—
Reign of Federigo of Naples—Claims of France and Spain to his
kingdom—The Pope attacks the Colonna—Alexander's rapa-
city—Double-dealing of Gonsalvo da Cordova—Siege of Capua
—Ill-treatment of the inhabitants by the French and Cæsar
Borgia—Fate of King Federigo—Piombino surrenders to Cæsar
—A third husband found for Lucrezia—Great celebrations in
Rome—Lucrezia sets out for her new home in Ferrara.

THE year 1500 was the year of Jubilee. Preparations
for its celebration were begun as early as 1498, for
Alexander VI. was a Pope who revelled in ceremonies
and public displays. Pilgrims thronged to visit the
tombs of the Apostles that they might gain the
indulgences granted for such expeditions. The disturbed state of northern Italy and the badness of
the roads doubtless prevented many from leaving
their homes, but the numbers who assembled in
Rome bore witness to the influence which religion
still held over men's minds, as well as to the respect
still maintained for the Holy See. On the Thursday
of Holy Week the number gathered together to receive
the papal benediction was estimated at 100,000.
"I rejoice," wrote Peter Delphinus, "that the
Christian religion does not lack the testimony of

277

pious minds, especially in these times of failing faith and depravity of morals."

The conditions prevailing in Rome at that time could not have contributed much to the edification of these pious pilgrims. Many scandalous tales about the Pope and his family were flying about the city, which was frequently the scene of brawling and bloodshed. It is said that, one day in May, no less than eighteen corpses were hung up on the Bridge of Sant' Angelo. One of the most prominent evildoers of the time was a doctor of the Hospital of San Giovanni in Laterano, who used to go out in the early morning to shoot the passers-by, and then plunder their dead bodies. He was associated in crime with the confessor of the hospital, who encouraged him to poison the wealthy among their patients, that they might share the spoils between them.

Spectacles of worldly splendour also greeted the pilgrims' eyes. One day a Frenchman and a Burgundian fought a duel on Monte Testaccio. One of the combatants was backed by Cæsar Borgia, and the other by the Princess of Squillace. On another occasion Cæsar gave a Spanish display in the Piazza of St. Peter's. Mounted on horseback, he slew five bulls with a lance, and beheaded a sixth with one stroke of the sword.

The Florentines were meanwhile making fresh preparations for the overthrow of the Pisans. Since they had concluded an alliance with the French King and sent a considerable force to his aid, they thought that they might reasonably count upon help from France. Cardinal de Rohan, governor of Milan, was at last induced to send them 600 cavalry, 8,000 Swiss, and a train of heavy artillery and other implements of war. The Florentines also enlisted the help of Italian warriors in order to besiege the unfortunate town still more effectively. The Pisans, not relying entirely upon their valour and the strong fortifications of their town, entered into negotiations with Beaumont, the leader of the French troops, offering to surrender to the King of France. But Beaumont continued the siege, and destroyed part of the walls. When, however, a riotous band of soldiers was about to rush upon the town, they found their progress interrupted by a deep trench, which was fortified by a rampart just erected by the Pisans. The French, unable to proceed, were greatly embarrassed, and Beaumont now felt inclined to consider the proposed offer. A mutual agreement was arrived at, and the French were received with open arms. Great confusion prevailed among the besieging troops, who broke all the bonds of discipline. The Pisans, thereupon, made a bold sortie, advanced upon Librafetta and took possession of the place, which was of great importance as the approach to Lucca.

Louis XII. was deeply indignant at this affront to his army. The Florentines sent ambassadors—among them Machiavelli—in the hope of soothing him, but not until they had promised him fresh subsidies did the King look upon them with favour. He even proffered renewed assistance, but the Florentines, who either harboured suspicions or were not in a position to continue the war, declined his support.

Cæsar stayed in Rome several months in order to raise money for his enterprises in the Romagna. His high-flown plans were, however, soon frustrated. On the day before the Feast of St. Peter and St. Paul the Pope had a very narrow escape from death through the fall of a piece of iron in the Basilica. The next day, as he was sitting in his room with the Cardinal of Capua and Monsignore Peto, his private secretary, a sudden and alarming hurricane arose and tore off the roof of the upper part of the Sala de' Papi. A quantity of masonry crashed into the room, but the Pope was protected by the balcony from injury. His two companions shouted to the watchman that his Holiness was killed, and the news immediately spread all over Rome. But when the clouds of dust had settled they were able to make their way to the place where he lay stunned and wounded. Three nobles, who had been precipitated from the upper story, were lying near, in an unconscious and dying condition. The Pope was carried into the adjoining hall, where he soon recovered consciousness. His injuries, it was found, were not serious. There was a slight wound on the head, and one of the right-hand fingers, on which he wore the papal ring, was badly crushed. The first night his temperature was high, but he soon began to mend. " If nothing unforeseen occurs," writes the Mantuan envoy on July 2, " he will recover."

Cæsar and Jofré hastened to express their joy at their father's rescue. The Pope, however, seems to have turned in his weakness to Lucrezia, than whom he would have no other nurse. When the Venetian ambassador visited him on July 3 he found with him Madonna Lucrezia, Sancia and Jofré, and one of Lucrezia's maids of honour, who stood high in the favour of the seventy-year-old Pope.

" Any other man would have been led to look into himself and consider his ways by such a series of narrow escapes ; but Alexander was a true Borgia ; he thanked God and the Blessed Virgin and SS. Peter and Paul for his preservation, and lived on as before." Writing of Alexander in September 1500, Paolo Capello says : " The Pope is now seventy years of age. He grows younger every day. His cares never last the night through   He is always merry, and never does anything that he does not like. The advancement of his children is his only care ; nothing else troubles him."[1]

A considerable sum of money was necessary for the execution of Cæsar's plans. Alexander entered

[1] Pastor

heart and soul into the raising of supplies for him.
People who paid one-third of the cost of a pilgrimage
to Rome were entitled to the privileges conferred
by the actual journey. From Venice alone were
received 799,000 livres in gold. As a pretext for
this unusual accumulation of money, it was given out
that the Pope wished to equip a fleet to support
the Venetians against the Turks. But this help was
of a less substantial kind, and consisted merely in the
command that all the faithful should say an *Ave
Maria* or the *Angelus* at the sound of morning, midday,
and evening bells.

Cæsar had long cherished an intense hatred of
Lucrezia's husband, Alfonso of Bisceglia, whom he
regarded as a hindrance in the way of providing himself with a more profitable brother-in-law. He therefore resolved to get rid of him.

On July 15, 1500, the news of a terrible deed spread
through the city of Rome Late at night Alfonso,
who was on his way from the Vatican to visit Lucrezia,
had been struck down on the steps of St. Peter's
by a band of masked men who attacked him with
daggers and left him for dead. The Duke, however,
revived and managed to drag himself as far as the
Pope's apartments, where Lucrezia, at the sight of
her husband covered with blood, fell on the ground
in a faint. Alfonso was carried to another room in
the Vatican, where a Cardinal immediately administered Extreme Unction. In spite of his severe wounds,
however, he began to recover. The Pope placed
sixteen sentinels at the door of his room, and, in order
to avoid the risk of poisoning, all his food was cooked
by his sister Donna Sancia and his wife Lucrezia,
though the latter was still suffering severely from the
effects of the shock.

All Rome was prating about the attempted murder.
On July 19 the Venetian ambassador wrote to his
Seignory : " It is not known who wounded the Duke,

but it is said to be the same person who murdered the Duke of Gandia and threw him into the Tiber. Monsignore of Valentinois has issued an edict that no one shall be found with arms between the Castle of Sant' Angelo and St Peter's, on pain of death."

To the same ambassador Cæsar remarked: "I did not wound the Duke; but, if I had done so, he would well have deserved it." To the great surprise of every one, he even paid a visit to the wounded man, though it was said that, as he left the sick-room, he was heard to mutter these pregnant words: "What is not accomplished at midday, may be done at night."

When the prospect of Alfonso's recovery was established beyond a doubt, Borgia lost patience. On August 18, at nine o'clock in the evening, he paid another visit to his brother-in-law, who was by this time allowed to sit up. Forcibly ejecting Lucrezia and Sancia from the room, Cæsar summoned his fiendish friend Michelotto, who, throwing the young Duke across his bed, strangled him without more ado. This gruesome deed done, they bore the dead man to St. Peter's, without priest and without prayers, amid the silence of the night.

Cæsar now threw off his mask of hypocrisy and declared openly that he had committed the murder in self-defence, as Alfonso had on one occasion tried to take his life. He had, he said, once been walking in the Vatican gardens, when one of the archers of the Duke of Bisceglia had directed an arrow at his ear.

The way in which the Pope regarded this crime shows clearly what a terrible power Cæsar wielded over his father. The Venetian envoy leads us to suppose that Alexander had even made some feeble attempt to protect Alfonso's life; but as soon as the murder was committed he glossed the matter over, partly from fear of his formidable son, and partly because the Duke's removal would afford him opportunities which he desired.

" Never," says Gregorovius, " was bloody deed so soon forgotten.   The murder of a prince of the royal House of Naples made no more impression than the death of a Vatican stable-boy would have done.   No one avoided Cæsar ; none of the priests refused him admission to the Church, and all the Cardinals continued to show him the deepest reverence and respect. Prelates vied with each other to receive the red hat from the hand of the all-powerful murderer, who offered the dignity to the highest bidders."

The unhappy Lucrezia, who had really loved Alfonso, was in a pitiable position.   That she was incapable of any very great depth of feeling is possible, but that the conduct of her father and brother did not fill her with impotent rebellion is hardly credible. On August 30 she turned her back on Rome, so full of hideous memories, and, accompanied by a retinue of six hundred riders, set out for Nepi, where she might indulge her grief unobserved.   Her father and brother were probably relieved to be rid of her tearful presence.   Paolo Capello, the Venetian ambassador, who left Rome on September 16, 1500, in his report to his Government, says : " Madonna Lucrezia, who is gracious and generous, formerly stood high in the Pope's favour, but now she is so no longer."

How long Lucrezia stayed at Nepi we do not know. Her father probably recalled her to Rome in September or October, when a reconciliation took place between them.   Lucrezia's buoyancy of spirit soon reasserted itself, and her mind became filled with visions of a brilliant future in face of which the sadness of her widowhood faded into nothingness.   That Lucrezia was a strong or noble character will hardly be maintained even by the most daring of her apologists, but that she was gentle and sweet, as well as affectionate, cannot be denied.   Far from being the vindictive, passionate heroine of romance, this unfortunate woman was little more than a passive agent in the hands of her father and her brother, whose strong and vigorous personalities easily dominated her colourless and plastic nature. She was essentially a child of circumstance, more sinned against than sinning.

The expenses of Cæsar's campaign were still very heavy, and all Alexander's extortions did not suffice to pay them. The Pope was, therefore, obliged to borrow considerable sums from merchants and others, in particular from a certain Agostino Chigi, a brother of Lorenzo Chigi, one of the nobles who met his end in the accident to the Vatican apartment. He was one of the wealthiest men in Rome, and not only lent Alexander many thousand ducats, but also gave him his plate, which the Pope immediately had melted.

The year 1500 was for Cæsar a year of good fortune. The Venetians, who were in close alliance with the King of France and the Pope, sent him a patent by which he became a Venetian noble. This mark of favour greatly encouraged him in his ambitious plans. Towards the end of September Cæsar advanced against the town of Pesaro, which received him without resistance, and he entered with public honours the Sforza Palace, where, hardly four years before, Lucrezia had lived with her husband, Giovanni Sforza, the hereditary Lord of Pesaro. A witness of Cæsar's entry was Pandolfo Collenuccio, who, having once been banished by Sforza, had found an asylum at Ferrara. He was now despatched by Duke Ercole to congratulate Cæsar on his capture of Pesaro. On October 29, 1500, Collenuccio wrote to the Duke the following letter, quoted by Gregorovius in his *Lucrezia Borgia* :

" MY ILLUSTRIOUS MASTER,

" Having left your Excellency, I reached Pesaro two and a half days ago, arriving there on Thursday at the twenty-fourth hour. At exactly the same time the Duke of Valentino (Cæsar) made his entry.

The whole population was gathered about the city gate, and he was received in the midst of a heavy storm of rain and presented with the keys of the city. He took up his abode in the palace, in the room formerly occupied by Signor Giovanni. His entry, from what my people tell me, was very impressive. It was orderly, and he was accompanied by many horses and foot-soldiers. The same evening I notified him of my arrival, and requested an audience as soon as it might suit his Majesty's convenience. About 2 o'clock at night [eight o'clock in the evening] he sent Signor Ramiro and his major-domo to call upon me and to ask me in the most courteous manner whether I was comfortably lodged and whether, owing to the great crowd of people in the city, I lacked anything. He also bade them tell me to rest myself thoroughly, and that he would receive me on the following day. Early on Wednesday he sent a courier to me with a sack of barley, a cask of wine, a wether, eight pairs of capons and hens, two large torches, two bundles of wax candles, and two boxes of sweetmeats. He, however, appointed no time for an audience, but he sent his apologies and begged me not to think it strange. The reason was that he had risen at the twentieth hour [two o'clock in the afternoon] and had dined, then had gone to the castle and spent the night, returning greatly exhausted in consequence of a sore in the groin.

" To-day, after he had dined, about the twenty-second hour [four in the afternoon], he sent Signor Ramiro to fetch me to him. With great frankness and amiability his Majesty first apologised for not having granted me an audience on the preceding day, owing to his having so much to do in the castle, and also on account of the pain caused by his ulcer. After these preliminaries, and when I had announced that the sole object of my mission was to wait upon his Majesty, to congratulate and thank him, and to offer your services, he answered me in very carefully chosen and fluent words, covering each point. The gist of it was that, knowing your Excellency's ability and goodness, he had always loved you and hoped to enjoy personal relations with you. He had looked forward to this when you were in Milan, but circumstances then prevented it. But now that he had come to this country, he—determined to fulfil his wish—had written the letter announcing his success, of his own free will and as proof of his love, feeling sure that your Majesty would have pleasure in it. He says that he will continue to keep you informed of his doings, as he desires to establish a firm friendship with your Majesty, and he offers to do everything in his power to help you in case of need. He desires, indeed, to look upon you as a father. . . .

" When I take both the actual facts and his words into consideration, I understand why he wishes to establish some sort of friendly alliance with your Majesty. I believe in his professions, and can see nothing but good in them. He was much pleased by your Majesty's sending a special messenger to him, and I heard that he had informed the Pope of it ; to his people here he mentioned it in a way which showed that he considered it of the greatest importance. . . . We came to the subject of Faenza. His Majesty said to me, ' I do not know what Faenza wants to do ; she can give us no more trouble than did the others ; still she may delay matters.' I replied that I believed she would do as the others had done ; but, if she did not, it could only redound to his Majesty's glory, for it would give him another opportunity to display his skill and valour in capturing the place. This seemed to please him, and he replied that he would assuredly crush it. Bologna was not mentioned. He was pleased with the messages from your people, from Don Alfonso and the Cardinal, of whom he spoke long and affectionately.

" Thereupon, having been together a full half-hour, I took my departure, and his Majesty rode forth on horseback. This evening he is going to Gradara; to-morrow to Rimini, and then farther. . . .

" In this place there are more than two thousand men quartered, but they have done no appreciable damage. The surrounding country is swarming with soldiers, but how much harm they have done we do not know. He has granted to the city no privileges or exemptions, and a certain doctor of Forli has been established as his deputy. He took seventy pieces of artillery from the castle, and the guard that he has left there is very small.

" I will tell your Excellency something which I have heard from several sources; it was, however, related to me in detail by a Portuguese cavalier, a soldier in the army of the Duke of Valentino, . . . an upright man who was a friend of our Lord Don Ferrantino when he was with King Charles. He told me that the Pope intended to give the town as a dowry to Madonna Lucrezia, and that he had found a husband for her—an Italian, who would always remain on friendly terms with Valentino. Whether this is true, I know not, but it is commonly believed.

" As to Fano, the Duke did not retain it. He was there five days. He did not want it, but the citizens presented it to him and it will be his when he desires it. They say that the Pope commanded him not to take Fano, unless the burghers themselves requested it. Therefore it remained *in statu quo*.

" *Postscript.*—The daily life of the Duke is as follows: he goes to bed at eight, nine, or ten o'clock at night [three to five o'clock in the morning]. Consequently the eighteenth hour is his dawn, the nineteenth his sunrise, and the twentieth his time for rising. Immediately on getting up he sits down to the table, and while there and afterwards attends to his business affairs. He is considered brave, strong, and generous, and is reputed to lay great store by straightforward men. He is terrible in revenge—so many tell me. A man of great good sense, and eager for greatness and renown, he seems more anxious to conquer States than to keep and administer them.

"Your illustrious ducal Majesty's servant,

"PANDULPHUS.

"PESARO,
   "*Thursday, October 29, six o'clock at night, 1500* "[1]

Cæsar took possession of Rimini, which was governed by the fierce and gifted Pandolfo Malatesta, just as easily as he had taken Pesaro. The conquest of Faenza presented greater difficulties ; its ruler, Astorre Manfredi, an attractive youth of seventeen or eighteen, was much beloved by his subjects, who valiantly repulsed the assaults of Cæsar's Generals Vitellozzo and Orsini, and, as winter approached, the siege had to be raised ; but, with the return of spring, Cæsar resumed the attack, and on April 25, 1501, the town surrendered under condition that Astorre's liberty should not be interfered with. His conquerors at first treated him as a distinguished guest, but before long he was carried off to the Castle of Sant' Angelo, where, in January 1502, he and his younger brother were put to death, being strangled by Cæsar's command. On June 9, 1502, the young Lord of Faenza was found drowned in the Tiber with a stone fastened round his neck. He was, says Burchard, of such fine stature and so charming of face that his like could scarcely have been found among a thousand youths of the same age.

A maid of honour of Elizabeth Gonzaga's, the wife of the Venetian General, Giovanni Caracciolo, had the misfortune to attract Cæsar's attention on her journey to Venice. She was one of the most beautiful women in Italy, and the Duke immediately

[1] Quoted by Gregorovius.

cast lustful eyes upon her. Well knowing that he could not hope to win her either by entreaties or by presents, he decided to use force, and sent a troop of soldiers to arrest her at Cesena. But her suite was determined to defend her at any risk. A fearful fight ensued, and not until most of her escort were slain did the small remainder take flight. The lady fell into Cæsar's hands, and thereupon her fate was sealed.

Caracciolo, on hearing the terrible news, was almost beside himself with rage and grief. Determined not to submit to this shameful treatment, he appealed to the Council of Ten, at that time presided over by the Doge Barbarigo. They immediately despatched Aloysius Manentino to Cæsar demanding that the lady should be restored to her husband. The French envoy was also informed of the occurrence, and complaints were lodged against Cæsar, who, under the King's auspices, had led the war into the Romagna. The envoy at once set out for Imola to express his displeasure at the Duke's behaviour and to assure him that Louis XII. would be greatly annoyed. The Senate also wrote to the Pope demanding satisfaction for the insult offered to the Republic of Venice. But both Alexander and Cæsar remained quite unmoved by these representations. Cæsar, who was a liar of the first magnitude, denied his guilt, and promised to investigate the matter, adding that there was no lack of beautiful maidens whose favours he could enjoy without having recourse to forcible means. Tomaso Tomasi, however, relates that when the bodies of Astorre and his brother were discovered in the Tiber, near them was the corpse of a woman who proved to be none other than the unhappy wife of Caracciolo. To Cæsar no human life was sacred, and all who stood in his way or afforded him any inconvenience were speedily doomed to die.

The capture of Faenza was the occasion of great
TB

joy at the Vatican, and Cæsar immediately adopted
the title of Duke of the Romagna, a dignity which
was recognised by other Powers, such as Hungary,
Venice, and even Castile and Portugal.

Puffed up with pride, Cæsar now journeyed to
Bologna with the intention of attacking it. But
on his approach, he received commands from the
King of France not to molest the town, as he had
pledged himself to protect it. His obligation, to be
sure, contained the restriction that the rights of the
Church should not be interfered with, but the King
thought it well to maintain that the Pope had no
rights over the district of Bologna. Cæsar was therefore obliged to acquiesce, but Alexander, through the
medium of Paolo Orsini, made an agreement with
Bentivoglio, the Governor, that Bologna should be
left unmolested on condition that Cæsar should have
a free passage and provisions for his troops, and that
Bentivoglio should pay an annual tribute of 9,000
ducats, provide a certain number of soldiers, and
surrender the castle to the Orsini. This treaty was
concluded in 1501, but Bentivoglio, on account of a
rumour spread by Cæsar that he had been invited
to come to Bologna by the family Marescotti, had
all the members of the family at that time in the
town put to death.

The French army had now to proceed to carry out
King Louis's plan of attacking the kingdom of Naples.
A thousand lances and ten thousand infantry were
despatched to Naples under the command of d'Aubigny.
Cæsar, on the other hand, with two hundred lances,
and two thousand foot soldiers, sent to his help by
Bentivoglio, turned in the direction of Florence.
Not waiting for a response to his request to the Floren-
tines for a free passage and provisions, he crossed over
the Apennines.

Arrived at Barberino, he threw off his mask, and
desired Florence to conclude an alliance with him,

and that the present government should be replaced
by another in which he could place more confidence.
Cæsar made this demand, not so much because he
had the power to insist upon it (for his army was
neither large nor suitably equipped, but because
Florence was just then in a defenceless condition,
with no soldiers but the inhabitants. The Florentines, too, were unhappy and suspicious because
in Cæsar's camp were the Orsini, Vitellozzo, the
brother of their ill-fated General, and Piero de' Medici,
who thought it a favourable opportunity to profit
by their interests. But Cæsar had not the slightest
intention of advancing Piero's reinstatement, for
he was by no means anxious to promote the fortunes of
the Orsini and Vitellozzo families, with whom the
Medici would undoubtedly have closely allied themselves in the event of their restoration in Florence.
He also nursed a private grievance against Piero, for,
while Cæsar was still a student at Pisa, he had journeyed
to Florence in the hope of enlisting Piero's interest on
behalf of a friend who was involved in a criminal
law-suit. Piero, however, kept him waiting in his
audience-chamber so long that Cæsar, no little offended,
left the city without having spoken to him. Nevertheless, in order to curry favour with the Orsini and the
Vitellozzi, and also to increase the alarm of the
Florentines, he pretended to fall in with their wishes,
always hoping that he would get an opportunity of
seizing for himself part of the Tuscan domain.

Borgia meanwhile fixed the conditions under which
alone he would depart. The most important were
that Florence should appoint him administrator-in-
chief, with a considerable salary, and not interfere
if he wished to attack the other States of Italy, in
particular the dominion of Piombino, which at that
time stood under Florentine's protection. Further,
that six of the foremost citizens, chosen by Vitellozzo,
should be delivered up to him, and that Piero de'

Medici should be reinstated in his former position. When these plans became public so much bitter feeling was aroused in Florence that the magistrates fell into extremely bad odour with the people.

Before matters were fully settled Cæsar received orders from Louis, who was not at all pleased that he should thus arbitrarily interfere with the method of government in Florence,. to leave Florentine domains. In the event of his disobedience, d'Aubigny was commissioned to drive him out by force.

With great unwillingness, Cæsar obeyed, and withdrew his troops. But first of all he was appointed administrator-in-chief of Florence, with a salary of 36,000 ducats, and exemption from personal service. He then journeyed slowly towards Piombino, carrying great havoc in his train. In places where he found nothing to plunder he had all the inhabitants slaughtered. As he possessed no artillery, he despatched Vitellozzo to Pisa to obtain some.

Once in the domain of Piombino, Cæsar took Sughereto, Scarlino, the island of Elba, and Pianosa. He then besieged the town of Piombino, where Appiano, lord of the princedom, had collected an army ; but he was soon obliged to join the troops of Louis XII., who was preparing to war against Naples. He, however, left garrisons and troops behind him in the province of Piombino.

Federigo, King of Naples, was extremely popular among his subjects, for he had both the power and the will to promote their happiness. Even those who had revolted and taken to flight under the rule of Ferrante I. and Alfonso II now returned to their native town, and the Princes of Salerno and Bisignano had been among the first to do homage to their new sovereign. The goods of those barons who had been on the French side were restored, and it seemed as if at last a time of peace and happiness had begun for Naples. But Federigo's reign was destined to be a short one. The Kings of France and Spain wished to divide the kingdom of Naples between themselves, and devised a disgraceful means of attaining their object. As the representative of the House of Anjou, Louis XII. was to assert his claim to Naples, thus forcing Federigo to seek help from Ferdinand the Catholic. The latter, under pretext of driving away the French, was to send a considerable force which would unite with the French soldiers and expel the House of Aragon. Naples would thus be divided between France and Spain. The French King was to receive the town of Naples, the provinces of Terra di Lavoro and Abruzzo, as well as half the revenue of the meadow-lands of Apulia, and to bear titles as Duke of Milan and King of Naples. On the other hand, Calabria and Apulia, together with at least half of the revenue of the pasture-lands, were to fall to the share of Spain. This compact, signed on November 11, 1500, is still extant, and gives strong evidence of the faithless character of both Kings concerned.

Louis gave the conduct of the war into the hands of his trusty General, d'Aubigny, who was to march into the dominion of Naples with an army of one thousand lances and ten thousand infantry. When Federigo heard of this he asked help from Gonsalvo da Cordova, who, with his troops, was in Sicily. Gonsalvo immediately hastened to seize upon all the fortified places in Calabria. Federigo had meanwhile collected a considerable army, which was joined by the Colonna and their troops.

A gory fight was expected, but before the French had entered Naples the French and Spanish envoys arrived in Rome and disclosed to the Pope and the College of Cardinals the contents of the treaty concluded by their masters and declared the partition of Naples to be inevitable. The defence of Naples against the Turks and the spread of the Christian faith among the infidels, for which the situation of this kingdom was particularly favourable, served as pretext under which the Most Christian and Catholic Kings sought to cloak their rapacity.

The Pope did not oppose this obvious injustice, for he was glad of the opportunity for indulging his hatred of Federigo. For Cæsar, too, the prospect of being able more freely to pursue his passion for conquest in the States of the Church was attractive. On July 15, 1501, a bull was published by which Federigo was deposed and his kingdom divided between the two monarchs. To Alexander it seemed a suitable time for seizing upon the goods of the Colonna, who clung to the cause of the Aragons. It became increasingly clear that no Prince without considerable resources of his own could dispense with the favour of the Borgias. The Colonna also realised that the only way of retaining their possessions, was to place themselves under the protection of the College of Cardinals. But the Pope declared that no favour could be shown them unless they surrendered to him the keys of their town. At the same time he forbade the Cardinals to interfere in the quarrel with the Colonna, whose goods he had made up his mind to seize, threatening with imprisonment and death all who opposed him. On June 22 Francesco Borgia was despatched to take possession, in the Pope's name, of Rocca di Papa and the other castles belonging to the Colonna, who, fearing the Borgia rage, thought it well to submit. On the day following some twenty vassals of the family came to Rome and took an oath of homage to the Papacy. Each of them was presented with a gold ducat and a pair of stockings.

At the same time it was decided that San Marino, which had always served as a citadel for the Colonna, should be entirely demolished, a sentence which Cæsar and the French troops proceeded to carry out.

The Savelli, who also adhered to the House of Aragon, knew that their turn would soon come, and sought refuge in flight from the danger which threatened their lives.

The death of Cardinal Domenico della Rovere gave Alexander an excellent opportunity for enriching his treasury. He sent the Cardinal of Capua to his palace at midnight for the express purpose of seizing upon the property of the deceased, especially the gold, silver, and precious stones, which he had strict injunctions to bring to the Vatican. The poor Cardinal of Capua, although himself concerned in the inheritance, was obliged to obey. A few days later he died from the effects of poison, and then the grasping Pope was able to prey upon the property of both Cardinals.

About the same time occurred the death of Cardinal Zeno of Santa Maria in Porticu. Alexander's predecessors had given him liberty to dispose of his property as he chose, with the result that he left 25,000 ducats to various pious objects, and 100,000 ducats to Venice in order to carry on the Turkish crusade. But the Pope, who could not endure to lose sight of so large a sum of money, informed the Venetian Republic that he had revoked the power granted to the Cardinal by former Popes, and declared the will invalid. He thereupon, in his capacity of Spiritual Lord, claimed all the property for himself. Although Venice took no heed of the Pope's action, he did not altogether fail in his object. The Cardinal had left, in a cloister of Ancona, two caskets containing 20,000 gold ducats as well as other valuables, with directions that they should be given to a youth who had once done him great service. This young man, however, died before the Cardinal, who made no mention of the caskets in his will. Alexander, upon hearing of this, sent to Ancona and seized upon the treasure.

A like fate overtook the Cardinal of Lisbon, who was seized with an apoplectic stroke while dining with a friend at the Vatican. He recovered sufficiently to be able to be taken to his own palace, but the Pope refused to allow him to make his will, hoping to be able to take possession of the inheritance himself. The Cardinal, deeply incensed, swore that the Borgias should have none of his money. He sent secretly for some of his friends, to whom he entrusted some 50,000 ducats for the promotion of good works ; among other friends and relations he divided considerable sums, as well as furniture and silver plate, commanding them to leave the States of the Church secretly. To the astonishment of all concerned, however, the Cardinal recovered, when he found himself without enough means to keep up the dignity of his position. But the thought that he had deprived the Borgias of his inheritance contributed much to cheer him in his misfortune.

This custom of appropriating the goods of the deceased rich was constantly exercised by the Pope's children, who not infrequently disputed the division of the treasure.

Meanwhile, d'Aubigny had marched into Rome at the head of his troops. He and his generals, Gajazzo, d'Allègre, and others, were richly entertained in the palace of Cardinal Sforza. Their soldiers, too, were treated with every consideration. On the Feast of SS. Peter and Paul the whole of the Roman clergy went in procession to the Basilica of St. Peter. First of all the Pope received d'Aubigny and the French Generals, and afterwards the terms of the already-mentioned treaty between Alexander VI. and the Kings of France and Spain. But care was taken to represent the alliance only as a union for the defence of Christendom against the Turks. In five or six days the French took their departure from Rome, and Alexander greatly rejoiced when he saw them disappear in the direction of Naples.

Federigo of Naples was terrified at the news that France and Spain had united against him, and, without beating about the bush, he appealed to Gonsalvo to know whether this alliance was a fact. Gonsalvo denied it most emphatically, and even promised Naples his support. But Federigo, whose suspicions were not quite allayed, withdrew in the direction of San Germano, in order to await the troops recruited by the Orsini. As soon as the French had arrived, Gonsalvo ceased to dissimulate, and sent six galleys to Naples to fetch the two widowed Queens, one of whom was a sister, the other a niece, of the King of Spain. Prospero Colonna advised Federigo to seize the opportunity and capture the galleys before all the troops had united. But the King lacked the necessary decision to follow this advice, and thought it more prudent to use his troops in defending his towns, though San Germano was already in a state of insurrection. He chose Capua as their citadel, and, leaving Prospero Colonna behind in Naples, he himself went with the rest of the army to Aversa.

D'Aubigny lost no time in laying siege to Capua, which his troops attacked with great violence. The garrison, however, defended itself so bravely that the French had perforce to retire with considerable losses. But the Capuans, at last realising that they could not hold out indefinitely, agreed to an interview with Fabricius Colonna. Relying upon overtures of peace, the defence was neglected, the sentry relieved, and the town left in disorder. This did not escape the notice of the enemy, who hastened to break open the gates, slaughter the inhabitants, and plunder the town. Even the cloisters were not spared, and many women were sent to Rome and sold in the market. Many of them, preferring honour to life itself, threw themselves into the wells or drowned themselves in the river.

Cæsar Borgia, who had also been engaged in the

invasion of Capua, learned that some women had taken refuge in a tower of the castle. Guicciardini relates that Cæsar, hastening thither with some of his suite, examined his victims carefully, and, choosing forty of the most beautiful for himself, abandoned the rest to the mercies of his men. Fabricius Colonna, Don Ugo di Cardone, and the other Captains were taken captive; among them was the famous *condottiere*, Rinuccio da Marciano, who was severely wounded and only survived his capture a few days. If we are to believe the historian Paulus Jovius, his end was accelerated by poison administered by Vitellozzo in revenge because Rinuccio's faction in Florence had condemned his brother to death.

After the fall of Capua Federigo gave up all hope of being able to defend his kingdom, especially as Gaeta had also yielded. Naples therefore entered into negotiations with the enemy, and bought itself off for 60,000 ducats of the plunder. The King had to retire to Castelnuovo, though he was compelled to surrender this fortress as well as his other towns and fortified places, with the exception of Ischia, to the French. Cast down from his high estate, he found himself and his numerous family reduced to great misery; his treasure had been snatched away from him, and his eldest son was imprisoned in Tarento without hope of release. Among his companions in misfortune were his sister Isabella d'Este, who had been cruelly repudiated by her husband Ladislaus of Hungary, and Isabella, Duchess of Milan, whose husband and eldest son had been poisoned by Ludovico the Moor, and who now had to look on helplessly at the degradation of her House of Aragon.

In describing the events of this period, Guicciardini recounts a remarkable example of filial love. When the French entered Naples the son of the Prince of Montpensier went to visit his father's tomb at

Pozzuoli. Throwing himself down by the tomb, he was overcome by a passion of grief so intense that he died from its effects.

Federigo, whose position had become untenable, now resolved to throw himself upon the mercy of Louis of France rather than entrust himself to his other enemy, the false Ferdinand of Spain. The French King willingly granted him a safe escort to France, whither he embarked after sending his son in Tarento as much help as possible. Louis received him graciously, and conferred on him the dukedom of Aragon, with a pension of 30,000 ducats. Thereupon Federigo commanded that Ischia should be ceded to the French.

The "Great Captain," Gonsalvo, meanwhile marched into Calabria, where the towns, with the exception of Manfredonia and Tarento, yielded without much resistance. After an obstinate defence, Tarento had finally to give in. When the Count of Potenza and Leonardo, Knight of Rhodes and Governor of Tarento, who had the guardianship of the young Duke of Calabria, saw that they could no longer hold out, they bound themselves to surrender the town in four months, provided no help arrived meanwhile. On the other hand Gonsalvo had to swear that the young Duke should be free to choose his own place of withdrawal. The latter had received orders to join his father in France, but Gonsalvo, notwithstanding his solemn oath, refused to let him go, but sent him under escort as a prisoner to Spain.

Cæsar, whose assistance was no longer necessary, now sent Giovanni Baglioni and Vitellozo with troops to Piombino. Appiano, who was in no condition to defend himself, hastened to France to demand help from Louis XII. on the ground of a former treaty. But the King explained that he could not oppose Cæsar's conquests on account of a reconciliation which he had concluded with the Pope.   Piombino therefore was obliged to surrender.

Already in 1501 rumours were afloat in Rome concerning a projected alliance between Lucrezia and Alfonso d'Este, the hereditary Prince of Ferrara. It was Alexander himself who had devised this plan, for he hoped by it to secure the possession of the Romagna for Cæsar, and at the same time to open a prospect of annexing Bologna and Florence. That Lucrezia might still harbour regrets for the other Alfonso did not affect the Pope's schemes. He commissioned Giambattista Ferrari of Modena, one of his staunchiest adherents to lay the proposal before Duke Ercole of Ferrara, " on account of the great advantage which would accrue to his State from it." The Duke was greatly embarrassed at the offer. His son Alfonso raised decided objections, and his daughter, the virtuous Isabella, Margravine of Mantua, and her sister-in-law Elisabetta of Urbino, were horrified at the idea of admitting a Borgia into their family. Thus influenced, Duke Ercole returned a decided refusal, but Alexander, undismayed, succeeded in overcoming the opposition of Louis XII. and winning him over to his side. Louis was most anxious to conciliate the Pope, for it was just at the time of his expedition to Naples, for which he needed the papal authority. At the same time he only gave a half-hearted consent to the furtherance of the match, and advised Duke Ercole not to be in a hurry, and even assured him that he would continue to favour the alliance between Alfonso and Louise of Angoulême. The Duke, therefore, made no haste to conclude matters, and when Alexander and Cæsar tried to urge him forward he insisted that the stipulated conditions should be carried out.

On July 27, 1501, the Pope, accompanied by a troop of soldiers, went to Sermoneta, leaving Lucrezia as his representative in the Vatican—a bold and extrordinary step to take. " Before his Holiness, our Master, left the city, he turned over the palace and all business affairs to his daughter Lucrezia, authorising her to open all letters which should come addressed to him. In all important matters she was to ask advice of the Cardinal of Lisbon " (Burchard's *Diary*) Alexander had just received news of Alfonso's consent to the union, and it was probably as a recognition of Lucrezia's political importance as the prospective Duchess of Ferrara that he placed her in so prominent a position.

Duke Ercole had experienced no little difficulty in overcoming his son's repugnance to an alliance with a woman of Lucrezia's ill repute, for the malicious rumours spread at the time of her divorce had sullied her fair fame so greatly that most honourable men and women looked at her askance.

But when Ercole threatened that he would marry her himself, Alfonso gave way. The marriage was regarded merely as a profitable piece of statecraft, and the honour of the house of Milan was bartered for the highest price obtainable. The Pope's agents in Ferrara, alarmed at the Duke's exorbitant demands, sent Raimondi Romolini to Rome to submit them to Alexander. The Duke's conditions have already been mentioned. The dowry which he demanded was an extravagant one, but so great was the Pope's desire to secure the throne of Ferrara for his daughter that, after some altercation, he finally consented to pay it. The Duke also insisted upon the remission of the annual tribute paid by the fief of Ferrara to the Church, as well as the cession of Cento and Pieve, which belonged to the Bishopric of Bologna. Cæsar and Lucrezia both urged their father to submit to whatever the Duke demanded. Lucrezia, we are told, was radiant at the prospect of this, her third marriage. With characteristic volatility, she forgot the sorrows of her widowhood in the anticipation of a brilliant future. Doubtless, too, she looked forward to her position in Ferrara as a release from the uncongenial atmosphere of Rome, where her life was darkened by the tyranny of Cæsar and the black shadow of the Borgia reputation.

The marriage contract was executed on August 26, 1501, and the nuptials were concluded on September 1.

When the news arrived that the nuptial contract had been signed in Ferrara, the Pope, in his jubilation, had the Vatican illuminated and the glad tidings proclaimed by the cannon of the Castle of Sant' Angelo. On September 5 Lucrezia, accompanied by four bishops and three hundred knights, passed through the streets of Rome on her way to a thanksgiving service at Santa Maria del Popolo. In accordance with a strange custom of the time, she presented the costly robe in which she had attended the ceremony, to one of her court fools, who ran gaily up and down the city, yelling out, " Long live the illustrious Duchess of Ferrara ! Long live Pope Alexander ! " .

The Vatican now became the scene of feasting and merriment. Dancing and music enlivened every evening, for it was one of the Pope's greatest delights to watch beautiful women at the dance, and he often so far forgot his sacred office as to be present at voluptuous displays such as had aroused the displeasure of Pius II. Lucrezia, fond as she was of gaiety, became worn out with all this dissipation, and it was a relief when her father left Rome in order to visit Civita Castellana and Nepi. On September 25 the ambassadors wrote to Ferrara : " The illustrious lady continues somewhat ailing and is greatly fatigued. . . . The rest which she will have while his Holiness is away will do her good ; for whenever she is at the Pope's palace the entire night, until two or three o'clock, is spent in dancing and at play, which tires her greatly."

The bride's outfit was of the most luxurious kind ;

her father told the Ferrarese ambassadors that he intended her to have " more beautiful pearls than any other Italian princess."

On December 23 the bridal escort, consisting of Alfonso's brothers, Sigismondi, Ferrante, and the Cardinal Ippolito d'Este, with a retinue of five hundred persons, arrived in Rome. On the same day the Ferrarese envoy, in a letter to his lord, expresses the following favourable opinion of Lucrezia : " She is singularly graceful in everything she does, and her manners are modest, gentle, and decorous. She is also a good Christian, and more, she is going to confession and to Communion on Christmas Day. As regards good looks she has quite sufficient, but her pleasing expression and gracious ways make her seem even more beautiful than she is. In short, she seems to me to be such that there is nothing to fear, but rather the very best to be hoped, in every way, from her."

On December 28 the marriage was celebrated by procuration in the Vatican amid gorgeous festivities. The bride's dress was of " gold brocade and crimson velvet trimmed with ermine. . . . A black band confined her golden hair, and she wore on her head a light coif of gold and silk. Her necklace was a string of pearls with a locket consisting of an emerald, a ruby, and one large pearl." Until her departure on January 6, 1502, Rome gave itself up to one long round of festivities, and for days only masked faces were to be seen out of doors. Dances, comedies, banquets, games, and bull-fights followed in quick succession, all paid for out of the funds of the reluctant city.

The Pope was determined that Lucrezia's departure should be attended by great pomp and magnificence, and that her progress through Italy should be truly regal. He said farewell to his daughter in the Chamber of the Parrots, where they spent some time alone.

As she left him, he called after her in a loud voice bidding her be of good cheer and to write to him whenever she wanted anything, adding that he would do more for her in the future than he had ever done for her while she was in Rome. He then wandered from place to place, watching her until she and her retinue were lost to view.

It was about three o'clock in the afternoon when Lucrezia set out for her new home. The Romans heaved a sigh of relief at her departure, for they had been sorely taxed by the expenses of her marriage festivities. The papal Court, the Cardinals, ambassadors, and magistrates accompanied her to the Porta del Popolo. Francesco Borgia, Archbishop of Cosenza, a most devoted retainer, had been chosen as legate to escort her through the States of the Church. The bride's own suite consisted of one hundred and eighty persons; in a list which is still preserved may be seen the names of many of her maids of honour; her first lady-in-waiting was the beautiful and charming Angela Borgia. Lucrezia, herself, was mounted on a white jennet caparisoned with gold, and she wore a riding habit of red silk and ermine and a hat trimmed with feathers. Her brother Cæsar accompanied her for a short distance and then returned to the Vatican.

The Pope had made detailed arrangements for the journey and had carefully noted all the places at which they were to stop. Their route was to comprise Castelnuovo, Civita Castellana, Narni, Terni, Spoleto, Foligno, Pesaro, Rimini, Cesena, Forli, Faenza, Imola, and Bologna. From the following letter to the Priors of Nepi we may see to what extortions the people were subjected:

" DEAR SONS,

" Greeting and the Apostolic Blessing. As our dearly beloved daughter in Christ, the noble lady and Duchess Lucrezia de Borgia, who is to leave here

THE TRIUMPH OF APOLLO.

THE TRIUMPH OF MINERVA.

THE TRIUMPH OF VENUS.

FRESCOES FROM THE SCHIFFANOIA PALACE, RESIDENCE OF LUCREZIA
BORGIA AT FERRARA.

next Monday to join her husband Alfonso, the beloved son and first-born of the Duke of Ferrara, with a large escort of nobles, and two hundred horsemen will pass through your district, therefore we wish and command you, if you value our favour and desire to avoid our displeasure, to provide for the company mentioned above for a day and two nights, the time they will spend with you. By so doing you will receive from us all due approbation. Given in Rome, under the Apostolic seal, December 28, 1501, in the tenth year of our Pontificate."[1]

[1] Gregorovius.

CHAPTER XIV

IN every city where Lucrezia and her convoy halted, they were, at the Pope's command, fêted and honoured at the expense of the commune. At Spoleto she was met by Duke Guidobaldi of Urbino, who escorted her to his city. Sumptuous quarters were allotted to her in the beautiful palace of Federigo, which the Duke and Duchess had vacated for the occasion. The famous Duchess Elisabetta also showed the bride great kindness and accompanied her to her journey's end.

Pesaro, which Lucrezia must have entered with much emotion, now belonged to Cæsar, who had commanded that a royal reception should be accorded to his sister. Her former subjects appeared delighted to welcome her, but, notwithstanding their demonstrations of joy, she took no share in the festivities. Pozzi, in writing to the Duke, says that she spent the whole time in her chamber " for the purpose of washing her head, and because she was naturally inclined to solitude." Even the buoyancy of Lucrezia's disposition, it seems, was weighed down by sorrowful memories of the past.

This washing of the head was probably connected in some way with the hair-dressing, for it appears to have been a frequent interruption to the progress of the cavalcade. Don Ferrante wrote from Imola that Lucrezia would stay there a day in order to wash her head, which, she said, had not been done for eight days, and she was therefore afflicted with headache.

At Bologna the bridal retinue was splendidly received by the Bentivoglio family, who, though in their hearts they must have loathed the Borgias, spared no pains to do Lucrezia honour.

On the evening of January 31 they reached the Castle of Bentivoglio, about twenty miles from Ferrara. Here Lucrezia was greatly surprised by the unexpected appearance of her bridegroom, Alfonso, who had hitherto displayed a morose and apathetic attitude towards the bride who had been thrust upon him During their short interview Lucrezia, by the silent commendation of her beautiful face, contrived to cast her spell upon him, and he left for Ferrara at the end of two hours, with his heart relieved and his misgivings much allayed.

The Pope was delighted to hear of this meeting, for he had experienced many qualms as to Lucrezia's reception by the House of Este, and had frequently begged Cardinal Ferrari to warn Duke Ercole to treat his daughter-in-law kindly.

On February 1 Lucrezia continued her journey to Ferrara by the canal. Near Malalbergo she found Isabella Gonzaga waiting to meet her. At the urgent request of her father the marchioness, much against her will, had come to do the honours during the festivities in his palace. " In violent anger," so she wrote to her husband, who remained at home, she greeted and embraced her sister-in-law.

The Duke, with Don Alfonso and his Court, awaited Lucrezia at Torre della Fossa   When she left the boat the Duke saluted her on the cheek, she having first respectfully kissed his hand.

Thereupon, all mounted a magnificently decorated dais, to which the foreign ambassadors and numerous cavaliers came to kiss the bride's hand.   To the strains of music and the thunder of cannon, the cavalcade proceeded to the Borgo San Luca, where they all dismounted.   Lucrezia took up her residence in the palace of Alberto d'Este.[1]

Ferrara was already filled with thousands of strangers, of whom part had come out of curiosity and part at the invitation of the Duke.   The Princes of Urbino and Mantua were represented by the ladies of their families, and the House of Bentivoglio by Annibale. France, Rome, Venice, Florence, Lucca, and Siena had all sent envoys.   Cæsar himself was still in Rome, but he was represented by a cavalier.   The Pope had desired that Cæsar's wife, Charlotte d'Albret, should go to Ferrara for the festivities, but she did not appear.

Lucrezia's entry into the city on February 2, 1502, was one of the most splendid pageants of the age. At two o'clock in the afternoon Duke Ercole and all the ambassadors repaired to Alberto's palace to fetch the bride.   On the way back Alfonso headed the procession, the bride came towards the middle, and the Duke last.   This arrangement was intended to show that Lucrezia was the most important personage of the parade.   " Just behind Alfonso came her escort, pages, and court officials, among whom were several Spanish cavaliers ; then five bishops, followed by the ambassadors according to rank ; the four deputies of Rome, mounted upon beautiful horses and wearing long brocade cloaks and black

[1] Gregorovius.

birettas, coming next. These were followed by six tambourines and two of Lucrezia's favourite clowns.

" Then came the bride herself, radiantly beautiful and happy, mounted upon a white jennet with scarlet trappings, and followed by her master of horse. Lucrezia was dressed in a loose-sleeved camorra of black velvet with a narrow gold border, and a cape of gold brocade trimmed with ermine. On her head she wore a sort of net glittering with diamonds and gold—a present from her father-in-law. . . . About her neck she had a chain of pearls and rubies which had once belonged to the Duchess of Ferrara— as Isabella noticed, with tears in her eyes. Her beautiful hair fell down unconfined on her shoulders. She rode beneath a purple baldachin, which the doctors of Ferrara, *i.e.* the members of the faculties of law, medicine, and mathematics, supported in turn.

" Behind Lucrezia came the Duke, in black velvet, on a dark horse with trappings of the same material. On his right was the Duchess of Urbino, clad in a dark velvet gown. Then followed nobles, pages, and other personages of the house of Este, each of whom was accompanied by one of Lucrezia's ladies. . . . Afterwards came fourteen vehicles upon which were seated a number of the noble women of Ferrara, beautifully dressed, including the twelve damsels who had been allotted to Lucrezia as maids of honour. Then followed two white mules and two white horses decked with velvet and silk and costly gold trappings. Eighty-six mules accompanied the train, bearing the bride's trousseau and jewels "

At the gate near Castle Tedaldo Lucrezia's horse was frightened by the discharge of a cannon, and she was thrown. She rose without assistance, and the Duke placed her upon another horse, whereupon the cortége started again. " In honour of Lucrezia there were everywhere triumphal arches, tribunes, orations, and mythological scenes. . . . When the cavalcade reached the Piazza before the church, two rope-walkers descended from the towers and addressed compliments to the bride—thus was the ludicrous introduced into public festivities at that time. . . . At the moment when the procession reached the palace of the Duke, all prisoners were given their liberty."[1]

At the ducal palace the bride was received by the Marchioness Gonzaga and other distinguished ladies, many of them bastard daughters of the House of Este. To the sound of music the bridal pair were conducted to the reception hall and seated upon a throne. Then followed the presentation of the court officials, and an orator delivered himself of an epithalamium. Afterwards the Duke accompanied Lucrezia to the rooms which had been prepared for her. She must have been pleased with her reception by the House of Este, for her charming appearance made a favourable impression on every one, and all the poets of the day, not excluding Ariosto, wrote effusively in her honour. The chronicler Bernardino Zambotto describes her in the following words: "She has a beautiful countenance, sparkling and animated eyes, and a slender figure; she is keen and intellectual, joyous and human, and possessed of good reasoning powers. She pleased the people so greatly that they are perfectly satisfied with her, and they look to her Majesty for protection and good government. They are truly delighted, for they think that the city will greatly profit through her, especially as the Pope will refuse her nothing, as is shown by the portion he gave her, and by presenting Don Alfonso with certain cities."

Cagnolo of Parma also speaks of her approvingly: "She is of medium height and slender figure. Her face is long, the nose well-defined and beautiful; her hair a bright gold, and her eyes blue; her mouth is somewhat large, the teeth dazzlingly white; her

[1] Gregorovius and Garner.

neck white and slender, but well rounded. She is always cheerful and good-humoured."

The wedding festivities were continued for six days, their attractions being greatly increased by the presence of the three most beautiful women of the day—Lucrezia, Isabella, and the Duchess of Urbino. On the last day of these celebrations, so minutely described by Gregorovius, the departing ambassadors presented the bride with valuable gifts of beautiful stuffs and silver ware. The Venetian envoys had been clad in most magnificent garments of crimson velvet trimmed with fur, which excited the astonishment of the multitude. One of them, it is said, contained twenty-eight, and the other thirty-two, yards of velvet. Following the instructions of the Seignory of Venice, these festive robes were bestowed on Lucrezia as a bridal gift. The manner of presentation was quaint. The envoys, having addressed discourses in Latin and Italian to Lucrezia, retired to an adjoining room, where they divested themselves of their splendid garments and sent them in to the bride. This performance excited great merriment at the Court of Ferrara.

In spite of the trouble and expense to which the Duke had gone, Isabella seems to have found the entertainments dull and slow. She was longing to get back to Mantua, where she would not be constantly irritated by the unwelcome presence of her new sister-in-law. There is, however, good reason to believe that her antipathy died away in the course of time, to be replaced by a genuine friendship for Lucrezia.

On September 15, 1501, long before his sister's marriage, Cæsar had returned to Rome, where he learned that his troops had captured Piombino. The Borgia star was now in the ascendant. Lucrezia was about to enter upon an honourable alliance

Alexander had established two dukedoms[1] out of the property which he had seized from the Colonna; Cæsar was master of nearly the whole of the Romagna, as he was virtually master of Rome. The Pope himself quailed before the iron will of this odious tyrant, by whom no human life was held sacred.

Burchard, in his *Diarium*, describes a scene of the most horrible debauchery at a feast given by Cæsar on October 31, 1501, at which both the Pope and Lucrezia are said to have been present.[2] This, however, is the only occasion on which Burchard represents Lucrezia in an unfavourable light. He makes not the remotest reference to the criminal intimacy with her father and brothers of which she has been accused—a fact which he is not likely to have concealed if he had entertained any suspicions of its probability.

At the end of the year 1501 a bitter and malignant letter attacking the Borgias in no measured terms was sent to Silvio Savelli, one of the exiled Roman barons. " You are mistaken, my dear friend," it

[1] Nepi and Sermoneta.

[2] "Buchard tells us how, for the amusement of Cesare, of the Pope, and of Lucrezia, . . . fifty courtesans were set to dance after supper, with the servants and some others who were present, dressed at first and afterwards not so. He draws for us a picture of those fifty women on all fours . . . striving for the chestnuts flung to them in that chamber of the Apostolic Palace "—by the Pope and his two children. " There is much worse to follow " (*The Life of Cesare Borgia*, by Rafael Sabatini, p. 305. See also *The Diary of John Burchard, Bishop of Orta*, vol. iii, entries under October 27 and November 11, 1501.) Mr. Sabatini discredits these stories, but, since Burchard resided in the Vatican, he had every opportunity of knowing whether or no they were true, and he could have had no conceivable object in recording, in his private diary and note-book, not for publication but merely for his own information, events of which he had not ascertained the full and accurate details. Entries of the kind are rare in the Diary, but when they occur they indicate no surprise on the part of Burchard.

ran, "if you think that you ought to attempt to come to terms with this monster. . . . Lay before the Emperor and the other Princes of the Empire all the evil that has proceeded from this cursed beast for the perdition of Christendom; narrate the abominable crimes by which God is set at naught, and the heart of religion pierced through." It goes on to accuse the Pope, Cæsar, and Lucrezia of every conceivable crime. "There is no sort of outrage or vice," it says, "that is not openly practised in the Palace of the Pope. The perfidy of the Scythians and Carthaginians, the bestiality and savagery of Nero and Caligula, are surpassed. Rodrigo Borgia is an abyss of vice, a subverter of all justice, human or divine."

Although the Pope had this libel read to him, he made no effort to check the circulation of the pamphlet or to prosecute its author. Cæsar, however, did not take things so calmly. At the end of November a masked man who had inveighed against the Duke in the Borgo was seized by his command and suffered the loss of one hand and the tip of his tongue. A Venetian who had translated some scandalous document from the Greek and sent it to Venice, was put to death. The Pope, in speaking of his son to the Ferrarese envoy, said: "the Duke is good-hearted, but he cannot bear injuries. I have often told him that Rome is a free country, where a man may say 'or write what he will; that much is said against me, but that I do not interfere. He answered: 'If Rome is accustomed to write and speak slanders, well and good; but I will teach them to repent.' For my own part, I have always been forgiving—witness the Cardinals who plotted against me when Charles VIII. invaded Italy. I might have rid myself many times of Ascanio Sforza and Giuliano della Rovere; but I have not done so."

Five weeks after Lucrezia's departure Alexander

and Cæsar set out for Piombino, which had surrendered in September, 1501. The aim of this expedition was to inspect the fortifications which were in construction, apparently under the supervision of Leonardo da Vinci. They were accompanied by the Cardinals Pallavicino, Orsini, Cosenza, d'Este, and Borgia, as well as by a number of prelates and servants. They afterwards visited the island of Elba, and also spent some time in the outlying districts of Piombino. Their own enjoyment was not neglected, and the most beautiful maidens of the neighbourhood performed their national dances in the market-place. The time was Lent, but the papal Court made no pretence of fasting. In order to win the favour of the country people and impress them with the Borgia munificence, feasts were organised and an astonishing amount of money lavished on them.

The return journey was begun on March 1, but, owing to the bad weather, their progress was slow, and they did not reach Ercole until the fourth. They continued as far as Corneto, but upon their arrival the storm was so violent that it was impossible to land, and they seemed in imminent danger of shipwreck. The crew were beside themselves with terror, and fell on their faces and wept. The Pope alone appeared calm and unaffrighted. He remained on deck, crossed himself from time to time, and called upon the Name of Jesus. The alarming situation did not affect his appetite, and he asked for dinner; but the winds and waves were too rough to allow the kindling of a fire at the time, though later on, during a lull in the storm, they were able to cook a few fish. Finally, with great difficulty, they effected a landing near Porto Ercole, where horses were sent for the Pope and his suite from Corneto.

Meanwhile disturbances had broken out in Tuscany, originated by Vitellozzo, Giampagnolo, Baglione, and the Orsini, who, with the help of Pandolfo Petrucci were anxious to reinstate Piero de' Medici in Florence. But Guglielmo de' Pazzi, the Florentine plenipotentiary in Arezzo, learned that some of the citizens were in treacherous communication with Vitellozzo, and were meditating a revolution. He thereupon had two of the leaders arrested ; but this measure only served to bring the rebellion to a head. The citizens of Arezzo rose up and openly renounced their allegiance to Florence. They liberated both prisoners, and imprisoned Pazzi and the other magistrates in their stead. The people ran up and down with cries of " Freedom ! Freedom ! " and all that remained in the hands of the Florentines was the citadel in which the Bishop of Arezzo, the governor's son, had taken refuge.

The rebels sent to ask help of Vitellozzo, who was anything but pleased at this rash outbreak of revolution before adequate preparations had been made. Nevertheless, he hastened with troops to the support of the citizens. A few days later he returned to Citta di Castello, leaving his forces behind at Arezzo, and promising to return shortly with considerable reinforcements.

The Florentines apparently did not recognise the importance of this rebellion, and were in no hurry to suppress it, thinking that peace could be restored by a handful of soldiers from the surrounding districts. Vitellozzo, quick to notice their remissness, immediately returned to Arezzo with fresh forces. Baglione, Cardinal Paolo Orsini, and Piero de' Medici came to his aid, and the besieged, realising that the Florentine troop under Bentivoglio was not strong enough to resist Vitellozzo, surrendered in a few days. The besiegers, however, detained the Bishop, in order that they might exchange him for a few prisoners taken by the Florentines. Afterwards the citizens razed the citadel to the ground. The Florentines, who now saw that their cause was hopeless, withdrew to Monte Varchi, whereupon Vitellozzo made himself master of the surrounding district.

The Borgias took no part in this rebellion; the reinstatement of the Medici could only have been to their advantage, since the unrest which prevailed among the Florentine citizens would have been favourable to their plans against Tuscany. Cæsar, not wishing to let the present opportunity slip, directed his attention to Urbino, within whose province lay four towns and thirty fortified castles. Duke Guidobaldi of Montefeltro had, however, given no cause of offence; on the contrary, he had often taken up arms on behalf of the Church. His courage was undoubted, and, by his amiable qualities, he had earned the affection of his subjects. Cæsar, who, since the troops of Vitellozzo and Baglione were otherwise engaged, was not in a position to attack Urbino, took refuge in cunning. Both he and Alexander displayed the greatest friendliness towards the Duke, and the Pope undertook to settle the difference which had arisen between Guidobaldi and the Apostolic See concerning his enfeoffment. His nephew, Francesco Maria, was appointed Prefect of Rome, and the Pope planned for him a marriage with his niece, Angela Borgia.

No sooner did Cæsar feel secure of the Duke's favour than he despatched part of his troops for the purpose of besieging Camerino. He sent two ambassadors to Guidobaldi, requesting the loan of his heavy artillery as well as a free escort for fifteen hundred of his men. The Duke was most obliging, and immediately sent one of his nobles to Cæsar at Spoleto with assurances of his support. Cæsar, not to be outdone in amiability, received the envoy graciously, asserting that he well knew how to prize the service and favour of the Duke of Urbino, adding that he could wish no other brother in Italy.

Directly the envoy had returned to Urbino, Cæsar

sent two thousand men to the province, under pretext of conveying the artillery and the provisions. At the same time he commanded the rest of his troops to press forward,' garrison all the routes, and hold themselves in readiness to occupy the States of the Duke. Cæsar himself lost no time in betaking himself and his cavalry to Nocera, which lay on the way to Camerino, and thence rushed with so much violence upon the domain of Urbino that no place escaped pillage. Leaving behind him destruction and desolation, he announced his intention of now proceeding against the town of Urbino.

Duke Guidobaldo was immediately informed of this unexpected hostility on the part of his supposed friend, and being unable to defend himself, was obliged to seek safety in flight, clad as a peasant. In spite of Cæsar's vigilance and craftiness, he managed to escape to Mantua.

Cæsar took possession of Urbino without meeting any resistance, though he felt that his dominion over it could never be secure until he had succeeded in annihilating the family of Montefeltro. Knowing Cardinal della Rovere, who was at that time in Savona, to be their most devoted friend, the Pope and Cæsar cast about for some way of capturing him. Their plan, which was to beguile him on to some galleys under a false pretence, and then to seize him, fell through, owing to the Cardinal's sturdy principle of completely ignoring the Borgia authority.

For some time longer Cæsar remained at Urbino, unable to decide whether to continue the siege of Camerino or to unite his troops with those of Vitellozzo, who had gained important advantages in Tuscany. Although he dreaded the displeasure of France, who had taken Tuscany under her protection, Cæsar could not resist throwing in his lot with Vitellozzo, whose successes aroused his most sanguine expectations. The Medici brothers and the Orsini united with him, and it seemed certain that Florence would soon have to yield. In this crisis the citizens assembled to consider how they could avert the danger which threatened them. Soderini declared that the only way of saving the situation was to turn to Louis of France, who, in the Treaty of Blois, November 1501, had promised the Republic his protection. The result of Soderini's representations was that King Louis sent hasty messengers to the Borgias, admonishing them to give up their designs on Florence. In the event of their disobedience, a French force was ordered to be in readiness to expel Vitellozzo from Tuscany and to deprive Cæsar of the conquered towns. The latter was therefore obliged, with great reluctance to withdraw his forces from Florence.

Cæsar, who was zealously continuing the siege of Camerino, after pretending to negotiate with Giulio Cesare da Varano, the ruler, seized upon the town. As he never considered himself secure of a conquest as long as the legal owner still lived, he had Varano and two of his sons immediately strangled.

When the Pope heard of the capture of Camerino he was "almost beside himself with joy," writes the Venetian ambassador. Cæsar was already beginning to think of turning his attention to Bologna when Louis XII., who was beset by complaints of the conduct of the Duke of Romagna, gave him to understand that his ambition was leading him too far. Cæsar, who counted much on the French King's favour, hastened to Asti to try to make peace, throwing the blame of the Florentine undertaking upon Vitellozzo, the Orsini, and the Medici. Louis was appeased by the plausibility of his representations, especially as strife had broken out between France and Spain, and he was anxious to be on good terms with the Pope. He not only received Cæsar graciously, but concluded an alliance with him and promised him support in his enterprises.

But the suspicions of Cæsar's generals were aroused, and they summoned an assembly at Perugia, justly fearing that, sooner or later, the Borgia craft or force would deprive them of all their possessions. A compact was made to protect themselves against Cæsar and to support the Duke of Urbino. At the same time they commissioned Cardinal Orsini to go to the King of France in order to justify themselves for the capture of Arezzo, and to lodge complaints against Cæsar.

The Cardinal begged Alexander, under pretext of private business, for permission to absent himself from Rome ; but the Pope refused, saying that he had need of him. Orsini therefore took French leave, which so enraged the Pope that he visited his displeasure on the other members of the Orsini family by depriving them of their lives and property.

Among those who united in the crusade against the Borgia tyranny were the Dukes of Ferrara and Urbino, the Marquis of Mantua, Cardinal della Rovere, the Bentivogli, the Venetians, and the Florentines, who were " afraid that the dragon was preparing to swallow them up one by one." They painted in vivid colours the treachery and disloyalty of Cæsar, and conjured the King to punish this most perfidious monster who revelled in the shedding of innocent blood.

But the King was more disposed to listen to the representations of the Borgia ambassadors, especially as they promised him the help of Alexander and Cæsar in the war which had broken out in Naples between France and Spain. The complaints of the allies fell on deaf ears, for Louis not only distrusted the Venetians, but he considered the Pope's friendship necessary for the maintenance of his power in Italy.

Public festivities were held in Rome in honour of

the taking of Camerino, and the Pope, assured of Louis' favour, took measures for frustrating the intentions of the malcontents. Cæsar, to plant himself still more firmly in the King's favour, went to visit him at Milan, accompanied only by Cardinal Borgia and Trocci, the ever-facile tool of the Pope. He stayed at Ferrara and took his brother-in-law, Alfonso d'Este, with him to Milan, where he arrived safe and sound. The rebels were greatly astonished at this move, for the King's attitude had not yet been made public. When they saw how cordially Cæsar was received they realised that they had nothing more to hope for from the French.

Cæsar, with glib and oily tongue, represented to the King that all the disturbances in Italy proceeded from the malcontents, and promised that both he and the Pope would lend him powerful aid in his fight against Spain. Louis was captivated by his eloquence and winning manners, not realising the depths of infamy that lay beneath his charming exterior. " No cat, purring by the winter fireside," says Dean Kitchin, " could be softer or gentler, or seem to think less of her claws and the mice. Machiavelli saw in him the strong man destined to pluck Italy out of the hand of the foreigner. To such a man, he thought, all things could be forgiven."

When the French King left Milan Cæsar repaired to Imola with the intention of assembling his whole army there. All the Princes of Italy were terribly concerned at the Borgia good fortune, especially when they heard of Louis' promise to support him in his attack upon Bologna. The Venetians, therefore, addressed a letter to the King, pointing out the undesirability of encouraging the Duke of Valentino (Cæsar), and how little it would redound to the credit of the House of France and the honour of the Most Christian King to support a tyrant of so barbarous and bloodthirsty a kind that he gave the

GROUP OF CAVALRY.

REWARDING A BUFFOON.

FRESCOES FROM THE SCHIFANOIA PALACE, LUCREZIA BORGIA'S RESIDENCE AT FERRARA.

whole universe a hideous example of inhumanity and faithlessness.

King Louis, however, remained unmoved by this communication, refusing to injure his position by breaking faith with the Borgias. After his departure from Milan, Cæsar's opponents thought it a favourable opportunity to provide for their safety For although the Orsini, Baglioni, and Oliverotto da Fermo were in the Duke's service, and had received money from him in order to enlist troops against Bologna, they nevertheless deemed it prudent to unite their forces in order to protect themselves against him. At the same time a certain Ludovico Paltroni, who was in secret communication with the troops occupying the castle of S. Leo at Urbino, incited the whole town to make an effort for the restoration of their beloved Duke.

The allies assembled at Magione, near Perugia. After mature deliberation they decided to defend the cause of the Duke of Urbino, and to place seven hundred lances and nine thousand infantry in the field, if Bentivoglio would begin the war in Imola, and the Malatesta and Sforza take the necessary measures for the reconquest of Rimini and Pesaro. In order, however, to avoid offending the King, they declared themselves ready to support him in his enterprises and to sacrifice their lives and property in the honour of his service.

The allies would have given much to induce the Venetians and Florentines to join them. But although both these Powers were deeply annoyed by Cæsar's usurpations, they wished to see what line the French King would pursue before taking any decisive step.

Cæsar was at Imola, preparing to surprise Bologna, when the news of this alliance reached him. Although greatly discomposed, he did not lose courage, hoping to give the world a convincing proof of his genius

WB

for overcoming obstacles. First of all he sent couriers to Louis XII. begging him to despatch troops without delay, and then he entered into negotiations with the allies, thus gaining time, and preventing any hasty move on their part.

Bentivoglio had in the meantime seized and plundered the Castle of San Pietro da Coccia, near Imola. At the same time the Duke of Gravina and Paolo Orsini had proceeded with their troops to the domain of Urbino, where they encountered Cæsar's generals, Michelotto and Ugo da Cardone, at Cagli. Michelotto, whose skill lay rather in assassination than in generalship, had the unhappy Giulio Cesare Varano murdered, and took possession of Fossombrone,. But the allies attacked him so vigorously that his troops were utterly routed. Cardone was among the captured, but Michelotto escaped to Fano. Cæsar commanded him to go to Pesaro to repress the inhabitants, who were showing signs of restiveness and ill-will. Camerino, too, had risen up and summoned Giovanni Maria, the eldest son of their late Duke, from Venice in order to undertake the government.

Universal joy was excited by the success of the allies, who, if they had only taken advantage of the favourable moment, would undoubtedly have succeeded in wresting all Cæsar's conquests from him. They allowed themselves, however, to be misled by his false representations of a union, and thus missed their chance. To their great consternation Cæsar raised a large army, including reinforcements from the King of France. Although he was now in a position to crush the allies, he preferred to dally with negotiations for a while longer. The Pope also entered into transactions with Bentivoglio and the Orsini. The latter were speedily won by fair words and promises, though it seems hardly credible that such crafty and experienced generals could be duped by a man whose falseness and barbarity were so well known to them.

Baglione and Vitellozzo showed great repugnance to the idea of a reconciliation with Cæsar. Vitellozzo, especially, mistrusted him, and, in order to incite the other allies to war, he sent his troops to Fossombrone to help the Duke of Urbino to reconquer his territory. The latter did all in his power to prevent the league from coming to terms with Cæsar, but, as Orsini and others had been won over to his side, the rest were obliged to follow suit. It was agreed that the past should be forgótten, that Cæsar should take back his former generals, that they should help him to reconquer Urbino and Camerino, though they did not bind themselves to take any personal part in this enterprise. A separate peace was concluded with Bentivoglio, by which Bologna bound itself to provide Cæsar for eight years with one hundred lances as well as an annual tribute of twelve thousand ducats. Bentivoglio's son also undertook to place at Cæsar's disposal, though only for a year, a hundred lances and a hundred mounted archers. France and Florence were to be sureties for this contract, and, to confirm the alliance, the son of Annibale Bentivoglio was to espouse a " niece " of the Pope, the reputed sister of the Bishop of Enna.

As soon as this agreement was concluded the Duke of Urbino, who seems to have had no great confidence in the promises of his people to defend him at the risks of their lives, returned to Venice. Before starting he had all the fortifications torn down, so that the enemy could not garrison them and keep the people in slavery.

The blind confidence which Cardinal Orsini placed in the Borgias, who had won him through cajolery and flattery, is very remarkable. He gave no heed to the repeated warnings which assailed him, especially as he continued in favour with the Pope.

Cæsar had taken Camerino and Urbino without any resistance, since the allies had not only abandoned these towns, but had even threatened to turn their weapons against them. He thereupon gave his generals orders to attack Sinigaglia, which was then under the regency of Giovanni da Montefeltro, for his son Francesco Maria della Rovere. The town soon surrendered, and Giovanni, abandoned by all, fled from the vengeance of the Borgias, leaving the citadel in charge of Andrea Doria ; but the latter, on hearing that Cæsar himself was bearing down upon them, took flight to Venice. The citadel refused to surrender to any one but Cæsar.

Although Vitellozzo found it hard to place any confidence in the villainous Duke who had slain his brother, he allowed himself to be persuaded by Paolo Orsini, who had succumbed to Cæsar's fawning flattery, to await the Duke with the others in Sinigaglia.

Cæsar, who had decided to leave Fano on December 30, 1502, communicated his intentions to eight of his confidants, including Michelotto and the Bishop of Enna. When he arrived at Sinigaglia on December 31 he was joined at the gates by Vitellozzo, Paolo Orsini, the Duke of Gravina, and Oliverotto da Fermo. Vitellozzo looked sad and depressed, almost as if his approaching death had cast its shadow upon him, and it is said that he had already taken farewell of his people as though for the last time. The Duke greeted them with every appearance of friendliness, and they all entered the town together. No sooner, however, had they arrived at the ducal palace than he had them arrested and thrown into prison. Cæsar then gave commands that the troops of Oliverotto and Orsini should be attacked without delay. Oliverotto's men, who were near at hand, were all slaughtered, but the Orsini and Vitellozzo forces, being farther off, had time to collect themselves, and offered a brave and successful resistance.

The same night Vitellozzo and Oliverotto met their fate. At Cæsar's command they were brought forth to the place of execution, where, seated back to back on two chairs, they were ruthlessly strangled. At this critical moment the unfortunate victims were deserted by their accustomed courage Oliverotto, bathed in tears, accused Vitellozzo of having brought about his downfall, while Vitellozzo entreated that the Pope would grant the remission of his sins.

Neither Paolo nor the Duke of Gravina (both Orsini) met with so speedy a vengeance, for Cæsar was awaiting news from Rome. But when he heard that the Pope had seized Cardinal Orsini, the Archbishop of Florence, and Giacopo di Santa Croce, both Paolo and the Duke were strangled in the same fashion by Michelotto, January 18, 1503.

On the morning of January 3, the blind and aged Cardinal Orsini, who had received news, through the Pope, of the capture of Sinigaglia, was hastening with his congratulations to the Vatican. On the way he encountered the Prefect of Rome, who, as if by chance, accompanied him to the palace. Arrived there, the mules and horses of the Cardinal's retinue were taken to the Pope's stables, and the Cardinal himself entered the Chamber of the Parrots. Here he found himself immediately surrounded by a band of armed men. Seeing him turn pale with fright, the soldiers sought to soothe him, begging him to accompany them to another room. With him were the Protonotary Orsini, Giacopo of Santa Croce, and the Abbot Alviano, and the Pope hastily sent for Rinaldo Orsini, Archbishop of Florence, to add to their number. When they were all secured, commands were issued to seize and plunder the Orsini Palace. The house of the Cardinal's mother, who had fled on hearing of her son's arrest, was also completely pillaged. "Everything was taken even to the straw from the stables," says Giustiniani. The booty was afterwards divided among the Borgias, Cæsar, of course, receiving the largest share.

The prisoners were conveyed to the Castle of Sant' Angelo. The Protonotary and Giacopo da Santa Croce found means to regain their liberty by binding themselves, on heavy security, to reappear at an appointed time ; but no sooner were they set free than the Pope issued orders for their rearrest, regardless of the compact that had been made with them.

The College of Cardinals, indignant at this treatment of the Orsini, attempted to remonstrate with the Pope. But the latter was much annoyed at their interference, and declared that the Orsini had disgraced the Holy See by conspiring against the Duke of the Romagna, and had given him every cause for revenge. "Since they had not seen fit to keep their word, there was no reason why he should keep his."

Cardinal Orsini was kept a prisoner in the Borgia tower until February 22, when he succumbed to poison, said to have been administered by order of the Pope. Such was the end of the man who, next to Ascanio Sforza, contributed most to bringing about the election of Alexander VI. He was borne to the grave in an open coffin, in order that it might appear that he had died a natural death. Burchard was authorised to superintend the obsequies, " but," writes the wary chaplain, " not wishing to know more than I was obliged, I stayed away and occupied myself in another manner." On February 24 the Pope summoned the physicians who had attended the dying Cardinal and forced them to swear that he had died from natural causes.

Tomasini describes the circumstances of his death

as follows: "When Alexander had taken Cardinal Orsini captive, he treated him as though he were only imprisoned as a hostage, and at first confined him to the rooms in the Vatican which lay on the upper side of the Papal Chapel. Afterwards he was taken to the Castle of Sant' Angelo, without being kept in very close custody. The Pope even allowed him to occupy the apartments of the governor, and gave his mother permission to provide him with food. But Alexander had determined to end his life by poison, and after a time the Cardinal was forbidden to accept his mother's culinary attentions. At the same time the Pope heard that a vineyard had been bought by an Orsini for 2,000 scudi, and that this money had been given over to the Cardinal, with a pearl of extraordinary size and beauty. As neither the money nor the pearl had been found during the plundering of the palace, Alexander demanded the surrender of both, under severe penalties, just as if they had been his own property. When this was refused, he commanded that no meat sent by the Cardinal's mother should be received. But maternal love triumphed. Dressed in man's clothes, she went to the Pope, and resigned to him the pearl and the 2,000 scudi which her son had given her. It was, nevertheless, too late. Poison had already been administered to the Cardinal, and the provisions which she was again able to send could profit him nothing."

How far Alexander VI. was concerned in the violent deaths just described is matter for conjecture. When news reached him of the despatch of Oliverotto and Vitellozzo he assured the ambassador Giustiniani that he knew nothing of the affair, and that he had even written to the Duke of Valentinois bidding him disband his troops and return to Rome. Afterwards he spoke to the Cardinals of a plot against the life of Cæsar, who had been obliged to arrest and execute the leaders. When on January 3, 1503, the Pope had arrested Cardinal Orsini, the Archbishop of Florence and Giacopo da Santa Croce, he justified himself by referring to these plots, supported secretly by Florence and Venice, and connived at by the Cardinal. In talking to the Ferrarese ambassador, Alexander mentions disapproval of Cæsar's conduct. " As soon as we heard of the Duke's intention," he said, " we wrote to tell him not to do anything with Vitellozzo until he had so settled affairs as to have the Duke of Urbino in subjection."

The accusation against Alexander VI. of having poisoned Cardinal Orsini is not easy to prove. Giustiniani, who was deeply attached to the Orsini and well posted in all the news of Rome, writes on February 15, 1503, that the Cardinal showed signs of frenzy ; on the 22nd, in announcing the sick man's critical condition, he says no word of any suspicion of foul play. Soderini, the Florentine ambassador, in his despatch, and Brancatalini, in his diary, simply mention the death of the Cardinal with no hint of poison. Burchard, in describing the Consistory of February 20, tells us that Cardinal Orsini had offered the Pope 27,000 ducats for his release, but that Alexander had replied that his health must first be restored, and warmly recommended him to the physicians. Hearing the reports that were spread after his death, the Pope had inquiries made concerning the illness, and the doctors who had attended the Cardinal swore that his death had been a natural one.[1]

Cæsar Borgia now turned his attention to his other foes. Hastening to Citta di Castello, from which the Vitelli had fled, he had no difficulty in taking possession of it. He next proceeded to Perugia, which had been abandoned by Baglione, and then

[1] See *Revue des Questions historiques*, April 1881.

made preparations to advance upon Siena. He sent ambassadors demanding the banishment of Pandolpho Petrucci, the Lord of Siena, promising, on his side, not to molest the Sienese boundaries, but to withdraw his troops to Roman territory. The Pope, for his part, tried to lull their suspicions, as he had already lulled those of others. He wrote very amiable letters and despatched envoys with messages full of loving kindness. But the suspicious disclosure that he had no intention of forcing a way into the town made the plot against Petrucci all the more difficult. For, although many of the citizens were dissatisfied with his government, they preferred the tyranny of a fellow-citizen to the rule of a foreigner. Cæsar, nevertheless, persisted in his hypocritical assertion that he only wished to compass the banishment of Petrucci, although he had already marched into the dominion of Siena, advanced as far as Pienza and Chiusi, and received the submission of the surrounding places.

Consternation sprang up and spread in Siena, and Petrucci decided, with a good grace, to yield his position, which sooner or later would have been forced from him, and left the town. Cæsar was thereupon informed that the Sienese were ready to comply with his wishes as soon as he and his troops had quitted their domains.

For various reasons, Cæsar agreed to their proposals. He realised the difficulty of conquering Siena, which was strongly garrisoned, and he was also conscious of falling into disfavour with the French King, who by no means approved his proceedings.

Meanwhile Cæsar received news from the Pope that the Duke of Pitigliano and the other Orsini had united with the Savelli and taken up arms. They had already taken the Bridge of Lamentano and distributed their troops throughout the neighbourhood. Cæsar immediately attacked the dominion of Gian

Giordano Orsini, in spite of the fact that the latter was under the protection of the French King. The Pope excused himself to Louis on the ground that it was impossible to leave this domain in possession of the Orsini, his deadly foes, and proposed to make over to him the dukedom of Squillace and other property as an equivalent.

The King, however, repelled this offer. He despatched envoys to Cæsar with a peremptory command that he should cease to molest the dominion of Gian Giordano, who at the risk of his life had escaped to Bracciano, the chief stronghold of the Orsini.

CHAPTER XV

Cæsar Borgia at the height of his power—Death of Cardinal Michieli
—Nomination of new Cardinals—Illness and death of Pope
Alexander VI., 1503—His burial—Anarchy in Rome—Decline
of Cæsar's fortunes—Election of Cardinal Piccolomini as Pius
III.—His character—Reconciliation of the Orsini and Colonna—
Flight of Cæsar—Death of Pius III. after a reign of twenty-seven
days—Election of Giuliano della Rovere as Julius II —The
Venetians attack the Romagna—Cæsar taken prisoner by the
Pope—He is betrayed by Gonsalvo da Cordova and sent to
Spain—Escapes from imprisonment and is received by his
brother-in-law, King of Navarre—Cæsar's death in battle, 1507
—His character compared with that of Alexander VI —Cæsar's
wife and daughter—His illegitimate children.

CÆSAR BORGIA was now near the zenith of his ambition. Having mastered the whole of the Romagna,
he turned a covetous eye towards Florence, Pisa, and
Siena. The Florentines quailed before his ever-
growing power, especially as the Pope proposed to
declare him King of the Romagna and Umbria.

The King of France was at this time faring badly
in Naples, with the result that the Borgias no longer
felt dependent upon him, and even went so far as
to declare themselves ill-satisfied with his conduct
towards them. But the peace which, through the
mediation of Philip, Duke of Austria, was concluded
at Blois between Louis XII. and Ferdinand of Castile,
put a stop to the enmity against Giordano. The
King, who had been chosen as arbitrator for the
contesting parties, arranged an agreement between
them, by which Giordano was to receive an equivalent
for the dominion of Bracciano.

Cæsar, who now had no further need of his troops, led them back to Rome ; but, before he arrived there, Cardinal d'Este quitted the city, having entered into an amorous intrigue with Sancia of Aragon, with whom Cæsar himself was also reported to be on terms of illicit intimacy. About the same time occurred the death of Cardinal Michieli, "nephew" of Pope Paul II. ; there can be little doubt that his end was caused by poison administered by command of the Borgias, who reaped a considerable harvest from his removal. "His Holiness," we are told, "shut himself up with doors firmly closed, that he might count up his gains." The fact that Michieli's fortune had contributed towards Alexander's election had no effect upon the rapacious Pope, whose avarice did but increase with his advancing years.

But the lucky star of the Borgias was already on the wane. In order to carry out their designs on Tuscany, much money was needed, and the most convenient way of raising the required amount seemed to be by nominating fresh Cardinals. Giustiniani, the Venetian ambassador, writes on May 31, 1503 : "To-day there was a Consistory. Instead of four new Cardinals, as people expected, and as the Pope had said, nine were nominated. . . . Most of them are men of doubtful reputation ; all of them have paid handsomely for their elevation, some 20,000 ducats and more, so that from 120,000 to 130,000 ducats have been collected. If we add to this 64,000 ducats from the sale of the offices in the Court and what Cardinal Michieli left behind him, we shall have a fine sum. Alexander VI. is showing to the world that the amount of a Pope's income is just what he chooses."[1]

Not content with this method of making money,

[1] Pastor warns us that Giustiniani's reports must be accepted with caution, though he admits that the bribes given at this creation of Cardinals are confirmed from other sources.

Alexander and Cæsar, it is said, made plans for poisoning not only the nine new Cardinals, but also some others of the richest prelates in Rome. With this object, they invited them to a supper at the Villa of Cardinal Adriano di Corneto, who, on account of his great wealth, was also condemned to die. Cæsar, in pursuance of this diabolical scheme, had despatched to the Pope's servant, who was to wait at table, some tankards of wine, " in which was mixed the poison called Cantarella." This was a " kind of white powder resembling sugar, which the Borgias had already often found an expeditious means of despatching their enemies. It was a poison of the deadliest kind, and Cæsar gave express commands that the wine should be offered to no one but the doomed persons " (see Appendix, p. 404).

On the evening of August 10, 1503,[1] the Pope and Cæsar repaired to Corneto's villa at la Vigna for supper. Some writers assert that the Pope was in the habit of carrying about a consecrated Host in a gold case, because an astrologer had once prophesied that he would never die as long as he had It upon him. On this particular evening it chanced that he had forgotten It, and upon discovering Its absence, he at once sent Cardinal Caraffa to fetch It. While Caraffa was gone, Alexander, owing to the extraordinary heat, felt thirsty and unable to wait until the meal was served. Just at that time the cupbearer who had received Cæsar's instructions with regard to the poisoned wine had gone to the Vatican in search of peaches which had been unaccountably forgotten. There only remained an under-servant who knew nothing of the subtlety of the situation. As he saw six flagons standing apart in a corner, he imagined that they contained the choicest wine, and presented a large glass of the poisoned beverage to the Pope, who, all unsuspicious, drained it to the

[1] Tomasi gives August 2 ; Yriarte gives August 5.

dregs. Cæsar also drank a glass of the same without the least suspicion.

The Pope had hardly seated himself at the table when the poison began to take effect. He was seized with pains so violent that he fell on the ground and was taken up as one dead. Cæsar exhibited much the same symptoms as his father.

Alexander, upon reviving a little, was plied with emetics ; phlebotomy was also tried, but all in vain. The fever and pain produced by the virulent poison continued, and, after having received the Holy Sacrament, he died. During his brief illness he made no mention of his children, for whose advancement he had set the whole Christian world in commotion.

Such, with slight variations, is the account which we get from contemporary writers such as Bembo, Guicciardini, Jovius, Platina, and Tomasi. Burchard, however, puts a different complexion on this affair. He maintains that the Pope, on August 12, 1503, fell sick of a fever; on the 16th a vein was opened, and it seemed that he was suffering from a tertian fever. On August 17 he took medicine, but the next day he became suddenly worse and it seemed that his life was in danger. He therefore received the Viaticum at the mass, during which five Cardinals were present, in his room. In the evening Extreme Unction was administered, and immediately afterwards he passed away.

Roscoe considers it extremely improbable that two such astute men as the Borgias should have made the safety of their lives dependent on the carelessness or loyalty of a servant. An impartial examination renders it more than likely that Alexander's death was not due to poison, but rather to a malignant fever. It is nevertheless remarkable that both he and Cæsar were at the same time attacked by severe illness which brought the father to death and the son to the edge of the grave.

It may be of interest to quote yet another account

of Alexander's last days.   " At the moment when the
Pope, forced to make a speedy decision between
France and Spain, hardly knew which way to turn ;
seeing himself on the eve of a disastrous war, of which
Venice would take advantage to invade the States
of the Duke, death came to relieve him of his embarrassments.   Already, on July 11, he was feeling indis-
posed, perhaps the result of indigestion , the Venetian
orator saw him lying on a couch, fully dressed, and
looking well "   On the 14th he received Antonio in
the Pontiff's Hall seated, "somewhat weak" but his
mind keenly alert.   But on August 7 the ambassador
found him rather depressed and more reserved than
usual.   Rome was at this time ravaged by fever, and
Alexander was alarmed at the number of deaths which
it had caused.   " We will take more precautions for
the safety of our person than we have hitherto done,"
he remarked.   On the 11th he celebrated, with his
accustomed *bonhomie*, the anniversary of his elevation, though in his heart of hearts he was perturbed
and uneasy.   As from his window he watched the
passing of a funeral, he said, " This is a fatal month
for stout people "[1]   Just at this moment an owl
fell at his feet, and he started back in terror, murmuring to himself, " Evil omen ! evil omen ! "   The same
day, Friday, he dined with a good appetite ; the bill of
fare—a dangerous one for the hot weather—has been
preserved : eggs, lobster, pumpkin *au poivre*, preserved
fruits, plums, and tart covered with leaves of gold.

Some days before he had supped at a late hour
with Cæsar and several Cardinals at the vineyard
of Cardinal Adriano.   On Saturday, August 12, he
was taken violently ill with sickness and fever.   Cæsar,
too, was confined to bed with fever, and all the other
guests suffered from the same alarming symptoms.
On the 14th the Pope was bled copiously, and the
Duke's condition grew worse.   On the 15th Giustiniani

[1] Alexander himself was portly.

was unable to obtain any reliable news. Those who entered the Vatican did not come out again; the Duke recalled his troops to Rome; the *habitués* of the palace feigned great nonchalance; but all these precautions were of evil portent. On the 16th the situation remained the same. On the 17th the Pope took medicine; his physician, the Bishop of Vanosa, did not conceal his anxiety. Towards evening the palace was topsy-turvy; every one sought in secret to save his own property. The tutors of the young Borgias, Giovanni and Rodrigo, sent to Piombino the valuables of their wards. On August 18 Alexander confessed and received the Holy Communion, in the course of the mass which was celebrated by his bedside. Then a strange hallucination overtook him: he imagined that a monkey was springing about his room. A Cardinal, in order to soothe him, said that he would capture the creature. " Leave it alone," said the dying man, " for it is the devil ! " At the hour of Vespers he received Extreme Unction, and then, in presence of a bishop, the datary, and the grooms of the palace, he expired. " Thereupon," says Burchard, " the Duke, who was in bed, despatched Don Michelotto with a large company of people; they closed all the doors of the papal apartments, and one of them drew a dagger, threatening to cut Cardinal Casanova's throat and throw him out of the window if he did not give up the Pope's keys. The Cardinal, terrified, surrendered them, and the intruders went into the room next the papal chamber and seized upon all the silver that they could lay hands on, as well as two coffers containing about 100,000 ducats. Towards evening Alexander's death was made known. The valets took possession of all that remained in his wardrobe and bedroom, leaving nothing of value except the arm-chair, a few cushions, and the tapestry nailed to the walls. The Duke never visited his father during his illness nor after his death, and the

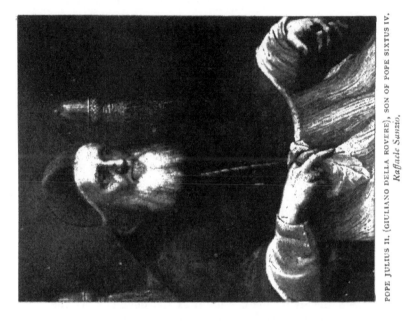

LUDOVICO SFORZA, "IL MORO," DUKE OF MILAN.
Boltraffio (Gallery of Prince Trivulzio, Milan).

POPE JULIUS II. (GIULIANO DELLA ROVERE), SON OF POPE SIXTUS IV.
Raffaele Sanzio.

336]

Pope, in his last days, did not once make mention either of Cæsar or Lucrezia."

The Cardinals remained absent from the bedside of their dead master, and the scandal of the obsequies of Sixtus IV. was repeated. Burchard dressed the corpse to the best of his ability, but he found no episcopal ring to place on the finger. The first night the Pope remained stretched out upon a table, between two wax tapers, quite alone, *et nemo cum eo*. When, the next day, he was carried to St. Peter's, accompanied by only four prelates, the palace porters fought the clergy of the basilica, who took refuge in the sacristy. Burchard's description of the terrible appearance presented by the corpse will not bear translation. It became, he says, " the colour of very black cloth." There was need for haste. Six porters and two carpenters, laughing and joking, placed it in a coffin which was both too narrow and too short. They took off the papal mitre, and covered the dead Pope with an old carpet, while with rough pulls and pushes the wretches adjusted his body to the ill-fitting coffin. " There were," says the Chaplain, " neither tapers, nor lights, nor priests, nor any one to watch over the dead Pontiff." [1]

In a letter to his wife, Isabella d'Este, the Marquis of Mantua gives particulars of Alexander's death. " There are some," he writes, " who maintain that at the moment he gave up his spirit seven devils were seen in his chamber. As soon as he was dead his body began to putrefy, and his mouth to foam like a kettle over the fire, which continued as long as it was on earth. The body swelled so that it lost all human form, and became nearly as broad as it was long. It was carried to the grave with little ceremony, a porter dragged it from the bed, by means of a cord fastened to the foot, to the place where it was buried, as all refused to touch it. It was given a wretched

[1] Gebhart, *Moines et Papes.*

X B

interment, in comparison with which that of the cripple's dwarf wife in Mantua was ceremonious. Scandalous epigrams are every day published regarding him."[1]

It is interesting to hear what Ercole of Ferrara really thought about the Pope, his daughter-in-law's father. In a letter to the Milanese ambassador, August 24, 1503, he says: "Knowing that many will ask you how we are affected by the Pope's death, this is to inform you that it was in no way displeasing to us. Once we desired, for the honour of God, our Master, and for the general good of Christendom, that God in His goodness and foresight would provide a worthy shepherd, and that His Church would be relieved of this great scandal. Personally we had nothing to wish for; we were concerned chiefly with the honour of God and the general welfare. We may add, however, that there was never a Pope from whom we received fewer favours. . . . It was only with the greatest difficulty that we secured from him what he had promised; but, beyond this, he never did anything for us. For this we hold the Duke of Romagna responsible; for, although he could not do with us as he wished, he treated us as if we were perfect strangers. He was never frank with us; he never confided his plans to us, although we always informed him of ours. Finally, as he inclined to Spain, and we remained good Frenchmen, we had little to look for either from the Pope or His Majesty. Therefore his death caused us little grief, as we had nothing but evil to expect from the advancement of the above-named Duke. We want you to give this our confidential statement to Chaumont, word for word, as we do not wish to conceal our true feelings from him—but speak cautiously to others about the subject, and then return this letter to our worthy councillor, Giantuca."

[1] Both Calixtus III. and Alexander VI. are buried in the church of Santa Maria de' Monserrato, where their monument with medallions is to be seen.

Alexander's death was followed by scenes of the direst confusion and anarchy in Rome. The insurrection was promoted mainly by those who had suffered loss of property at the hands of the Borgias ; in particular the Colonna, who with Gonsalvo's permission, had come back to the States of the Church to recover their possessions. Cæsar, who likewise had much to fear from the Orsini, was obliged to restore the property of both families. The Duke of Urbino, too, lost no time in taking possession of his State again. Francesco Maria della Rovere, the Lords of Pesaro, Camerino, Citta di Castello, and Piombino did the same. Malatesta, who was not greatly beloved by his subjects, met with some resistance in Rimini, whose fortress was still occupied by Cæsar's soldiers ; but Baglione, Ludovico Orsino, the Counts of Pitigliano and Alviano, with the help of the Venetian troops, succeeded in recapturing Perugia.

The Vatican was invested by the troops of Cæsar, who during his illness had given the command to Michelotto. The ravages committed by his soldiers produced the greatest alarm in Rome. The Bishop of Nicastro, Commander-in-Chief of the Castle of Sant' Angelo, was anxious to check their depredations by distributing weapons and ammunition among the Romans. The Cardinals, however, rejected this proposal, fearing that it would cause too much bloodshed. They would have preferred to enlist a regiment for the protection of themselves and their city, but the treasury was so much exhausted that there hardly remained money enough to summon a Consistory for the election of the new Pope.

Finally the Cardinals succeeded in raising a force of 2,000 soldiers, who were placed under command of Carlo Tanco. He received the title of Captain of the Sacred College, and finally, not only the garrison of the Castle of Sant' Angelo, but also Cæsar's soldiers, had perforce to swear allegiance to the commands of

the College of Cardinals. But the disturbances in
Rome continued. Although the Cardinals had commanded the Orsini and the Colonna not to set foot
in Rome, Prospero Colonna, with a considerable
number of Spanish troops, entered the city, though
he explained that he had no intention of insulting
the Sacred College. The Count of Pitigliano and
Fabio Orsini also advanced upon Rome at the head
of two hundred lances and over a thousand infantry.
Their sole object was to revenge themselves on Cæsar
and Michelotto, who had burned down the Orsini
Palace on Monte Giordano

The Orsini adherents pressed into the houses of
the Borgias and their friends, pillaged them thoroughly,
and committed the greatest barbarities. When a
Borgia fell into their hands Fabio had him slain
immediately, and, not content with having taken his
life, washed his hands and mouth in his blood. In
the meantime Cæsar's people were not idle ; they
also had a share in the shocking dramas which were
being enacted, and the Eternal City became one
hideous scene of murder and bloodshed. A rumour
arose that Cæsar's soldiers had seized upon the Cardinals and that Rome was to be burned and plundered.
The citizens were so much terrified at this report
that they armed themselves, closed the shops, and
barricaded the streets with chains and heavy beams.

This frightful anarchy continued until the Cardinals,
in desperation, turned to the ambassadors of the
Emperor, the Kings of France and Spain, and the
Republic of Venice, to beg their protection. This
step was the more effective because both the French
and Spanish troops were at that time in the neighbourhood of Rome   The ambassadors promised the help
of their sovereigns, who declared themselves ready to
maintain the privileges of the Conclave. The Cardinals charged them, above all, to rid the city of the
seditious troops who were causing such havoc, and

especially to remove Cæsar and his followers from their midst.

Cæsar Borgia, depressed both in mind and body, and exposed to the rage of his enemies, was filled with constant apprehensions for his safety. The College of Cardinals and the ambassadors issued in the name of their sovereigns a proclamation that all the party-leaders were quietly to withdraw from Rome without offering any obstacle to the papal election. The Orsini followed this command, and Prospero Colonna also submitted on condition that he should first be apprised of Cæsar's decision. But the latter could not bring himself to leave Rome and begged, as a favour, permission to remain. He pleaded his bad state of health, adding that his life would be endangered if he were to leave the city or even the Vatican. He offered to withdraw to the Castle of Sant' Angelo if the Cardinals would give security for his safety, so that the Conclave might be held in the Vatican. He would, however, much prefer to remain where he was, and promised to disband his troops under this condition. But the Cardinals, who mistrusted him and yet could not fathom his true intentions, decided that he and his troops must leave Rome without delay. They, however, offered him a safe escort through the States of the Church, and allowed him to take his baggage and artillery with him. Cæsar, therefore, could do nothing but obey this decree. The Cardinals, moreover, obliged him to swear to quit the city within three days, as well as not to engage in any enterprise against Rome or any other part of the States of the Church, and to remain at least ten miles from Rome during the Conclave. Prospero Colonna also bound himself to the same conditions. The ambassadors of the Emperor and of the King of Spain offered security for Cæsar.

After these stipulations were concluded Cæsar resolved to march towards Tivoli. He took with him eighteen cannon and had an escort of eight hundred infantry provided by the Cardinals. First of all came his vanguard, and then his baggage, which comprised about one hundred waggons. He was carried through the Vatican door in a litter, under a crimson canopy, borne by twelve of his halberdiers. Nevertheless, he took the precaution of having a page to ride close to his litter, on one of his fleetest horses, with the idea that he himself, in spite of his illness, could mount it in case of any sudden attack. For greater safety, he occupied a place in the middle of the procession. Cardinal Cesarino came to see him off at the city gate, but Cæsar sent a message to say that he was not in a condition to speak to anybody. Prospero Colonna also arrived with the same object, but found Cæsar in such a miserable plight that he openly offered him his pardon for all the injustice he had received through him, at the same time proposing to accompany him with his own troops as far as Tivoli. Cæsar made answer that he was not going in that direction, but would be pleased to see him at Pontemolle.

But Colonna dare not venture, on account of the number of French troops, to be found in the neighbourhood. Cæsar continued his way to Nepi, first halting at Citta Castellana, which was still in his possession. The French army lay only a short distance from Rome, between Nepi and Isola. The command had now been taken by the Marquis of Mantua in the place of la Trémouille, who was ill. Under pretext of protecting the Conclave, their real intention was to prevent the election of a Spanish Pope.

Some thirty-six Cardinals met together for the purpose of arranging the Conclave and celebrating the obsequies of the deceased Pontiff. When the Papal Chair had been vacant for about a month the Cardinals assembled in order to elect a new occupant. The Conclave began on September 16, and by the scrutiny taken on the 21st, Giuliano della Rovere had the highest number of votes, though it fell far below the requisite majority of two-thirds; Caraffa came next, and then d'Amboise, who, four days before, had declared, with his usual assurance, that either he or another Frenchman could not fail to be chosen; but as soon as he saw that he was out of the reckoning, he joined forces with Soderini, Ascanio Sforza, and Medici, and proposed the name of the aged and infirm Cardinal Francesco Piccolomini. Their idea was that his reign would of necessity prove a short one, and that, after his death, they would have more freedom in a new election. They were supported by the Spanish Cardinals, and the affair was immediately settled. On the following morning (September 22) Piccolomini, nephew of Pius II., was declared Pope under the title of Pius III.

The new Pope was a man of temperate and reputedly virtuous life, and his election filled the hearts of the Romans with joy and relief. "Our hearts rejoice and our eyes are filled with tears," writes Piero Delphinus, "because God our Lord has had mercy on His people and has given them a Chief Shepherd who is a holy man, innocent, and of untarnished name. Our deep sorrow has been turned to joy, and a day of sunshine has followed a night of storm. We are all filled with the highest hopes for the reform of the Church and the return of peace." And on September 28, 1503, Cosimo de' Pozzi, Bishop of Arezzo, in a letter to the newly elected Pontiff, says: "When all hope of release seemed shut away, God has given us in you a Pope whose wisdom, culture, and learning, whose religious education and virtuous life, have filled all good and God-fearing men with consolation. Now we can all hope for a new era in the history of the Church."

But the position of successor to the Borgias was fraught with difficulties for the gentle and peace-loving

Pius III. The Vatican had been robbed in the most shameless manner, and the papal treasury was in a lamentable state. " I wish no harm to the Duke," he said, " for it is the duty of a Pope to have loving-kindness for all, but I foresee that he will come to a bad end by the judgment of God."

This prediction was soon fulfilled, for, with the departure of the French army for Naples, Cæsar's last refuge failed him. Bartolomeo d'Alviano and Baglione raised troops with the object of attacking him, and the Orsini and Savelli were also preparing to bear down upon him. Cæsar, who was still far from well, besought the kind-hearted Pope to allow him to return to Rome. " I never thought," said Pius to the Ferrarese ambassador, " that I should feel any compassion for the Duke, and yet I do most deeply pity him."

Cæsar, therefore, obtained permission to re-enter Rome, greatly to the disapproval of many of the citizens, especially of Cardinals Giuliano della Rovere and Riario. The Pope himself, on October 7, acknowledged that he had made a mistake in allowing him to return. " I am neither a saint nor an angel," he remarked, " but only a man, and liable to err ; and I have been deceived."

The Orsini, who were also in Rome, would hear of no reconciliation. They challenged Cæsar to appear before the Pope and the Sacred College and justify himself from the crimes laid to his charge. Their idea was to join forces with Alviano and Baglione and avenge the murderous deeds of which he was guilty. Every day there were bloody skirmishes between Cæsar's soldiers and those of the Orsini.

Although the Orsini received pressing invitations to join the Spanish army, some of them yielded to the blandishments of Cardinal d'Amboise, and allied themselves with the French. The latter made overtures to Alviano, but met with a decided rejection, for it was obvious that d'Amboise, with an eye to a future election, was determined to remain on friendly terms with Cæsar. Alviano and the Orsini were so much incensed at this behaviour that, notwithstanding the fact that Giulio Orsini had already declared for the French, they concluded a treaty with the Spanish ambassador. On October 12 the reconciliation between the hitherto hostile houses of Orsini and Colonna was publicly announced.

Cæsar was now beset by foes on all sides, and his only hope lay in flight   But, just as he was about to leave Rome to seek refuge at Bracciano, the Orsini made a violent attack upon him. On October 15 two of his companions turned traitor, and his troops became scattered. Cæsar, not knowing how to escape, begged the Pope to allow him to take refuge in the Vatican. His request was granted, but his enemies quickly followed him. Alviano joined Orsini in the pursuit, crying, " Dead or alive ! " By setting fire to the Porta Torrione it was easy to gain access to the Vatican, and Cæsar was very near his doom when, with the help of his brother Jofré, Duke of Squillace, and three or four Cardinals he succeeded in escaping along a secret passage to the Castle of Sant' Angelo.

On October 18, after a brief reign of twenty-seven days, Pope Pius III laid down the burden of the flesh. His death, it was said, was hastened by the unskilfulness of a physician, who, by an ill-judged operation on his leg, brought on the inflammation to which he succumbed. A rumour also arose that his end was due to a poisoned plaster applied to his leg at the instigation of Pandolfo Petrucci, Lord of Siena. " The death of this Pope," wrote the Ferrarese ambassador, " will be lamented at all the Courts of Europe, for he was, by universal consent, held to be good, prudent, and pious. In spite of the rainy weather at the time, all Rome hastened to kiss the feet of the dead Pope, whose features were quite unaltered."

The papal election was put off for a few days in order to give the Orsini troops time to withdraw from Rome. The choice of the new Pope was practically certain before the assembly of the Conclave, for Giuliano della Rovere, though hated by many and feared by all, had bought so large a proportion of the Cardinals' votes that the others were in no position to withstand him. On November 1, 1503, the news of his election, under the title of Julius II., was made public.

Much astonishment was caused by the almost unanimous choice of a man who was well known for his dangerous and turbulent characteristics. It is true that he was one of the oldest as well as the richest and most powerful of the Cardinals, and also that he possessed a certain magnanimity which gained for him a considerable number of partisans. By tempting promises he persuaded d'Amboise to give him his vote, and the Spaniards, who were in the minority and feared to make an enemy of him, also supported his election. He won over Cæsar Borgia by promising to appoint him Gonfaloniere of the Church, and to allow one of his daughters to espouse Francesco Maria della Rovere. Cæsar was also greatly influenced by the new Pope's promise to help him in regaining possession of the Romagna, for Perugia, Castello, Urbino, Pesaro, Camerino, Piombino, and Sinigaglia had been recaptured as speedily as they had once been conquered. Some few towns still remained faithful to Cæsar, for they had experienced the advantages of uniting under his rule, since their former masters had been too weak to protect them, though, at the same time, powerful enough to oppress them. To his severe administration of justice they owed relief from a band of robbers who had formerly laid waste the country with rapine and slaughter.

The Venetians now made plain their intention of taking possession of the Romagna. Immediately upon the death of Alexander VI. they had despatched a large number of troops to Ravenna, which was already in their possession. By night they made a sudden and stealthy attack upon Cesena, but encountered such a stubborn resistance that they were compelled to withdraw. Notwithstanding this repulse, they seized upon Faenza, whose inhabitants turned for help to the Pope. The latter was not a little irate at the impudence of the Venetians, but had neither troops nor money enough to oppose them. All he could do was to send the Bishop of Tivoli to Venice to protest against this usurpation.

The Venetians would also have seized upon Imola and Forli had they not feared to exasperate the Pope too greatly. They were, however, masters of Rimini, and her province, Monte Fiore, Sant' Archangelo, Verucchio, Cattera, Savignano, Solaruolo, and Monte Bataglia, so that Cæsar remained in possession of nothing but the citadels of Forli, Cesena, Forlimpopoli, and Bertinoro

Realising that he must inevitably lose these places, Cæsar offered them to the Pope on condition that they should be restored to him as soon as his affairs were set in order. But Julius would not accept this stipulation, and desired the Duke to leave Rome. On November 19 he embarked for Ostia, whence he intended to set sail for Leghorn to negotiate with Florence for help in conquering the Romagna. Meanwhile the Pope, repenting him of his hastiness in refusing Cæsar's offer, sent messengers to him stating his readiness to agree to the aforesaid conditions. But Cæsar now refused to come to terms, whereupon the Pope, infuriated, had him taken prisoner upon the boat which was equipped for his departure, and taken to Rome, where he was placed in strict custody. This treatment seems, for the time, to have completely broken Cæsar's haughty spirit ; the Mantuan ambassador relates that he was even reduced to tears. Julius, however, treated him kindly, and gave him rooms in the Vatican, hoping to obtain the surrender of the keys from his governors without any fuss. Cæsar apparently sent the required orders, but the Governor of Cesena refused to take any commands from him while he was still a prisoner, and detained the papal messengers When the Pope heard this he was upon the point of casting Cæsar into one of the dungeons of Sant' Angelo, but he relented and sent him to the Torre Borgia instead. His goods were all confiscated, and his adherents were filled with terror of the Pope's vengeance.

Cæsar's few remaining troops were obliged to surrender, and their leader, Michelotto, was sent as a prisoner to the Pope. The latter, however, set him at liberty, greatly to the surprise of all who knew how strong was his antipathy to all those who had served as tools for the Borgia malice and cunning.

But the Pope, without committing an open breach of faith, determined to delay Cæsar's release for a time. He was probably afraid that the Governor of Forli would refuse to surrender the town if the Duke were at liberty, and was also perhaps influenced by memories of the injustices which he had suffered from Alexander VI. Cæsar, becoming suspicious, made a secret appeal to Gonsalvo, begging him to provide him with a safe escort to Naples, and two ships to call for him at Ostia. This request was willingly granted. Meanwhile, the Cardinal of Santa Croce received news that the required sum had been paid, and both Cesena and Bertinoro delivered to the Pope He, thereupon, without the Pope's knowledge, set Cæsar at liberty The latter, without waiting for Gonsalvo's ships, went secretly to Nettuno ;

thence in a little boat to Mondragone, and then by land to Naples. Here he received a cordial welcome from Gonsalvo, who entered with apparent interest into his plans, and even undertook to furnish him with troops and ships to escort him to Pisa. Thus did the Great Captain contrive to keep his dangerous visitor quiet until he had received instructions from King Ferdinand of Spain.

The ships were ready equipped to start the next day. Cæsar had had a long interview with Gonsalvo, who displayed every sign of amity, finishing with an affectionate embrace. Nevertheless, the Duke had hardly left the room when, by Gonsalvo's command, he was seized and confined in the citadel.

Gonsalvo excused himself for this breach of faith by saying that the command of his sovereign to take Cæsar prisoner was to be more esteemed than his own word. Not only this, but it was absolutely necessary to capture Cæsar, who, not content with his former injustices, intended to overthrow the other States and to set all Italy in an uproar On August 20, shortly after his arrest, Cæsar was sent to Spain on a small galley, attended by a single page. During the voyage he was guarded by his old enemy Prospero Colonna, who was in command of the vessel. Prospero, however, seems to have displayed great tact and magnanimity on this occasion, and, so far from triumphing over his fallen foe, he avoided meeting him for fear that he might seem to be rejoicing in his humiliation.

But all the cruel buffets of fortune did not succeed in reducing Cæsar's spirit and energy for any length of time, and he busied himself with plans for escape. Ferdinand had him first of all confined in the Castle of Chinchilla,[1] but as this was not considered a safe enough prison for so restive a prisoner, he was removed to the Castle of Medina del Campo, in the

[1] Not, as Gregorovius says, Seville.

north of Spain. Here he was kept in rigorous captivity, deprived of every luxury, and allowed no visitors. "All his plans had failed, nothing remained of all that he had sought to achieve by his crimes, his cruelties, and his murders." His only recreation was in flying his falcons, watching them seize upon a helpless bird and tear it to pieces with their talons. No one in Italy made any effort to procure his release except Lucrezia, whose desires met with little sympathy from her husband's family. The Gonzaga alone appear to have maintained a not unfriendly attitude towards him, and Isabella, who was now warmly attached to Lucrezia, seconded her appeals to her husband on Cæsar's behalf.

In spite of the strict watch kept over him, on October 25, 1506, Cæsar, with the help of his chaplain and a servant of his jailer, contrived to escape from his window. The Count of Benevento was awaiting him with horses, and, after a month's rest under the Count's sheltering roof in order to give some wounds in his hands time to heal, the fugitive made his way towards Pampeluna, where he was kindly received by his brother-in-law, Jean d'Albret, King of Navarre. On October 7, 1506, Cæsar, in a letter to the Marquis of Mantua, says: "After so many vicissitudes, it has pleased the Lord God to deliver me and to enable me to leave my prison. My secretary, Federigo, the bearer, will explain how it happened Through the infinite mercy of the Lord, may it be for His great glory."

Cæsar had intended to proceed to France with the idea of obtaining the support of Louis XII., but the latter, having just entered into a truce with Spain, refused to receive him. Not only so, but the King also snatched from him his yearly income and his dukedom of Valentinois in order to confirm himself in the good graces of the King of Spain.

The King of Navarre was at this time engaged in

a war with one of his vassals, the Prince of Alarino. Cæsar, who was now deprived of all other resources, offered to serve as volunteer in his brother-in-law's army. A terrible skirmish took place under the walls of the fortress of Viana, during which Cæsar received a fatal blow. His dead and naked body, covered with wounds, was discovered at the bottom of a ravine. The King, greatly distressed, had him covered with a cloak and carried to Viana. After a pompous ceremony, the corpse was laid in front of the high altar in the parish church of Santa Maria of Viana, and during the course of the same year, 1507, an imposing and elaborate tomb was erected to his memory.

Tomasi is of opinion that Cæsar's manner of death was too honourable for a man whose record was so black with crime. When, however, we consider his deep humiliations, the sufferings which he bore manfully, the miserably dependent condition in which he found himself after his father's death, the loss of all his possessions, as well as the treachery which was shown towards him, it is difficult to avoid a feeling of compassion for the unfortunate wretch whose fortunes so miserably failed him at the last. Neither must it be forgotten that he lived at a time when a human life was of less account than we now consider the life of a dog, and that even the most appalling of the charges laid to his account are not to be judged by twentieth-century standards. [1]

Cæsar's courage and endurance were of a rare kind. He pursued his ends, with incredible persistence, undaunted by the greatest difficulties. Brave in war, amazingly ambitious, energetic, and of irresistible eloquence, it was little wonder that he, with the help of his father Alexander VI., rose to such eminence. His administrative talent was remarkable, and, though he sought to extirpate the most important families of Italy, he governed his conquests with skill and ability.

[1] See *Cesare Borgia*, by R. Sabatini.

While former princes had troubled little about their subjects except to practise extortions upon them, Cæsar introduced a severe system of jurisdiction, and had all those who threatened the peace of the community executed The adherence and loyalty shown to him even after his fall, by several towns, are a proof that they had fared better under his rule than under that of their former legitimate masters. The worst of men have some redeeming quality, and, though Tomasi, Guicciardini, and other historians have condemned him with no sparing hand, an impartial judge cannot but admit that, in spite of their many and monstrous crimes, both Cæsar Borgia and his father were not wholly beyond the pale of humanity. Cæsar certainly has less claim to forbearance than Alexander, who from the year 1497 was thoroughly under the influence of a mind stronger and even more determined than his own.   The Pope, as we have seen, was afraid of his powerful son, and followed his lead along the paths of wickedness.   To quote M. Émile Gebhart in his essay on the Borgias : " Alexandre est digne de quelque pitié. Il n'a pas goûté grâce à Cæsar, toute la joie qu'il s'était promise du pontificat ; il a perdu, dans l'âpre labeur auquel son fils l'avait asservi, sa gaîté naturelle et un vague instinct de grandeur d'âme que manifestaient encore, dans les premières années de son règne, quelques paroles vraiment nobles. Le Valentinois fut le démon de la famille. Il doit porter la plus lourde part de la gloire maudite des Borgia."

Many and bitter were the tears which Lucrezia, now Duchess of Ferrara, shed for her brother.   It would seem that Cæsar could not have been utterly devoid of grace to have caused so much sisterly regret. Pope Julius II., on the other hand, must have rejoiced to be rid of so dangerous an enemy, who had many faithful followers in the Romagna.

1. MEDAL STRUCK TO COMMEMORATE THE CORONATION OF
ALEXANDER VI. (*British Museum.*)

3. ALEXANDER VI. CLOSING THE HOLY DOOR, DECEMBER 31,
1500. (*British Museum.*)

4. MEDAL COMMEMORATING THE RESTORATION OF THE CASTLE
OF SANT' ANGELO BY ALEXANDER VI. (*British Museum.*)

2. ALEXANDER VI. OPENING THE HOLY DOOR AT ST. PETER'S,
FOR THE YEAR OF JUBILEE, 1500. (*British Museum.*)

352]

According to Zurita, Cæsar left only one legitimate child—a daughter, Louise—who was born in 1504, and was destined never to see her father. Her mother, Charlotte d'Albret, lived for some time at the Court of the beautiful Anne of Brittany, but soon after the birth of her baby-girl she withdrew to a quieter life in the vicinity of her friend, the repudiated Queen Jeanne. Having found the world unsatisfactory, she turned to the religious life. She lived like a saint in her château near Bourges, and, though her stingy father had given her but a meagre dowry, the poor of the neighbourhood had good cause to bless her name. In 1507, the year of her husband's death, Charlotte lost her faithful protectress, Jeanne. The double loss seemed to overwhelm her, and she refused to be comforted. She had the walls of her house hung with black, and, though only twenty-five years of age, retired into these mournful surroundings, only emerging at intervals to distribute her bounty to her needy neighbours. On March 11, 1514, this pious lady said farewell to earth, and departed this life in the odour of sanctity. Her little daughter, who was with her during her last moments, was, at Charlotte's wish, entrusted to the care of Madame d'Angoulême, mother of King Francis I. A few years later she became the wife of Louis de la Trémouille, the knight " sans peur et sans reproche." He was killed at the battle of Pavia in 1525, and some years later the widowed Louise found a second husband in Philip of Bourbon, Baron de Busset.

It is known that Cæsar was also the father of two natural children—a son, Girolamo, and a daughter, Lucrezia. Girolamo probably died in boyhood, but Lucrezia, dedicated to the cloister from her early youth, lived on, until 1573, in Ferrara, where she had become Abbess of San Bernardino. Gregorovius relates that, as late as February 1550, an illegitimate son of Cæsar's appeared in Paris. He was a priest,

YB

and gave his name as Don Luigi. On the strength of his father's having met his death in the service of the King of Navarre he had journeyed from Rome to ask assistance of the French King The latter gave him a hundred ducats, whereupon he returned to his native place, and was heard of no more.

CHAPTER XVI

ALREADY before the death of Cæsar there had arisen
between France and Spain differences which were to
have the most disastrous consequences for Italy. It
had been arranged that, in the division of Naples,
France should receive the provinces of Terra di
Lavoro and both the Abruzzi, while Spain was to
take possession of Apulia and Calabria; but, when it
came to the point, it was evident that neither monarch
knew the country well enough to settle the exact
boundry-line. The divisions of Alfonso I.—Terra
di Lavoro, Principato, Basilicata, Calabria, Apulia,
and Abruzzo were no longer recognised. The province of Basilicata was the first source of discord.
The Spanish General, Gonsalvo, maintained that
both Basilicata and Principato belonged to Calabria
because they lay exactly between the two Calabrias,
and therefore must be attributed to Spain. The
French viceroy, Louis d'Armagnac, Duke of Nemours,
declared, on the other hand, that these provinces had
never belonged to Calabria. A like dispute arose
about Capitanata, a subdivision of Apulia, and also
about the division of the pasture-lands of the same

province which were the source of considerable crown-revenues. In the first year these were equally divided between the monarchs, but the next year each party sought to grasp as much as possible for itself, with calamitous results.

The Neapolitan nobles sought to mitigate the strife, and the Duke de Nemours had a personal interview with Gonsalvo. But, as no agreement could be arrived at, the decision was referred to the two Kings, though only upon condition that, before the passing of the sentence, weapons should be laid down. But the Duke of Nemours, whose forces were stronger than those of Gonsalvo, refused to be bound by the compact, fearing that the latter might, in the meanwhile, strengthen his resources. He informed Gonsalvo that he would again begin hostilities if the district of Capitanata were not surrendered, and immediately garrisoned Tripalda and all the fortified places of which he could possess himself. A reinforcement of two thousand Swiss, sent by Louis to the Duke, clearly showed his intention of continuing the war and of taking advantage of his present superior position. His troops were very successful. Canosa, in spite of a plucky resistance, was forced to yield; the town of Cosenza was plundered, and Gonsalvo had perforce to evacuate not only Capitanata, but also the greater part of Calabria and Apulia. Destitute of money, and scantily provided with provisions and ammunition, he retired to the fortified town of Barletta, where he was surrounded and hard pressed by the troops of the Duke of Nemours.

The French captains, however, maintained that for divers reasons, among others the lack of water, the whole army could not besiege Barletta; but though d'Aubigny thought otherwise and protested against this idea, it was decided that part of the French army should continue the siege, while the rest should be devoted to the conquest of Naples.

The Viceroy now conquered the whole of Apulia, with the exception of Otranto, Gallipoli, and Tarento, and then turned back to the investment of Barletta. At the same time d'Aubigny entered Calabria and conquered and plundered Cosenza, though the citadel still remained in the possession of the Spaniards. Troops from Sicily united with Gonsalvo's forces, and a fight ensued, resulting in a signal victory for d'Aubigny.

But a change in the fortunes of war now seemed to be approaching. A French officer named Charles de Torgues, who, through an exchange of prisoners, had come to Barletta, was invited by Don Enrico of Mendoza to supper. Inigo Lopez and Don Piero d'Origno, the Prior of Messina, were also present During the meal a discussion arose over the incapacity of the Italian soldiers, and de Torgues called them " an effeminate and degenerate people." Lopez replied that he had in his service troops who were just as brave and trustworthy as his Spaniards In order to settle the dispute, it was decided to select thirteen French and the same number of Italians, who, on horseback and fully armed, should be put to a fighting test. The conquerors were to receive, as a reward, the horses and armour of the conquered, together with a hundred golden crowns. Each side was allowed to choose four arbitrators, and hostages were provided to ensure the proper observance of the stipulated conditions.

On February 13, 1503, the first trial took place in a plain between Andre and Corrato. Both armies were present at the spectacle, and Gonsalvo, in an address which has been perpetuated by a Spanish poet, urged the Italians to put forth their whole strength to vanquish their opponents. After a prolonged and dangerous struggle, in which strength, courage, and perseverance were displayed by both sides, the Italians gained the day. But the French had felt so secure of victory that no one among them could produce the hundred golden crowns which were to have been the prize of the conquerors. They were therefore taken captive to Barletta, where Gonsalvo, with considerable magnanimity, paid their ransom,

Henceforward the good fortune of the French seems to have abandoned them First, the inhabitants of Castellanetta, in the neighbourhood of Barletta, took up arms, angered by the insolence of the French, over whom they gained important advantages.

Then Gonsalvo, hearing that the village of Rubos, some twelve miles distant from Barletta, was carelessly guarded, descended upon it by night. He attacked the French with such fierceness that they, totally unprepared for the onslaught, offered only a feeble resistance. They were utterly defeated, and la Palisse, their commander, was taken prisoner. Gonsalvo returned to Barletta, without being pursued by the Duke of Nemours.

Although Louis, secure in the hope of a peaceful termination, had instructed the Duke to remain on the defensive only, the latter considered it a favourable juncture to enter upon a decisive action Moreover, the two armies were now so close together that an encounter was inevitable. The Spanish had received reinforcements under the command of Ugo da Cardone, and had assembled all the troops in Calabria, while the French were stationed at Seminara. D'Aubigny was in Gioia, three miles away, endeavouring to block the way of the Spanish troops. He fortified his camp with four cannon, which he had posted on the bank of the river on which Gioia stands. The Spanish vanguard, under Manuel Benavida, now advanced to the bank which was not garrisoned by the French. Their leader began negotiations with d'Aubigny, but while they were thus engaged the Spanish rearguard were traversing the river.

D'Aubigny, upon hearing of this, hastened without

his artillery to the point where the Spaniards were
crossing, with the intention of attacking them before
their troops had reached the other side. But it
was too late. The Spaniards had already effected
a landing and were ready in battle-array. D'Aubigny,
in spite of having no artillery, thought it his duty
to attack them, but was utterly crushed even before
the Spanish rearguard had got across the river. Several
of the French commanders and many Neapolitan
barons were taken captive. D'Aubigny himself fled
to the Castle of Angitola, but was obliged to surrender
to the Spaniards, who hemmed him in on every
side.

The downfall of their greatest General was most
detrimental to the French, especially as it moved
their Viceroy, the Duke of Nemours, to rash proceedings which he would perhaps otherwise not
have entered upon. Gonsalvo, who knew nothing
of the success of his countrymen, marched secretly
towards Carinola, about ten miles distant from
Barletta. The plague, as well as lack of provisions,
had driven him to abandon the latter place. Carinola
is about midway between Barletta and Canosa, where
Nemours had assembled his forces. The Duke was
uncertain as to whether he should attack the Spaniards,
and held a council of war. Several of the officers
were against an assault, since the French troops had
been reduced by their previous reverses, while the
Spanish army had been reinforced by fresh troops.
They advised a withdrawal to Melfi until help could
be sent to them from France. Others, again, thought
it risky to remain idle, especially as reinforcements
could not be relied upon. They were anxious to
venture an attack, considering that the honour of
the French arms demanded it.

Nemours, who knew that the Spaniards were
marching upon Carinola, decided to begin the attack,
and despatched his troops in great haste. But he

could obtain no reliable news as to whether Barletta was completely evacuated, for Fabricius Colonna had arranged his troops so cleverly that the French were cut off from the town, and the height of the fennel, which grows luxuriantly in Calabria, concealed the view of the Spanish army as it marched along.

The Spaniards arrived in Carinola at almost the same time as the French, but, as the latter were in possession of the town, Gonsalvo had the neighbouring vineyards garrisoned. On Colonna's advice, the Spanish troops began digging entrenchments, but before their task was finished the French approached their camp. It was already night, and Yve d'Allègre and the Prince of Melfi advised postponing the attack to the following day, since the Spaniards would be shortly obliged to yield from lack of provisions. Nemours, however, ignored the advice, and proceeded with great vigour to the attack. The Swiss, in particular, distinguished themselves by their valour in the obstinate fight which ensued. Suddenly a powder magazine exploded, causing the utmost consternation and confusion. Gonsalvo, nevertheless, retained his self-possession, and called out, " The victory is ours. God has declared Himself for us; we have no more need of our artillery." His prediction was fulfilled, and the Spaniards actually won the day. Owing to the varying accounts of this event it is difficult to assign the cause of this victory. The French were completely disarrayed by the death of the Duke of Nemours, who, fighting courageously in the foremost rank, was struck down by a musket-shot, which immediately killed him.

D'Allègre, the Prince of Salerno, and several of the Neapolitan barons withdrew to Gaeta and Trajetto, and the rest of the French troops were dispersed to various parts. Gonsalvo, however, marched immediately upon Naples. He offered the Prince of Melfi the half of his kingdom if he would ally himself

with the Spaniards. But nothing would have induced the Prince to accept this proposal. At Naples
Gonsalvo was received with open arms, and the
French fled to Castelnuovo. Capua and Aversa,
abandoned by the French commanders, surrendered
to Spain on May 14, 1503

Louis XII. still clung to the hope of reconquering
Naples. He not only sent reinforcements, under
la Trémouille, towards Naples, by way of the States
of the Church, but he attacked Ferdinand of Spain
himself. His numerous troops advanced into Roussillon and Fontarabia, while his fleet threatened the
coasts of Catalonia and Valencia. But Ferdinand,
placing himself at the head of his army, drove the
enemy back into French territory. Neither did the
French fleet accomplish anything, and, after several
futile attempts to land men, it was obliged to return
to Marseilles

The French fared no better in Italy. The Viceroy,
the Marquis of Saluzzo, who had succeeded Nemours,
united his troops with those which were still lying
round Gaeta, and received, besides, reinforcements
from the Duke of Mantua, who had allied himself
with France. With the united strength of all these
forces he invested Trajetto and Fondi as far as the
river Garigliano.

Gonsalvo now left San Germano, where he had
withdrawn with his men, and garrisoned the opposite
bank of the river, in order to prevent the French
from crossing. The latter, however, had ferried
over in flat boats, with the intention of attacking
the Spaniards, while cannon were mounted on the
bank. But the Spaniards defended themselves with
the greatest vigour, and forced the French to
retreat

Gonsalvo had encamped near Cintra, about a
mile away from the river, but, as the district was
marshy and the weather extremely stormy, his troops

suffered grievously from damp and cold. The captains wanted to withdraw to Capua in order to refresh their men, instead of awaiting a second onslaught from the French, who far exceeded them in number. But Gonsalvo replied that he would prefer to die at once, having advanced only a handsbreadth against the enemy, rather than to live a hundred years, having retreated only two paces.

The French had constructed a bridge, which they fortified at the end with bastions, but they were prevented from attacking the Spaniards, because their camp was surrounded by morasses which the heavy rains had rendered impassable. They also suffered much from the badness of the weather, as well as from lack of provisions. Consequently the troops were attacked by sickness, and the Italians abandoned them. Day by day their numbers visibly decreased, so that they only had courage to engage in petty skirmishes with the Spaniards, in which the latter were nearly always victorious.

The Spanish army, on the other hand, was reinforced by the troops of Bartolomeo d'Alviano and the Orsini. Gonsalvo now made an onslaught upon the French, encouraged by hearing that their corps were placed at very wide intervals. He decided to cross the river, if possible, without the enemy's knowledge, and entrusted this difficult task to d'Alviano. A wooden bridge was surreptitiously built in the camp and, during the night, conveyed to Suio (some four miles from the French camp), where it was placed across the river. On December 27, 1503, Gonsalvo crossed the bridge with his men, in the darkness. He gave command that the next morning his rearguard should attack the *tête de pont* of the French. When the latter heard of this bold stroke they were seized with terror. The Marquis of Saluzzo despatched d'Allègre to prevent the passage of the Spaniards, but it was too late. At

the same time Alviano attacked the *tête de pont*
on the other bank of the Garigliano with great
violence, hunting the French from their posts.

The Viceroy immediately withdrew his troops to
Gaeta, though he was obliged to leave behind a large
part of his ammunition, nine cannon, and the sick
and wounded Gonsalvo, on perceiving the flight,
sent Prospero Colonna with his light cavalry, in order
to hinder their progress as much as possible. They
were overtaken at Seandi, where a slight skirmish
took place, but the French continued their march
directly afterwards. After much fighting, they reached
a bridge near Gaeta, where the Viceroy found
it necessary to call a halt. A violent encounter
took place. The Spanish rearguard had by this
time come up, and had crossed the river in boats.
The French resisted as well as they could, but the
fear of being attacked by Gonsalvo in the rear undermined their courage. Closely pursued by the
Spaniards, they took flight in the direction of Gaeta.
Not far from the latter place the road branches into
two, one of which leads to Itri, and the other to
Gaeta. Those who took the Itri path were for the
most part captured or slain, and the others were
pursued through the very gates of Gaeta itself.

In this battle Piero de' Medici fought valorously,
and, when the cause seemed hopeless, he embarked
on a galley to fetch four heavy cannon which he had
saved out of the hands of the enemy. But their
weight, as well as that of the great number of people
who had sought refuge on the vessel, caused it to
sink. Piero and many others were drowned, and
his corpse was not found until several days had passed.
His death was a clear gain to the House of Medici,
since the hatred of the Florentines had been mainly
directed against him personally. His widow Alfonsina
received permission to return to Florence. She
married her daughter to Filippo Strozzi, a nobleman

whose renown had penetrated the whole of Italy. It is true that, upon hearing of this marriage, the magistrates of Florence condemned the bridegroom to pay a penalty of five hundred golden crowns, and to three years' banishment. Strozzi, however, returned to the city before the stipulated time had elapsed, without any inconvenient results.

Gonsalvo, who was in very low water, was only too glad to conclude a treaty which made over to him the possession of the important fortress of Gaeta together with all the artillery and military stores. A free passage was granted to the remnant of the French army, which, sick and woe-begone, made its retreat. With those who had taken the land route it fared almost as ill as with those who embarked at Gaeta. The greater part of their fleet was wrecked upon the French coast during a violent storm, while those who were on land were stricken down by pestilence, hunger, and cold, so that the roads were strewn with corpses. After the surrender of Gaeta, a treaty was concluded between the two Kings. (October 12, 1505.) Ferdinand who, after the death of Isabella, had quarrelled with his son-in-law, Philip the Fair, and longed eagerly for a male heir, was to marry Louis XII.'s niece, Germaine de Foix, a spoilt young beauty of eighteen. Any children of this marriage were to inherit Sicily, Aragon, and Naples, but, should the union prove fruitless, Naples was to be divided between France and Aragon. Ferdinand, on the other hand, was to pay Louis a million gold ducats as indemnity for the late war.

Of all the generals who had distinguished themselves in the last Italian campaign, none stood so high as the Great Captain, Gonsalvo Aguilar da Cordova. By his courage, endurance, and military genius he had conquered the whole of Naples, and his kindness, generosity, and love of justice had made him beloved of the Neapolitans. Ferdinand well realised how much he owed to Gonsalvo, and not only appointed him Viceroy of Naples, but bestowed on him crown-land revenues to the amount of 20,000 gold ducats. Notwithstanding these tokens of favour, the King in his heart cherished suspicion and jealousy of the Great Captain, fearing that he might constitute himself unconditional lord of Naples. In all Gonsalvo's dealings, even the wisest, he only saw a desire to gain the affection of the Neapolitans in order that he might one day possess himself of the crown. His uneasiness, indeed, became so uncontrollable that he recalled Gonsalvo to Spain under pretext of asking his advice. But the General begged to be excused, saying that the affairs of the kingdom were not yet completely arranged. Ferdinand repeated his command, but again Gonsalvo refused to obey. The King's agitation thereupon became so intense that he made up his mind to journey to Naples to see for himself what was going on. He arrived there, in company with his young wife, in October 1506. Although during his journey he received news of the death of his son-in-law Philip, and the regency of Castile devolved upon him on account of the mental incapacity of his daughter Joan, even then he could not bring himself to forego his undertaking. He stayed seven months in Naples, replaced Gonsalvo's chosen officials by others, made a few arrangements for the government of the town, and started on his homeward way, accompanied by the source of his anxiety—Gonsalvo.

In Savona Ferdinand had a meeting with the King of France. Gonsalvo was treated with the greatest honour. Louis, indeed, could not conceal his admiration even for one who had robbed him of a kingdom. Ferdinand restrained his annoyance until they reached Spain, when he commanded Gonsalvo to retire to his country house, and not to appear at the Court without permission. This was the way in which he rewarded a General who had served him well and faithfully, esteeming neither his life nor possessions in comparison with the welfare of his King and country   He died in 1515, and the only recognition made of his greatness by the King was a magnificent funeral at the royal expense.

Gonsalvo, in reviewing his past life, was accustomed to say that he reproached himself for three great mistakes : firstly, for having broken his promise to the royal House of Aragon ; secondly, for having sent Cæsar Borgia as prisoner to Spain ; and thirdly, for a mistake which he would not mention, but which may have been his removal from Naples when at the height of his power, and his retirement into the loneliness of private life. Ferdinand's ingratitude must have wounded him deeply, and the fact that he took his unjust sentence of banishment with so little resentment gives proof of the nobility of his character.

From the time of Lucrezia's marriage with Alfonso d'Este, her life seems to have been beyond shadow of reproach. After the excitement of the wedding festivities she had many difficulties to overcome on the threshold of her new life, but by her gentle and affectionate nature and winning manners she succeeded in gaining all hearts. Pietro Bembo, the famous Venetian, fell a victim to her charms, and though there can be no doubt of his absorbing passion for Lucrezia, there is no reason to suppose that it ever passed the bounds of propriety Lucrezia, for her part, evidently regarded him with an affection which, according to Gregorovius, was more than platonic. Bembo was an attractive man of handsome presence and courtly manners, which stood out in pleasing contrast to the somewhat uncouth deportment of Alfonso. From 1503 to 1506 they enjoyed the closest friendship—a fact which did not fail to excite the jealousy of Lucrezia's husband, and probably led to Bembo's removal in 1506 to the Court of Urbino. They nevertheless continued to keep up a correspondence, much of which is still preserved. Lucrezia's letters are inscribed : " Al mio carissimo M. Pietro Bembo."

Bembo's infatuation has not escaped the notice of the two Strozzi, at whose villa near Ferrara he spent much of his time. But both father and son appear also to have fallen under Lucrezia's magic spell, and the verses which they dedicated to her are even more full of passion than those of Bembo. Tito Strozzi, the father, sang of a rose which his lady-love had given him, but his son surpassed him in an epigram on " Rose of Lucrezia," which could hardly have been the one bestowed upon his father.

Many other poets celebrated Lucrezia's beauty and virtue in verse. The great Ariosto dedicated to her a stanza of his *Orlando Furioso*, in which he represents her as a pattern of modesty and beauty ɪ

> Lucrezia Borgia di cui d'ora in ora
> La beltà, la virtù e la fama honesta,
> E la fortuna, va crescendo non meno
> Che giovin pianta in morbida terra.

Even making allowances for the flattery of a court poet, it is highly improbable that he would have written anything directly inconsistent with the public opinion of the time.

Living at the Court of Ferrara was a kinswoman of Lucrezia's—Angela Borgia, who by her grace and comeliness threw a glamour over all who came into contact with her. She had at one time been betrothed to Francesco Maria della Rovere, but for some reason or other the contract had been annulled. Among Angela's adorers were two brothers of Alfonso's— Cardinal Ippolito d'Este, and Giulio, a bastard son of the old Duke Ercole. One day, when Ippolito was paying court to her, she began to praise the beauty of Giulio's eyes. This so inflamed the Cardinal's jealousy that he hired assassins and commissioned them to lie in wait for his brother as he returned from hunting, and to tear out the beautiful eyes which had excited Donna Angela's admiration. His command was carried out, November 3, 1505; but the depraved Ippolito was - not .allowed to enjoy the complete success of his plan, for the physicians were able to save one of his · victim's eyes. The whole of Ferrara burned with indignation at the Cardinal's atrocity, and he was punished by a temporary banishment. Giulio, who considered that the Duke had dealt too leniently with him, longed for a deeper revenge. Ippolito, however, had many friends in Ferrara, for he was a jovial man of the world, while the Duke, by his morose and surly manners, was unpopular with the nobility.

Giulio succeeded in winning the support of several disaffected nobles and others who were in Alfonso's service, among them Count Albertino Boschetti, the captain of . the palace guard, a chamberlain, and one of the Duke's minstrels. Even Don Ferrante, the Duke's own brother, entered into the plot. Giulio's plan was to despatch Cardinal Ippolito by means of poison, and then to destroy the Duke himself and set Don Ferrante on the throne.

The Cardinal, however, who was well supplied with spies, got an inkling of what was going on, and lost no time in informing his brother, Duke Alfonso. The conspirators, with the exception of. Don Ferrante, sought refuge in flight, but only Giulio and the minstrel succeeded in escaping. Count Boschetti was seized in the neighbourhood of Ferrara. When Don Ferrante was brought before the' Duke he cast himself .at his feet and begged for mercy. But Alfonso, in a frenzy of rage, struck out one of-

3. ALFONSO, DUKE OF FERRARA, OBVERSE; LUCREZIA HIS
WIFE, REVERSE.
(South Kensington Museum.)

4. POPE PIUS III., COMMEMORATING HIS CORONATION.
(British Museum.)

1. GIOVANNI SFORZA, FIRST HUSBAND OF LUCREZIA BORGIA.
MEDAL COMMEMORATING HIS RETURN TO HIS STATES.
(British Museum.)

2. CATERINA SFORZA.   *(South Kensington Museum.)*

his eyes with a staff which he had in his hand. He then had him imprisoned in the tower of the castle, where he was soon joined by Giulio, who had been surrendered by the Marquis of Mantua, from whom he had sought protection. The trial for treason resulted in sentence of death for all the guilty. Boschetti and two of his companions were beheaded in front of the Palazzo della Ragione The execution of the two Princes was arranged for August 12, 1506. The scaffold was erected in the courtyard of the castle, the Duke took his place, and the people thronged to witness the revolting sight. The wretched victims had already been led to the block when Alfonso made a sign that a reprieve would be granted. More dead than alive, they were borne back to their dungeons, where they were condemned to a life-long imprisonment. They both survived their brother. Don Ferrante died in 1540, at the age of sixty-three, and Don Giulio, who was liberated after Alfonso's death, died in 1561, in his eighty-fourth year.

Duke Alfonso's hopes of an heir had twice been disappointed, but on April 4, 1508, his heart was gladdened by the birth of a baby son, who was named Ercole, after his grandfather. The younger poet Strozzi celebrated the advent of the little heir in the most exuberant and flattering verses. They were, however, his final effort, for on the morning of June 6 the dead body of the poet was found near the d'Este Palace, wounded in two-and-twenty places, and with part of his hair torn out by the roots The whole of Ferrara was filled with resentment, for Strozzi, who had only reached his twenty-eighth year, was a general favourite, and indeed had contributed much to the fame of the city.

This foul deed has, by some, been ascribed to Alfonso on the grounds of an infatuation for his young wife, Barbara. Others maintain that he was

ZB

jealous of Lucrezia's attitude towards him. One of the strongest proofs of the Duke's guilt is that he apparently made no effort to discover and punish the murderer.

Even Lucrezia has not escaped being charged with the murder, though none of the later historians have attributed any importance to this accusation. The motives ascribed to her were jealousy of Barbara, or the fear that Strozzi might reveal her relations with Bembo.

Meanwhile, what had become of the little Rodrigo, Lucrezia's son by Alfonso of Naples? For some reason it was not considered suitable that the child should be brought up at the Court of Ferrara. Yriarte quotes a letter from Duke Ercole to Lucrezia, strongly advising his separation from her, and he was therefore placed under the guardianship of the Patriarch of Alexandria and Francesco Borgia, Archbishop of Cosenza. He was well equipped, from a worldly point of view, for he not only owned his father's inheritance of Bisceglia, but he was also Duke of Sermoneta and lord of Guadrata. He appears to have been confided to the care of his aunt, Donna Sancia of Aragon, a somewhat unsuitable person to whom to entrust the education of a child, one would think! Upon her death in 1506 Rodrigo was probably placed under the protection of another aunt, Isabella of Aragon, Duchess of Bari, whose acquaintance we have already made as the unhappy wife of Gian Galeazzo of Milan, the victim of Ludovico Sforza's jealous ambition.

There is an entry in the household accounts of the Duchess of Ferrara for March 26, 1505, mentioning "a suit of damask and brocade which her Majesty sent to her son Don Rodrigo in Bari, as a present." The little Rodrigo appears to have had, as companion, the mysterious Giovanni *Infans Romanus*, who was about the same age. Alexander VI., it is said, enjoyed the company of these two children and often had them with him. In 1508 Giovanni and Rodrigo are again mentioned as being together in Bari, and sharing the instructions of a certain Don Bartolommeo Grotto. In August 1512 the inconvenient little Duke, Rodrigo, was removed by the hand of death. Lucrezia appears to have grieved over his loss, for in a letter to an unknown correspondent, dated October 1, she speaks of her continued tears and sorrow "per la morte del Duca di Bisselli, mio figliuolo carissimo."

In 1510 occurred the death of Lucrezia's first husband, Giovanni Sforza of Pesaro, who had been living a quiet and studious life at the Castle of Gradara. He had ruled his State with considerable wisdom and had made many improvements in Pesaro. In 1504 he had married Ginevra, daughter of a Venetian noble, and their union resulted in the birth of a son, Costanzo. This fact proves that the ostensible reason for his divorce from Lucrezia was unfounded.

Meanwhile Pope Julius II. had made peace with Venice and commanded Alfonso d'Este to withdraw from the league with France and to cease hostilities against the Republic. This the Duke refused to do, and was therefore placed under the papal ban. Ferrara and France were thus drawn into a war, which led to the celebrated battle of Ravenna, on Easter Sunday, April 11, 1512, in which Alfonso's artillery won the day. This is said to have been the most bloody battle fought on Italian soil since the days of the Huns and Goths. It was during this war that Lucrezia made the acquaintance of the celebrated Bayard. His biographer writes : " The good Duchess who was a pearl in this world, received the French with special marks of favour. Every day she gave the most wonderful festivals and banquets in the Italian fashion. I venture to say that neither in her time, nor for many years before, has there been such a glorious princess, for she is beautiful and good, gentle and courteous to every one, and there is no doubt that, although her husband is a skilful and brave prince, this lady, by her gracious character, has been of great service to him."

Lucrezia's relations with Alfonso, though never of a passionate nature, seem to have become more affectionate with the passing of time. In April 1514 she bore him a second son, Alessandro, who, however, died when he was two years old. In a letter to her friend and sister-in-law, Isabella Gonzaga of Mantua, she makes touching reference to her loss: "Yesterday," she writes, "at the fourth hour of the night, the poor little man (*poverino*) yielded his blessed soul into the hands of our Lord God, leaving me much afflicted and full of sorrow, as your Excellency, being a woman and a tender mother yourself, may easily believe." In July 1515, she had her first baby-girl—Leonora—and on November 1, 1516, arrived another little son, Francesco. Alfonso was delighted to have a legitimate family springing up around him; he was also much gratified by the respect and admiration accorded to his wife, who, though she had outlived the zenith of her beauty, was honoured for her womanly charm and virtue.

It appears from the official correspondence of Leo X. that Lucrezia sought from him spiritual consolation and advice. She also wrote to him on one occasion begging him to intercede with her husband on behalf of a citizen who was unjustly imprisoned. The Pope, in his reply, says: "Because you are universally esteemed to be prudent and discerning beyond other women, and have the reputation of being adorned with all the virtues, I doubt not that you will accomplish your will with your husband, by whom, I believe, you are warmly loved for these reasons."

It cannot be disputed that the once defamed and execrated Lucrezia had now become one of the most

honoured women of the day, and even the fierce light
which beats upon a throne reveals no taint of discredit.   Caviceo dedicated his work, *Il Pelegrino*, to
her in 1508, and considered it honour enough, when
he wished to praise the celebrated Isabella Gonzaga,
to say that she approached in perfection the Duchess
of Ferrara.

The historian, Jovius, tells us how entirely Lucrezia
cast away her former luxurious habits in order to
live a simple and pious life.   In time of famine her
kindness to the poor was remarkable, and she actually
pawned her jewels in order to help them.

In the year 1518 occurred the death of Lucrezia's
mother, Vannozza.   Although the days of the Borgia
greatness were over and past, Vannozza had lived on
in Rome—a noted, and, to a certain extent, an esteemed
personality.   She had never seen her daughter, of
whom she was both fond and proud, since her marriage
with Alfonso d'Este, though she continued to corres-
pond with her.   Her last letter to Lucrezia, dated
December 19, 1515, refers to Agapito of Emilia,
Cæsar's former secretary.   The formality with which
she thinks fit to address her daughter, the Duchess,
strikes quaintly upon modern ears   It runs as follows :

" ILLUSTRIOUS LADY, GREETING AND RESPECTS !

" Your Excellency will certainly remember with
favour the services which Messer Agapito of Emilia
rendered to his Excellency our Duke, as well as the
love which he has always shown us especially.   He
therefore deserves that his kinsmen should be supported
and favoured in every possible way.   Shortly before
his death he relinquished all his benefices in favour
of his nephews to Giambattista of Aquila ; among
them are some of little value in the Archbishopric
of Capua ;   the deceased acted thus in order to further
the interests of his nephews, for he never imagined
that they would be injured by the most reverend

and illustrious Cardinal who is Archbishop of that town If your Excellency wishes to do me a kindness, I beg, for the above-mentioned reasons, that you will recommend the said nephews to the favour of his most revered lordship Niccolo, the bearer of this letter, himself the nephew of the said Agapito, will furnish your Excellency with all necessary explanations. And now farewell to your Excellency, to whom I recommend myself.

" *Postscript*.—Your Excellency will do in this matter as you think best, for I have written the above from a sense of obligation Do, therefore, only what you know will please his Worthiness, and, for the moment, answer as you think discreet.

" VANNOZZA,
" Who prays for you constantly."

From the above it will be seen, remarks Gregorovius, that Vannozza did credit to the Borgias and the diplomatic lessons which they had taught her

Like many others of her kind, this woman who had been a great sinner devoted the latter years of her life to piety and good works She was a familiar figure in the churches, and in her will she endowed a number of religious foundations For many years there were inscriptions in the hospitals of the Lateran and of the Consolazione referring to her legacies as well as to provisions for masses on the anniversaries of her death and those of her two husbands.

Vannozza breathed her last at Rome, November 26, 1518, at the age of seventy-six. She was buried with conspicuous honours—" almost like a Cardinal "—in the Church of Santa Maria del Popolo, near her son, the Duke of Gandia An official character was imparted to the ceremony by the presence of the papal Court Pope Leo X in this way recognised Vannozza either as the widow of Alexander VI. or as the mother of the Duchess of Ferrara.

The manuscript of a memorial drawn up by Marcantonio Altieri, one of the most prominent men in Rome, and Guardian of the Company of the Gonfalone *ad Sancta Sanctorum*, is still preserved among the archives of the Association. It runs as follows :

" We must not forget the charitable foundations established by the respected and honoured lady, Madonna Vannozza of the House of Catanei, the happy mother of the illustrious Duke of Gandia, the Duke of Valentino, the Prince of Squillace, and of Madonna Lucrezia, Duchess of Ferrara. As she wished to endow the Company with her worldly goods, she bequeathed it her jewels of great value, and so much more that the Company in a few years was able to discharge certain obligations, with the help of the noble gentlemen, Messer Mariano Castellano and my dear Messer Rafael Casate, who had recently been guardians. She made an agreement with the great and famous silversmith Caradosso, by which she gave him 2,000 ducats so that he might, with his exceptional talent, carry out the desire of that noble and honourable woman. She also left us so much property that we shall have a revenue of 400 ducats with which to feed the sick and miserable who, alas ! abound. Out of gratitude for her piety and devotion and for those meritorious and charitable endowments, our honourable Society unanimously and cheerfully decided not only to celebrate her obsequies with great pomp, but also to honour the deceased with a magnificent and splendid monument. It was also decided to celebrate mass in the Church de Popolo, where she is buried, on the anniversary of her death, and to provide for other ceremonies with an assembly of men bearing torches and tapers, for the purpose of commending her soul's salvation to God, and to prove to the world that we hate and despise ingratitude."

It is not certain whether a marble monument was

ever erected to Vannozza's memory, but the following mendacious inscription was placed over her grave :

" To Vannozza Catanei, ennobled by her children, Duke Cæsar of Valentino, Jofre of Squillace, and Lucrezia of Ferrara, and equally conspicuous for her goodness, her piety, her age and her wisdom. Girolamo Picus, Fiduciary-Commissioner and Executor of her will, erected this monument in memory of the great services rendered by her to the Lateran Hospital. She lived seventy-six years, four months, and thirteen days. She died on November 26, 1518."

For more than two hundred years the priests in Santa Maria del Popolo sang masses for the repose of the soul of this famous woman, who, doubtless, hoped to propitiate heaven with her gold and silver and precious stones. Much evil has been spoken and written about Vannozza, but an impartial examination leads us to suppose that the chief accusation which can be justly supported is that of her amorous relations with Rodrigo Borgia before he became Pope. Afterwards, though, owing to her increasing years, she ceased to wield the same kind of attraction over him, she still influenced him (even when he had fallen a victim to the charms of Giulia Farnese), by her amiability, good sense, and discrimination.

When the Duke of Ferrara returned from France, where he had been trying to gain the support of Louis XII against the Pope's claims upon Reggio and Modena, he found Lucrezia in an extremely serious state of health On June 14, 1519, she gave birth to a still-born child. It was evident that she could not recover, and she herself clearly realised her danger. The following letter written to Pope Leo X. two days before her death, sheds light upon the state of mind in which she approached the Valley of the Shadow :

" Most Holy Father and Honoured Master,

" With all respect I kiss the feet of your Holiness and commend myself in deep humility to your holy mercy. Having suffered severe pain for more than two months, early on the morning of the 14th of this month, as it pleased God, I was delivered of a daughter. I hoped then to find relief from my sufferings, but it has been otherwise and I shall be obliged to pay the debt of nature And so great is the favour which our merciful Creator has shown me that I realise that my end is approaching, and know that in a few hours, after having received the Holy Sacraments of the Church, I shall be no longer of this world. Having arrived so far, I desire as a Christian, although a sinner, to beg your Holiness to deign mercifully to give me all possible spiritual consolation and support, and your blessing upon my soul. This I ask in all humbleness, and I commend to your Holiness my husband and children, all of whom are your servants.

" Your Holiness's humble servant,
" Lucrezia d'Este.

" Ferrara,
" 22nd June, 1519, 24th hour."

It is hardly credible that this letter, so full of calm and dignity, could have been written on her death-bed by any woman guilty of all the crimes which have been laid to the charge of the unhappy Lucrezia.

On the night of June 24 the soul of Lucrezia escaped from the envy and calumny of this troublesome world. Alfonso immediately sent the news of his loss to his nephew, Federigo Gonzaga, in a letter from which we quote the following .

" It has just pleased our Lord to recall to Himself the soul of the illustrious lady, the Duchess, my much-loved wife. . . . I cannot write this without tears, so much do I suffer at the thought of losing so dear and sweet a companion; for such her exemplary conduct and the tender love which existed between us, made her to me. On the occasion of this severe loss, I would indeed seek consolation from your Excellency, but I know that you will share my sorrow, and I prefer that you should mingle your tears with mine rather than that you should endeavour to console me. . . . "

The Marquis Federigo sent his uncle, Giovanni Gonzaga, to Ferrara. In sending news of Lucrezia's funeral to his nephew, Giovanni says: " Her death has caused great grief throughout the entire city, and his ducal Majesty, in particular, has manifested the keenest sorrow. Wonderful things are reported concerning her life, and it is said that she has worn the *cilice*[1] for about ten years; also that she has confessed daily for the last two years, and has received the Communion three or four times every month."

Among the many letters of condolence received by Alfonso was one from the mysterious *Infans Romanus*, Giovanni Borgia; he mourns the loss of his " sister," who had also been one of his principal patrons. There is documentary evidence to prove that he had remained at the Court of Ferrara until 1517, and that the following year he went to France, with an introduction from Duke Alfonso to the French King.

From the union of Lucrezia and Alfonso d'Este were born five children—Ercole, who succeeded his father as Duke of Ferrara, and married a daughter of Louis XII. of France; Ippolito, who became a Cardinal and died in 1572 at Tivoli; Eleonora, who entered upon a religious career and died a nun in the Cloister of Corpus Domini, June 1575; Francesco

---

[1] A penitential hair garment.

afterwards Marquis of Massalombardo, who died in 1578, and Alessandro, the little boy who died in 1516, when only two years old. The history of these children, however, belongs to the House of Este and we will not pursue it further.

CHAPTER XVII

MANY and fierce are the controversies which have raged about the life and character of Pope Alexander VI. Illustrious scholars such as Rinaldi, Matagne, Hergenroether, Moehler, and Mansi have taken the darkest possible view of him, and at one time the name of Borgia went forth to the world as a synonym of all that was vile and debased. " It is easier," says Mansi, " to be silent about this Pontiff, than to speak of him with moderation, since in him all vices were exaggerated, and he was, one might say, devoid of virtue." On the other hand, the researches of von Reumont and Gregorovius have made it probable that many of the crimes imputed to Rodrigo Borgia have been invented or exaggerated, and several writers, such as Padre Leonetti, Baron Corvo, and the Abbé Clement, have even sought to depict him as a maligned and injured saint. Dr. Ludwig Pastor, himself a Roman Catholic historian of high repute, demonstrates the absolute hopelessness of trying to rehabilitate a character whose vices and excesess are confirmed by a stndy of the cocuments accessible to the present-day historian. He particularly refers to valuable information contained in papers of the Milanese Archives which were not investigated by Gregorovius Much light, too, has been thrown upon Alexander VI and his family by the publication of the Diary of John Burchard, Bishop of Orta,[1] who was Master of the Ceremonies under Sixtus IV., Innocent VIII., and Alexander VI. A lymphatic, egotistic, unimaginative man, his detailed narrative bears the stamp of truth, and there can be little doubt that he is one of the most trustworthy contemporary witnesses whose evidence is obtainable.

That Alexander was the father of at least ten illegitimate children is now established beyond a doubt. He followed the profligate and immoral mode of life which, alas! was all too common in his time among all ecclesiastics, especially those in high places. Many influential men, while leading private lives of revolting depravity, continued their public careers with brilliancy and satisfaction. The moral and social conscience of the time was feeble and atrophied. It is almost impossible for the average decently-brought-up Briton of the present age to realise the unwholesome moral atmosphere in which the Italians of the fifteenth and sixteenth centuries lived, moved, and had their being. "The exceptional infamy that attaches to Alexander," remarks Bishop Creighton, "is largely due to the fact that he did not add hypocrisy to his other vices." "Les vices d'Alexandre VI. ne choquent que parce qu'il est Pape : ailleurs ils seraient tolérés, acceptés, peut-être applaudis."[2]

The extraordinary thing about these men of the Renaissance is that many of them appeared to combine a deep religious fervour with a life of appalling wickedness. They were "so constituted that to turn from

[1] An English translation has been published in three vols.

[2] *Revue des Questions historiques* (April, 1881).

vice and cruelty and crime, from the deliberate corruption and enslavement of a people, by licentious pleasures, from the persecution of an enemy in secret, with a fervid and impassioned movement of the soul to God, was nowise impossible Their temper admitted of this anomaly, as we may plainly see from Cellini's autobiography." [1] Alexander himself is reported to have cherished a particular devotion for the Blessed Virgin, and in her honour he revived the custom of ringing the bell during the recitation of the Angelus thrice a day.

Alexander VI. has been called the " most characteristic incarnation of the secular spirit of the Papacy of the fifteenth century." It must, however, be remembered that the secularisation of the Papacy had been begun by Sixtus IV , and that it was as remarkable under Innocent VIII. as under Alexander, though certainly during the latter's pontificate the materialisation of religion reached its highest point.

Of his ability—of his genius even—there can be no two opinions ; indeed, if vigour of body and mind were all that was required of a Pope, Alexander VI. would have been among the greatest. He had a remarkable capacity for hard mental work, and his buoyant, jovial nature enabled him to bear his burden of vice and crime, with a lightness impossible to a man of a less sanguine disposition.

In every-day life Alexander VI. was genial and pleasant, fond of talking, and almost incapable of keeping a secret. He was impetuous, but he rarely bore malice, and he had but little sympathy with the vindictive spirit constantly displayed by his son Cæsar. Naturally unreserved and expansive, he showed a frank and almost boyish glee at the success of his schemes. As we have seen, he was an affectionate father, and his dominating passion was the advancement of his family. Although in the highest degree

[1] Symonds, *Renascence.*

sensual, he does not appear to have been intemperate in eating or drinking. To inferiors he showed himself plausible and affable, and it is said that " he liked to do unpleasant things in a pleasant manner." In spite of these amiable characteristics, however, the populace detested their Pope with a deadly loathing. Indeed, as Yriare remarks, the fact that Rodrigo Borgia was permitted to occupy the throne of St. Peter for a space of ten years affords remarkable proof of the strength of the later mediæval Papacy.

Alexander was an excellent man of business and a good organiser. He regulated the Curia and arranged that the salaries of all officials should be paid punctually, a matter in which many of the former Popes had been remiss. In times of famine he minimised the suffering in the city by providing a supply of corn from Sicily. His administration of justice after his accession has already been commented upon.

The prevalent belief that Alexander poisoned his Cardinals when his treasury needed replenishing " can neither be proved nor disproved ; it is bad enough that the Pope's conduct did not make such stories incredible. Men saw the Pope greedily seizing on the goods of dying Cardinals without any attempt to conceal his pressing need of money and his readiness to receive it from every source They can hardly be blamed for not stopping to reflect that even Cardinals must die, and that the number who died during Alexander's pontificate was not above the average."[1]

Unlike his son Cæsar, Alexander does not appear to have been wantonly inhuman. He did not revel in cruelty as cruelty, though he certainly never let any humane scruples stand in the way of his own advancement. In the ordinary sense of the word he was no tyrant ; his natural geniality, as a rule, preserved him from that form of vice.

The pontificate of Alexander VI. is indeed dark

[1] Creighton.

with a terrible darkness. But the gloom is not absolutely unrelieved, for, in some ways at least, he contributed to advance the good and the beautiful. Under his rule painting and architecture flourished, and many monuments still abide to bear witness to his patronage of the arts. Scientists and men of letters found protection and encouragement at the papal Court, and the Pope did much to forward the cause of education.

Among the arrivals in Rome during the year of Jubilee was a clever but impecunious youth who, to earn his daily bread, was obliged to give lessons in mechanics and mathematics. Alexander VI., on hearing of him, summoned him to the Vatican, and, after making inquiries, installed him in the Chair of Astronomy at the Roman Gymnasium. Sometimes the Pope himself would go and listen to his lectures, for the young man was no other than the great Copernicus. In later years the astronomer, as a recognition of the Pope's kindness, dedicated to him his work *On the Motion of the Heavenly Bodies*.

Almost immediately after his accession the Pope set about the renovation of his apartments in the Vatican. He also had a square tower built on to them—the Torre Borgia—the upper part of which was used as his private chapel. The decoration of the rooms was entrusted to the painter Pinturicchio, who, though he probably had many assistants in the work, superintended it so capably that his influence is plainly visible in the whole scheme of decoration. "As a whole," says Schmarsow, "the work should be justly ascribed to him, and deserves the highest praise for the evenness of its execution, and the careful schooling and sagacious selection, in regard to the parts assigned to them, of the pupils whom he evidently employed."

Alexander occupied five of these apartments for living purposes—the Hall of Mysteries, the Hall of

ST. FRANCIS BORGIA, S.J., FOURTH DUKE OF GANDIA, THIRD GENERAL OF THE
SOCIETY OF JESUS, GREAT-GRANDSON OF POPE ALEXANDER VI.

From the old Ducal Palace at Gandia, now a Jesuit College.

The tapestry on the right represents his baptism, the one on the left his departure
from home to join the Jesuits.

384]

Saints, the Hall of Arts and Sciences, and two "withdrawing" rooms   It was in the Hall of the Arts that Lucrezia's first husband was assassinated, and the apartment next to it witnessed the last scene of Alexander's life.

It is supposed that Pinturicchio had no share in the decoration of the Hall of the Pontiffs, the first room of the suite.   It was here that Alexander VI. had such a narrow escape from being killed by the falling in of the roof during the summer of 1500.   The three rooms which open out of this Hall are to be seen to-day exactly as they were in the time of the Borgias, and are now the apartments of Cardinal Merry del Val.   In the rich decorations of gold and stucco-work the Borgia Bull continually appears.   In the first of these three—the Hall of Mysteries—the pictures are entirely drawn from religious subjects.   There are seven principal paintings—the Annunciation, the Nativity, the Adoration, the Resurrection, the Ascension, the Descent of the Holy Spirit, and the Assumption of the Virgin.   The Annunciation is probably the work of Pinturicchio.   Its design is simple and graceful, a religious tone pervades the whole conception, and the colouring is exquisitely soft and beautiful.   The figures of the Virgin and Child in the Nativity are also thought to be due to the master's hand, though other portions of the picture point to the work of pupils.   The painting of the Resurrection is of special interest in that it contains a striking full-length portrait of Pope Alexander himself.   Although he is so completely swathed in a superb jewel-embroidered and brocaded cope that only his head and hands are visible, yet, by the wonderful art of the painter, we are made to feel the figure beneath the drapery.   "It is in the face and hands, however, that the artist reveals himself as a portrait-painter of high rank.   The face is in direct profile—a position that shows as little as may be

AAB

the fat cheeks and extra layers of flesh running from cheeks and chin to neck. But a square full face would not more truly have given the character of this Borgian Pontiff An insufficient, sloping forehead, full eyes, too close to the nose, which is large and with a high Roman arch to it, long upper lip over a heavy lower one, a chin that leads by one diagonal line without a curve into the wide, short neck, a most abnormal development of the lower back part of head and neck—these are the salient points of this portrayal, which can be no caricature. For it must have pleased the Pope, or it would not have remained on the walls, and perforce it must have done him full credit. The hands, with their smooth taper fingers, would be nearly ideally perfect if the flesh had not made them puffy. Not the kind of hands likely to be found on a strong, noble man, but of charming line and colour for a—soulless dilettante perhaps " [1]

The Hall of Saints contains the finest of all Pinturicchio's works—the Dispute of St. Catherine. In a large and brilliant assembly of people, St. Catherine is the only adult woman. She stands " straight, willowy, and undismayed, robed in a magnificent brocaded gown, her long fair hair hanging to her waist," declaring her beliefs before the Emperor Maximilian and fifty philosophers. It appears that many members of the crowd are portraits of well-known people. Catherine herself has been taken as a likeness of Lucrezia Borgia, but it is more probable that she represents Giulia Farnese. One of the most conspicuous figures is a Turk on a white charger. He is supposed to be a portrait of Djem, the son of Mohammed II., but is more probably Juan Borgia, Duke of Gandia. Cæsar is also there as King, and Jofré, with his girl-wife, appears in the centre of the picture.

The ceiling of this hall is decorated with scenes

[1] Mary Knight Potter, *The Art of the Vatican.*

from the myths of Isis and Osiris and the Bull of Apis—subjects suggested by the Borgia arms. Over the doorway leading into the Hall of Arts and Sciences is a round medallion of a Madonna and Child Vasari is probably right in supposing the Madonna to be a portrait of Giulia Farnese, for it is the same face as that of St Catherine's in the Disputa. His statement that Alexander VI. was painted kneeling in adoration before her appears, however, to be quite unfounded.

In the lunettes of this third apartment, which was probably the Pope's study, are painted personifications of Mathematics, Dialectics, Jurisprudence, Geometry, Arithmetic, Music, and Astronomy. Next to the figure of Geometry is the Borgia escutcheon surmounted by the keys and the tiara, and supported by three angels who make one of the most charming groups in the whole set of apartments.

From the Hall of Arts and Sciences a marble staircase leads to the chambers in the Borgia Tower. These two rooms are less elaborately decorated than the others. In the first is a frieze of apostles and prophets. Each apostle bears a scroll inscribed with a sentence from the Creed, while each of the prophets carries one with a prophecy written upon it.

In the second room, which was probably the Pope's bedchamber, there are sibyls and prophets in pairs, and the spaces are filled up with ribbons on which are written the early prophecies concerning the birth of Christ. Though these apartments are on a less magnificent scale than the others, they harmonise well with the conception of the whole. Pinturicchio, though not one of the great masters of the Renaissance, understood the rare and potent art of " space composition," which will cause his works to be remembered when those, perhaps, of greater men are forgotten.

Pinturicchio's gay and fanciful style was particularly congenial to the luxurious and sensual age of th

Borgias, when a higher form of art might have lacked appreciation. Mr. Berenson, in speaking of his work, says : " But if mere prettiness pleased so well, why then, the more pretty faces, the more splendid costumes and romantic surroundings per square foot, the better ! And so Pinturicchio, never possessing much feeling for form and movement, now, under the pressure of favour and popularity, forgot their very existence, and tended to make of his work an *olla podrida*, rich and savoury, but more welcome to provincial palates than to the few *gourmets*. And when such an opulent and luxurious half-barbarian as Pope Alexander VI was his employer, then no spice nor condiment nor seasoning was spared, and a more gorgeously barbaric blaze of embossed gold and priceless ultramarine than in the Borgia Apartments you shall not soon see again ! "

Alexander made special efforts for the improvement of the Trastevere, the northern part of Rome, which had grown to be the most important division of the city. During his pontificate it was transformed into a remarkably handsome quarter Sixtus IV. had already made a wide street running from the moat of the Castle of Sant' Angelo to the Papal Palace. Alexander added another, parallel with it ; it was then called the Via Allessandrina, but is now known as Borgo Nuovo. This new street was really planned in order to accommodate the great crowd of pilgrims expected to assemble for the Jubilee celebrations of 1500.

Substantial alterations were made by Alexander VI. in the Castle of Sant' Angelo, which he had thoroughly well fortified and surrounded by a wall and moat. Five subterranean prisons were also dug out, and, by a special arrangement, the Pope reserved the right of appropriating anything of value which might be found in the course of the excavations—a stipulation which resulted in his possession of the bust of Hadrian, which is now in the Rotonda of the Vatican.

By the Pope's orders, a fountain was placed in the Piazza of Santa Maria in Trastevere, while the one erected by Innocent VIII in the Piazza of St Peter's was decorated by Alexander with four gilt bulls, the Borgia arms.

In Rome itself Alexander finished the roof of Santa Maria Maggiore, which had been begun by his uncle, Pope Calixtus. It is said that the first gold brought from America was employed in the decoration of its beautiful panels. As Cardinal he had already built the colossal Palazzo Borgia, now the property of the Sforza Cesarini. It had its origin in the ancient buildings of the Papal Chancery, which Borgia transformed into one of the finest palaces in Italy   He also set on foot restorations in St Peter's, the Church of San Niccolo in Carcere, and the Church of the SS. Apostoli, as well as in the city walls.   The rebuilding of the University is also due to him.

The architectural zeal displayed by the Pope gave an impetus to building throughout the whole of the city, and new churches and palaces arose on every hand.   The celebrated Cancellaria, the abode of the wealthy Cardinal Riario, was a product of this time, and Cardinal Giuliano della Rovere also built a palace for his own occupation.

The year 1502 saw the completion of the celebrated Tempietto in the court of the Franciscan Convent near the S. Pietro in Montorio.   It was the work of the great Bramante, who had come to Rome in 1499 and thoroughly imbued his mind with the spirit of classic architecture as exemplified in the antiquities of the ancient city.

Besides the already mentioned churches, many others were erected during Alexander's pontificate. Among them were the Church of San Rocco on the quay of the Ripetta, and that of SS. Trinità dei

Monti, on the Pincio, founded by Cardinal Briçonnet. The Porta Settimiana was restored by order of the Pope, whose architect, Antonio da Sangallo, also designed the fortresses of Civitella, Tivoli and Civita Castellana.

For the encouragement of education Alexander VI. did much. He enlarged the buildings of the University of la Sapienza at Rome, regulated the method of conferring degrees at Pisa, and commissioned the Archbishop of Toledo and the Bishop of Salamanca to reform the Universities of their respective towns. He also made a grant from the ecclesiastical revenues to help the foundation of the University of Lisbon. The founding of Aberdeen University was sanctioned by him, and the Latin bull issued at Rome for this purpose, in 1495, is still in possession of the authorities. It sets forth " the many blessings that flow from the acquisition of the priceless pearl of knowledge," which " conduces to the clear understanding of the secrets of the universe," and " raises those of humble origin to the loftiest rank " Howbeit, in the northern districts of the realm of James IV., " there are certain localities cut off from the rest of the kingdom by firths and very lofty mountains, where dwell rude and ignorant men, almost uncivilised," so that it is difficult to find suitable men for preaching the Word of God and administering the sacraments. If, however, a school of general learning were established in these parts, " large numbers—ecclesiastics and laymen alike—would willingly incline to the study of letters." Moreover, in the " renowned city of Old Aberdeen," there is " a healthy climate, no lack of provisions, and abundance of all the necessaries of life." Therein, therefore, we " do by these presents appoint and ordain " that " from henceforth and for ever, there do flourish a School and University of General Learning, alike in Theology, Canon and Civil Law, Medicine, Polite Letters, and any authorised

faculty, whatsoever, wherein clergy holding church
benefices, and laymen, doctors, and masters, may
lecture and teach, and those desirous to study (come
whence they may) may do so and qualify." The
deed further enacts that the Bishop of Aberdeen, for
the time being, is to be Chancellor, and shall " confer
the degrees of Bachelor and Licentiate in any or all
of the aforementioned faculties on students of praiseworthy life, who have been deemed suitable for that
honour by the Rector, the Regents, the Masters, the
Doctors, or a majority of the faculty in which they
severally desire to graduate." The further degrees of
Master or Doctor are to be granted to Licentiates
after due examination by the Masters or Doctors of
the *Studium*, with the assent of the other Doctors or
Masters of the faculty. All graduates are to have
full licence to teach in this or any other University
without further examination or test. The Chancellor
and the Rector, assisted by certain of the resident
Doctors and others, are empowered to make statutes
for the good government of the University. The
malediction of St. Peter and St. Paul is invoked against
any infringement of the deed.

Such was the legal document placed by Alexander VI. in the hands of Bishop Elphinstone. It is,
however, more than likely that the Bishop himself
inspired the terms of the bull, and that the Pope merely
gave it his official sanction.[1]

Strange though it may seem, this paradoxical Pope
was by no means indifferent to the spiritual interests
of the Church. In his Censorial edict for Germany,
June 1, 1501, he declares that, though the art of
printing is valuable for the spread of good literature,
it may also be a means of propagating works directed
against the Catholic faith and help in the dissemina-
tion of erroneous doctrines. Steps are to be taken,
therefore, for the suppression and prevention of

[1] Robert Walker, M.A., *Aberdeen University Handbook*, Pt. 1.

such publications. Strict supervision is to be enforced, especially in the Dioceses of Cologne, Mayence, Trèves and Magdeburg. " In virtue of our authority," continues the bull, " we charge the said Archbishop, Vicars, and officials to command all printers and other persons residing in their respective Dioceses, whatever may be their dignity, position or condition, within a certain fixed time, to notify all printed books in their possession to the said Archbishops, Vicars, or officials, and, without prevarication of any kind, to deliver up whatever books or treatises shall be judged by them to contain anything contrary to the Catholic Faith, or to be ungodly, or capable of causing scandal, or ill-sounding in any way, equally under pain of excommunication and a fine to be determined as aforesaid "

It is also noteworthy that in the bull decreeing the limits of Spain and Portugal, Alexander urgently enjoins the sending of wise and pious men to spread the Catholic religion among the infidels. When plans were made for the conquest of Africa, he was emphatic as to the need for introducing Christianity among the natives   He confirmed the appointment of the self-denying monk, Mathias, as Bishop of Greenland, where, without this spiritual leader, the people would have relapsed into the darkness of heathenism. In preparing for the second voyage of Columbus, Alexander joined with Ferdinand and Isabella in providing missionaries for the evangelisation of the native races.   The Militia of St. George, a military order which was supposed to keep two or three thousand men in readiness to take up the defence of Christendom, was confirmed by him, and he did much for the Order of St. Michael and that of the Militia of Christ. Finding that the worship of Satanic power was widely spread, and having an injurious effect upon the development of Catholicism, the Pope published an edict condemning the magicians and wizards who practised the black arts. He often posed as the champion of convents against their oppressors, and he took measures for the reform of the Austrian monasteries. He supported the efforts of Cardinal Ximenes in Spain and tried to improve the state of the clergy in Portugal. After the death of his son, Juan, Duke of Gandia, he was heard to cry aloud in his grief : " God has perhaps permitted this blow as a punishment for one of our sins," and he reiterated his wish to reform the papal Court and the Church of Rome, which, he said, ought to serve as an example to all the Churches in the world.

But in men of Alexander's temperament a fit of remorse and repentance is far from being synonymous with reform, and, in spite of his protestations, the grossly corrupt morals of the whole papal Court were not materially improved. His good deeds were of the spasmodic order, and his predominating interests were distinctly secular. The formalities and ceremonies of the religious offices were as nothing to this light-minded Pope, and, at the solemn mass sung on Charles VIII.'s arrival in Rome, he is said to have confused all the ceremonies   While travelling, he placidly ate meat, regardless of the rules for Lenten abstinence, and it is not surprising that his callousness and levity in these respects should have brought reproach upon the Church.

To repeat—although modern research has, to some extent, lightened the burden of guilt with which history has charged Pope Alexander VI., and has proved him to be somewhat less black than he is painted, yet there is such undoubted proof of his iniquities, that no unbiassed person can do otherwise than agree with von Reumont when he says : " The reign of this Pope, which lasted eleven years, was a serious disaster, on account of its worldliness, openly proclaimed with the most amazing effrontery, on account of its equally unconcealed nepotism, and lastly, on account of his utter absence of all moral sense both in public and private life, which made every sort of accusation credible, and brought the Papacy into utter discredit, while its authority still seemed unimpaired. Those better qualities which Alexander undoubtedly did possess shrink into nothing in the balance when weighed with all this."

CHAPTER XVIII

The great-grandson of Pope Alexander VI., St Francis Borgia,
fourth Duke of Gandia.

IT seems a contradiction of the accepted laws of
heredity that from Borgia ancestry should have
sprung a man of pure and holy life—Francis Borgia,
the Saint As we have already seen, Alexander's
son, the murdered Duke of Gandia, left a widow,
Maria Enriquez, who lived a pious and praiseworthy
life. Her eldest son Juan, third Duke of Gandia,
was the child of many prayers, and he grew up to be an
upright and virtuous prince. He married Joan, an
illegitimate daughter of the Archbishop of Saragossa,
Alfonso of Aragon (himself a bastard son of King
Ferdinand the Catholic), and the eldest son of their
union was Francisco Borgia, whose fame as a saint
has outlived many generations

The little Francisco was born at Gandia in 1510.
Very early in his career he showed a distinctly religious
bent. At an age when other children were playing
with toys, the future saint delighted to raise miniature
altars and imitate the ceremonies of the Church.
When he was ten years old his mother died, an event
which cost the sensitive boy many tears and fervent
prayers, and gave him, it is said, the idea of flagellating
himself. Shortly afterwards, owing to social disturbances in his father's duchy, Francisco was entrusted to the care of his uncle, Don Juan of Aragon,
who had succeeded Alfonso as Archbishop of Saragossa. Don Juan received his young charge with
kindness and geniality, and made excellent provision
for his education.

Francisco's disposition was remarkably gentle and lovable, and the reports of his character were so attractive that his grandmother, Doña Maria Luna, felt that she could not die without having seen him. The boy and his little sister were therefore sent to her at Baza. He had hardly arrived there when he was seized with an illness from which he did not recover for six months. When he was well, Doña Maria, with the consent of his father and uncle, sent him to Tordesillas to be with Joan the Mad's youngest child. This little girl was living under the strict discipline of the Marquis of Denia, and sadly needed a companion of her own age. Three years later, when he was about fifteen, Francisco went back to Saragossa, where he studied philosophy under the Doctor Gaspard de Lax. In 1527 he was removed to the Court of Charles V., where he soon became a general favourite, for his character was such that no breath of calumny could touch it. At the age of nineteen he married Eleanora de Castro, a Portuguese damsel of high rank and considerable attractions. At the same time he was made Marquis of Lombay by Charles V. Francisco accompanied the Emperor upon two disastrous expeditions—to Provence 1536, and to Algiers later.

In 1539 occurred the death of the Empress Isabella, for whom Francisco cherished a chivalrous devotion. Charles V. was at Toledo at the time, and he commissioned Francisco and Eleanora to go with her corpse to Elvira, where the burial was to take place. Upon their arrival Francisco was called upon to identify the body, and the coffin lid was removed. The sight of her face, changed almost beyond recognition by the ravages of death, made the deepest impression upon him. Realising the transitoriness of even the most beautiful of earthly things, he determined to leave the world as soon as God should remove the hindrances in his path.

The same year Francisco was made Viceroy of Catalonia, an office which he filled with justice and ability, while at the same time he did not neglect the culture of his spiritual life. He succeeded in ridding the province of the dangerous brigands who infested it, and established schools and hospitals for the good of his people.

While Francisco was Viceroy his father died, and the family estates descended to him. He shortly afterwards obtained leave to resign his office and accepted the position of major-domo to the Infanta Maria of Portugal, then about to be married to the Emperor's son Philip. Before this marriage took place, however, she died, and Francisco was set at liberty. He retired to Gandia, where he built a Dominican convent and a Jesuit college.

In 1546 Eleanora was taken ill. Francisco at first prayed for her recovery, but, realising that if she recovered he would not be able to sever himself from the world, he ceased his prayers. On March 27 Eleanora died, and her husband, though feeling her loss keenly, now rejoiced at the thought of yielding himself up entirely to the religious life. The death of the Empress seven years before had withdrawn him from the Court and the vanities of the world, but the death of his wife detached him from the world itself. A few days later Father Peter Lefèvre came to Gandia to lay the foundation-stone of the College of Jesuits. Francisco went through the spiritual exercises of St. Ignatius with him, and gained so much benefit that he wrote to the Pope begging him to seal them with his apostolic approval. At the same time he made up his mind to join the Society of Jesus. St. Ignatius, however, advised him to wait until his children were settled in life. For the next three years, therefore, he watched over their education and development until they were all able to dispense with his fatherly care. Francisco himself lived the simplest of lives and daily grew in grace so that the very sight of him " was like a benediction "

In August of the Jubilee year, 1550, Francisco set out for Rome, accompanied by his second son Juan and a retinue of thirty servants. He was enthusiastically received in Italy, and his uncle, Ercole II. (son of Lucrezia Borgia), invited him to the Court of Ferrara. The Pope, Julius II., offered him rooms at the Vatican, but Francisco refused them in order that he might sit at the feet of Ignatius, at whose saintliness he never ceased to marvel. " Until now," he confessed, " I thought Lefèvre a giant and myself a child ; but, compared with Ignatius, Lefèvre himself is but a child."

Francisco's stay in Rome was not a long one. In February 1551 he returned to his native country, not to Gandia, but to Ognate in Guipuscoa. With the Emperor's consent he resigned his duchy in favour of his eldest son, and then definitely withdrew from secular affairs. His hair was cropped and tonsure shaven, his ducal robes cast off, and the Jesuit's habit put on The same year, 1551, he was ordained priest, and he preached his first sermon at Vergara on June 29.

The people of Ognate gave Francisco a hermitage about a mile from their town. Here he made wooden cells for himself and his companions, but, instead of leading the retired life which he had planned, he found himself the centre of attraction Crowds of visitors invaded his solitude, curious to see the Duke who had been transformed into a hermit. When St. Ignatius heard of this, he sent him on a preaching expedition in Portugal, where, by the humility and sweetness of his life, he gained much influence. In Spain, too, he enlisted many disciples for his Order.

In 1554 Francisco was appointed Vicar-General of Spain by St. Ignatius, a responsibility which was distasteful to his meek and lowly spirit, though he nobly fulfilled the duties connected with it. He continued to live an austere and devoted life, charitable towards others and severe towards himself. His sunny disposition never changed, though the mortifications to which he subjected himself became so intense that his friends complained to St. Ignatius, who commanded him to modify them for his health's sake.

In April of the next year (1555) Francisco soothed the last hours of the unfortunate Queen, Joan the Mad, sister of our Catherine of Aragon, who for many years had shown the greatest repugnance to the things of religion. Francisco's gentle and loving ministrations had the desired effect, and on Good Friday, April 12, her sad life ended with the prayer, " Christ Crucified be with me."

Francisco, in consequence of this happy influence, became more beloved than ever, for all Spain was grateful for his goodness to Queen Joan. To the sick he was a god-send, for no service, however distasteful or menial, was disdained by this saintly man.

St. Ignatius died in 1556, but the election of his successor did not take place until nearly two years later. Francisco, for some reason, was not present, a fact which led to a disagreement with Padre Nadal, who, in his journal, represents our hero in a less favourable light than is generally shed upon him. It must always be remembered that Francisco was, after all, human, and that his gracious and beautiful life was the outcome, not of his natural temperament, but of a continual and obstinate struggle with his lower self, in which he never faltered.

In 1565 Francisco was elected General of the Society of Jesus, upon the death of Father Laynez.

Pope Pius IV. rejoiced at the news, and all the Catholic Courts congratulated him Francisco alone was dismayed. The entry in his journal for the day of the election is simply, " Day of my crucifixion ! " His habit of submission to the divine will, however, stood him in good stead, and he entered upon his new responsibilities with courage and cheerfulness. He removed to Rome, the headquarters of the Society, and, by his energy and enterprise, the institution grew and flourished. In 1572 we hear of Mary, Queen of Scots, appealing for the prayers of the Society and those of its holy General. In 1571 Francisco was sent by Pope Pius V. on an embassy to France, Spain, and Portugal to stir up the Christian Powers in the defence of Christendom against the Mohammedans. He was at this time in bad health, and the long journey and excitement proved too much for him. Having accomplished his mission and arrived at Ferrara, he was taken so seriously ill that his cousin Duke Alfonso sent him back to Rome in a litter. Two days after his arrival, September 30, 1572, Francisco Borgia passed calmly and peacefully to his rest. Eventually he was raised to the altars of the Catholic Church by canonisation.

ALEXANDER VI., ADORING THE RISEN SAVIOUR.
Pinturicchio (Borgia Apartments, the Vatican).

APPENDIX

NOTE ON THE DEATH OF DJEM SULTAN

A word remains to be said on the question of the death of Djem Sultan. The prevalent opinion among Turkish students is that his decease was brought about by foul means, and that a cumulative poison, probably arsenious acid or white arsenic, was employed.

Cæsar Borgia was a hostage in the army of Charles VIII , as was also Djem Sultan The Turkish Prince having been transferred from the Pope's custody to that of the French King, his Holiness could no longer draw the pension of 40,000 ducats per annum paid for Djem's maintenance by the Sultan Bajazet II. He would, therefore, lose nothing by the death of Djem, who was no longer in his power.

On the other hand, it is undisputed that Bajazet had offered large bribes to both Charles VIII. and Alexander VI. in return for the death of Djem, although his letter to the Pope in which an offer of 300,000 ducats was made, provided Djem's soul could be " released from the cares of this troublesome world," having been intercepted, was not actually delivered to his Holiness. The contents of the letter are recorded and were, therefore, known more or less publicly. It is not improbable that the Pope was made aware of them, since they concerned him particularly.

Cæsar Borgia is said, by Mr. Sabatini, to have escaped from Charles VIII. on the night of January 29, 1494, and on February 25 following Djem Sultan died. Mr. Sabatini, consequently, concludes (1) that Cæsar could not have administered any poison to Djem ; (2) that Djem's death involved a heavy loss to the Pope, who thereby forfeited the pension of 40,000 ducats ; (3) that cumulative poisons are unknown ; (4) that the offer of a money reward for Djem's death never actually reached the Pope ; (5) that no money was eventually paid to the Pope for Djem's corpse Djem, he says, died at Capua on February 25, 1494, and his death " was natural," whatever the disease causing it may have been ; (6) that the " secret poison " referred to by many contemporary writers could not have had any existence in fact, since, if it had existed, it would have been unknown outside the Borgia family.

The obvious reply to these statements is the following :

1. Cæsar, being a fellow-hostage with Djem, may have had opportunities of administering doses of poison to him, if not by his own by another's hand. Djem was ill for a week, and the malady from which he suffered and died was some painful affection of the intestines or stomach It is described by contemporaries as "dysentery" It was quite possible for Cæsar to have instructed one of his faithful retainers accompanying the forces of Charles VIII. to administer very small doses of white arsenic to Djem which would not destroy the life of his victim for several weeks, but take effect gradually. Examples of this kind of poisoning are not at all rare. Having provided the poison and the instruction required for its administration, Cæsar withdrew, probably leaving the accomplishment of his nefarious design in trustworthy hands.

2. Djem, having passed out of the Pope's custody and into the hands of the King of France, Alexander VI., as we have said, could no longer draw the pension paid for the Prince's maintenance by Bajazet II. Therefore it is incorrect to say, with Sanuto, that Djem's death involved loss to his Holiness If the Pope, by his agents, were able to inform Bajazet that Djem had been murdered, in accordance with Bajazet's suggestion, then Alexander could claim the reward offered to him by the Sultan for the commission of this foul crime. The blood-money named by the Sultan as the price he was willing to offer for his brother's life was 300,000 ducats, more than seven years' pension at the rate Bajazet was paying The temptation to obtain such a sum down, rather than lose both Djem and his 40,000 ducats a year altogether, must have been irresistible to men like Alexander VI. and Cæsar Borgia, whose money-hunger was insatiable

3. Cumulative poisons are few in number, and arsenious acid, or white arsenic, is one of them. It resembles powdered sugar or flour. When ordered medicinally, in minute quantities, patients are always directed to discontinue the medicine for at least a week, after taking it for fourteen days, the reason being that cumulative poison remains in the system, and, if persevered in regularly and without intermission, will cause death slowly but surely, in course of time, however small the doses taken may be. The *existence* of arsenious

acid, or white arsenic, was not the secret of the Borgias. The *manner of its administration*, as a slow poison, difficult, at that period, to detect, was the Borgia secret ! Every one knew what was meant by " cantarella," but only few were aware that it was cumulative in its action. On this point Mr. Sabatini appears to have been misinformed.

4. That money rewards for Djem's death had been offered by Bajazet is admitted by Mr Sabatini. He says " Bajazet had offered such bribes to Charles for the life of Djem, as had caused the Knights of Rhodes to remove the Turk from French keeping "[1] He also does not deny that Bajazet made a similar offer to Alexander VI. But he thinks that " for Djem's death in the hands of France, the Pope could make no claim upon Bajazet."[2] Now the reverse appears to be the case, as Mr. Sabatini himself shows. He states that the Pope, fearing a French invasion, had actually appealed for help to Bajazet [3] The Sultan was frantic at the prospect of Djem's falling into the hands of Charles VIII , who proposed to " make a raid " upon Bajazet. It was in consequence of this wholesome fear that Bajazet appealed to Alexander to murder his brother Djem The bribe was to be paid on delivery of the Prince's body in Constantinople, and was to be the reward for removing Djem from risk of capture by the French King The intercepted letter from the Sultan to the Pope was delivered by Giovanni della Rovere to his brother the Cardinal, who, detesting Alexander, promptly laid it before Charles VIII. The King immediately demanded and obtained the surrender of Djem, whose death was now the only solution of the Pope's difficulty.

The circumstantial evidence against Alexander is, therefore, strong.

5. As to whether Alexander received the bribe of 300,000 ducats in return for Djem's dead body, the evidence that his Holiness did receive it is equally circumstantial The body, having been returned to the papal agents, was embalmed and shipped to Constantinople, where Bajazet received it with great pomp and parade of mourning.[4]

This is undisputed. It was, moreover, accompanied by papal representatives On what grounds was Djem's body surrendered to and taken possession of by Alexander VI ? It was manifestly of no utility to Charles VIII. Why was

[1] *Cesare Borgia*, p 118   [2] *Ibid*   [3] *Ibid* , p 112
[4] See *Djem Sultan*, by L Thuasne.

it sent by the Pope to Bajazet II ? There can be only one opinion on this point.

6. As we have shown above, it has never been pretended that " cantarella," or white arsenic, was a " secret poison " unknown to any except the Borgias. It was its cumulative property that was known to them, and not generally known at the time.

" Cases of chronic poisoning are the result usually of the repeated administration of small doses of lead, copper, mercury, phosphorus, or arsenic.

" Chronic poisoning may be caused by inhaling vapours in factories, or arsenical dust from green wall-papers, making artificial flowers, etc , etc

" Persons continuing in this atmosphere show all the indications of arsenical poisoning, and will gradually die, if not removed from it."[1]

THE OPINION OF CONTEMPORARY WRITERS ON DJEM'S DEATH

" On Wednesday, 25th of the month of February last, Gem, *alias* Zizimi, brother of the Grand Turk . . . died through eating or drinking something disagreeable to which his stomach was not accustomed   His corpse was then, at the importunate request of the Grand Turk, sent to him with all the household of the deceased   The Grand Turk is said to have paid or given a large sum of money on this account, and to have received this household with favour."[2]

Thuasne says   " L'opinion générale des contemporaires est que le prince turc fut empoisonné."

Burchard states that he died " in the State of Naples *at the Castle of Capua* " (vol 11 *in loco*). This explains the difficulty raised by Mr Sabatini, who finds the following discrepancies in the contemporary accounts of the tragedy :

1. Sagredo states that Djem died at Terracina, which is a town on the coast about fifty miles north of Naples, through which the forces of Charles VIII. passed. He attributes the death on January 31 to poison, administered by direction of the Pope, in return for money promised by Bajazet

2. Paulus Jovius, the Bishop,[3] gives a later date, and

---

[1] *Dictionary of Medicine,* p 1296
[2] *Diary of John Burchard,* vol 11 , entry for February 25, 1495.
[3] Of Nocera

says the Prince died, from the same cause, at Gaeta, which
is about ten miles south of Terracina on the way to Naples

3 Guicciardini and Corio tell the same story, but place
the death at Naples.

4 Burchard's entry, quoted above, states that he died
in the State of Naples at the Castle of Capua, and his statement, though guarded, agrees with the others.

5. Panvinio " tells us positively that Djem died of dysentery
at Capua "

6. Sanuto says death resulted from " a catarrh which
descended to the stomach," at Capua

Thus we find that, out of seven authors quoted by Mr.
Sabatini, five agree as to the place where and the date when
the death occurred. The two others fix the death as occurring
en route to Naples. The discrepancy appears to be unimportant.

7 Priuli, who is not quoted by Mr Sabatini, says :

" On February 26, 1495, four days after the King of France
entered Naples, Ziem Sultan, brother of the Grand Turk,
died. He was poisoned "[1]

According to Burchard, Cardinal Cæsar Borgia fled from
the camp of Charles VIII. on Friday, January 30, in the
disguise of a stable-man.

The full text of Bajazet's letter to the Pope is given in
the Diary, in the Latin text of Thuasne, on pp 209–10.
Monsieur Thuasne, in a note, says . " The Cardinal de Gurck,
Raymond Perrault, affirmed to the Florentine Notary,
Alessandro Bracci, that he had seen the original letter, and
Bracci writes, ' moreover he knew that the Turk had offered
three hundred thousand ducats if the Pope would cause
the death of his brother (Djem), and that many believed
Djem's death was due to poison.' "[2]

" The ' white powder ' might very well have been Arsenious
Acid, or some preparation containing it ; but Dr. Willcox
thinks it improbable that that substance was prepared in
anything approaching a pure form at that time, and that
it was more likely to have been present in a mineral such as
limestone or chalk He does not think that it will be possible
to identify the substance by the name ' Cantarella.'

" The symptoms resembling those of dysentery would do
very well for a case of acute arsenical poisoning The poison
would not, strictly speaking, have a cumulative effect, but a
single dose, unless very large, would probably take several

[1] *Rer Ital Script* , t xxiv , *Chronicon Venetum,* col 16.
[2] *Arch Fiorent Letteri ai X di Balie,* clas x , dist 4, no 26, a, c 103

days to produce fatal results. In this case, if arsenic was the poison, it is probable that more than one dose was administered."[1]

The famous Catherine Sforza left a book in manuscript written by herself It contains more than 550 receipts relating to hygiene, medicine, cosmetics, magic, etc , and is included by Count Pasolini in his volume of " Documents " appended to his Life of Catherine Sforza The receipts contain directions for administering poison " slowly, or by degrees."[2]

[1] Extract from a letter from Sir Bernard Spilsbury, to the Author

[2] *Catherine Sforza*, French text by Marc Hélys (Per*in & Cie, Paris, 1912), page 410.

INDEX

A

Lightning Source UK Ltd.
Milton Keynes UK
UKHW011510120520
363145UK00017B/457